ISSUES IN EDUCATIONAL PLACEMENT

Students with Emotional and Behavioral Disorders

Issues in Educational Placement

Students with Emotional and Behavioral Disorders

Edited by

James M. Kauffman
John Wills Lloyd
Daniel P. Hallahan
University of Virginia

Terry A. Astuto
New York University

LEA LAWRENCE ERLBAUM ASSOCIATES, PUBLISHERS
1995 Hillsdale, New Jersey Hove, UK

Lawrence Erlbaum Associates, Inc., Publishers
365 Broadway
Hillsdale, New Jersey 07642

Library of Congress Cataloging-in-Publication Data

Issues in educational placement : students with emotional and behavioral disorders / edited by James M. Kauffman . . . [et al.].
p. cm.
Includes bibliographical references and index.
ISBN 0-8058-1532-5 (alk. paper). — ISBN 0-8058-1533-3 (pbk. : alk. paper)
1. Mentally ill children—Education—United States. 2. Behavior disorders in children—United States. 3. Problem children—Education—United States. 4. Mainstreaming in education—United States. I. Kauffman, James M.
LC4181.I86 1995
371.94'0973—dc20 94-34112
CIP

Books published by Lawrence Erlbaum Associates are printed on acid-free paper, and their bindings are chosen for strength and durability.

Printed in the United States of America
10 9 8 7 6 5 4 3 2 1

CONTENTS

FOREWORD

Frank H. Wood
University of Minnesota

Americans believe that the common good is served by supporting and advancing each individual's efforts to realize his or her potential, regardless of her or his present status. One way in which this belief has been expressed is the effort to provide every child with an appropriately individualized education. Cost has discouraged the complete implementation of a one-on-one tutoring model in the public school system, although the strength of the present home-schooling movement demonstrates the attraction that model has for many parents. As a compromise, we have attempted to provide a more fully individualized education for the most needy students, those who are not easily accommodated in regular classrooms without special support or who are not benefiting from the regular program. The editors of this book have brought together a set of excellent chapters discussing what we have achieved and where we should be going in adapting educational programs to meet the needs of students with emotional or behavioral disorders. Although focused on the needs of students with this disability, the discussion addresses important issues that affect all of special education.

Our efforts to achieve more fully individualized educational programs for our children are remarkably successful when compared with those of other societies. But the results are not fully satisfactory. Few students reach the level of achievement that their parents and teachers think possible for them, and many students fail to achieve self-sufficiency in basic skill areas. Although most Americans will agree that the answer to raising achievement levels lies in meeting the emotional, physical, and educational needs of children through more fully individualized attention and caregiving, they differ in their views on how and at what cost in public money this end can be achieved.

Fortunately for students who were foundering in our educational system, legislators representing perspectives ranging from liberal to conservative came together in 1975 to pass a remarkable piece of legislation, Public Law 94-142, the Education for All Handicapped Children Act (EAHCA). Extending the provisions of earlier, less comprehensive bills, and incorporating the best thinking of parents, judges and legal scholars, legislators, educators, and advocates for students denied an appropriate education because of type or severity of their educational disabilities, the EAHCA and its implementing regulations established fundamental guidelines for special education that have benefited thousands of students whose education needs had previously been neglected. As Bateman and Chard point out in their chapter on the legal framework within which special education takes form, the basic principle put forward in P.L. 94-142 is that every child has the right to an appropriately individualized program of education at public expense. That educational program is to be described in an individualized education plan approved by the child's parents or guardians. Professionals are charged with coming up with the plan; parents have the responsibility to decide whether or not the proposed plan is in the best interest of their child. These important principles have been retained in subsequent versions of the legislation, including the current Individuals with Disabilities Education Act (IDEA).

The spirit of compromise that made the passage of P.L. 94-142 possible soon dissolved as differences in perspective affected how different groups interpreted what its provisions meant. The largest group of special educators and parents turned their attention to assisting local school districts to implement the bill's provisions, following up by monitoring the results. Through a process of incremental reform, they have been able to demonstrate increasing, although by no means total, success in achieving the goal of improving the educational performance of students with special needs. Although I am sometimes discouraged by the apparently rapid increase in the number of students with severe emotional and behavioral disorders in our schools, the authors of the chapters in this book encourage me to believe that we are still on the right path in our response to their needs. That we often fall short of what is required is in part a result of our imperfect knowledge, but the lack of resources to implement what we already know is an equally important factor.

Those who believe the problem of our limited success with some students can be remedied by making fundamental changes in how special education is delivered in our schools have continued their efforts to extend the application of key principles contained in the law to additional groups of students. Concerned about the stigmatization of students with special needs resulting from the application of disability labels and the use of segregated placements, they urged that the principle of making placements in least restrictive environments become a mandate that all special education services should be provided in the regular classroom. These special educators believe that for social reasons the only appropriate placement for any student is the "mainstream"; placement at other points along the continuum of services is to be avoided if at all possible. For some advocates, this interpretation of the principle of education in the least restrictive environment became the basis for demands for "full inclusion" of all students in regular classroom settings. Others have advocated extending the goal of individualizing education to include all students, whether or not they fit the eligibility categories recognized by the EAHCA. Combined with the goal of full inclusion, this proposal has been called the "Regular Education Initiative."

Disagreement can be productive, producing a tension that moves a field forward, but the result of the conflict between those calling for radical reform and those placing their faith in more incremental change has been a public relations disaster for special education. To attract public support, the critics have exaggerated the failures of present programs without acknowledging the difficulties of the problems being addressed. The individualized programs called for by EAHCA have proved to be costly, and although many students with special needs have benefited from special education, their progress often continues to be slower than their peers' because of the effects of severe, persisting learning and behavior problems. Individualization is an aid to learning but not a cure for disability.

Attracted by the noise of the arguments between special educators, reporters and TV commentators have developed feature stories focused on special education's failures, characterizing its programs as costly, ineffective, and even abusive. Many special education professionals, parents, and students have been confused and demoralized by these one-sided, negative presentations. In this climate, the innovative programs proposed by some critics appeal to those searching for immediate solutions to difficult problems in spite of the absence of evidence that they will bring better results than current programs. Americans are by nature an impatient people, quick to criticize the status quo and ready to believe in the advantage of radical change—if they are assured that it will not be too expensive.

What has been urgently needed to help the field retain its balance is a thoughtful, honest description of the outcomes of the strategy of incremental change in special education to date, its accomplishments, its limitations, its costs, and the potential for its improvement. The fact that such a statement should come from the combined efforts of a group of special educators who have specialized in the education of students with severe emotional and behavioral disorders is not a result of chance. The disabilities limiting these students' educational progress have social as well as personal implications, often making them the most difficult to include in typical classroom settings as well as the most frustrating to educate in segregated settings. With their challenging behavior, they provide the test case for any educational program intended to promote the best interests of the child.

Because they are writing in the context of the debate over calls for a "Regular Education Initiative" or "full inclusion," Kauffman, Lloyd, Hallahan, Astuto, and their collaborators in the preparation of this book begin by focusing on issues related to placement of students. Citing the published empirical evidence—or, as in the cases of Lakin and Stephens and Denny, Gunter, Shores, and Campbell, presenting new data—the authors move away from simply arguing for or against a call to place all students in one setting, the regular classroom, to explore the possibilities and problems of realizing in practice the more complex concept of maximizing the appropriateness of education while minimizing the restrictiveness of the setting so as to provide the best match for the needs of an individual student. The role of supportive and related services and important factors such as cultural differences are brought into the discussion. The overriding purpose is to recover the broad vision which the authors of the EAHCA sought to capture in law. Together, the authors raise the discussion of what can be learned from special education's successes and failures to a level that informs the reader about the complexities of the decisions that parents and educators face in seeking the best interests of individual students, particularly those with emotional and behavioral disorders.

My comments to this point have addressed the content of this collection of chapters. I think it important to comment also on the various methodologies of which they provide examples. Without attempting an exhaustive catalog, I would call readers' attention to chapters dealing with semantics (chap. 1), history (chap. 2), demographics (chap. 3), and a research synopsis based on a systematic literature sampling methodology (chap. 4). There is more—the results of empirical investigations, policy papers, a through legal review—providing rich substance for students in an advanced seminar in education or public policy.

A friend of mine once wrote that "optimism is essential for human life even when it may not seem justified by the evidence." Optimism and courage are required to continue to study and report fully, "warts and all," the results of our efforts to individualize education for all students while observing how easily parents and the general public can be mislead by the promise of a quick, cheap fix for complex problems. We should be grateful to the authors of this book for the integrity with which they have undertaken and completed their task.

PREFACE

Issues regarding the placement of students in specific classes and schools have, for over a century, absorbed a substantial proportion of the energy devoted to the structure of U.S. public education. Many of the great controversies about education during the past five decades have been centered on questions about where students should to go school—to what buildings and to what classrooms. The buildings and classrooms to which students are assigned have been points of controversy because these placements determine in large measure what and how students will be taught and the peer groups with which students will associate. Student placement is the focus of controversies regarding the racial integration of public schools, heterogeneous ability grouping, and the appropriate education of students with disabilities in the least restrictive environment (LRE), as prescribed by the Individuals with Disabilities Education Act (IDEA) and prior federal legislation.

Placement of students with disabilities is a matter of great concern to advocates of special education for two primary reasons. First, appropriate education is extremely unlikely, if not impossible, for students with certain disabilities in some settings. Therefore, placement alternatives in which appropriate education is both possible and likely must be available to all students with disabilities. Second, all students with disabilities are entitled by law to an appropriate education in the setting that is least restrictive. Therefore, care must be taken in choosing for each student the appropriate placement alternative that entails the least personal restriction. Placement decisions are critically important both when the decision is to place a pupil in a more restrictive setting and when it is to return the pupil to a less restrictive environment. The difficulty of defining *appropriate* education and the *least restrictive* alternative placement has led to considerable professional controversy, a great deal of litigation, and a critical need for information regarding the criteria and procedures for determining placements.

Many issues involving student placement cut across all disabilities. Some disabilities, however, offer especially difficult challenges to those who must make placement decisions. Students with emotional or behavioral disorders, referred to as *serious emotional disturbance* in federal documents, have been described as an underserved population of children and youth with particularly complex needs. One of the most complex aspects of these students' needs is the determination and selection of the placements in which appropriate education and related services are most likely to occur. Students identified as having emotional or behavioral disorders and requiring special education are placed frequently in settings seen as more restrictive than their home schools and regular classes. Nevertheless, the reasons that parents, educators, and other professionals select these placements are poorly understood. The poor understanding of these placement decisions is a serious problem because such decisions substantially affect the opportunities students have for learning academic and social skills and participating in everyday activities with their nonhandicapped peers.

This volume brings together a series of chapters intended to further our understanding of how and why decisions are made to place students with emotional or behavior disorders in particular educational environments. We begin with two chapters that set the problem of placement in contemporary and historical context, as we believe that understanding placement decisions requires knowledge of the dimensions of current issues and the history of their development. In Part II, chapters 3 through 9, we review current realities—what we know about where students with emotional and behavioral disorders are placed, what the literature indicates about these placements, what policies constrain decision making, the teachers who work in various types of placements, and findings and perspectives regarding participants in placement decisions. Part III contains five chapters dealing with special problems and options—topics that crystalize concerns about multicultural issues, postsecondary education, law and regulation, demands on teachers, and policy choices. We end with two chapters recapitulating the issues and looking toward the future.

This book is a product of work conducted under the auspices of the Virginia Behavior Disorders Project. The Virginia Behavior Disorders Project, launched in 1986, has focused on improving our understanding of the nature and treatment of emotional and behavioral disorders by conducting research and providing technical assistance. Two of us (J.M.K. and J.W.L.) serve as co-directors for the project. The project activity that resulted in this work was funded under the title Placement Issues in Educating Children and Youths with Emotional and Behavioral Disorders and was supported in part by a grant (H237A10002-91) from the Office of Special Education Programs of the U.S. Department of Education; the views expressed in this book do not necessarily represent the views of the funding agency.

Our hope is that this book will further our understanding of the decision processes leading to placement of pupils with emotional or behavioral disorders and that this understanding will lead, in turn, to improvements in these pupils' lives in school and elsewhere. We hope also that our efforts will lead to further research of the many placement issues that are left unresolved.

J. M. K.
J. W. L.
D. P. H.
T. A. A.

PART I

OVERVIEW

CHAPTER

1

A Sense of Place: The Importance of Placement Issues in Contemporary Special Education

James M. Kauffman
John Wills Lloyd
University of Virginia

Place has many meanings. We may use *place* to indicate that something is in disarray, as when we say, "His hair was all over the place." When we want to say that someone thoroughly bested another person, we might assert, "She really put him in his place." In a similar sense, we say, "The president has earned a place in history," and it may be either a glorious or an infamous place. Yet, if a horse finishes first, second, or third in a race, we say that it "placed." More narrowly, if the horse finishes immediately after the winner, then we say that it did not "win" or "show" but "placed." In business, we might refer to the fact that someone holds a position in a company by saying, "He has a place with the Smith Corporation." Or, if an employment agency has secured a job for someone, we might say, "The agency placed him." Furthermore, if someone is advancing in the corporate structure, we might say, "She is going places."

All of these diverse meanings for the word *place* illustrate the breadth of uses for the word. In education, however, the term *place* carries special connotations. Understanding the issues surrounding the placement of children and youths with disabilities requires consideration of the role of *place* in language and culture. Placement is not an issue anchored merely in special education regulations or the deeper ground of controversies regarding educational equity, but instead in the bedrock of human history. Accordingly, we must examine the meanings of the word *place* beyond those given in the previous paragraph. Table 1.1 provides several definitions of *place* that are pertinent to our subsequent discussion.

As these varied definitions suggest, decisions to place students in specific physical locations are but one aspect of the larger issues of the power and authority

TABLE 1.1
Relevant Definitions of *Place*

As a noun, *place* may mean:
- The physical environment or physical surroundings.
- An indefinite region or area, a building or locality used for a special purpose, or where something is.
- A particular region, an individual dwelling, or a scene.
- A relative position in a social scale or a step in sequence.
- A proper or designated niche.
- An available seat or accommodation, an empty or vacated position, or a position dictated by circumstance.
- In an original or proper place or in a suitable environment.

As a transitive verb, *place* may mean:
- To distribute in an orderly manner.
- To put into a particular position or to present for consideration.
- To put into a particular condition or state.
- To direct accurately to a desired area or predetermined spot.
- To appoint to a position.
- To find a place for.
- To assign to a position, rank, or category.
- To attribute or ascribe.

Note. Drawn from *Webster's Third New International Dictionary* (1971). Springfield, MA: Merriam, p. 1727.

of special education within the system of general education (i.e., special education's "rightful place" in public education), the social status of students receiving special education, the social environments and roles to which students are assigned, and the procedural processes by which decisions are reached. Although the relative power of special education and the social status of students served thereby are indeed important issues related to the placement of students and cannot be avoided in any comprehensive treatment of placement issues, in the present discussion we give primary attention to the physical locations in which students are taught. Location has historically been a symbol of authority and rank, if not a key to acquiring and maintaining power and status, and it is, therefore, not surprising that the locus of special education services has come to occupy center stage. Moreover, location is central to the concept of ecology. All the literal and metaphorical meanings of place are connected to the physical location of individuals in a social or behavioral ecology. Before turning to the centrality of location and placement in contemporary special education issues, therefore, we comment briefly on the importance of location in the history of human affairs and the critical role of location in ecological analyses of social and behavioral phenomena. Our very cursory treatment of these topics is intended only to suggest further study of the importance of place in human affairs and, more particularly, to provide context for studying the role place plays in special education. We think that such study must be founded on careful, systematic analyses rather than on looser arguments based primarily on imagery. That is, productive study demands words conveying carefully crafted ideas and scrupulous attention to scientific evidence, not just appealing images (cf. Kauffman, 1993).

THE PLACE OF LOCATION IN PSYCHOSOCIAL HISTORY

A sense of physical place—location in space, where things are and where things happen—is basic to much of human thought. Place as a set of coordinates in the physical world is a central issue in identity or belonging. One can hardly imagine an existence without being somewhere, and the where of being is nearly always a partial determinant of the quality of being. Home, homeland, homecoming, and many associated concepts are related to identity and quality of being, and arouse intense emotions in many individuals, if not most. Homelands and holy places are the issues underlying many national, ethnic, tribal, class, and religious conflicts, and many religions attach special significance to the assignment of place after death. In short, individual and group identities—the perception and presentation of self, community, and quality of life—are inextricably bound to location (cf. Goffman, 1973).

Physical location is so fundamental a dimension of the world as we know it that nearly all communication regarding nearly every aspect of social structure involves reference to it. Every society is structured both by assumptions and rules governing the behavior that is considered appropriate in certain locations and by the observation that some events or outcomes are probable in some locations but improbable in others. Children go to a place called "school" because we believe that certain things are likely to happen there, things unlikely to happen elsewhere. Places called "courtrooms," "prisons," "laboratories," "surgical suites," "offices," "restaurants," "no smoking areas," and so on are designated and maintained under the assumption that certain behavior or outcomes are more appropriate or likely in these locations. What is said to be possible, probable, desirable, or permissible in certain places may change, either based on empirical findings or because social values change, or both. Nevertheless, every society communicates rules for censure or approbation of specific behavior in certain locations.

Rules or conventions for granting individuals access to and exit from specific locations, necessarily grounded in assumptions about the reciprocal influences of location and person, are the primary stuff of social control and many controversies. Holding office, for example—both the power or authority entailed by accession to the office and the officeholder's occupation of designated space—is a universal phenomenon of organized societies. Office as location sets the occasion for certain types of behavior of the officeholder, and the officeholder's behavior affects the physical and psychological trappings of the office. Governments, businesses, religions, clans, and families grant access and exit privileges or make entrance or exit demands as means of controlling behavior and maintaining a social order deemed appropriate, profitable, right, or self-enhancing. That is, they create social ecologies designed to support certain types of behavior and thwart others, presumably under the assumption that certain types of behavior strengthen the social fabric and others threaten the social good.

Psychosocial history could thus be analyzed as the access and exit rules governing locations and the rationale for these locations' known or presumed influences on the behavior of individuals and communities. In fact, some histories of the treatment of mental illness and of institutions and schools for individuals with emotional or behavioral disorders provide such analyses for specific places or types of environments (e.g., Bockoven, 1956; Caplan, 1969; Grob, 1973, 1983; D. Rothman, 1971; E. P. Rothman, 1967). Implicit or explicit in these histories are appraisals of the mutually interactive effects of the behavior of individuals in specific social environments, that is, of the sociobehavioral ecologies in the locations of interest.

THE ROLE OF LOCATION IN SOCIOBEHAVIORAL ECOLOGIES

Scientists have long been interested in studying the totality or pattern of relationships between organisms and their environments—the ecologies of living things. Educators and social scientists with an ecological bent have for decades investigated the development and structure of human communities and the ways in which the presence of certain individuals or behavioral characteristics alters the pattern, rhythm, or course of social interactions or relationships. In fact, an explicitly ecological conceptual model of emotional or behavioral disorders emerged in the 1960s (e.g., Hobbs, 1966; Rhodes, 1967), and contemporary psychological and behavioral technology suggests relatively sophisticated ecobehavioral analyses of the problems of maintaining individuals with emotional or behavioral disorders in specific social environments (e.g., Kamps, Leonard, Dugan, Boland, & Greenwood, 1991).

Two concepts critical to the understanding of sociobehavioral ecologies are *niche* and *ecodeme*. Niche refers to a site or habitat supplying the support necessary for an individual to survive. It also refers to an organism's role in an interdependent community, especially its way of life in a community and the effects of its behavior on the environment. Thus, an ecological niche involves both location and interaction. An ecodeme is a population occupying a particular ecological niche. In sociobehavioral ecology, the ecodeme is comprised of the group occupying the location and forming the community and structure within which an individual of interest might be introduced or from which an individual might be ejected.

Certain ecological niches are notoriously hospitable to some species and individuals, and equally notoriously inhospitable to others. Moreover, an ecosystem may be thrown out of balance or destroyed by the introduction of certain organisms, and individuals or species finding a hospitable niche may, if uncontrolled by others, destroy the ecosystem that initially sustains them. The uncontrolled behavior of homo sapiens, in fact, threatens the entire ecosphere. Natural scientists concerned with ecologies study the limits of individual and species adaptability to various habitats and the effects of niches on survival. Social and behavioral scientists, however, are interested in more than survival; they study also how the quality of human life is altered by occupying a given niche. Moreover, social ecologists are interested in how humans create and maintain ecodemes and niches for themselves and others. In a similar vein, special educators have undertaken studies of the relationship between behavior and characteristics of the settings in which it occurs (e.g., Repp, Barton, & Gottlieb, 1983).

Congregation and segregation of individuals (which are not peculiar to homo sapiens) are two means by which ecologies, including human social ecologies, are constructed and maintained. The conceptual bases and strategies for clustering individuals in certain locations—the rationales for and the construction of ecodemes and niches—are the turning points for controversies about placement. The ideals of a democratic society include the freedoms of movement and association; therefore, the assignment of ecodeme or niche is viewed with great caution, if not suspicion. The contemporary ideals of American society also include tolerance if not deliberate maintenance of a rich sociobehavioral diversity; consequently, the removal of individuals from an ecodeme or niche is also viewed with great wariness, if not misgiving. The primary focus of human sociobehavioral ecological interventions is thus on altering the behavior of individuals within a given location—refurbishing the existing social habitat rather than moving individuals to new locations in which a different ecodeme is present and a new niche may be established. A common suggestion, for example, is that special services should be brought to students in the habitat of their regular classroom and school; students should not be brought to services offered at another place.

Location is fundamental to the concept of ecology, yet the forced relocation of individuals is a suspect means of addressing problems of human ecologies. Thus, the extent to which the capacity of one place to accommodate sociobehavioral diversity can be expanded in ways that provide equal nurturance for all members of its ecodeme is the fundamental issue underlying much of the controversy regarding educational placement. The great challenge of applied social sciences is answering this question: How do we maintain sociobehavioral diversity—both within and among a diversity of social ecologies—that gives rise to and sustains desirable human behavior? Moreover, the social conditions of the United States in the late 20th century demand consideration of the following question: Might we create, inadvertently and in the pursuit of tolerance of difference, a social ecology in which sociobehavioral diversity along critical dimensions is inimical to the nourishment of desirable conduct? Moynihan's (1993) analysis clearly suggests that we might—and sometimes have.

Moynihan submitted that U.S. social scientists have sometimes redefined deviance, urging that it be viewed merely as a behavioral difference falling within the bounds of normalcy and, therefore, deserving of no particular concern; deviancy has thus been "defined down." Moreover, social scientists have sometimes made unwarranted claims of having the technical knowledge required for dealing effectively with behavioral difference or deviance in specific settings. The consequences have in some cases included substantial increases in socially problematic behavior and decrements in quality of life for many or all members of the ecodeme, but particularly for the individuals exhibiting unwelcomed behavior. A case in point explored by Moynihan and others (e.g., Bachrach, 1986; Sacks, 1991) is the deinstitutionalization of persons who are mentally ill, in the justification of which social scientists contended that communities would become more tolerant of behavioral "difference" and that the technology of effective community-based treatment of severe and chronic mental illness had been developed. The social ecology of the typical U.S. community seems unable—at least with today's psychopharmacological and behavioral technologies—to nourish desirable behavior of or toward persons with certain forms of mental illness. The behavioral diversity introduced into the community by these individuals results in a less hospitable niche for them and fewer nurturant responses from the ecodeme than might be found in the typical psychiatric hospital. We should ask whether students with certain emotional or behavioral disorders and the ordinary school communities in which they might be placed are faced with similar ecological problems.

THE CENTRALITY OF LOCATION AND PLACEMENT IN CONTEMPORARY SPECIAL EDUCATION ISSUES

Psychosocial history and sociobehavioral ecology suggest that where students go to school will be a matter of great concern to social scientists and to those who make educational policy. The history of education is replete with discussions of the significance of place, and the place in which a student is taught provides a social ecology that is critical for learning and socialization. In attempting to understand placement issues in contemporary special education, however, one must begin by examining the background of place as a center point of controversies in general education.

Where students go to school has long been understood to be important in determining their life opportunities. Attendance at a particular school determines the student's ecodeme, and the personal relationships so formed often play an important role in the nexus of social contacts on which social status, privilege, and power often depend. The school attended—indeed, perhaps as much as what the student has learned—influences how others perceive the individual and may thereby affect future opportunities for schooling and employment. In short, some have assumed that in obtaining social rank and financial security, where one studies may be as important as what one studies; in opening doors to social and economic development, where and with whom one learns may equal or exceed what one learns. For a variety of reasons that we discuss here, the where of education has become a preoccupation of U.S. educators, and this preoccupation with place has led to neglect of the what—content, curriculum, what transpires between teacher and student—of both general and special education (see Edgar & Polloway, 1994; Zigler, Hodapp, & Edison, 1990).

One reason for the centrality of location and placement is that these are easily verifiable and measurable dimensions of educational experience. In contrast to many of the more ephemeral goals and measures of education, location and placement offer a metric about which there has been relatively little controversy. Second, the objective of placement—changing the location of a student or students—is more readily accomplished than many other objectives of education that are not only more subjective in nature but technically demanding, such as engendering learning. Goals that are more readily attained and progress that is more easily measured induce behavior that is more immediately reinforced; changing students' placements is, thus, likely to be one of the more reliably rewarding acts of educators. Finally, location and placement are issues with very strong emotional components. As we noted, place involves connotations of power, privilege, identity, and belonging, and it is, thus, a central issue in perceptions of merit, fairness, civil rights, and opportunity.

Notwithstanding the U.S. ideals of equal opportunity and meritocracy, public schooling in the United States has a history of discrimination against students differing in nonacademic credentials—race, gender, religion, or social or economic status—from those who are privileged. Preferred or privileged places of learning have not been accessible only on the basis of academic merit; they have been partialed to those already among the social and economic elite (Kozol, 1991). Placement issues in special education have been shaped in part by larger social forces, especially those involving discrimination against minorities and others placed at a disadvantage in the social fabric (Gallagher, 1994; MacMillan, Semmel, & Gerber, 1994; Semmel, Gerber, & MacMillan, 1994). Where students with disabilities should be taught has been, since the late 1960s, a matter with conceptual and legal ties to the civil rights movement.

Racial Segregation and Its Legacy of Concern for Place

Racial segregation of the schools was the most egregious form of discrimination practiced in U.S. public education until its abolition. Its legacy for special education as well as other compensatory programs is a profound, perhaps justifiable, suspicion of any place of learning that is restricted to any category of pupils (except, perhaps, categories of chronological age, and even these are questioned by some). Legal racial segregation of the public schools was ended in 1954 with the decision of the U.S. Supreme Court in *Brown v. Board of Education of Topeka*. The question before the court was whether segregation of pupils in public schools solely on the basis of race, even if physical facilities and other tangible variables are equal for the races, deprives minority students of equal educational opportunity. The decision drew heavily on the U.S. Constitution's Fourteenth Amendment, which grants equal protection of laws as a civil right. The Court's opinion included language particularly relevant to our discussion of placement. Regarding the effects of segregation on children of color, Chief Justice Warren wrote:

> [Segregation] generates a feeling of inferiority as to their status in the community that may affect their hearts and minds in a way unlikely ever to be undone. . . . We conclude that in the field of public education the doctrine of "separate but equal" has no place. Separate educational facilities are inherently unequal. (cited in Bartholomew, 1974, p. 47)

The end of arguments that education could be separate but equal for pupils differing in race led directly to a focus on achieving a near identity of racial proportion in each school with racial proportion in the larger society (not necessarily the racial proportion within the school's attendance boundaries). That is, communality of place was assumed to be at least a necessary, if not sufficient, condition for equality of education of children differing in race. Particularity of place associated with race—even if students were not assigned a location based on race—was assumed to nullify any and all efforts to make education equal for the races. Consequently, *de facto* racial segregation, marked by disproportional representation of pupils of given race in a school, was viewed as inherently racially discriminatory, and substantial and protracted efforts were made to redress such discrimination through several means, primarily busing, to achieve racial balance.

That efforts to achieve racial balance in the schools have not produced equal educational outcomes for children of all races is hardly arguable. The reasons that racial balance in school enrollment, where it has been achieved, has not always brought equal educational outcomes likely include but are not restricted to the following: given that all children have equal educational opportunity to learn in school, there will remain variability in outcomes due in part to the conditions of life outside the school, and students experiencing serious disadvantages in their homes and communities (i.e., environmental risk factors) will therefore remain at a disadvantage in school learning; a more fine-grained analysis of locations may show that within a particular school system, building, or classroom there are places differing in racial proportion or in the opportunities they afford particular individuals or groups; and educational opportunity is determined not only by the schools and classes students attend but by more subtle forms of equal or unequal treatment involving interactions with peers and teachers. Concern has been refocused, unsurprisingly, on disproportionate placement of ethnic minority and poor students in particular classes and programs within the schools.

In the 1980s and the early 1990s, analyses of place shifted in large measure from issues of racial balance in general school enrollments to issues of tracking and ability grouping (e.g., Oakes, 1985, 1992). Placement in remedial, lower level, vocational, or advanced classes or tracks was assumed to be discriminatory, especially if the placement of any group of concern (e.g., African-American students, students of lower socioeconomic status, males) was not proportional to its representation in the school's enrollment. Some analysts proposed the correction of this apparent discrimination by homogenous placement achieved through heterogeneous grouping (e.g., Hastings, 1992; Oakes, 1985, 1992). The argument was that if placement in any given class is equally probable for all students, then opportunity to learn will be equalized, and hence the civil right to equal protection of law will be realized.

But homogenous placement (i.e., similar placements for all, creating heterogeneous grouping) presents a great dilemma for educators. It is difficult, if not impossible, to offer all curricula with equal finesse in the same place at the same time, and it is generally acknowledged that students may differ not only in what they know but in what they need to know, what they want to learn, and perhaps how they are best taught (cf. Grossen, 1993). How, then, should students be grouped for instruction? Indeed, educators must now examine more carefully the meaning of *Brown v. Board of Education of Topeka* and its implications for policies regarding public school choice, magnet schools, schools designed to accommodate the characteristics of males or African-American students, and so on, in which students may be segregated *de facto* according to any of a variety of characteristics. In short, to what distinguishing student characteristics does the *Brown* decision apply (e.g., to gender, age, academic interests, performance on academic tasks, and disability as well as race)? To what level of placement does *Brown* apply (e.g., to classrooms and to locations within classrooms as well as to school buildings and school systems)? And, under what conditions or circumstances of placement does *Brown* prohibit separation or segregation of students (e.g., when it is voluntary, follows informed consent, or follows due process of law on a case-by-case basis as well as when it is forced and uniform)?

Granted that legal racial segregation of public facilities, including public schools, is despicable, hyperextension of the notion that it is inherently inequitable to separate students on any basis brings us recursively to the issue of fairness. Gallagher (1994) noted that "fairness does not consist of educating all children in the same place at the same time (and with the same curriculum?) but in ensuring that the student has basic needs met and is travelling a well thought-out road to a career and a satisfying life style" (p. 528).

How to achieve Gallagher's definition of fairness in the education of students differing along dimensions directly relevant to instruction is a difficult problem to solve, the more so when the assumption undergirding placement is that separation of students by any criterion is inherently unequal treatment and therefore illegal. To the extent that students are assigned to different places on the basis of characteristics not relevant to learning and instruction, such separation may be inherently unfair. Conversely, to the extent that the student characteristics prompting separation into different places are directly relevant to learning and instruction, such separation may in some cases be required to achieve fairness (cf. Grossen, 1993). These are important considerations for framing the issue of special education placements in the context of the civil rights movement.

Special Education Placement as a Civil Rights Issue

Following the lead of the civil rights movement, special educators of the 1960s made parallel arguments regarding the placement of students with disabilities (e.g., Dunn, 1968; see MacMillan et al., 1994; Semmel et al., 1994, for further discussion). Dunn's (1968) article reflected the primary social concerns of the 1960s for avoiding discrimination and achieving racial balance by raising the issue of disproportional placement of African-American students in special classes for those with mild mental retardation.

Following the publication of Dunn's article, and perhaps in part because of it and similar publications, in the 1970s most students with mild disabilities were removed from special self-contained classes and placed part time in resource rooms (cf. MacMillan et al., 1994; Semmel et al., 1994). Although Dunn's treatise captured the civil rights movement's interest in racial equality, it did not represent the central concerns of the movement for civil rights for persons with disabilities. The objective of those advocating for what was to become the Education for All Handicapped Children Act of 1975 (now known as the Individuals with Disabilities Education Act [IDEA]) was not to open the door to a universal place irrespective of students' disabilities, but to establish a civil right to individual consideration of placement in a variety of possible environments to meet unique needs (Hocutt, Martin, & McKinney, 1991). As Semmel et al. (1994) noted, the law emanating from the civil rights movement for people with disabilities had two parts:

> First, find and provide *appropriate* public education for individual students with disabilities based upon their *unique* needs, not the characteristics associated with some broad class of disabilities. The second was, don't discriminate; children and their families have a right not to be mistreated. (p. 487)

Placement in environments in which appropriate education could not be provided or that were more restrictive than necessary to achieve appropriate education or placement without parental involvement in the decision are types of mistreatment to which Semmel et al. referred.

The differences between the civil rights movement for racial minorities and that for persons with disabilities have often been confused, leading to a collision of advocacy regarding placement. The civil rights movement of disenfranchised racial minorities was intent on achieving educational placement without regard for race (except to achieve racial balance) under the assumption that differential placement of a broad class of individuals was unfairly discriminatory; advocacy was for placement decisions made by group identification, not individual-by-individual determination of appropriateness of placement. The civil rights movement for persons with disabilities, however, asked for differential educational programs, including differential placement of individual students based on assessment of their unique needs, under the assumption that universal placement of individuals without regard for their uniqueness was unfairly discriminatory; advocacy was for a placement decision only after determination of individual characteristics and needs, and placement decisions made according to group membership were strictly forbidden. In Dunn's era, misunderstanding of these differences in civil rights advocacy—with its focal concern that placement decisions were being made on the basis of a broad class criterion (African American) rather than individual need—led to the widespread decertification of students as having mild mental retardation. Misunderstanding of these differences led in the 1980s and early 1990s—an era of emphasis on persons with disabilities as a broad class (like a racial or ethnic group) rather than a heterogeneous category that must be treated on a case-by-case basis—to the widespread attempt to devise a universal placement for all students with disabilities.

In the 1980s and early 1990s, some people argued on the basis of *Brown* that—as in the case of any skin color or ethnic origin, so in the case of disability of any description—separate education is inherently unequal (e.g., Gartner & Lipsky, 1989; Stainback & Stainback, 1991; Will, 1984). If the assertion that separate education is inherently unequal is interpreted to apply absolutely and equally not only to all manner of placement decisions but all types of differences among students, then communality of place will be the central issue in achieving equal opportunity in schooling. Indeed, some special educators argue, " 'place' is the issue" (Blackman, 1992, p. 29). Moreover, in the 1980s and early 1990s, the focus has been on placement in the least restrictive environment (LRE) as mandated by IDEA, and some people have argued that the LRE for all students with disabilities is a regular classroom in their neighborhood schools (e.g., Laski, 1991; Stainback & Stainback, 1991).

Certainly, according to IDEA place is an issue, but a secondary issue, awaiting, first, a determination of the appropriateness of education. LRE is not the first requirement of the law; it must be secondary to and balanced against the primary objective of providing an appropriate education (Barbara D. Bateman, personal communication; see also chap. 12, this volume; Bateman, 1994). Defining *appropriate* is no small matter; much of the current controversy regarding placement hinges on what this word means (Hocutt et al., 1991).

One line of argument is that appropriate education includes only that which can be achieved by universal placement in the neighborhood school and regular classroom, that is, that placement elsewhere precludes appropriate education (cf. Laski, 1991; Stainback & Stainback, 1991). Such reasoning is clearly at odds with the framers and advocates of IDEA and a substantial body of case law (cf. chap. 12, this volume; Bateman, 1994); it substitutes end for means by making place the first and overriding concern in achieving fairness for students with disabilities. Semmel et al. (1994) observed that "confusing the social *goal* of equal opportunity with *place* of opportunity distracted social scientists as well as the lay public from attention to what were appropriate educational means to reach desired ends" (p. 485).

What are the desired ends of education for students with disabilities? One might take the position that the foremost end is for students to be together—in the same place at the same time. From this perspective, it matters not whether other goals than placement itself are achieved. As one speaker in a widely distributed video says:

> It really doesn't matter whether or not it [placement of students with disabilities in their neighborhood schools and in regular classrooms] works. It does work, and that's great. But even if it didn't work it would still be the thing to do, because it's right. (Goodwin, Wurzburg, & Biklen, 1987)

If, however, the desired ends are a combination of academic and social outcomes—"ensuring that the student has basic needs met and is travelling a well thought-out road to a career and a satisfying life style" (Gallagher, 1994), for example—then we must ask in what environment these may be best achieved. That is, if it is admitted that the question of placement is subordinate to achieving desired outcomes, then evidence of the effects of various placements on outcomes will be a matter of serious import. Moreover, IDEA requires that questions of placement be framed by the larger issue of appropriateness. Thus, place cannot be the overriding civil rights issue for students with disabilities unless this federal law is rewritten.

Special Education Placement as an Efficacy Issue

That the academic and social outcomes of special education leave much to be desired is not arguable. Special education programs and their outcomes have been particularly disappointing for students with emotional or behavioral disorders (cf. Colvin, Greenberg, & Sherman, 1993; Knitzer, Steinberg, & Fleisch, 1990). Research does not, however, support the contention of some (e.g., Gartner & Lipsky, 1989; Lipsky & Gartner, 1991) that special education has failed to achieve its desired ends primarily because of students' placement in settings other than neighborhood schools and regular classrooms, and that the available data show consistently the adverse effects of special class placement.

Decades of research in special education have provided no definitive answer to most questions about the effects of placement on the achievement of desired outcomes. The available research data regarding the efficacy of various placement options contain a lot of "noise," or unexplained variance. The "noise" might be an artifact of the outcome measures used, a confound of place with the instruction and social transactions occurring in the placements studied, a function of the heterogeneity of characteristics of the students in the sample, or some combination of these and other factors (cf. Gottlieb, Alter, & Gottlieb, 1991; Gottlieb, Alter, Gottlieb, & Wishner, 1994; Hallahan, Keller, McKinney, Lloyd, & Bryan, 1988; MacMillan et al., 1994; Semmel et al., 1994; Zigler et al., 1990). Although not definitive, the available data suggest that place per se is a weak variable in explaining variability in educational outcomes (Gamoran, 1992; Grossen, 1993).

Of late, some have made the claim that we now have the technical means of producing the desired academic and social outcomes of education for all children when all are placed in general education settings (e.g., Blackman, 1992; Gartner & Lipsky, 1989; Stainback & Stainback, 1991). Researchers who have examined the outcomes for special education students placed in regular classrooms in which attempts were made to produce maximum social and academic gains have not, however, been able to confirm this claim (e.g., Fuchs, Fuchs, & Fernstrom, 1993; Jenkins, Jewell, Leicester, Jenkins, & Troutner, 1991; Ysseldyke, Christenson, & Thurlow, 1993; Zigmond et al., in press).

It may be that questions of the efficacy of special education placement have been seriously miscast in most research to date. As we have discussed, place is an important constraint on personal experience and on educational practices and their outcomes. Nevertheless, it is clear that place alone is not the critical ingredient in helping students attain important social and academic goals. What goes on in placements—the social and academic curricula—are more critical variables (Colvin et al., 1993; Grossen, 1993). We need, therefore, to inquire more carefully into how place constrains the achievement of educational ends and how placement, thus, might be a means to those ends.

OLD QUESTIONS REFRAMED

Our hope is that the subsequent chapters will advance our ability to answer three fundamental questions about the placement of students with emotional or behavioral disorders: What is? What could be? What should be? In addressing these questions, we must first be clear about the objectives of general and special education for individual exceptional students. Only after knowing what outcomes we seek for each individual student who needs special education can we pose the first critical question relevant to placement: What conditions and behavioral interactions are required to move the student toward those goals as effectively and efficiently as possible? When we know what conditions and interactions we wish to foster, then we are ready to ask the placement question: In what place are we most likely to be able to create the conditions and foster the behavioral interactions we wish to produce? The answer to the first question will help us determine what is appropriate education; the answer to the second will reveal what environment is least restrictive.

By necessity, general education answers these questions of goals and placement for the general case (Bateman, 1994; Kauffman & Hallahan, 1993). Special education's role as a part of the broader system of public education is to address questions of goals and place for exceptional cases. Inevitably, general education must acknowledge particularity but serve communality, whereas special education by definition acknowledges communality but serves particularity. In general education, goals and places conducive to them are designed for what is average, typical, or most highly predictable, just as general merchandise stores and general construction companies or general law or medical offices and so on are designed to address the commonplace. Predictably, education has its unusual and particularly demanding cases. The suggestion that all cases are unique or that all cases must be treated with the same degree of individual attention not only begs the question of general education but proposes malpractice. What is, what could be, and what should be in education, with reference to goals and places arranged to facilitate their achievement, are questions answerable only if we ask for each student with a disability an additional question: What exceptions to the general practice of education are required in this case?

Contemporary critiques of special education commonly lament the stigma of special placement; for example, "what is so wrong about special education is the stigma and isolation that result from being removed from the regular education class for so long" (Blackman, 1992, p. 29). In a strangely ironic twist, those who would alleviate the stigma associated with disability overlook both the negative message inherent in proscribing the congregation of students with a shared identity and the potential for self-enhancement resulting from such congregation (cf. Bateman, 1994; Edgar, 1988; Hallahan & Kauffman, 1994; see also chap. 11, this volume). As Bateman (1994) noted,

> The parents, advocates, and courts who urge that a child who has a disability must be placed with those who do not have a disability too often send the message that children who have disabilities are not peers and are not fit to be with. Something is terribly and not very subtly insulting about saying a bright learning disabled student ought not attend a special school with other students who have learning disabilities because he needs to be with non-disabled students. (p. 516)

If the relationship between the appropriateness of education and the place in which it occurs is complex, such that appropriateness is not universally achieveable in the same type of placement, then how might we approach the problem of stigma? Old questions about place and stigma might be reframed (cf. Hallahan & Kauffman, 1994). What can we do to help students understand that their personal worthiness is unrelated to the place of their instruction? What can we do to help students, teachers, parents, and others celebrate not only the unavoidable and positive differences in students' characteristics but also the necessary and habilitative differences in places of instruction? How can we induce a positive identity for students with emotional or behavioral disorders, regardless of where they are placed for their education, and fashion a supportive, self-enhancing culture of those who are working toward more successful management of their emotional or behavioral disorders?

REFERENCES

Bachrach, L. L. (1986). Deinstitutionalization: What do the numbers mean? *Hospital and Community Psychiatry, 37*, 118–119, 121.

Bartholomew, P. C. (1974). *Summaries of leading cases on the Constitution* (9th ed.). Totowa, NJ: Littlefield, Adams.

Bateman, B. D. (1994). Who, how, and where: Special education's issues in perpetuity [Special issue, Theory and Practice of Special Education: Taking Stock a Quarter Century After Deno and Dunn]. *Journal of Special Education, 27*, 509–520.

Blackman, H. P. (1992). Surmounting the disability of isolation. *The School Administrator, 49*(2), 28–29.

Bockoven, J. S. (1956). Moral treatment in American psychiatry. *Journal of Nervous and Mental Disease, 124*, 167–194, 292–321.

Brown v. Board of Education of Topeka, 347 U.S. 483 (1954).

Caplan, R. B. (1969). *Psychiatry and the community in nineteenth-century America: The recurring concern with the environment in the prevention and treatment of mental illness.* New York: Basic Books.

Colvin, G., Greenberg, S., & Sherman, R. (1993). The forgotten variable: Improving academic skills for students with serious emotional disturbance. *Effective School Practices, 12*(1), 20–25.

Dunn, L. M. (1968). Special education for the mildly retarded—is much of it justifiable? *Exceptional Children, 35*, 5–22.

Edgar, E. (1988). Congregate. *Habilitation News, 8*(3), 6–7.

Edgar, E., & Polloway, E. A. (1994). Education for adolescents with disabilities: Curriculum and placement issues [Special issue, Theory and Practice of Special Education: Taking Stock a Quarter Century After Deno and Dunn]. *Journal of Special Education, 27*, 438–452.

Fuchs, D., Fuchs, L. S., & Fernstrom, P. (1993). A conservative approach to special education reform: Mainstreaming through transenvironmental programming and curriculum-based measurement. *American Educational Research Journal, 30*, 149–177.

Gallagher, J. J. (1994). The pull of societal forces on special education [Special issue, Theory and Practice of Special Education: Taking Stock a Quarter Century After Deno and Dunn]. *Journal of Special Education, 27*, 521–530.

Gamoran, A. (1992). Is ability grouping equitable? *Educational Leadership, 50*(2), 11–17.

Gartner, A., & Lipsky, D. K. (1989). *The yoke of special education: How to break it.* Rochester, NY: National Center on Education and the Economy.

Goffman, E. (1973). *The presentation of self in everyday life.* New York: Overlook Press.

Goodwin, T., Wurzburg, G. (Producers and Directors), & Biklen, D. (Executive Producer). (1987). *Regular lives.* [Videocassette]. Syracuse, NY: Syracuse University.

Gottlieb, J., Alter, M., & Gottlieb, B. W. (1991). Mainstreaming academically handicapped children in urban schools. In J. W. Lloyd, N. N. Singh, & A. C. Repp (Eds.), *The regular education initiative: Alternative perspectives on concepts, issues, and models* (pp. 95–112). Sycamore, IL: Sycamore.

Gottlieb, J., Alter, M., Gottlieb, B. W., & Wishner, J. (1994). Special education in urban America: It's not justifiable for many [Special issue, Theory and Practice of Special Education: Taking Stock a Quarter Century After Deno and Dunn]. *Journal of Special Education, 27*, 453–465.

Grob, N. (1973). *Mental institutions in America: Social policy to 1875*. New York: Free Press.

Grob, N. (1983). *Mental illness and American society, 1875–1940*. Princeton, NJ: Princeton University Press.

Grossen, B. (1993). Focus: Heterogeneous grouping and curriculum design. *Effective School Practices, 12*(1), 5–8.

Hallahan, D. P., & Kauffman, J. M. (1994). Toward a culture of disability in the aftermath of Deno and Dunn [Special issue, Theory and Practice of Special Education: Taking Stock a Quarter Century After Deno and Dunn]. *Journal of Special Education, 27*, 496–508.

Hallahan, D. P., Keller, C. E., McKinney, J. D., Lloyd, J. W., & Bryan, T. (1988). Examining the research base of the regular education initiative: Efficacy studies and the adaptive learning environments model. *Journal of Learning Disabilities, 21*, 29–35.

Hastings, C. (1992). Ending ability grouping is a moral imperative. *Educational Leadership, 50*(2), 14.

Hobbs, N. (1966). Helping the disturbed child: Psychological and ecological strategies. *American Psychologist, 21*, 1105–1115.

Hocutt, A. W., Martin, E. W., & McKinney, J. E. (1991). Historical and legal context of mainstreaming. In J. W. Lloyd, N. N. Singh, & A. C. Repp (Eds.), *The regular education initiative: Alternative perspectives on concepts, issues, and models* (pp. 17–28). Sycamore, IL: Sycamore.

Jenkins, J. R., Jewell, M., Leicester, N., Jenkins, L., & Troutner, N. M. (1991). Development of a school building model for educating students with handicaps and at-risk students in general education classrooms. *Journal of Learning Disabilities, 24*, 311–320.

Kamps, D. M., Leonard, B. R., Dugan, E. P., Boland, B., & Greenwood, C. R. (1991). The use of ecobehavioral assessment to identify naturally occurring effective procedures in classrooms serving students with autism and other developmental disabilities. *Journal of Behavioral Education, 1*, 367–397.

Kauffman, J. M. (1993). How we might achieve the radical reform of special education. *Exceptional Children, 60*, 6–16.

Kauffman, J. M., & Hallahan, D. P. (1993). Toward a comprehensive service delivery system. In J. I. Goodlad & T. C. Lovitt (Eds.), *Integrating general and special education* (pp. 73–102). Columbus, OH: Merrill/Macmillan.

Knitzer, J., Steinberg, Z., & Fleisch, B. (1990). *At the schoolhouse door: An examination of programs and policies for children with behavioral and emotional problems*. New York: Bank Street College of Education.

Kozol, J. (1991). *Savage inequalities: Children in America's schools*. New York: Crown.

Laski, F. J. (1991). Achieving integration during the second revolution. In L. H. Meyer, C. A. Peck, & L. Brown (Eds.), *Critical issues in the lives of people with severe disabilities* (pp. 409–421). Baltimore: Brookes.

Lipsky, D. K., & Gartner, A. (1991). Restructuring for quality. In J. W. Lloyd, N. N. Singh, & A. C. Repp (Eds.), *The regular education initiative: Alternative perspectives on concepts, issues, and models* (pp. 43–57). Sycamore, IL: Sycamore.

MacMillan, D. L., Semmel, M. I., & Gerber, M. M. (1994). The social context of Dunn: Then and now [Special issue, Theory and Practice of Special Education: Taking Stock a Quarter Century After Deno and Dunn]. *Journal of Special Education, 27*, 466–480.

Moynihan, D. P. (1993). Defining deviancy down. *American Scholar, 62*(1), 17–30.

Oakes, J. (1985). *Keeping track: How schools structure inequality*. New Haven, CT: Yale University Press.

Oakes, J. (1992). Can tracking research inform practice? Technical, normative, and political considerations. *Educational Researcher, 21*(4), 12–21.

Repp, A. C., Barton, L. E., & Gottlieb, J. (1983). Naturalistic studies of institutionalized mentally retarded persons: II. The effects of density on the behavior of profoundly and severely retarded persons. *American Journal of Mental Deficiency, 87*, 441–447.

Rhodes, W. C. (1967). The disturbing child: A problem of ecological management. *Exceptional Children, 33*, 449–455.

Rothman, D. (1971). *The discovery of the asylum: Social order and disorder in the new republic.* Boston: Little, Brown.

Rothman, E. P. (1967). The Livingston School: A day school for disturbed girls. In P. H. Berkowitz & E. P. Rothman (Eds.), *Public education for disturbed children in New York City.* Springfield, IL: Thomas.

Sacks, O. (1991, February 13). Forsaking the mentally ill. *The New York Times*, p. 23.

Semmel, M. I., Gerber, M. M., & MacMillan, D. L. (1994). Twenty-five years after Dunn's article: A legacy of policy analysis research in special education [Special issue, Theory and Practice of Special Education: Taking Stock a Quarter Century After Deno and Dunn]. *Journal of Special Education, 27*, 481–495.

Stainback, W., & Stainback, S. (1991). A rationale for integration and restructuring: A synopsis. In J. W. Lloyd, N. N. Singh, & A. C. Repp (Eds.), *The regular education initiative: Alternative perspectives on concepts, issues, and models* (pp. 226–239). Sycamore, IL: Sycamore.

Will, M. C. (1984). Let us pause and reflect—but not too long. *Exceptional Children, 51*, 11–16.

Ysseldyke, J. E., Christenson, S. L., & Thurlow, M. L. (1993). *Final report: Student learning in context model project.* Minneapolis, MN: University of Minnesota College of Education.

Zigler, E., Hodapp, R. M., & Edison, M. R. (1990). From theory to practice in the care and education of mentally retarded individuals. *American Journal on Mental Retardation, 95*, 1–12.

Zigmond, N., Jenkins, J., Fuchs, L., Deno, S., Fuchs, D., Baker, J., Jenkins, L., & Couthino, M. (in press). Special education in restructured schools: Findings from three multi–year studies. *Phi Delta Kappan.*

CHAPTER

2

The Legacies of Placement: A Brief History of Placement Options and Issues with Commentary on Their Evolution

James M. Kauffman
Karen Smucker
University of Virginia

Misconceptions abound regarding the history of the placement and treatment of children and youths with emotional or behavioral disorders. Some of these misconceptions are the result of a disregard for history; others are the outcomes of inadequate methods of historical research. All too often, literature searches cover only sources published in recent years, ignoring sometimes highly significant events or insights from an earlier era. As Kauffman (1976) showed in the 1970s, consultation of original 19th-century sources reveals a much richer and more sympathetic literature than most reviews and commentaries had suggested (e.g., Despert, 1965; Kanner, 1962; Rubenstein, 1948). We suspect that misconceptions about the more recent history of placement as well are formed and perpetuated by lack of attention to original sources. In preparing this chapter, we have given most of our attention to literature published prior to 1980, in contrast to our focus in chapter 4 on more current literature.

The history of education of children with emotional or behavioral disorders cannot be studied outside the context of several other disciplines, particularly psychiatry, psychology, criminology, and social work (Kauffman, 1993; Lewis, 1974). Nevertheless, we have attempted to emphasize the educational facets of placement. Further, placements in hospitals, foster families, and detention centers, whether determined by personnel in departments of health and social services or the juvenile justice system, are not strictly educational placements, but they are intimately connected to the educational problems of many children and youths with emotional or behavioral disorders. Neither can the history of education of children with emotional or behavioral disorders be studied outside the context of other special education categories, particularly mental retardation and learning disabilities. As Kauffman (1976, 1993) showed, ignoring the links among special education categories results in a shallow and deceptive image of the history of education of children with emotional or behavioral disorders. In this chapter we keep emotional or behavioral disorders at the center of our interest, but broaden our scope to include relevant information about children having a variety of labels.

We have organized our discussion around two major questions about the history of placement. First, when and why did placement options emerge in the United States? Second, how have placement issues evolved over the past 150 years? We must add two disclaimers regarding the scope and depth of our portrayal of history. First, constraints on our time and space limit the full treatment of the topic, which easily deserves an entire volume of its own. Second, our perspective is prone to the inevitable biases of history writers. We are reminded that "we all invent our pasts, more or less, as we go along, at the dictates of Whim and Interest; the happenings of former times are a clay in the present moment that will-we, nill-we, the lot of us must sculpt. Thus Being does make positivists of us all" (Barth, 1960, p. 743).

THE EMERGENCE OF EDUCATIONAL PLACEMENT OPTIONS

There is good reason to believe that children with emotional and behavioral disorders have been present in every era and in every society. Prior to the development of special places assumed to offer therapeutic advantages for children with these disorders, they were left in their natural habitats—kept in their typical social ecologies, which were seldom the sites of relationships having any therapeutic intent or effect. That many or most of these children's natural social ecologies were hostile environments in which they were rejected, segregated, ridiculed, severely punished, grotesquely abused, or killed is not open to serious question (cf. Bremner, 1970, 1971; Despert, 1965; Kanner, 1962; Kauffman, 1976). Neither is it deniable that many or most children with emotional or behavioral disorders suffer such treatment in their natural social ecologies today (Jackson, 1993; Kauffman, 1993; Knitzer, 1982).

Alternative placement options were devised to address what concerned adults saw as the inability of people in the places occupied by these children to deal effectively and humanely with their behavior. Clearly, the adults concerned with these children believed that a change of venue might significantly increase the probability that these children could be dealt with more effectively and humanely. Consequently, they devised alternative placements—sites that would offer more humane treatment and the conditions required for desirable changes in children's emotions and behavior. In reading the historical literature, we searched for the reasons that people devised these alternative placements. Why did they believe a different place was required for kinder or more effective treatment? What did they believe was possible or likely to happen in this new place that was impossible or unlikely to happen in the place from which the child was being removed? To what extent did they believe that the place per se was important to the child's welfare? To what extent did they believe that what was to occur in the place was the key therapeutic ingredient? How was the site of one's work with children assumed to be related to intended social interactions, relationships, and therapeutic outcomes?

Definitive answers may never be obtainable from the historical record for most placement options, because those first devising placement options did not often address these questions directly. Proponents or opponents of a type of placement may note that no defensible present-day rationale exists (e.g., Lundy & Pumariega, 1993). This should not be interpreted to mean that the placement option never had a rationale, nor should we judge the defensibility of a treatment offered in a prior era solely in terms of today's context.

Psychiatric Hospitalization and Residential Placement

We begin by noting that hospitalization became the preferred mode for treating "madness" in the 19th century. For reasons that go beyond the scope of this chapter, 19th-century physicians became the arbiters of grossly deviant behavior that had been called *madness* or *lunacy*—behavior they were given the social authority to label as reflecting "insanity" or "mental illness" (Scull, 1975). Physicians, particularly those specializing in the branch of medicine now known as psychiatry, also became the arbiters of how mental illness should be treated, and psychiatry continues to be the professional group given most credence in matters of classification and treatment of adults and children with emotional or behavioral disorders (cf. Phillips, Draguns, & Bartlett, 1975; Prugh, Engel, & Morse, 1975). Like other serious illnesses, mental illnesses came to be seen by the end of the 19th century as disorders often requiring treatment in hospitals, where the ministrations of trained personnel and prescribed regimens of activity, diet, and medication could be carried out.

Psychiatric hospitalization has gone through periods of popularity and periods of disrepute. Rationales for hospital treatment and perspectives on its virtues and vices have varied from era to era in the history of psychiatric hospitalization (cf. Bockoven, 1956; Caplan, 1969; Carlson & Dain, 1960; Dain & Carlson, 1960; Deutsch, 1948; Grob, 1973, 1983; Rhodes & Sagor, 1975; Rothman, 1971). The most despised rationale of the present era is that hospitalization will rid the community of its undesirables and protect citizens from the unpredictable, nonconformist, distasteful, or disruptive behavior of those who are mentally ill. Today, the emphasis is on the legal right of those who are mentally ill to live in the community unless their behavior is a clear and present danger to themselves or others.

One reason for hospitalizing persons with mental illness has always been the community's unwillingness to accept and live with them—a rationale that has become not only unpopular among advocates for mentally ill people but legally suspect. An important consideration, however, is the other rationales for hospitalization that are consistent with putting the mentally ill person's individual interests first. That is, what rationales focused on the quality of life of the individual with mental illness and on achieving therapeutic effects?

General Psychiatric Hospitals. The leading psychiatric hospitals of the mid-19th century employed an approach to mental illness (then called *lunacy* or *insanity*) known as moral treatment (Bockoven, 1956; Brigham, 1847). As Bockoven noted, moral treatment was something like a combination of what today might be called *physical, occupational, recreational, psychological*, and *educational* therapies. Two aspects of the rationale for hospital placement in the practice of moral treatment are pertinent here: removing the patient from the community in which symptoms of mental illness were problematic, and providing an intensive, kind regimen of constructive activities. A change of venue from community to hospital was considered necessary both to terminate morbid psychological associations and patterns of interaction in the home and community and to ensure that patients would participate in scheduled therapeutic activities. That the intent of hospitalization was kind and effective treatment in an environment approximating that of a good boarding school is evident from the writings of moral therapists (Brigham, 1847; Mayo, 1839; see also Bockoven, 1956). Two excerpts from Brigham illustrate:

> The removal of the insane from home and former associations, with respectful and kind treatment under all circumstances, and in most cases manual labor, attendance on religious worship on Sunday, the establishment of regular habits and of self-control, diversion of the mind from morbid trains of thought, are now generally considered as essential in the Moral Treatment of the Insane. (p. 1)

> By means thus indicated [i.e., various forms of constructive activity] institutions for the care and cure of those affected by mental disorder will be made to resemble those for education, rather than hospitals for the sick, or prisons for criminals, and when we call to mind that the greater part of those committed to such establishments are not actually sick, and do not require medical treatment, but are suffering from deranged intellect, feelings and passions, it is evident that a judicious course of mental and moral discipline is most essential for their comfort and restoration. (p. 15)

Kind, effective treatment in an institutional setting and return to a community setting were clearly the intentions of moral therapists. Their plans were frequently subverted by the same factors undermining good intentions of interventionists today: negative public attitudes, personnel problems, fiscal constraints, exaggerated or overly optimistic claims of treatment outcomes, and lack of technical knowledge and skill (Ray, 1852).

The general psychiatric hospital of the 19th century is typically assumed to have been populated exclusively by adults. However, it is apparent from 19th-century hospital records that children and youths were included among the patients in psychiatric hospitals in which moral therapy was practiced, those under the age of 20 comprising perhaps 5% to 10% of the population (see Kauffman, 1976). Moreover, moral therapists were known to work with both youths and adults (e.g., Mayo, 1839).

Hospital Schools and Units for Children and Adolescents. Early moral therapists noted the importance of schools and classes as part of hospital treatment for both adults and children, and as an ameliorative treatment for both emotional and behavioral disorders and mental retardation (Brigham, 1845, 1847; Ray, 1846). Instruction, in addition to other productive activities, was seen as indispensable, as indicated by Brigham's (1845) commentary on his observations of schools in European institutions:

> If no other end were answered by the formation of schools, they ought to be established as recreative, palliative, remedial even, in every Lunatic Asylum (p. 339). . . . The patients in the schools, even some of the epileptic and idiotic, work when the weather permits it; and for some, who are employed nearly every day, there are evening classes. Thus every objection is removed, which can be raised against the instruction of the insane, even those who regard economy as the first consideration. (p. 340)

Exercising the mental "faculties" and learning functional academic, self-care, vocational, and recreational skills were viewed by moral therapists as a critical aspect of hospitalization.

In the later development of child psychiatry and related disciplines, the school was seen as an important aspect of children's lives. Even in treatment centers or hospitals with the most psychodynamic orientations, much of child psychiatric treatment tended to be framed by a school or schoollike environment (cf. Berkowitz & Rothman, 1960; Bettelheim, 1950; Bettelheim & Sylvester, 1948; Fenichel, Freedman, & Klapper, 1960; Hirschberg, 1953; Kornberg, 1955). The classroom in the hospital or residential center was assumed to be a place in which critical relationships and insights could be formed.

Attention to the special needs of children hospitalized for emotional or behavioral disorders has its origins in the 20th century. As we have already noted, children and adolescents were included in general psychiatric hospital populations of the 19th century. Special units for children and adolescents in psychiatric hospitals were inventions of the 1930s (Crespi, 1989; Kanner, 1957). Although the Menninger Clinic's Southard School was organized in 1926, it first served primarily as a "small residential school whose program centered around the training of young children who were functioning at a retarded level" (Menninger Foundation, 1969, p. xii). Only later was it expanded to include children and adolescents with a wide range of psychiatric disorders. In 1934, the first children's ward was established at Bellevue Psychiatric Hospital, and in 1935 the New York City Board of Education began providing teachers for a school program on the unit (see Berkowitz, 1974; Rothman, 1974; Wright, 1967).

The development of pediatrics and the establishment of pediatric hospitals presaged the development of child psychiatry and pediatric units in psychiatric hospitals and clinics. "In 1930, the first full-time psychiatric clinic was established as an integral part of a pediatric hospital" (Kanner, 1957, p. 14). The rationale for placement of children and adolescents in special units within a psychiatric facility was that youngsters and adults have different needs and deal with different emotional and behavioral issues. However, this rationale was challenged. The controversy regarding placement in all-adolescent or mixed wards included a variety of arguments: Adult psychiatric patients are poor role models for adolescents, but adolescents are better behaved when their unit includes adult patients; a mixed ward is more familylike, but a hospital designed to treat adults does not have programs and facilities appropriate for adolescents; staff and adults in units designed for adults will not tolerate adolescent behavior, but a mixed ward provides a more realistic social environment (Crespi, 1989). Consensus was reached on one point: If adolescents are placed in units with adults, then at least part of the adolescents' daily program needs to be conducted separately from adults. Nevertheless, the dimensions (e.g., age, gender, type of problem) and extremes of heterogeneous and homogeneous grouping remain controversial issues.

Child Psychiatric Hospitals and Residential Centers. In the era of moral treatment, residential centers for juvenile delinquents (very broadly defined) were founded. These were called *houses of refuge* or *reform schools*, and their purpose was both to protect the larger society from troublesome youths and to provide corrective training. That the rationale for these institutions included humanitarian aims is not questionable; neither is it questionable that these aims were often made secondary or forgotten almost completely (see Bremner, 1970; Rhodes & Sagor, 1975; Rothman, 1971). In general, placement in psychiatric hospitals resulted in greater dedication to treatment, as delinquent and incorrigible youths were assumed to be "bad" and deserving of punishment, whereas those with psychiatric disorders were assumed to be "sick" and in need of therapeutic care. The attitude toward "bad" children, including those who were homeless or truant, was that they should be removed from the community and placed in special schools where they would not bother others and would learn to behave themselves. For example, a special commission report to the City of Chicago in 1899 included the following statement regarding the responsibility of the public education system to provide alternative residential schools:

> By all means the board of education should have the power to establish and maintain one or more such schools, and thereby break up or avoid the formation of bad habits and character, and thus save many children from becoming criminals. . . . We should rightfully have the power to arrest all the little beggars, loafers and vagabonds that infest our city, take them from the streets and place them in schools where they are compelled to receive education and learn moral principles. (cited in Hoffman, 1975, p. 418)

Interest in the special mental health needs of the pediatric population culminated, predictably, in hospitals and residential centers devoted exclusively to children and adolescents. The first psychiatric hospital for children in the United States was established in 1931 (Davids, 1975). Early hospital and residential programs, including classroom activities, were psychodynamic in philosophy, and much attention was given to the importance of psychotherapy and personality reorganization (Berkowitz & Rothman, 1960; Bettelheim, 1950; Bettelheim & Sylvester, 1948; Kornberg, 1955). In the late 1940s, the psychodynamic model was expanded by the work of Redl and colleagues, in a residential program for aggressive children, to include attention to "surface" behavior and greater concentration on use of the milieu as a therapeutic tool (Redl, 1966a, 1966b; Redl & Wineman, 1952a, 1952b). The blending of concern for education and psychological well-being, of attention to both the underlying meanings of behavior and its moment-to-moment management, became known as a "psychoeducational" approach (see Fenichel, 1966, 1974; Morse, 1953, 1965a, 1965b, 1974). By the early 1960s, the concept of *ecological psychology* and the European model of the *educateur* were offered by Hobbs and others who developed the Re-ED program (Hobbs, 1965, 1974). Prototypic behavioral analysis approaches to schooling were developed in psychiatric hospitals at about the same time (Hewett, 1967, 1968), and such approaches were subsequently moved into community classroom settings (Hewett & Forness, 1974).

The reasoning behind the establishment of hospital and residential placements varied, depending on conceptual orientation and type of facility. In all cases, however, the hospital or residence was to provide a more stable, predictable, and mentally healthful environment than could be achieved in the home and community. The assumption was that some children cannot be managed and taught in their communities, but that through living in a carefully structured environment for a period of time with trained personnel most can discover or recover the attitudes and patterns of behavior that would allow their reintegration into the larger society.

Space does not allow the reiteration here of the full explanations of hospital and residential programs. We would be remiss, however, not to repeat two statements regarding Project Re-ED, arguably the residential program with the most elegantly formulated rationale. First, a commentary on why some children need 4 to 6 months in a residential school:

> A four-month's experience in a residential school makes sense only if one appreciates objectives of the Re-ED program. The purpose is not to effect a "cure" or a profound reorganization of the child's character and personality, but rather to give the child a special 24-hour-a-day environment in which he can grow in trust, competence, confidence, and joy, and give the child's family, school, and community an opportunity to regroup their forces in the interest of the child's development in a relatively normal setting. Re-ED assumes that normal life circumstances are more conducive to healthy growth than is an institutional placement; it further assumes that there are occasions when a period of partial disengagement may be good for a child and for his family, school, and community as well. (Hobbs, 1965, p. 293)

It is important to recognize that since the early decades of the 20th century, hospital and residential programs have been assumed to be only one type of placement in an array of needed mental health services for children. Following is an explanation of how a residential program might fit into an array of other services for children:

> Schools such as proposed in Project Re-ED should not be thought of as replacements for psychiatric services for children. Indeed, the operation of the school should increase public awareness of the need for other specialized services. It has a clearly complementary function to the residential treatment center which requires the services of the traditional psychiatric team. It should serve as a buffer against hospitalization and as a means of speeding the return to school and community of the child who has been hospitalized for psychiatric reasons. (Hobbs, 1965, p. 289)

Community- and School-Based Special Services and Programs

Hospital and residential treatment programs for children were launched in an era of burgeoning concern for mental health. The early decades of the 20th century saw the rise of mental hygiene programs, the establishment of child guidance clinics, and attempts to help regular classroom teachers become more adept at managing and teaching students with behavior problems.

By the 1930s, child guidance and counseling services were relatively common in major cities. Kanner (1973) noted that child guidance clinics brought three innovations in dealing with children: (a) collaboration among disciplines concerned with children's development; (b) concern for children whose behavior was annoying to parents and teachers but not cases of obvious psychopathology, opening the door to primary and secondary prevention; and (c) concern for the effects of interpersonal relationships and adults' attitudes on child behavior. Mental hygiene clinics in some public schools were staffed by a variety of professional personnel, and their objectives included offering mental health courses for high school students, taking referrals from teachers and parents, studying referred children and their problems and discussing the findings in an interdisciplinary conference, and devising programs of management to be carried out in the home or classroom with the help of a social worker or visiting teacher (Haines, 1925). Ryan (1928) described attempts to imbue the training of all classroom teachers with knowledge that would enable them to manage behavior problems without removing students from regular classes.

School-based programs had their origins in early special ("ungraded") classes for truant, disobedient, and insubordinate children (Hoffman, 1975). These early classes had protection of order and learning in regular classes as a primary aim; their therapeutic or corrective purposes received relatively little attention. By the middle of the 20th century, however, placement in special classes was often accompanied by the rationale of assisting the student's emotional and behavioral development (e.g., Hay, 1967; Krugman, 1953; Stullken, 1950). In fact, the necessity of collaboration among school personnel and mental health professionals for the benefit of the child was generally acknowledged:

> The basic prerequisite for the effective utilization of available resources and the structuring of new and powerful tools is *sustained involvement in the school on the part of a team* that minimally incorporates both educational and clinical personnel. (Hay, 1967, p. 199)

A study of special public school classes in the 1960s found programs with a variety of theoretical and philosophical underpinnings and modes of operation (Morse, Cutler, & Fink, 1964). These conceptual orientations included psychodynamic and psychoeducational rationales, as well as approaches that Morse et al. called *educational* (mostly traditional teaching methods) and *naturalistic* (just provide a good, empathic teacher who can deal with problems ad hoc). Some classes were found to be *primitive* (behavior kept under control by threat and coercion) or *chaotic* (little semblance of order, sometimes rationalized as therapeutic permissiveness). Particularly important as a new direction in the 1960s were special classes organized around principles of respondent and operant behavior (Haring & Phillips, 1962; Hewett, 1968). Placement in these classes was intended to teach students appropriate behavior, primarily through the systematic application of consequences, so that they could return to regular classes.

In the 1960s and 1970s, the role of the crisis, helping, resource, or consultant teacher of students with emotional or behavioral disorders was further developed by Morse (1965a, 1971a, 1971b). This kind of teacher, acting as a teacher–therapist hybrid, was to give attention to both the academic and the emotional–behavioral problems of students. In this model, teachers were to remove students from the classroom only to the extent necessary to manage a crisis and lay the groundwork for avoiding future crises. Consultation and collaboration with other teachers and school personnel were critical means of influencing the student, and also a means of working preventively to improve the socioemotional and academic environment of the regular classroom and the school. Morse's contributions to the development of this model were based on a psychoeducational approach. Others have described the same basic modus operandi from the behavioral perspective (e.g., Bergan, 1977; Nelson & Stevens, 1981).

Other developments of the late 19th and early 20th centuries relevant to the educational placement of students with emotional or behavioral disorders were the establishment of juvenile courts and other social welfare programs for children and adolescents, such as placement in foster homes. The creation of juvenile courts and the scientific study of juvenile delinquency were intended to provide more humane and effective treatment than had been maintained in juvenile detention centers (see Healy, 1915a, 1915b). In the early decades of the 20th century, foster home placements were devised such that juvenile courts had authority "to remove children from homes in which they suffered from proven parental brutality, neglect, and other major and disastrous forms of irresponsibility" (Kanner, 1957, p. 10; see also Healy, 1931). That juvenile courts were invented with the best of intentions is clear. Equally clear is their failure to achieve in most cases what was hoped for, and the failure in many cases of alternative placements such as foster care and probation (Sheehan, 1993a, 1993b; Silberman, 1978).

Special Day Schools and Partial Hospitalization. The availability of hospital and residential care on the one hand and, on the other, programs in regular or special classes in neighborhood schools, left a gap in placement options in the first half of the 20th century. In 1953, the first day school for severely emotionally disturbed children was opened in New York City (Fenichel, 1966, 1974; Fenichel et al., 1960). The purpose of the day school was to prevent the need for hospital or residential care, to keep children in the community with their families, and to provide a hopeful and therapeutic environment. As hospitals and treatment centers developed outpatient clinics, day treatment or partial hospitalization programs became viewed as an alternative to inpatient hospitalization or residential care. The advantages seen in day schools and day treatment were maintaining family relationships, keeping the child in contact with the community, avoiding many of the problems of generalizing treatment gains from hospital to home, allowing work with the child's family in situ, and lower costs (see Morse, 1985).

Special Classes in Public Schools. We have already commented on the origins of special class placements in the late 19th century and their growth in the post-World War II decades of the 1950s and 1960s. By the early 1960s, special classes for "the emotionally handicapped" had become common enough that the Council for Exceptional Children (CEC) disseminated guidelines for planning such classes (Hollister & Goldston, 1962). CEC also sponsored a large-scale study of special public school classes (Morse et al., 1964). Morse and colleagues reported findings from a mail survey of 117 programs and site visits to 54 programs across the United States. Included in the Morse et al. monograph were findings on the impetus for programs, program goals and aims, operational characteristics, personnel experience and training, and placement processes (both entrance into and exit from special classes).

Morse et al. found that although special classes seemed typically to be organized with good intentions and to have a defensible rationale, their staffing and operation often left much to be desired. A high percentage of teachers had little or no special training, the teachers often worked in isolation with little support from anyone other than their building principal, programs were often poorly articulated with mental health and other necessary services, and the curriculum and instructional methods were much like those used in general education. Twenty years later, relatively little appeared to have changed (Grosenick, George, & George, 1987). Although the characteristics of effective special programs, including special classes, are known (cf. Peacock Hill Working Group, 1991), programming for students in special classes is often grossly inadequate, especially in teacher preparation, support services for students and teachers, and curriculum (Knitzer, Steinberg, & Fleisch, 1990).

Mainstreaming and Inclusive Schools. Special education's mainstreaming movement of the 1970s affected the placement of all categories of students with disabilities. Based largely on the extension of racial minorities' demands for equal treatment to students with disabilities, the mainstreaming movement resulted in efforts to make certain that those with emotional or behavioral disorders spent as much of their school experience as possible in contact with students without disabilities—in mainstream classes and activities (see chap. 1). Concern for placement in the most normalized or least restrictive environment (LRE) was embodied in Public Law 94-142 (enacted in 1975, known since its 1990 amendments as the Individuals with Disabilities Education Act [IDEA]). The primary requirement of IDEA is that every student with a disability be provided a free, appropriate education; a secondary requirement is that the appropriate education be provided in the LRE (see chap. 12, this volume; Bateman, 1992, 1994).

LRE became the preoccupation of some mainstreaming advocates, often appearing to overshadow the primary aim of appropriate education. In the 1980s, emphasis on returning responsibility for more students with disabilities to neighborhood schools and regular classroom teachers and averting placement elsewhere became known as the *regular education initiative* (cf. Lloyd, Singh, & Repp, 1991). In the 1990s, these ideas culminated in movement toward "inclusive" schools in what some have termed the *inclusion revolution* (Rogers, 1993). Inclusive schools are neighborhood schools that ostensibly provide appropriate education for literally all children in their catchment areas, regardless of any disabling conditions children may have (cf. Lipsky & Gartner, 1991; Rogers, 1993; Stainback & Stainback, 1991). Thus, placement issues became focused on whether one place—at least the neighborhood school, if not the regular classroom—could and would become the site of appropriate education for all students with emotional or behavioral disorders. That one type of placement can provide appropriate education for all students with emotional or behavioral disorders strains the credulity of some (e.g., Berkowitz, 1974; Braaten, Kauffman, Braaten, Nelson, & Polsgrove, 1988; Idstein, 1993; Morse, 1985, 1994; Walker & Bullis, 1991).

Placement Concerns of the 1990s: Recurrent Themes

The level of concern in the 1980s and early 1990s for placement in the LRE appears not to have been matched by concern for effective intervention (see Morse, 1994). As Morse (1984) observed, "the worship of the 'least restrictive' [is] myopic: the goal should be to find the most productive setting to provide the maximum assistance for the child" (p. 120). Furthermore, Morse (1985) asked:

> What should govern the placement service is a match between the needs the pupil has and the resources to meet those needs. How many interventions will be necessary to maximize the pupil's potential for growth? Where can these interventions be expeditiously brought to bear? (p. 268)

Questions of "segregation" versus inclusion in neighborhood schools and regular classes became the center of reform rhetoric in the 1990s, but these questions were not new in the education of students with emotional or behavioral disorders. The literature of the 1950s speaks to the point. Hay (1953) commented on the question of segregation of children in New York City's special school channel of "junior guidance" classes (see also Hay, 1967):

> Two questions that have been raised repeatedly deserve consideration. There is some fear that such a channel has segregative features. Segregation is usually viewed as a coerced deprivation of valuable opportunities in contrast to those of a more favored group. Deprivation is intensified when there is little or no mobility in the relationships. As this project has been envisaged from its inception there has been a keen awareness of this aspect. We feel, however, that since none of the elements usually associated with segregation is intrinsic here, the term does not apply. There is no coercion; neither child nor parent who is resistive need be included. Periodic reassessment allows for optional continuation. We have discovered that the reservoir of such children is so large as to allow for the inclusion of only those who are accepting. Furthermore the opportunities for these children are richer than usual. Hence there is neither coercion or deprivation.
>
> There is, however, a type of segregation that is extensively current and is seriously traumatic, namely, the functional segregation that is the lot of many of these unhappy children. The child who is not functioning well, academically or socially, stands out frequently as the proverbial sore thumb. Such an arrangement is much more segregative than the one in which an attempt is made by specialists to assess the child's needs and provide a healthful climate. (pp. 682–683)

Another placement concern of the 1990s is presaged in professional literature of earlier decades: maintenance of a continuum of alternative placements. A continuum of placement options is a way of ensuring that one does not have to decide between hospital or residential care on the one hand and the neighborhood school or regular classroom on the other (cf. Hallenbeck, Kauffman, & Lloyd, 1993; Morse, 1985, 1994). A continuum of options is necessary, in fact, to operationalize the basic idea of LRE. "Translating 'least restrictive environment' into practice requires the establishment of service programs that contain a variety of alternative settings and the fewest in the most non-normal or restrictive settings" (Abeson, Burdorf, Casey, Kunz, & McNeil, 1975, pp. 275–276). Two decades before this statement by Abeson et al., in discussion following a symposium on the education of emotionally disturbed children (Krugman, 1953), a symposium participant commented that:

> there are some youngsters for whom these special [junior guidance] classes will not be sufficient and where residential treatment or concomitant psychotherapy in a clinic is desirable. But I wonder if some of the youngsters now needing residential care might not be handled without such an expensive and drastic move before the residential care, if we could have this type of resource as a part of our general balance, a medicine chest variety of treatment resources. (p. 711)

In many ways, the placement issues of the 1990s are merely a revisitation of the issues of earlier decades. The observations of Berkowitz (1974) might well be attributable to the 1990s:

> Recent thinking in the field of childhood psychopathology suggests that no disturbed youngster should be isolated from the mainstream of education but, rather, should be offered all types of treatment services while living at home and being maintained somehow in some neighborhood school. This point of view is founded on stressing the normal aspects of daily living and conceptualized in terms of the need of the educator to work, not just with the youngster who is being treated, but also with his relationship to home, school, and community while he is living there and experiencing it. . . .
>
> Regardless of the infinite variety of treatment and educational settings available, the prime goal of all of these is to return youngsters to the community as rapidly as is practicable. Because the earlier this return occurs the lower the treatment costs and the greater the population for whom treatment can be available, this concept, unfortunately, has been condensed into recommendations that children with all types of psychopathology remain in the community in the first place. The emphasis, therefore, has been mistakenly placed on reducing the cost of individual treatment. My own experience leads me to believe that, while more people can be serviced on a much lower budget by keeping the child in the home, the severely disturbed youngster eventually ends up in residential treatment regardless of how much outpatient, community-based care he has had.
>
> In addition to the advantages I see for residential treatment for psychotherapeutic reasons, the potential educational gains are immeasurable. A special setting with small classes, staffed by learning disability specialists, allowing experimentation

> with new methodology and equipment, and offering resources for vocational training and guidance as well as that intensive kind of interaction between clinical staff and school staff provides a valuable multidisciplined approach not available in an outpatient, community-based treatment program. (pp. 43–44)

Yet another placement concern of the 1990s with roots in earlier decades is returning children from more restrictive to less restrictive environments. Children are sometimes kept unnecessarily long in special classes, schools, residential centers, or hospitals; other times they are returned too quickly or even precipitously to more normal or less restrictive settings. In either case, the negative consequences for the child and others can be serious. Delaying the return too long is not only an inefficient use of costly resources but may exacerbate the child's difficulty in making the transition to a less restrictive setting. Returning the child too early, however, may leave both the child and persons in the community to which he or she is returned unequipped for living successfully with each other, leading to recursive bouts of blame and conflict, charges that the placement was ineffective, and eventually to an even more restrictive placement. Hobbs (1975) captured what may be the consensus of mental health workers in his statement that, "As a rule, it is better to err in the direction of a too-early return of the child to a normal setting than to err in the direction of a too-late return" (p. 11).

A continuing challenge for special education and other professions serving children and youths with emotional or behavioral disorders is to make community-based treatment programs more effective—both to circumvent more often the need for residential or hospital care and to make earlier and more successful return to home communities possible. The overriding concern in the 1990s for placement in the LRE has brought new urgency to research questions posed in chapter 1: How do we maintain sociobehavioral diversity—both within and among a diversity of social ecologies—that gives rise to and sustains desirable human behavior? What conditions and behavioral interactions are required to move the student toward desired goals as effectively and efficiently as possible? In what place are we most likely to be able to create the conditions and foster the behavioral interactions we wish to produce?

COMMENTARY ON THE EVOLUTION OF PLACEMENT ISSUES

Placement issues have evolved in the 20th century in the context of the professional cultures of psychiatry, psychology, social work, and related disciplines, in addition to professional education. In describing the growth of child psychiatry in the 20th century, Kanner (1957) suggested that the first four decades of the century could be portrayed as follows: The first decade was characterized by thinking *about* children—developing professional cultures, including psychometry, dynamic psychiatry, juvenile courts, and the mental hygiene movement; the second by doing things *to* children—developing better community facilities, special classes, probation, and organized foster home care, for example;

the third by doing things *for* children—studying and working with families and schools to help children with emotional or behavioral problems; and the fourth by working *with* children—including children themselves as participants in therapeutic programs. Since the mid-20th century, it appears that changes in service delivery models have been limited to variations in emphasis on these four themes.

As we reviewed the history of placement, we arrived at two conclusions. First, no new placements per se have been proposed and no radically different placement ideas have been formulated since about 1950. We believe that there may be no unexplored therapeutic or habilitative places for children with emotional or behavioral disorders. The key to resolving placement issues is quite unlikely to be found in devising a new placement scheme; it seems much more likely to be found in better implementation of the placement ideas already available. Second, each placement option seems both inherently unable to accommodate every child—even when implemented with the greatest available expertise and finesse—and invariably to be corrupted by human failures in implementation.

Hoffman (1974) concluded two decades ago, regarding the history of service delivery systems, that "in each case, what began as sincere, humanistic efforts toward change were turned into near caricatures of their original purposes" (p. 71). We have found no evidence of an exception to this conclusion for any placement option. Nearly three decades ago, Redl (1966b) described how professionals too often act as if they really don't care how well interventions are implemented or how carefully a special environment is constructed to support an intervention, often justifying a cavalier attitude about implementation in economic terms. In fact, his commentary on "implementational sins" still rings true:

> If I intended to build a plant for the production of atomic energy, for instance, nobody would come around and call me a fool because I insisted on getting uranium or whatever it takes instead of being nice and cooperative and doing it with strawberry juice, which is much more "reasonable" because it grows right here, is cheaper, and supports the local industry to boot. My demand for just the type of material—and just the type of container and storage atmosphere—I need would be considered, although admittedly exorbitant, quite "realistic." In a parallel case in the field of services to emotionally sick children, I would much more likely be called an "unrealistic fool who probably thinks money grows on trees." The result of our widespread disease of "implementational psychopathy" is that we are often not really doing what we said we would undertake and that we are all too elegantly hopping over our implementational sins, just because we don't think we have to care. (Redl, 1966a, pp. 14–15)

Given the problem of making any placement work reliably and effectively for all students, one must review the evolution and current array of options. Selected landmarks in the evolution of placement options and sources of information about them are shown in Table 2.1. The landmarks listed in Table 2.1 are not necessarily the first or earliest account of each option. However, each is among the earliest accounts we were able to locate.

By the early 1960s, every type of placement option now employed (cf. Knitzer et al., 1990, p. 11) had been initiated (cf. Berkowitz & Rothman, 1967). These options included at least the following:

- Regular classroom with supports, including aides, counselling, or mental health services.
- Crisis or resource teachers in regular schools, including consultation with regular classroom teachers and students spending minimum time in the resource room.
- Self-contained special class in a regular school, including mainstreaming for part of the school day.
- Special day schools, including those organized on a cooperative or regional basis.
- Day treatment or partial hospitalization programs attached to hospitals or residential centers, including those placing some students in regular classrooms in the community.
- Residential treatment centers and inpatient hospitals, including those sending some students home on weekends and to regular classrooms in the community.

TABLE 2.1
Selected Landmarks in the History of Placement

Year/Decade	*Landmark*
1840s	Moral therapy used in asylums including children and youth (Brigham, 1847; Mayo, 1839)
1850s	State institutions for delinquents (Bremner, 1970; Rothman, 1971)
1871	Public school ungraded class established for truant, disobedient, and insubordinate children (Hoffman, 1974)
1920s	Mental hygiene and guidance programs in public schools (Bremner, 1971, pp. 947–957, 1040–1057; Haines, 1925; Kanner, 1973)
1931	Psychiatric hospital for children (Davids, 1975)
1935	Special classes established at Bellevue Psychiatric Hospital (Wright, 1967)
1937	All-adolescent psychiatric hospital unit at Bellevue (Crespi, 1989)
1944	Residential program organized around psychodynamic principles (Bettelheim, 1950; Bettelheim & Sylvester, 1948)
1946	Residential program organized around milieu and psychoeducational principles (Redl & Wineman, 1952a, 1952b)
1953	Day school for severely emotionally disturbed children (Fenichel, Freedman, & Klapper, 1960)
1961	Residential program organized around principles of ecological psychology (Hobbs, 1965, 1974)
1962	Special public school classes organized around behavior principles (Haring & Phillips, 1962)
1964	National survey of special public school classes (Morse, Cutler, & Fink, 1964)
1965	Crisis, helping, or resource teachers (Morse, 1965a)
1968	Special public school classes with specific behavioral curriculum (Hewett, 1968)

- Homebound instruction, in which teachers visit students' homes to provide instruction.
- Schools in juvenile detention centers and prisons.

Making public schools into clinical schools—centers of clinical services, including health, mental health, welfare, research, and training—was proposed in the 1960s by Rothman and Berkowitz (1967). Every conceivable combination of place and treatment seems to us to have been considered and attempted, and each appears to have been found successful for some children and unsuccessful for others. Understanding the issue of placement in dealing with children whose behavior is extremely problematic demands that one reconsider the general purposes of placing students in various settings.

Throughout the history of programs for children with emotional or behavioral disorders, the general purposes of placement have been to control or create a social ecology conducive to appropriate behavior and mental health, both of the children and of the families and communities from which they are removed or in which they are kept (see chap. 1). We believe that in all cases these purposes have been expressed as one or more of the following:

- Protecting others (family, community, schoolmates) from children's uncontrolled or intolerable behavior.
- Protecting children from themselves or others.
- Educating or training children in academics and other life skills and appropriate emotional responses, attitudes, and conduct.
- Educating or training children's families or teachers and peers in order to provide a more supportive environment.
- Keeping children available and amenable to therapies—psychotherapy, pharmacotherapy, or behavior therapy.
- Providing opportunity for observation and assessment of children's behavior and its contexts.

The pursuit of any or all of these purposes requires altering children's social environment through two strategies: injecting necessary and sufficient services into the places in which the children live, and moving children to or keeping children in the places where these services can be delivered most reliably, effectively, and efficiently (cf. Morse, 1985; Redl, 1966a). Controversy about placement begins with the varying answers professionals give to two questions: What services are necessary and sufficient to resolve the student's difficulties? Where can these services be delivered with greatest reliability and effect and at lowest cost? In special education and related fields, there is little agreement regarding what is required to address students' problems—the *what* of intervention. There appears to be even less agreement about *where* intervention is best accomplished, given a consensus about what is needed.

The controversy does not stop with questions about necessary and sufficient services and the places in which they are best delivered. It continues with varying answers to two additional questions: To what extent should placement decisions be made primarily in the immediate interests or crises of children? To what extent should placement options other than children's "natural" home and neighborhood school be abandoned in favor of long-range preventative strategies and noncrisis interventions? In commenting on her ethnographic study of foster placements in New York City, Sheehan (1993a, 1993b) captured two essential problems common to all placement options: unpredictable effects and the dilemma presented by considering both long-term solutions and immediate approaches:

> The achievements and the failures of the foster-care system are as varied as the children, parents, and foster parents it comprises. . . . The effects of foster care on any child are as unpredictable as its effects were on Florence and Crystal [two women whose foster care experiences were described]. The simple remedy one hears proposed most often is that the money spent on foster care—whose wards in New York City have nearly tripled in the past ten years—would be better spent trying to solve its root causes: poverty, drug addiction, and homelessness. Yet experience has shown that these social problems are amenable only to slow, expensive, and hard-thought-out measures. In the meantime, something has to be done to take care of the children. (Sheehan, 1993b, p. 79)

The legacies of educational placement include not only success but failure and uncertainty as well. Hobbs commented on Project Re-ED: "From one perspective, Project Re-ED could be declared a success. Yet it is just as readily manifest that Re-ED does not offer a solution of what to do about the disturbed child" (1974, p. 161).

Although every placement option has its shining examples of success, each also has for many been a nightmare of failure to achieve the equality of opportunity that was desired. To some extent, the preoccupation with place per se—the LRE as an end, not a means—has cloaked the legacy of success of many placement options in suspicion and denial. Preoccupation with place has, in fact, allowed some to turn the legacy of failure into an argument for uniform placement. If one denies the success of alternative placements for some students, then the LRE appears always to be the neighborhood school and regular classroom. Thus, goals and means are confused: "Confusing the social *goal* of equal opportunity with *place* of opportunity distracted social scientists as well as the lay public from attention to what were appropriate educational means to reach desired ends" (Semmel, Gerber, & MacMillan, 1994, p. 485).

The legacy of uncertainty, too, plays to the argument for universal and uniform placement decisions. "Often, all things considered, we are unable to predict just what placement would be best for a given pupil" (Morse, 1985, p. 270). This statement, although true in terms of extremely accurate prediction, might be misinterpreted to mean that there is typically no basis for making alternative placement decisions. Experienced professionals can often predict what type of placement is better for helping a child.

We might reconsider the question raised by Redl's (1966b) commentary on our "implementational sins." Do we care enough to find out not only what we must do to help children, but where we can make those things happen reliably and safely, regardless of the cost? Indeed, "A *place*—mainstream, special class, institution, or whatever—does not define needed treatment" (Morse, 1985, p. 270). Nor can all forms of needed treatment be provided in every place. Place does not define treatment, but it does constrain it. The history of failure and uncertainty of all types of placements should lead us into more careful research and analyses that return our attention to the successes of each alternative. The abandonment of alternative placements that work for some is inappropriate, as is the determination to standardize for all what some have termed students' "social address" (see Zigler, Hodapp, & Edison, 1990).

The great challenge of the 21st century will not be reconceptualizing services and placements for students with emotional or behavioral disorders, but instead bringing to fruition the concept of effective services in an array of alternative placements, with each student placed in the least restrictive alternative (cf. Huefner, 1994). This concept was articulated in the 1960s by Hobbs (1964, 1974), as demonstrated in this passage:

> One of the cardinal principles of the Re-ED idea is that the disturbed child should be removed the least possible distance from his home, school, and community—in time, in geographical space, and in the psychological texture of the experience provided. Logically extended, this concept leads to keeping children out of the Re-ED schools whenever possible and seeking, instead, to work with the child and significant other people in his life in their natural settings. Special residential placement would thus be indicated only when a child needs intensive, around-the-clock re-education or when the family is so fragile as to be unable to sustain him. (Hobbs, 1974, p. 163)

Hobbs's eloquently stated principles and goals are not outdated, nor will they be. Achieving what he described, however, is an especially daunting challenge in a society in which an escalating number of children's natural settings are increasingly abusive, chaotic, coercive, and dangerous; a rising number of families are fragile or unable to offer a protective and nurturing environment; and public funding of social services is under siege. Moreover, in the summary report of his monumental Project on Classification of Exceptional Children, Hobbs (1975) offered, along with his appeal for the least restrictive, least stigmatizing, most normalized treatment, a caveat:

> These arguments should not be construed as opposing special classes or special institutions for exceptional children who need the intensive assistance that such arrangements can provide, who have difficulty sustaining for long periods the

> demands of normal environments, who have unsatisfactory and irremediable living arrangements at home and thus require special residential placement, or who are so disruptive of regular classes or so burdensome to their families that a special placement is necessary. (pp. 10–11)

The history of placement suggests that those of us in the helping professions will not be able in the forseeable future to avoid making personal, often agonizing judgments regarding which students need intensive assistance in a special class, which students are unable to sustain the demands of normal environments, which home environments are irremediable, when the disruption and burden of a youngster's behavior is intolerable to a teacher or family and a special placement is necessary, and when the child placed in a restrictive setting should be returned to a more nearly normal environment. History also suggests that intelligent programmatic research could eventually provide far more reliable bases than we now have for making these judgments. Such research cannot be accomplished easily or quickly; it will require extraordinary efforts to accumulate, over a period of decades, reliable data indicating how *where* children are placed affects *what* and *how* interventions can be delivered most effectively.

REFERENCES

Abeson, A., Burgdorf, R. L., Casey, P. J., Kunz, J. W., & NcNeil, W. (1975). Access to opportunity. In N. Hobbs (Ed.), *Issues in the classification of children* (Vol. 2, pp. 270–292). San Francisco: Jossey-Bass.

Barth, J. (1960). *The sotweed factor*. New York: Doubleday.

Bateman, B. D. (1992). *Better IEPs*. Creswell, OR: Otter Ink Press.

Bateman, B. D. (1994). Who, how, and where: Special education's issues in perpetuity [Special issue, Theory and Practice of Special Education: Taking Stock a Quarter Century After Deno and Dunn]. *Journal of Special Education, 27*, 509–520.

Bergan, J. R. (1977). *Behavioral consultation*. Columbus, OH: Merrill.

Berkowitz, P. H. (1974). Pearl H. Berkowitz. In J. M. Kauffman & C. D. Lewis (Eds.), *Teaching children with behavior disorders: Personal perspectives* (pp. 24–49). Columbus, OH: Merrill.

Berkowitz, P. H., & Rothman, E. P. (1960). *The disturbed child: Recognition and psychoeducational therapy in the classroom*. New York: New York University Press.

Berkowitz, P. H., & Rothman, E. P. (Eds.). (1967). *Public education for disturbed children in New York City*. Springfield, IL: Thomas.

Bettelheim, B. (1950). *Love is not enough*. New York: Macmillan.

Bettelheim, B., & Sylvester, W. (1948). A therapeutic milieu. *American Journal of Orthopsychiatry, 18*, 191–206.

Bockoven, J. S. (1956). Moral treatment in American psychiatry. *Journal of Nervous and Mental Disease, 124*, 167–194, 292–321.

Braaten, S., Kauffman, J. M., Braaten, B., Nelson, C. M., & Polsgrove, L. (1988). The regular education initiative: Patent medicine for behavioral disorders. *Exceptional Children, 55*, 21–27.

Bremner, R. H. (Ed.). (1970). *Children and youth in America: A documentary history: Vol. 1, 1600–1865*. Cambridge, MA: Harvard University Press.

Bremner, R. H. (Ed.). (1971). *Children and youth in America: A documentary history: Vol. 2, 1866–1932*. Cambridge, MA: Harvard University Press.

Brigham, A. (1845). Schools in lunatic asylums. *American Journal of Insanity, 1*, 326–340.

Brigham, A. (1847). The moral treatment of insanity. *American Journal of Insanity, 4*, 1–15.

Caplan, R. B. (1969). *Psychiatry and the community in nineteenth century America.* New York: Basic Books.

Carlson, E. T., & Dain, N. (1960). The psychotherapy that was moral treatment. *American Journal of Psychiatry, 117*, 519–524.

Crespi, T. D. (1989). *Child and adolescent psychopathology and involuntary hospitalization.* Springfield, IL: Thomas.

Dain, N., & Carlson, E. T. (1960). Milieu therapy in the nineteenth century: Patient care at the Friend's Asylum, Frankford, Pennsylvania, 1817–1861. *Journal of Nervous and Mental Disease, 131*, 277–290.

Davids, L. (1975). Therapeutic approaches to children in residential treatment: Changes from the mid-1950s to the mid-1970s. *American Psychologist, 84*, 161–164.

Despert, J. L. (1965). *The emotionally disturbed child—then and now.* New York: Brunner.

Deutsch, A. (1948). *The shame of the states.* New York: Harcourt Brace.

Fenichel, C. (1966). Psychoeducational approaches for seriously disturbed children in the classroom. In P. Knoblock (Ed.), *Intervention approaches in educating emotionally disturbed children* (pp. 5–18). Syracuse, NY: Syracuse University Press.

Fenichel, C. (1974). Carl Fenichel. In J. M. Kauffman & C. D. Lewis (Eds.), *Teaching children with behavior disorders: Personal perspectives* (pp. 50–75). Columbus, OH: Merrill.

Fenichel, C., Freedman, A. M., & Klapper, Z. (1960). A day school for schizophrenic children. *American Journal of Orthopsychiatry, 30*, 130–143.

Grob, G. N. (1973). *Mental institutions in America: Social policy to 1875.* New York: Free Press.

Grob, G. N. (1983). *Mental illness and American society, 1875–1940.* Princeton, NJ: Princeton University Press.

Grosenick, J. K., George, M. P., & George, N. L. (1987). A profile of school programs for the behaviorally disordered: Twenty years after Morse, Cutler, and Fink. *Behavioral Disorders, 13*, 108–115.

Haines, T. H. (1925). State laws relating to special classes and school for mentally handicapped children in the public schools. *Mental Hygiene, 9*, 545–551.

Hallenbeck, B. A., Kauffman, J. M., & Lloyd, J. W. (1993). When, how, and why educational placement decisions are made: Two case studies. *Journal of Emotional and Behavioral Disorders, 1*, 109–117.

Haring, N. G., & Phillips, E. L. (1962). *Educating emotionally disturbed children.* New York: McGraw-Hill.

Hay, L. (1953). A new school channel for helping the troubled child. *American Journal of Orthopsychiatry, 23*, 678–683.

Hay, L. (1967). The junior guidance classes program. In P. H. Berkowitz & E. P. Rothman (Eds.), *Public education for disturbed children in New York City* (pp. 197–224). Springfield, IL: Thomas.

Healy, W. (1915a). *The individual delinquent.* Boston: Little, Brown.

Healy, W. (1915b). *Mental conflicts and misconduct.* Boston: Little, Brown.

Healy, W. (1931). *Reconstructing behavior in youth: A study of problem children in foster homes.* New York: Knopf.

Hewett, F. M. (1967). Establishing a school in a psychiatric hospital. *Mental Hygiene, 51*, 275–283.

Hewett, F. M. (1968). *The emotionally disturbed child in the classroom.* Boston: Allyn & Bacon.

Hewett, F. M., & Forness, S. R. (1974). *Education of exceptional learners.* Newton, MA: Allyn & Bacon.

Hirschberg, J. C. (1953). The role of education in the treatment of emotionally disturbed children through planned ego development. *American Journal of Orthopsychiatry, 23*, 684–690.

Hobbs, N. (1964). Mental health's third revolution. *American Journal of Orthopsychiatry, 34*, 823–824.

Hobbs, N. (1965). How the Re-ED plan developed. In N. J. Long, W. C. Morse, & R. G. Newman (Eds.), *Conflict in the classroom* (pp. 286–294). Belmont, CA: Wadsworth.

Hobbs, N. (1974). Nicholas Hobbs. In J. M. Kauffman & C. D. Lewis (Eds.), *Teaching children with behavior disorders: Personal perspectives* (pp. 142–167). Columbus, OH: Merrill.

Hobbs, N. (1975). *The futures of children.* San Francisco: Jossey-Bass.

Hoffman, E. (1974). The treatment of deviance by the educational system: History. In W. C. Rhodes & S. Head (Eds.), *A study of child variance: Vol. 3. Service delivery systems.* Ann Arbor, MI: University of Michigan.

Hoffman, E. (1975). The American public school and the deviant child: The origins of their involvement. *Journal of Special Education, 9,* 415–423.

Hollister, W. G., & Goldston, S. E. (1962). *Considerations for planning classes for the emotionally disturbed.* Washington, DC: Council for Exceptional Children.

Huefner, D. S. (1994). The mainstreaming cases: Tensions and trends for school administrators. *Education Administration Quarterly, 30,* 27–55.

Idstein, P. (1993). Swimming against the mainstream. *Phi Delta Kappan, 75,* 336–340.

Jackson, D. (1993, March 28–April 2). Failure track. *Chicago Tribune.*

Kanner, L. (1957). *Child psychiatry* (3rd ed.). Springfield, IL: Thomas.

Kanner, L. (1962). Emotionally disturbed children. A historical review. *Child Development, 33,* 97–102.

Kanner, L. (1973). Historical perspective on developmental deviations. *Journal of Autism and Childhood Schizophrenia, 3,* 187–198.

Kauffman, J. M. (1976). Nineteenth century views of children's behavior disorders: Historical contributions and continuing issues. *Journal of Special Education, 10,* 335–349.

Kauffman, J. M. (1993). *Characteristics of emotional and behavioral disorders of children and youth* (5th ed.). Columbus, OH: Merrill/Macmillan.

Knitzer, J. (1982). *Unclaimed children: The failure of public responsibility to children and adolescents in need of mental health services.* Washington, DC: Children's Defense Fund.

Knitzer, J., Steinberg, Z., & Fleisch, B. (1990). *At the schoolhouse door: An examination of programs and policies for children with behavioral and emotional problems.* New York: Bank Street College of Education.

Kornberg, L. (1955). *A class for disturbed children: A case study and its meaning for education.* New York: Teachers College Press.

Krugman, M. (Chair). (1953). Symposium: The education of emotionally disturbed children. *American Journal of Orthopsychiatry, 23,* 667–731.

Lewis, C. D. (1974). Introduction: Landmarks. In J. M. Kauffman & C. D. Lewis (Eds.), *Teaching children with behavior disorders: Personal perspectives.* Columbus, OH: Merrill.

Lipsky, D. K., & Gartner, A. (1991). Restructuring for quality. In J. W. Lloyd, N. N. Singh, & A. C. Repp (Eds.), *The regular education initiative: Alternative perspectives on concepts, issues, and models* (pp. 43–57). Sycamore, IL: Sycamore.

Lloyd, J. W., Singh, N. N., & Repp, A. C. (Eds.). (1991). *The regular education initiative: Alternative perspectives on concepts, issues, and models.* Sycamore, IL: Sycamore.

Lundy, M., & Pumariega, A. J. (1993). Psychiatric hospitalization of children and adolescents: Treatment in search of a rationale. *Journal of Child and Family Studies, 2,* 1–4.

Mayo, T. (1839). *Elements of pathology of the human mind.* Philadelphia: Waldie.

Menninger Foundation, Children's Division. (1969). *Disturbed children: Examination and assessment through team process.* San Francisco: Jossey-Bass.

Morse, W. C. (1953). The development of a mental hygiene milieu in a camp program for disturbed boys. *American Journal of Orthopsychiatry, 23,* 826–833.

Morse, W. C. (1965a). The crisis teacher. In N. J. Long, W. C. Morse, & R. G. Newman (Eds.), *Conflict in the classroom* (pp. 251–254). Belmont, CA: Wadsworth.

Morse, W. C. (1965b). Intervention techniques for the classroom teacher. In P. Knoblock (Ed.), *Educational programming for emotionally disturbed children: The decade ahead.* Syracuse, NY: Syracuse University Press.

Morse, W. C. (1971a). Crisis intervention in school mental health and special classes for the disturbed. In N. J. Long, W. C. Morse, & R. G. Newman (Eds.), *Conflict in the classroom* (2nd ed., pp. 459–464). Belmont, CA: Wadsworth.

Morse, W. C. (1971b). The crisis or helping teacher. In N. J. Long, W. C. Morse, & R. G. Newman (Eds.), *Conflict in the classroom* (2nd ed.). Belmont, CA: Wadsworth.

Morse, W. C. (1974). William C. Morse. In J. M. Kauffman & C. D. Lewis (Eds.), *Teaching children with behavior disorders: Personal perspectives* (pp. 198–216). Columbus, OH: Merrill.

Morse, W. C. (1984). Personal perspective. In B. Blatt & R. J. Morris (Eds.), *Perspectives in special education: Personal orientations* (pp. 101–124). Glenview, IL: Scott, Foresman.

Morse, W. C. (1985). *The education and treatment of socioemotionally impaired children and youth.* Syracuse, NY: Syracuse University Press.

Morse, W. C. (1994). Comments from a biased viewpoint [Special issue, Theory and Practice of Special Education: Taking Stock a Quarter Century After Deno and Dunn]. *Journal of Special Education, 27,* 531–542.

Morse, W. C., Cutler, R. L., & Fink, A. H. (1964). *Public school classes for the emotionally disturbed: A research analysis.* Washington, DC: Council for Exceptional Children.

Nelson, C. M., & Stevens, K. B. (1981). An accountable consultation model for mainstreaming behaviorally disordered children. *Behavioral Disorders, 6,* 82–91.

Peacock Hill Working Group. (1991). Problems and promises in special education and related services for children and youth with emotional or behavioral disorders. *Behavioral Disorders, 16,* 299–313.

Phillips, L., Draguns, J. G., & Bartlett, D. P. (1975). Classification of behavior disorders. In N. Hobbs (Ed.), *Issues in the classification of children* (Vol. 1, pp. 26–55). San Francisco: Jossey-Bass.

Prugh, D. G., Engel, M., & Morse, W. C. (1975). Emotional disturbance in children. In N. Hobbs (Ed.), *Issues in the classification of children* (Vol. 1, pp. 261–299). San Francisco: Jossey-Bass.

Ray, I. (1846). Observations on the principal hospitals for the insane in Great Britain, France and Germany. *American Journal of Insanity, 2,* 289–390.

Ray, I. (1852). The popular feeling towards hospitals for the insane. *American Journal of Insanity, 9,* 36–65.

Redl, F. (1966a). Designing a therapeutic classroom environment for disturbed children: The milieu approach. In P. Knoblock (Ed.), *Intervention approaches in educating emotionally disturbed children* (pp. 79–98). Syracuse, NY: Syracuse University Press.

Redl, F. (1966b). *When we deal with children.* New York: Free Press.

Redl, F., & Wineman, D. (1952a). *Children who hate.* New York: Free Press.

Redl, F., & Wineman, D. (1952b). *Controls from within.* New York: Free Press.

Rhodes, W. C., & Sagor, M. (1975). Community perspectives. In N. Hobbs (Ed.), *Issues in the classification of children* (Vol. 1, pp. 101–129). San Francisco: Jossey-Bass.

Rogers, J. (1993, May). The inclusion revolution. Phi *Delta Kappa Research Bulletin No. 11.*

Rothman, D. (1971). *The discovery of the asylum: Social order and disorder in the new republic.* Boston: Little, Brown.

Rothman, E. P. (1974). Esther P. Rothman. In J. M. Kauffman & C. D. Lewis (Eds.), *Teaching children with behavior disorders: Personal perspectives* (pp. 218–239). Columbus, OH: Merrill.

Rothman, E. P., & Berkowitz, P. H. (1967). The clinical school—a paradigm. In P. H. Berkowitz & E. P. Rothman (Eds.), *Public education for disturbed children in New York City* (pp. 355–369). Springfield, IL: Thomas.

Rubenstein, E. A. (1948). Childhood mental disease in America. *American Journal of Orthopsychiatry, 18,* 314–321.

Ryan, W. C. (1928, July). *The preparation of teachers for dealing with behavior problem children.* Minneapolis, MN: National Education Association.

Scull, A. T. (1975). From madness to mental illness: Medical men as moral entrepreneurs. *Archives of European Sociology, 16*, 218–251.

Semmel, M. I., Gerber, M. M., & MacMillan, D. L. (1994). Twenty-five years after Dunn's article: A legacy of policy analysis research in special education [Special issue, Theory and Practice of Special Education: Taking Stock a Quarter Century After Deno and Dunn]. *Journal of Special Education, 27*, 481–495.

Sheehan, S. (1993a, January 11). A lost childhood. *The New Yorker*, pp. 54–85.

Sheehan, S. (1993b, January 18). A lost motherhood. *The New Yorker*, pp. 52–79.

Silberman, C. E. (1978). *Criminal violence, criminal justice*. New York: Random House.

Stainback, W., & Stainback, S. (1991). A rationale for integration and restructuring: A synopsis. In J. W. Lloyd, N. N. Singh, & A. C. Repp (Eds.), *The regular education initiative: Alternative perspectives on concepts, issues, and models* (pp. 226–239). Sycamore, IL: Sycamore.

Stullken, E. H. (1950). Special schools and classes for the socially maladjusted. In N. B. Henry (Ed.), *The education of exceptional children* (pp. 281–301). Chicago: University of Chicago Press.

Walker, H. M., & Bullis, M. (1991). Behavior disorders and the social context of regular class integration: A conceptual dilemma? In J. W. Lloyd, N. N. Singh, & A. C. Repp (Eds.), *The regular education initiative: Alternative perspectives on concepts, issues, and models* (pp. 75–93). Sycamore, IL: Sycamore.

Wright, W. G. (1967). The Bellevue Psychiatric Hospital school. In P. H. Berkowitz & E. P. Rothman (Eds.), *Public education for disturbed children in New York City* (pp. 78–123). Springfield, IL: Thomas.

Zigler, E., Hodapp, R. M., & Edison, M. R. (1990). From theory to practice in the care and education of mentally retarded individuals. *American Journal on Mental Retardation, 95*, 1–12.

PART II

Current Realities

CHAPTER

3

WHERE STUDENTS WITH EMOTIONAL OR BEHAVIORAL DISORDERS GO TO SCHOOL

Susan A. Stephens
The Center for Assessment and Policy Development,
Bala Cynwyd, PA

K. Charlie Lakin
University of Minnesota

Probably no category of disabling condition within the special education classifications creates more controversy and confusion than that of "serious emotional disturbance" (emotional or behavioral disorders).[1] Similar behaviors or presenting problems may have a number of different causes, ranging from brain and metabolic disorders to situationally induced disorders associated with family dysfunction (including abuse and neglect as well as breakdown in family functioning), to labeling based on race or gender, to theoretical biases or differential thresholds for appropriate or tolerable behavior. Evidence abounds that there is no common perception of the manifestations or causes that should define "serious emotional disturbance," or the means to differentiate it from "social maladjustment" as is required under current federal special education statutes. In fact, there are long-standing efforts to modify the federal definition to recognize behavior or conduct disorders and to focus on the effects of emotional and behavioral disorders on personal, vocational and social—as well as academic—skills (Viadero, 1992).

The results of these ambiguities in the definition of emotional and behavioral disorders and how it is applied in educational systems are clearly evident in the December 1, 1990, reports of the prevalence of emotional or behavioral disorders among school-age students (ages 6–17) receiving special education under the Individuals with Disabilities Education Act (U.S. Department of Education,

[1]In addition to the diversity and ambiguity within special education about the definition and diagnosis of emotional disturbance, other service systems—including social service, mental health, and juvenile justice—also use similar labels to identify children and youth, and may use their own criteria for such a designation.

1991). Those statistics show that states vary in the reported proportion of students identified as having special education needs associated with emotional or behavioral disorders among all enrolled students, from a low of .04% to .05% (in Mississippi and Arkansas, respectively) to a high of 2.2% (in Connecticut and Massachusetts), with the national average being .89%.

Further evidence of the ambiguity in the definition of emotional or behavioral disorders is indicated by the state-by-state variation in the changes of the number of students classified with this disability. Between 1977 and 1990, the number of students identified as having emotional or behavioral disorders in the special education system decreased by more than 50% in 3 states, while increasing by more than 200% in 15 others. In 1990, 26 states had more than twice the prevalence of emotional or behavioral disorders among their special education population than they had reported in 1977, and nationally the increase was 38.5%. During the same period, the total number of school-age students identified as having disabilities for the purposes of receiving special education increased by only 23.7%.

Such statistics strongly suggest that the practice of identifying students as having emotional or behavioral disorders for the purposes of receiving special education is fraught with ambiguity and instability. The dramatic differences among states seem likely to reflect differences in the extent to which special education programs for students with emotional or behavioral disorders are used as mechanisms of isolation and control of students whose behavior is disturbing within the typical school environment and for whom school-related services are perceived as preferable to other efforts at control (chiefly, expulsion and punishment). These differences may also reflect the differences in state and regional perceptions of the ability and responsibility of schools to develop and carry out effective intervention programs. Further, they may also reflect differences among states in the extent to which children and youth placed by their families, physicians, and social service agencies in private schools and other settings for treatment of emotional or behavioral disorders are concurrently identified within the special education system as having these disorders. Finally, differences in funding arrangements across the states may define which populations are the primary responsibility of particular agencies, specifically, the extent to which children and youths with emotional or behavioral disorders are considered to be primarily the responsibility of the education, mental health, child welfare, or juvenile justice agencies.[2]

All these factors combine to create a situation in which there is no definitive understanding of what constitutes emotional or behavioral disorders.[3] For exam-

---

[2]As noted in a recent report to Congress on the implementation of the Education of the Handicapped Act (U.S. Department of Education, 1990), there are various factors that affect variation in the reporting practices of states—misunderstanding of federal definitions, inability of data systems to produce data in line with the definitions, and varying interpretations of ambiguous situations, for example, students placed at residential facilities but who receive education in the local public school.

[3]See Wells (1991b) for a discussion of these issues as they apply specifically to placement of students with emotional or behavioral disorders in residential treatment settings.

ple, we do not know how many school-age children might meet some established diagnostic standards of emotional or behavioral disorders (or, under an expanded definition, having "social maladjustment"), where students who meet some established standards are being educated, whether such students are being educated appropriately (or indeed whether they are receiving any educational services while in private treatment settings), or what proportion of students who meet a diagnostic standard for emotional or behavioral disorders could benefit from receiving specific special education services.

In this chapter, we present a statistical profile of where students with emotional or behavioral disorders are placed. More specifically, we profile placement in separate educational facilities, that is, day or residential facilities that exclusively or primarily serve students with disabilities and at which students receive educational services. We also describe the characteristics of students with emotional or behavioral disorders who have been placed in such facilities. These descriptions provide a context for subsequent chapters focusing on placement decisions themselves and the impact of placement decisions on students, educators, and parents.

WHERE ARE STUDENTS WITH EMOTIONAL OR BEHAVIORAL DISORDERS EDUCATED?

Students with emotional or behavioral disorders receive educational services in a variety of settings, as do students with other disabilities. As used for the purposes of reporting by the states to the U. S. Department of Education under P.L. 94-142 (the Education of the Handicapped Act [EHA]) and its extensions (most recently, the Individuals with Disabilities Education Act [IDEA]), these settings include:

- Regular classrooms (i.e., classroom settings in which nondisabled students as well as those with disabilities receive instruction)—students are considered to be placed in regular classrooms if they receive special education and related services for less than 21% of the school day.
- Resource rooms as a supplement to education in regular classrooms (in which students with disabilities receive special instruction outside the regular classroom on a regular basis for some portion of the school day)—students are considered to be placed in resource room settings if they receive special education and related services between 21% and 60% of the school day.
- Separate classes within a regular school building (i.e., classes in which only students with disabilities are enrolled, but which are held in the same school building or campus as classes for nondisabled students)—students are considered to be placed in separate classes if they receive special education

and related services for more than 60% of the school day and are in self-contained special education classes for all or part of the day.

- Separate public day schools (public schools that only students with disabilities attend).
- Separate private day schools.
- Public residential facilities at which on-site educational services are provided (these include state-supported or operated residential schools for students with hearing or vision impairments, as well as state- and locally funded residential facilities for children and adults with cognitive impairments such as mental retardation, physical impariments, and emotional or behavioral disorders).
- Private residential facilities at which on-site educational services are provided (including residential treatment programs in which on-site educational services are provided).
- Correctional facilities.[4]
- Homebound or hospital-based instruction.

Placements as Reported by the U.S. Department of Education

Each year, states must report to the U.S. Department of Education the number of students receiving special education under Part B of the Individuals with Disabilities Education Act (IDEA-B), formerly known as the Education of the Handicapped Act (EHA-B), and under Chapter 1 of the Elementary and Secondary Education Act (ESEA for State Operated Programs, or SOP), by primary disabling condition, age, and primary educational placement.

As shown in Table 3.1, most students with disabling conditions whose education is funded with federal special education funds are placed in regular classrooms (about 30%, depending on the reporting year) or in regular classrooms with resource room supplements (another 40%, depending on the reporting year). Further, another quarter of all special education students are in separate classrooms, but within school buildings housing regular classes. Only about 6% or 7% of all students with disabilities are placed in separate facilities or are educated at home or in hospital settings.

The placement patterns for students reported with emotional or behavioral disorders are quite different from those for special education students in general. Within regular school settings, only about six students with emotional or behavioral disorders are placed in regular classrooms (with or without resource room support) for every 10 special education students in general. The ratio of students with emotional or behavioral disorders to all special education students in separate classrooms within regular schools is about 1.4 to 1.0. Thus, compared to the more

[4]Correctional facilities have not been uniformly included as a separate reporting category.

TABLE 3.1
Students Whose Education is Partially Funded Through IDEA and Chapter 1 of ESEA (SOP), Students With Emotional or Behavioral Disorders and All Students
(Percentage of Students in all 50 States and the District of Columbia)

	1986–87	*1987–88*	*1988–89*
Students with emotional or behavioral disorders as percentage of all students under IDEA[a] and ESEA (SOP)[b] combined, ages 6–21	*8.5*	*9.1*	*9.1*
Percentage of students[c] under IDEA and ESEA (SOP) by type of educational setting			
Regular classroom			
Students with emotional or behavioral disorders	9.9	12.6	14.1
All students	27.4	29.1	30.7
Resource room			
Students with emotional or behavioral disorders	34.5	32.9	30
All students	40.9	39.9	38.9
Special class			
Students with emotional or behavioral disorders	36.5	34.5	35.8
All students	24.8	24.6	24.2
Public separate day facility			
Students with emotional or behavioral disorders	7.1	8.9	8
All students	3.3	3.5	3.2
Private separate day facility			
Students with emotional or behavioral disorders	4.8	5.4	5.4
All students	1.6	1.4	1.3
Public residential facility			
Students with emotional or behavioral disorders	1.6	1.8	2.1
All students	0.5	0.5	0.6
Private residential facility			
Students with emotional or behavioral disorders	2.2	1.7	1.7
All students	0.4	0.3	0.3
Other[d]			
Students with emotional or behavioral disorders	3.3	2.2	2.9
All students	1.1	0.7	0.8

Notes. [a]IDEA refers to Part B of the Individuals with Disabilities Education Act. The original legislation was known as the Education of the Handicapped Act (EHA).

[b]ESEA (SOP) refers to Chapter 1 of the Elementary and Secondary Education Act (State Operated Programs).

[c]Ages 3 through 21 in 1986–87, ages 6 through 21 in 1987–88 and 1988–89.

[d]Home-based or hospital instruction, correctional facilities. Correctional facilities not included in total in 1987–88 or 1988–89.

Sources. U.S. Department of Education (1988, 1989, 1990, 1991).

than 90% of all special education students who attend classes within regular schools, only about 80% of students with emotional or behavioral disorders do so, and many more of the latter students are separated from other students for all or part of the school day.

When we look at the placement of special education students in separate facilities, day or residential, the differences in the experience of students with emotional or behavioral disorders compared to special education students generally are even more striking. The proportion of students with emotional or behavioral disorders in public day schools solely or predominantly serving students with disabilities is more than twice that for special education students in general. For private separate day schools, the ratio of students with emotional or behavioral disorders to all special education students placed in these settings is about 3 or 4:1. Although the numbers are small, the ratio between the rates of placement into residential facilities, both public and private, for students with emotional or behavioral disorders and for all students with disabilities served with federal special education funding is even greater. Students who have emotional or behavioral disorders are considerably more likely than special education students in general to be placed in separate facilities, where they are educated apart from nondisabled peers and often, especially in the case of residential placements, in settings at a considerable distance from their family, neighborhood, or community.

Another way to illustrate the same pattern is to look at the proportion of students with emotional or behavioral disorders among all students placed in separate facilities. Although students categorized as having emotional or behavioral disorders account for only about 8% to 9% of all special education students (see Table 3.1), Table 3.2 indicates that about one fourth of all students placed in separate facilities are classified as having emotional or behavioral disorders. Of students placed in residential facilities, particularly private facilities, as many as 40% to 50% may have emotional or behavioral disorders. Thus, in the most restrictive environments, students with emotional or behavioral disorders far outstrip what would be expected based on their proportion in the special education population.

Placements as Estimated by a 1988–89 National Survey

Disproportionate representation of students with emotional or behavioral disorders among all those placed in separate facilities was also found in a survey of such facilities conducted during the 1988–89 school year (Lakin, Stephens, Hill, & Chen, 1990; see appendix for more details of this survey). The results from this survey are also presented in Table 3.2. In this survey, conducted among 1,941 separate facilities randomly selected to be representative of all such facilities nationwide, more than one fourth of students were described by staff[5] of the

[5]The survey obtained reports from officials or key staff at the facilities, many of whom were professionals in special education or related fields. However, the reports should not be interpreted as diagnoses by mental health professionals. Further, the reports may not necessarily reflect the criteria specified in regulations governing special education funding.

TABLE 3.2

Students With Emotional or Behavioral Disorders as Percentage of All Students Placed in Separate Facilities, by Type of Facility (Percentage of Students in All 50 States and the District of Columbia)

	In All Separate Facilities	*In Separate Day Facilities*	*In Separate Residential Facilities*	*In Separate Public Facilities*	*In Separate Private Facilities*
Reports from states on placement of students under IDEA and ESEA (SOP)					
1986–87[a]	23.5	20.9	37.2	19.7	30.7
1987–88[b]	28.9	27.2	39.7	24.6	39.4
1988–89[c]	28.9	26.8	40.3	24.2	40.2
Estimates from 1988 survey of separate facilities					
1988[d]	28.8	19.3	51.7	20.5	41.7

Notes. [a]Students age 3 through 21.
[b]Students age 6 through 21.
[c]Students age 6 through 21.
[d]Students from infancy through 21.
Sources. U.S. Department of Education (1989, 1990, 1991), Lakin et al. (1990).

facility in which they were placed as having emotional or behavioral disorders. As with the students cited in the reports from the states, survey responses from separate facilities indicate that these students were much more likely to represent a large proportion of the population in residential facilities than in day programs, and in private rather than public facilities.

Although confirming the general patterns of placement in separate facilities as reported by the states for students for whom federal special education funds are used, the 1988–89 survey of separate facilities also revealed an area of striking contrast to these reports. Table 3.3 shows the number of students with emotional or behavioral disorders reported by the states to be placed in separate facilities over several years, as well as the estimates from the 1988–89 survey. Looking first at the total column in the far right side of the table, it is apparent that the survey estimated that there were almost 30,000 more students with emotional or behavioral disorders placed in separate facilities in the 1988–89 school year than were reported to receive federal special education funds. The bulk of this difference was in the number of students reported in separate residential facilities, particularly private facilities.

There are a number of reasons for the differences between the state reports of students with emotional or behavioral disorders receiving special education services and the estimates from the survey of separate facilities. Some have to do with the latitude given respondents to the survey to use whatever categories of disabilities they felt best fit their students, rather than more restrictive categories associated with federal regulations or professional theories. However, a major factor is likely to be funding arrangements associated with how children and youth come into the child-serving systems of the states, and which paths are likely to result in placements through the special education system. For example, children whose behavior causes them to be labeled *delinquent* and who are served in separate residential facilities are especially unlikely in many jurisdictions to have their placements paid for with special education funds.

Summary of Placement Patterns for Students with Emotional or Behavioral Disorders

From these analyses we learn the following about where students with emotional or behavioral disorders are placed:

- Although most (about 80%) are in regular school settings, more students with emotional or behavioral disorders, compared to special education students in general, are in segregated classrooms within regular school settings.
- The contrast between the proportion of all special education students who are placed in separate facilities and the proportion of those with emotional or behavioral disorders in such facilities is even greater.

TABLE 3.3

Number of Students With Emotional or Behavioral Disorders in Separate Facilities, by Type of Facility (Students in All 50 States and the District of Columbia)

	Separate Day Facilities			*Separate Residential Facilities*			*All Separate Facilities*		
	Public	*Private*	*All Day Facilities*	*Public*	*Private*	*All Residential Facilities*	*Public*	*Private*	*All Facilities*
Reports from states on placement of students under IDEA and ESEA (SOP)									
1986–87[a]	26,557	18,110	44,667	6,163	8,430	14,593	32,720	26,540	59,260
1987–88[b]	33,425	20,181	53,606	6,638	6,282	12,920	40,063	26,463	66,526
1988–89[c]	29,815	20,211	50,026	7,975	6,288	14,263	37,790	26,499	64,289
Estimates from 1988 survey of separate facilities									
1988[d]	27,830	16,355	44,185	12,427	36,850	49,277	40,257	53,205	93,462

Notes. [a]Students age 3 through 21.
[b]Students age 6 through 21.
[c]Students age 6 through 21.
[d]Students from infancy through 21.
Sources. U.S. Department of Education (1989, 1990, 1991), Lakin et al. (1990).

- The differences in placement rates into separate facilities vary by type of facility, with the largest disparity between students with emotional or behavioral disorders and all special education students being in placements into private residential facilities, where the ratio is as high as 7 to 1.
- The differential placement of students with emotional or behavioral disorders in separate facilities results in that group of students comprising a much larger than expected proportion of the total population of separate school students—as much as 40% to 50% in private and/or residential facilities.
- When national estimates based on reports directly from separate facilities are used, it appears that a much larger number of children and youth with emotional or behavioral disorders are placed in such facilities, particularly in private residential facilities, than are supported with federal special education funding through the IDEA and Chapter 1 of the Elementary and Secondary Education Act.

Factors that may account for these placement patterns include the belief that children and youth with emotional or behavioral disorders are seen as less amenable to treatment within the regular school setting than other students with disabilities. Further, there is ambiguity in the application of the federal special education definition of severely emotionally disturbed such that students with similar emotional or behavioral disorders may or may not be receiving special education funds. Also, the fact that in many cases children and youth with emotional or behavioral disorders may be no longer actively engaged in education may mean that they have come to the attention of child-serving agencies other than the educational system with their communities. Finally, the funding arrangements across agencies responsible for children and youth with emotional or behavioral disorders may result in special education funds being used for only a portion of that group.

The remainder of this chapter uses information from the 1988–89 survey of separate facilities to describe characteristics and experiences of students with emotional or behavioral disorders who are placed in separate day and residential facilities.

CHARACTERISTICS OF STUDENTS WITH EMOTIONAL OR BEHAVIORAL DISORDERS WHO ARE PLACED AT SEPARATE FACILITIES

The 1988–89 survey of separate facilities asked facility administrators to provide information on the sociodemographic characteristics and primary and secondary disabling conditions of their students. Estimates from the survey reports of the distribution of these characteristics among students with emotional or behavioral disorders at separate facilities are presented in Tables 3.4 through 3.8.

Disabling Condition

Of the students reported as having emotional or behavioral disorders as their primary disabling condition, the 1988–89 survey of separate facilities found that close to half were reported to have as their primary type of impairment a serious behavior or conduct disorder (see Table 3.4).[6] This was true both for students placed in day programs as well as those in residential placements. The next most frequently reported type of emotional or behavioral disorder was attention deficit disorder, reported for somewhat less than 20% of the student population in separate facilities. The other types of emotional or behavioral disorders (anxiety or withdrawal disorder, pervasive developmental disorder, substance abuse or dependence, psychotic or schizophrenic thought disorder, or other disorders) were each reported to be the principal type of disorder for 10% or less of the day and residential students at separate facilities.

The differences in placement rates for students with each type of emotional or behavioral disorder between public and private facilities are relatively small, although they suggest some modest specialization between such facilities. It appears that private day facilities have somewhat disproportionately more students with every type of emotional or behavioral disorder, except those specifically related to conduct or behavior problems.[7] On the other hand, among residential programs, private facilities have somewhat more students with substance abuse problems, whereas public programs have more students with developmental and psychiatric disorders.

Most (about two thirds) of students with emotional or behavioral disorders placed in separate day and residential facilities were reported to have no secondary disability (see Table 3.5). Among students with secondary disabilities, the most frequently reported were learning disabilities (14% and 17% of all students with emotional or behavioral disorders in day and residential facilities, respectively), mild or moderate mental retardation (10% and 8%, respectively), and speech or language impairments (8% and 3%, respectively). Overall, nearly one third of students with emotional or behavioral disorders in separate facilities bring with them some kind of cognitive difficulties, although we cannot determine whether these are the cause or result of emotional or behavioral disorders.[8]

---

[6]"Social maladjustment" is specifically excluded from coverage under IDEA-B. The large proportion of students reported to have conduct or behavior disorders in the 1988 survey may be one factor explaining the differences in total number of students with emotional or behavioral disorders in separate facilities between the survey estimates and the federal statistics. Further, it suggests that many such placements may be made for social control reasons.

[7]Private day facilities may include partial hospitalization programs that tend to focus on psychiatric diagnoses rather than behavioral disorders.

[8]Students with emotional or behavioral disorders placed in private facilities, whether day or residential, were somewhat less likely to be reported with a secondary handicap of mental retardation and somewhat more likely to be reported with a secondary handicap of learning disabilities. There are many possible explanations for this, including greater reluctance among private schools to describe

TABLE 3.4

Distribution of Separate School Students With Emotional or Behavioral Disorders, by Type of Primary Handicapping Condition

	In Separate Day Facilities				*In Separate Residential Facilities*			
Primary Handicapping Condition	*Percentage of Students With Emotional or Behavioral Disorders*[a]	*Percentage in Public Facilities*[b]	*Percentage in Private Facilities*[b]	*Percentage of Total Separate Day Facility Population*	*Percentage of Students With Emotional or Behavioral Disorders*	*Percentage in Public Facilities*[b]	*Percentage in Private Facilities*[b]	*Percentage of Total Separate Residential Facility Population*
Attention Deficit Disorder	17.4	52.3	47.7	3.4	19.1	29.9	70.1	9.9
Serious conduct or behavior disorder	47.6	67.4	32.6	9.2	43.7	25.8	74.2	22.6
Anxiety or withdrawal disorder	9.8	52.7	47.3	1.9	9.6	25.5	74.5	5
Pervasive developmental disorder	5.8	51.6	48.4	1.1	4.4	32.5	67.5	2.3
Substance abuse or dependence	3.1	57.1	42.9	0.6	6.4	16.2	83.8	3.3
Psychotic or schizophrenic thought disorder	7.2	59.9	40.1	1.4	6.5	36.5	63.5	3.4
Other emotional or behavioral disorder	9.2	58	42	1.8	10.3	30.8	69.2	5.3
All separate school students with emotional or behavioral disorders	100	63	37	19.3[c]	100	25.2	74.8	51.7[c]

Notes. Data for this table were reported by day facilities with 70.3% (unweighted) of the students in the day facility sample and by residential facilities with 69.5% (unweighted) of the students in the residential facility sample.

[a]Sums to 100%, within rounding error, within the column.

[b]Sums to 100% across public and private facilities.

[c]Differs from sum within column due to rounding error.

Source. Lakin et al. (1990; Tables II.1 and II.2).

TABLE 3.5

Secondary Handicapping Conditions of Separate School Students With Emotional or Behavioral Disorders, by Type of Facility (Percentage of Students)

	No Secondary Disability	*Mild or Moderate Mental Retardation*	*Severe or Profound Mental Retardation*	*Orthopedic or Other Health Impairment*	*Hearing Impairment*	*Vision Impairment*	*Speech or Language Impairment*	*Learning Disability*	*Other*
In separate day facilities	64.4	9.6	2.4	0.4	0.2	<0.1	8.2	13.6	1.1
In separate residential facilities	67.9	8	0.5	0.2	0.2	<0.1	2.9	17.7	2.6

Note. Data for this table were reported by day facilities with 35.6% (unweighted) of the students in the day facility sample and by residential facilities with 32.5% (unweighted) of the students in the residential facility sample.

Source. Lakin et al. (1990, Tables II.8 and II.9).

TABLE 3.6
Percentage[a] of Separate School Students by Age, Students With Emotional or Behavioral Disorders, and All Students

	In Separate Day Facilities		*In Separate Residential Facilities*	
Ages	*Students With Emotional or Behavioral Disorders*	*All Students*	*Students With Emotional or Behavioral Disorders*	*All Students*
0–2	0.6	6.9	1.1	2.5
3–5	11.8	16.3	5.8	5.3
6–11	25.4	25.3	19.2	19.4
12–17	53.6	35.3	66.4	50
18–21	8.6	16.2	7.5	22.8

Notes. Data for this table were reported by day facilities with 38.2% (unweighted) of the students in day facility sample and by residential facilities with 37.7% (unweighted) of the students in the residential facility sample.

[a]Sums to 100% within column.

Source. Lakin et al. (1990, Tables II.22 and II.23).

Age

Compared to all students placed at separate facilities, students with emotional or behavioral disorders are disproportionately adolescents between the ages of 12 and 17. More than half of students with emotional or behavioral disorders reported in the 1988–89 survey of separate facilities were between the ages of 12 and 17 (Table 3.6). Among students with emotional or behavioral disorders at residential facilities, almost two thirds were within that age range. About 20% to 25% of such students in separate facilities were reported to be between the ages of 6 and 11, with the larger percentage in day facilities. Few students with emotional or behavioral disorders younger than age 6 or older than age 17 were reported to be in separate facilities, particularly in residential facilities.

Reports from the states about students served with federal special education funds, regardless of placement, also confirm the predominance of adolescents among those identifed as having emotional or behavioral disorders (see Table 3.7). In the reports for the 1988–89 school year, states reported that 58.4% were in the age range of 12 through 17, whereas 36% were age 6 through 11, and only 5.6% were between 18 and 21. In contrast, among all special education students, the majority (52.3%) were in the youngest age group (6 through 11) and 42.1% were adolescents.

---

their students as having mental retardation, perhaps in part to accommodate parents' wishes to avoid such a label, or an expansion of the populations served by public facilities for students with mental retardation to include students with emotional or behavioral problems. Private facilities also tend to avoid accepting students with a dual diagnosis of emotional disorder and mental retardation, as such students are often victimized by other students.

TABLE 3.7
Percentage of Students Served Under IDEA and ESEA (SOP) in 1988–89, by Age

Ages	*Students With Emotional or Behavioral Disorders*[a]	*All Students*[b]	*Students With Emotional or Behavioral Disorders as a Percentage of All Students in Each Age Range*
6–11	36	52.3	6.2
12–17	58.4	42.1	12.6
18–21	5.6	5.6	9.1
Total	100	100	9.1

Notes. [a]Percentages sum to 100% within this column.
[b]Percentages sum to 100% within this column.
Source. U.S. Department of Education (1990).

Thus, both the survey estimates and the reports from the states suggest that, in contrast to students with other disabling conditions, some emotional or behavioral disorders may not be evident in students' elementary school years. In part, this may be due to later age of onset of certain disorders that may not be manifested until adolescence. Adolescence may also pose situational issues (e.g., those related to sexual development and expression as well as physical strength and the threat of aggression) that are associated with the onset of emotional and behavioral disorders or with the labeling of students as having such disorders. However, lack of appropriate training and support within the school and other child-serving systems may mean that emotional and behavioral disorders in some younger students may go unidentified and untreated.

Gender and Ethnicity

The 1988–89 survey of separate facilities, in addition to collecting data on individual groups of students, categorized facilities by the disabling condition of the majority of students at each facility. Table 3.8 presents the distribution of students by gender and ethnicity for those facilities where more than 50% of the students were reported to have emotional or behavioral disorders.

There are more male than female students in facilities primarily serving students with emotional or behavioral disorders, as is true for separate facilities in general. In particular, separate day schools primarily serving students with emotional or behavioral disorders are much more likely to have male students than are other facilities serving the same type of students.

Close to three fourths of the students in separate facilities primarily serving students with emotional or behavioral disorders were reported to be White and non-Hispanic. This was true for both day and residential as well as public and private facilities, and parallels the patterns for separate facilities in general.

TABLE 3.8
Percentage of Students in Separate Facilities by Gender and Ethnicity, by Primary Disability Served by the Facility

	Separate Day Facilities		*Separate Residential Facilities*	
	Facilities Primarily Serving Students With Emotional or Behavioral Disorders[a]	*All Separate Day Facilities*	*Facilities Primarily Serving Students With Emotional or Behavioral Disorders*	*All Separate Residential Facilities*
Gender of students				
Male	76.9	64.3	67.1	64.6
Female	23.1	35.7	32.9	35.4
Ethnicity of students				
White, not Hispanic	65.5	70.8	72.6	74.8
African American, not Hispanic	24.9	19.4	20.6	18.2
Hispanic	4.8	6.9	4.5	4.1
American Indian or Alaskan native	4.3	1.6	1.6	1.8
Asian or Pacific Islander	0.5	1.4	0.6	1.1

Notes. Data for this table were reported by day facilities with 38.1% (unweighted) of students in the day facility sample and by residential facilities with 37.9% (unweighted) of students in the residential facility sample.

[a]Defined as facilities with more than half of current students reported as having emotional or behavioral disorders as their primary handicapping condition.

Source. Lakin et al. (1990, Tables II.26 and II.27, gender; and Tables II.28 and II.29, ethnicity).

MOVEMENT OF STUDENTS INTO AND OUT OF SEPARATE FACILITIES

A critical issue in placements for students with disabilities is the stability of placement versus movement to reflect the changing educational and other needs of the student. Placement in separate facilities is generally believed to be appropriate in limited circumstances to address highly specialized needs of students. This would suggest that students would generally not spend their entire educational career in separate facilities. Data from the 1988–89 survey of separate facilities support this assumption, particularly for students with emotional or behavioral disorders.

Compared to all separate facilities for students with disabilities, those primarily serving students with emotional or behavioral disorders reported considerably greater turnover of students and shorter average lengths of stay (see Table 3.9). The rate of new admissions and discharges per 100 students reported to have taken place in 1987 was about 10 points higher for day facilities for students with emotional or behavioral disorders than for all separate day facilities, and about 25 points higher for residential facilities primarily serving students with emotional or behavioral disorders than for all residential facilities. Conversely, the average length of stay in separate day facilities was 2.7 years in facilities primarily serving students with emotional or behavioral disorders, compared to 6.4 in all day facilities, and 1.8 years for residential students in facilities for students with emotional or behavioral disorders, compared to 4.2 for all residential facilities.

Possible explanations for the greater student movement and shorter lengths of stay for separate facilities primarily serving students with emotional or behavioral disorders include unsuccessful placements in which students are so disruptive that they are released prior to completion of the treatment program, and restrictions by public agencies funding placements on the time individual students may spend in particular separate facilities. Shorter stays may also, of course, reflect the later average age of admission to facilities serving students with emotional or behavioral disorders. Such stays are also in keeping with the medical orientation of many approaches to treating emotional and behavioral disorders. In contrast to the educational models used in programs for students diagnosed as having learning disabilities or mental retardation that expect to provide long-term interventions, many treatment programs for students with emotional or behavioral disorders are designed to be intensive but short in duration.

Characteristics of Entering Students

Mirroring the current age distribution at separate facilities for students with emotional or behavioral disorders, most new admissions (about two thirds in both day and residential facilities) were reported to be in the 12- to 17-year age

TABLE 3.9
Summary of Student Movement in Separate Facilities in 1987, by Primary Disability Served by the Facility

	Separate Day Facilities		*Separate Residential Facilities*	
	Facilities Primarily Serving Students With Emotional or Behavioral Disorders[a]	*All Separate Day Facilities*	*Facilities Primarily Serving Students With Emotional or Behavioral Disorders*	*All Separate Residential Facilities*
First admissions per 100 students	34.1	23.2	56.5	31.1
Readmissions per 100 students	2.2	1.7	2.9	2.3
Discharges per 100 students	32.1	20.7	54.3	28.8
Average length of enrollment (years)[b]	2.7	6.4	1.8[c]	4.2[d]

Notes. Data for this table were reported by day facilities with 72.2% (unweighted) of students in the day facility sample and by residential facilities with 58% (unweighted) of students in the residential facility sample. A few "short-term" facilities (with more than 100% annual student turnover) were excluded from this table and included as nonresponse. Facilities with reported net change (admissions plus readmissions less discharges) of less than −25% or greater than +25% were excluded from this table and included as nonresponse. Average length of stay of "less than 1 year" was coded as 0.5 year.

[a]Defined as facilities with more than half of current students reported as having emotional or behavioral disorders as their primary handicapping condition.

[b]Among students leaving the facility in 1987.

[c]Residential students only.

[d]Residential students only.

Source. Lakin et al. (1990, Tables IV.1 and IV.2).

range, with another one fourth of new admissions in the 6- to 11-year age range (Table 3.10). This contrasts sharply with the age distribution of new admissions to separate facilities generally, particularly into day facilities. Overall, one third of new admissions to separate day facilities are students between infancy and the age of 6, one fourth between 6 and 11, and 30% between 12 and 17 years of age. Although the contrast between all residential facilities and those serving students with emotional or behavioral disorders is not as great, there are fewer admissions to the latter facilities before the age of 6 and after the age of 18 than to separate residential facilities generally.

Movement of Students in and out of Separate Facilities

Of students who had previously had an educational placement, most (about 50% to 60%) entering separate facilities serving students of varying disabilities were previously enrolled in regular schools. Similar to students entering other separate facilities, approximately 20% to 30% of all those enrolling in facilities primarily serving students with emotional or behavioral disorders were transferring from another separate facility (Table 3.11). When school-age students leave separate facilities, most return to a regular school setting; the same general pattern is true for those leaving facilities primarily serving students with emotional or behavioral disorders, although a number are placed in another separate school (see Table 3.12).

There are some striking differences in the next placements for students leaving facilities primarily serving students with emotional or behavioral disorders compared to those leaving separate facilities as a whole. Almost twice as many students leaving day facilities for students with emotional or behavioral disorders as exiting day students in general either have no next placement or that placement is unknown to the facility's staff, suggesting that, although some may have graduated, others may have dropped out when they left the facility. It is also the case that more students leaving day facilities for students with emotional or behavioral disorders take jobs in the competitive or sheltered labor market or take part in vocational training programs than exiting students in general, perhaps reflecting their older average age as well as a lack of interest in school.

At the same time, for those students who continue in school, it is also the case that about 20% of students leaving separate facilities for students with emotional or behavioral disorders, either day or residential, transfer to another separate facility.

SUMMARY AND IMPLICATIONS

This chapter has used data collected from the states by the U.S. Department of Education and a survey conducted in 1988–89 of special schools serving students with disabilities to undertake some preliminary analyses of issues related to the placement of children and youth with emotional or behavioral disorders.

TABLE 3.10
Age Distribution of New Student Admissions in 1987, by Primary Disability Served by the Facility

	Separate Day Facilities		*Separate Residential Facilities*[a]	
Age at First Admission	*Facilities Primarily Serving Students With Emotional or Behavioral Disorders*[b]	*All Separate Day Facilities*	*Facilities Primarily Serving Students With Emotional or Behavioral Disorders*	*All Separate Residential Facilities*
0–2	0.3	13.1	1	3.6
3–5	5.4	22.3	4.8	6.4
6–11	25.1	25.3	21.3	22.5
12–17	63.5	30.1	67.5	51.3
18–21	5.7	9.1	5.3	16.3

Notes. Data for this table were reported by day facilities with 36.9% (unweighted) of students in the day facility sample and by residential facilities with 38.7% (unweighted) of students in the residential facility sample.

[a]Residential admissions only.

[b]Defined as facilities with more than half of current students reported as having emotional or behavioral disorders as their primary handicapping condition.

Source. Lakin et al. (1990, Tables IV.3 and IV.4).

TABLE 3.11

Previous Educational Placement of New Student Admissions in 1987, by Primary Disability Served by the Facility

	Separate Day Facilities		*Separate Residential Facilities*[a]	
	Facilities Primarily Serving Students With Emotional or Behavioral Disorders[b]	*All Separate Day Facilities*	*Facilities Primarily Serving Students With Emotional or Behavioral Disorders*	*All Separate Residential Facilities*
Regular class (with or without resource room)	22.8	11.7	28.4	19.8
Special class in regular school	37.7	26.6	26.7	32.1
Separate day school	10.8	16.1	8.7	14.2
Residential school	6.4	3.8	16.4	13.7
Home-based instruction	2.7	3.8	2.1	2.2
Other educational placement	13.2	10	8.1	5.7
No instruction	5	25.1	8.8	10
Unknown	1.5	2.9	0.9	2.4

Notes. Data for this table were reported by day facilities with 34.5% (unweighted) of students in the day facility sample and by residential facilities with 35.4% (unweighted) of students in the residential facility sample.

[a]Residential admissions only.

[b]Defined as facilities with more than half of current students reported as having emotional or behavioral disorders as their primary handicapping condition.

Source. Lakin et al. (1990, Tables IV.5 and IV.6).

TABLE 3.12
New Placements of Students Age 0–17 Leaving Separate Facilities in 1987, by Primary Disability Served by the Facility

	Separate Day Facilities		*Separate Residential Facilities*[a]	
	Facilities Primarily Serving Students With Emotional or Behavioral Disorders[b]	*All Separate Day Facilities*	*Facilities Primarily Serving Students With Emotional or Behavioral Disorders*	*All Separate Residential Facilities*
Regular class (with or without resource room)	20.7	19	29.8	22.9
Special class in regular school	32.1	42.5	34.2	37.5
Separate day school	8	16.3	4.9	7.7
Residential school	6.7	5.1	13.1	15.7
College or university degree program	1	0.5	0.4	0.6
Home-based instruction	2.2	1.5	0.6	1.4
Competitive work	6	1.9	2.3	1.3
Supported or subsidized work	0.2	0.2	0.2	0.1
Sheltered employment	2.8	1.7	0.3	0.3
Day activity center	0.1	0.6	0.6	0.4
Vocational training	3.2	1.4	4.4	2.9
No placement or program	8.4	3.9	3.4	2.4
Unknown	8.6	5.6	5.9	6.9

Notes. Data for this table were reported by day facilities with 38.2% (unweighted) of students in the day facility sample and by residential facilities with 36.7% (unweighted) of students in the residential facility sample.

[a]Both day and residential students.

[b]Defined as facilities with more than half of current students reported as having emotional or behavioral disorders as their primary handicapping condition.

Source. Lakin et al. (1990, Tables IV.9 and IV.10).

Most children and youth identified as having emotional or behavioral disorders are educated in separate classrooms or schools, 53% in the 1988–89 school year according to the U.S. Department of Education (1991). Based on both federal statistics and a recent survey, these students are disproportionately placed in separate facilities and form a substantial proportion of all students in separate facilities. In addition, students with emotional or behavioral disorders are particularly likely to be placed in private residential facilities, in many cases through channels other than the special education system. Further, there are increasing numbers of children and youth placed in residential treatment settings for emotional and behavioral disorders (see various statistics cited in Wells, 1991a), a fact that has caused considerable concern in the professional and policy communities.

Placement of children with disabilities into educational environments that are separate from those serving nondisabled children is a decision that can have broad ramifications for an individual's educational experience, socialization, family relationships (particularly if the placement is at a distant residential facility), and the costs borne by the community for educational services. Such placements are arguably sought because of the judgment among professionals and family members that the educational and other (e.g., emotional) needs of the child can best be met in a specialized facility. Thus, day schools and residential programs serving children with emotional or behavioral disorders often report that their students can benefit from a pervasive treatment milieu that is difficult to achieve in a more integrated setting. For example, teachers and therapeutic staff can be recruited and trained to mutually support treatment approaches so that a holistic approach to the child, and thus, positive outcomes, are more likely.[9]

However, placement patterns noted here appear to reflect the fact that some children and youth with emotional or behavior disorders are placed in residential settings for reasons other than those dictated by their educational needs. Such placement decisions are often made by parents and public or private agencies outside the educational system in response to behavior patterns, episodes, disorders, or family problems considered to be of more immediate, short-term concern than any chronic conditions affecting educational performance. In some cases, no public special education funds may be used for these placements, particularly if made for short-term diagnostic or therapeutic reasons or if initiated by the family or by a public agency other than the school. Thus, the number of students who are considered by some professionals to have emotional or behavioral disorders is considerably higher than the number reported to receive federal special education support.

---

[9]Small et al. (1991) argued that many residential treatment programs for children and youth with emotional and behavioral disorders have experienced changes in the severity of impairment among their students that have put tremendous pressure on the staff and other resources of such programs, making the expectation (or hope) that placement in such programs can successfully change the life course of such students more problematic than ever.

This leaves us with two questions that we cannot answer, but that should concern us. The first is whether students placed in programs for persons with emotional or behavioral disorders are being denied special education services to which they have a right and from which they would benefit. The second question is whether the tens of thousands of school-age children and youths being placed in separate settings are being denied the due process that they and their parents would be afforded if the placement were covered under the IDEA.[10]

Some students placed in separate facilities, particularly in residential treatment programs, may not have been previously identified as having special education needs. This is suggested by the fact that most students enter separate facilities as adolescents and many come from regular classroom settings. There is concern that insufficient attention is paid to prevention or to identification and early intervention with children and young adolescents and with their families. Equally, there is concern that placement in separate facilities may be a "last ditch" effort for many students with emotional or behavioral disorders, whose problems have become more severe and more difficult for families, schools, and other community institutions to handle. After leaving such facilities, many drop out or are otherwise "lost" to the formal service systems. In many cases, they appear to receive neither transitional nor long-term support.

Many students with emotional or behavioral disorders are placed in settings in which their daily routine takes place apart from nondisabled peers and, in many cases, from their families. There is concern that separation of children from their peers and their families, based on the existence of a physical, mental, or emotional condition, creates conditions that make truly equal access to educational and developmental opportunities difficult and reinforce the social isolation experienced by many children with disabilities. Such separation during the years of childhood and adolescence is certainly counter to the efforts to integrate adults with disabilities more fully into the mainstream of American life.

These concerns have been especially prominent with regard to the placement of children and youth with emotional or behavioral disorders. These students are likely to be difficult to handle in the classroom, as well as at home and in the community, and there is concern that these factors, rather than consideration of the best educational and treatment approach, may unduly affect the choice of educational setting for these children. Another concern is that insufficient atten-

---

[10]A recent study (U.S. General Accounting Office, 1991) of the quality of monitoring of out-of-state placements made by special education agencies compared to those made by child welfare agencies found that all 42 placements were monitored according to the federal requirements for reporting and case reviews. Although there are no federal requirements for in-person visits with the placed children and youth, state and local requirements for such monitoring were often not met due to budgetary constraints. This was as true of special education placements as of placements made by child welfare agencies. Thus, within this study's very limited scope, there is no support for the belief that placement through the special education system guarantees that more attention will be paid to monitoring the progress of the child.

tion has been given to efforts to work with these children within the context of their families to relieve some of the situational stresses and circumstances that may lead to placement in a foster home or residential facility, or that will hinder their development once they leave such placements. Small, Kennedy, and Bender (1991) noted that many children with emotional or behavioral disorders leaving residential treatment programs, and their families, will need ongoing, comprehensive supports. Small et al. maintained that a rigid distinction between being in placement and being in the community must be recognized as inappropriate in the many cases where strong family bonds and functioning cannot be assumed to exist as a natural support system for returning students. They supported the development of a continuum of supportive care settings outside of residential placements.

Together, these patterns suggest that children and youth who exhibit emotional or behavioral disorders are especially vulnerable to the effects of a fragmented, crisis-oriented service system. Although they may be served through child welfare, juvenile justice, and mental health systems, some are apparently not covered by the protections built into the IDEA until they are placed in a separate school. Many others suffer from the lack of comprehensive supports to children and their families that might help some, at least, avoid the severe problems or crises that lead to placements in separate—particularly residential—facilities. Given that such placements put a tremendous financial burden on society, and that the success of interventions for many children and youth with severe or long-standing emotional or behavioral disorders is often not great, considerably more attention and effort needs to be given to prevention, early intervention, and coordination of efforts across education and other service systems, with the hope of lessening the need for the restrictive placements and intensive interventions represented by separate day and residential facilities.

APPENDIX: SURVEY METHODOLOGY

1988–89 Survey of Separate Facilities

The Survey of Separate Facilities was conducted during the 1988–89 school year as part of the "Study of Programs of Instruction for Handicapped Children and Youth in Day and Residential Facilities" by Mathematica Policy Research, with the University of Minnesota as a subcontractor, under contract number 300-85-0190 from the U.S. Department of Education. The survey was designed to provide quantitative data on the current status and recent changes in the characteristics of students and educational programs from a nationally representative sample of day or residential facilities providing special education and other services exclusively or primarily to students with disabilities.

The facilities included in the survey were selected from a sample frame compiled from a large number of sources, including published directories, lists from advocacy groups and other research projects, commercially available lists of schools, and lists maintained by state departments of education. The sample frame was designed to include facilities serving students with all types of disabilities and contained almost 10,000 facilities. From this frame, a sample of 6,451 facilities was selected for initial screening.

A brief telephone screening interview was conducted with the principal, director, or other administrator of each sampled facility. A total of 5,928 facilities completed the screening interview, out of 6,451 in the sample, for an overall completion rate of 92%.

The screening interview determined whether the facility provided special education services and whether the student body was primarily or exclusively composed of persons with disabilities. A large proportion (60%) of the sample was screened as ineligible for the follow-up survey, due primarily to the large numbers of administrative offices, programs not providing special education services, and facilities serving both disabled and nondisabled students that appeared on the sample frame.

The screening interview obtained information necessary to administer distinct but congruent follow-up questionnaires to residential and day schools and to determine which of 10 detailed population modules should be administered based on the specific disabilities served at each facility. These modules covered each of the categories of disabilities recognized by the Department of Education, that is, mental retardation, learning disabilities, speech and language impairments, emotional disturbance, hearing impairment (including deaf and deaf–blind), orthopedic (physical) impairment, health impairment (including autism), visual impairment (including deaf–blind), multiple impairments, and noncategorical or other impairments.

Facility directors were mailed a survey packet containing a main questionnaire for the appropriate type of facility (day or residential) and a set of population modules corresponding to the disabilities reported among their student population. Reminder letters and telephone calls were made to facilities not responding to the initial mailing. Facilities not responding to the reminders were contacted by telephone and administered an abbreviated version of the main questionnaire and population modules. All facilities, regardless of whether responding by mail or telephone, were asked to provide information on the total number of students, the types of educational programs provided to students on and off campus, operating budget and per student costs, average length of stay, administrative problems facing the facility, changes in student and facility characteristics since 1976, and a number of other important data items. Other items, such as location of parents' residence, noninstrumental activities, frequency of staff and facility evaluations, detailed data on new admissions and releases, and changes in the number of students and staff since 1976 were asked only on the longer mail quesionnaire.

The following are definitions of several key terms used in the mail and telephone instruments:

> *Separate facility* was defined as a residential or day facility exclusively serving handicapped persons in buildings physically separate from programs for nondisabled age peers. Eligible separate facilities may be operated by state education agencies, other state agencies, local education agencies, county or regional agencies, or private for-profit or not-for-profit organizations. The special education services at these facilities may be provided by the operating agency or by another agency. Correctional facilities and those with average lengths of stay of less than 30 days were excluded from this study.
>
> *Residential school* was defined as a separate facility at which at least some persons with disabilities reside *and* at which at least some students age 0 to 22 receive educational services on the grounds of the facility during the usual school day.
>
> *Day school* was defined as a separate facility at which no persons with disabilities reside *and* at which students age 0 to 22 receive educational services during the usual school day.
>
> *Primary disability* was defined as the single type of disability that most directly or most seriously affects the functioning and developmental potential of the student.
>
> *Secondary disability* was defined as a condition serious enough that, in the absence of the primary disability, the individual would still be considered disabled on the basis of the secondary disability. If an individual had more than one secondary disability, the facility respondent was asked to provide information on the one considered to result in the greatest impairment to the student's academic, social, or vocational development.

Of the 2,580 facilities screened as eligible, 1,941 provided survey data on either the mail questionnaire or the telephone interview, for an overall response rate of 75%. The overall distribution of mail versus telephone completions was 872 to 1,069 respectively, a 1:1.2 ratio. Analysis of data provided on all facilities during the screening interview indicated that generally there were few large or statistically significant differences between eligible facilities that did or did not complete either the mail or telephone instrument. However, larger facilities were less likely than those serving fewer numbers of students to respond to the survey. The same patterns were found when comparisons were made between mail and telephone responders. In the absence of external information on the universe of separate facilities, it is not possible to statistically evaluate or correct for nonsampling errors (e.g., the effects of nonresponse). However, weights applied during analysis take into account nonresponse, and the responses to items answered only by facilities responding to the mail questionnaire were also weighted to represent the full sample.

More details on the survey methodology and results, definitions of survey items, the analysis of nonresponse, and the computation and presentation of standard errors are provided in Lakin et al. (1990).

REFERENCES

Lakin, K. C., Stephens, S. A., Hill, B. K., & Chen, T. H. (1990). *The study of programs of instruction for handicapped children and youth in day and residential facilities: Volume II. Current status and changes in separate facilities for students with handicaps.* Princeton, NJ: Mathematica Policy Research, Inc.

Small, R., Kennedy, K., Bender, B. (1991). Critical issues for practice in residential treatment: The view from within. *American Journal of Orthopsychiatry, 61*(3), 327–338.

U.S. Department of Education, Office of Special Education and Rehabilitative Services. (1988). *Implementation of the Education of the Handicapped Act. Tenth annual report to Congress.* Washington, DC: Division of Innovation and Development.

U.S. Department of Education, Office of Special Education and Rehabilitative Services. (1989). *Implementation of the Education of the Handicapped Act. Eleventh annual report to Congress.* Washington, DC: Division of Innovation and Development.

U.S. Department of Education, Office of Special Education and Rehabilitative Services. (1990). *Implementation of the Education of the Handicapped Act. Twelfth annual report to Congress.* Washington, DC: Division of Innovation and Development.

U.S. Department of Education, Office of Special Education and Rehabilitative Services. (1991). *Implementation of the Education of the Handicapped Act. Thirteenth annual report to Congress.* Washington, DC: Division of Innovation and Development.

U.S. General Accounting Office. (1991). *Child welfare: Monitoring out-of-state placements* (Rep. No. HRD-91-107BR). Washington, DC: U.S. Government Printing Office.

Viadero, D. (1992, April 29). New definition of "emotionally disturbed" sought. *Education Week*, p. 24.

Wells, K. (1991a). Long-term residential treatment for children: Introduction. *American Journal of Orthopsychiatry, 61*(3), 324–326.

Wells, K. (1991b). Placement of emotionally disturbed children in residential treatment: A review of placement criteria. *American Journal of Orthopsychiatry, 61*(3), 339–347.

CHAPTER

4

A Synopsis of Research and Professional Literature on Educational Placement

Kerri F. Martin
Betty A. Hallenbeck
James M. Kauffman
John Wills Lloyd
University of Virginia

Although the educational placement of students with emotional or behavioral disorders has been a critical issue in special education for decades, as discussed in chapter 2, few systematic or comprehensive reviews of the research and professional literatures have been reported. The virtual absence of such reviews may be due in part to the substantial size of the task of pulling together sources varying widely in intended audience and research methodology. Research findings and commentaries on placement issues are scattered throughout the literatures of several professions, including special education, school and clinical psychology, social work, psychiatry, hospital administration, and others involved in mental health. Within each of the various professions involved in placement issues, the literatures include both discussions of policy and theory or opinion (i.e., professional literature) and empirical work (i.e., research literature). Within the empirical work, the literatures include a variety of quantitative and qualitative research methods.

Our purpose was to bring together the scattered research and professional literatures on the topic of placement to form a base of knowledge that can be examined for its implications for policy and future research. We reviewed the research and professional literatures to (a) determine the location and nature of these sources, (b) summarize their content, (c) describe areas of agreement and disagreement about placement options, and (d) suggest areas of needed investigation. Although we cannot claim to have accomplished an exhaustive search, we believe that our search strategies netted the great majority of the research and professional literatures bearing on placement issues and published between about 1965 and 1992.

METHODS

Databases and Search Strategies

We searched the University of Virginia electronic library access system, ERIC, PSYCHLit, MedLine, Sociofile, and Congressional Information Service. University of Virginia librarians with training and expertise in the use of each database advised us on the selection of search terms and other technical aspects of the electronic searches. The terms we used in searching each electronic database are shown in Table 4.1. We conducted our search beginning in 1992 and ending in 1993. The searches of the electronic databases yielded references dating from about 1965.

Although some of the sources emerging from the electronic searches were books, monographs, or microfiche documents, the majority were journal articles. Therefore, we handsearched all the journals for which our electronic search located two or more articles. We searched the tables of contents of these journals for likely titles, beginning with the most recent issue of each journal and going back to the first issue published in 1980. In addition, we searched the reference list of each selected source for citations not already identified. The criterion for selection of sources up to this point was a title or abstract indicating that the source might contain information relevant to placement issues.

The electronic search and the handsearch resulted in a list of nearly 200 sources that we identified as potentially containing information relevant to placement settings and changes in placement. After reading each source and eliminating those not containing such information, we were left with 170 sources to code and enter in our own database. We compiled our own database of selected references using Q&A (version 4), an electronic program designed to allow entry, nonduplication, sorting, aggregation, and retrieval of information.

Coding

Reviewers read and coded each article according to a set of coding instructions and using a coding form. Some of the information coded was purely descriptive, such as the type of article (research or professional), information about the number, age, and gender of subjects, type of placement or placement change, labels used, and dependent measures used (for research articles). Other, more substantive information was also coded, including information about the design of the study (or a synopsis of professional articles), results, and important issues related to placement (administrative, interagency collaboration, programming, legal or pol-

TABLE 4.1
Search Terms Used in Databases Searched

Database	*Search Terms*
ERIC & VIRGO	emotional disturbances* emotionally disturbed emotional problems mental disorders behavior disorders* personality problems psychiatry clinical psychology psychopathology clinics* residential schools* institutional schools* special schools* placement* student placement* least restrictive environment*
PSYCLit	emotionally disturbed behavior disorders behavior problems treatment facilities residential care institutions institutional schools educational placement childhood psychosis handicapped treatment
MedLine	child behavior disorders* attention deficit disorder juvenile delinquency acting out dissociative disorders child development disorders child psychiatry mental disorders + children* adolescent behavior child, hospitalized* child, institutionalized* commitment of mentally ill*
Sociofile	behavior-disordered, disorders, problems, student behaviorally disordered child and youth services child-placement child-psychiatric emotionally disturbed psychiatrically hospitalized placement hospitalization special education special school
Congressional Information Service	[no specific search terms required]

*Major terms in which other terms are embedded. All terms were used in searching by key word.

icy matters, subject-specific, and ethical issues). Information about specific settings in which children and adolescents with emotional or behavioral disorders were placed (regular schools, alternative or day schools, residential settings, and psychiatric hospitals) was coded in the last section of the coding form.

Graduate students in special education at the University of Virginia coded the articles. We checked for intercoder agreement (using simple agreement and disagreement percentages) by recoding 20 of the articles: Ten had initially been coded by one person, 10 by the other. Percentages of exact agreement were: type of article, 70%; ages of subjects, 75%; grade levels of subjects, 100%; gender, 80%; total number of subjects, 80%; labels used, 70%; placement setting or change, 70%; method of inquiry, 65%; research design or professional synopsis, 80%; and results, 90%.

The information about issues, settings, and dependent measures was rated twice, once to determine the percentage to which coders agreed on the occurrence of information about issues, settings, or measures in an article, and again to determine the percentage of agreement on the content of those occurrences (occurrence and content). We obtained the following results: interagency collaboration issues, 85% and 50%; administrative issues, 85% and 80%; programming, 75% and 70%; subject-specific issues, 50% and 13%; ethical issues, 90% and 60%; regular school settings, 95% and 33%; day or alternative schools, 95% and 80%; residential schools, 80% and 56%; psychiatric hospital settings, 85% and 56%; academic measures, 100% and 100%; social or psychological measures, 90% and 50%; medical measures, 95% and 0%; familial measures, 100% and 100%; and cognitive measures, 100% and 100%.

It was evident from the results of the agreement check that there was ambiguity in some of the coding instructions, especially regarding subject-specific issues and dependent measures (some of the results for dependent measures reported are unrealistically high due to the small number of measures actually recorded). Therefore, all of the articles were recoded on those points after agreements were reached by the coders concerning how the coding instructions should be interpreted. Coders consulted with each other to construct tables summarizing much of the information in the database, including the 85 research articles and 85 professional articles.

LOCATION AND NATURE OF THE LITERATURES

Research Literature

Table 4.2 summarizes characteristics of the 85 research studies we reviewed. In 80 of the 85 research studies, authors used specific labels to identify groups. Table 4.3 lists the 68 different labels used in these 80 studies, illustrating the diversity in descriptions of the population of people with emotional or behavioral disorders.

TABLE 4.2
Characteristics of Research Studies

	Type of Study			Ages of Subjects					Gender Studied			Total Ns of Studies					Type of Setting or Change				Dependent Measures				
Citation	*Quantitative*	*Qualitative*	*Combination*	*0–12 Years*	*Children and Teens*	*13–19 Years*	*Older Teen, Adults*	*Full Range*	*Male*	*Female*	*Both*	*30 or less*	*31–100*	*101–450*	*451–850*	*+4,000 & +14,000*	*Single Setting*	*Single with Change*	*Multiple Settings*	*Multiple with Change*	*Academic*	*Social/Psychological*	*Medical*	*Familial*	*Cognitive*
Alessi & Magen (1988)	x													x			x					x			
Alexson & Sinclair (1986)	x				x										x			x			x	x			x
Apsler & Bassuk (1983)	x														x							x			
Askew & Thomas (1987)		x																x			interviews with heads, teachers, and students				
Balla, Lewis, Shanok, Snell, & Henisz (1974)	x				x				x						x		x					x			
Barack (1986)	x			x									x						x		x	x			x
Barber, Allen, & Coyne (1992)	x											29 staff members					x				coded vignettes				
Barker (1968)		x		x								x						x						x	x
Beitchman & Dielman (1982)	x			x							x				x		x					x		x	
Bergquist (1982)	x			x									x					x			x				x
Bloom & Hopewell (1982)	x				x						x		x				x					x		x	x
Burns (1991)	x																		x		data from NIMH surveys				
Cheek & Wolcott (1969)	x				x						x				x		x					x	x	x	
Christ, Adler, Merling, & Gershansky (1981)	x				x						x					x	x					x		x	

(Continued)

TABLE 4.2
(Continued)

	Type of Study			*Ages of Subjects*					*Gender Studied*			*Total Ns of Studies*					*Type of Setting or Change*				*Dependent Measures*				
Citation	*Quantitative*	*Qualitative*	*Combination*	*0–12 Years*	*Children and Teens*	*13–19 Years*	*Older Teen, Adults*	*Full Range*	*Male*	*Female*	*Both*	*30 or less*	*31–100*	*101–450*	*451–850*	*+4,000 & +14,000*	*Single Setting*	*Single with Change*	*Multiple Settings*	*Multiple with Change*	*Academic*	*Social/Psychological*	*Medical*	*Familial*	*Cognitive*
Clarke, Schaefer, Burchard, & Welkowitz (1992)	x			x					x			x							x			x		x	
Cohen et al. (1990)	x				x						x		x						x			x		x	
Coleman, Pfeiffer, & Oakland (1992)	x				x						x		x				x				x	x		x	x
Connolly (1987)	x				x						x		x					x				x			x
Cooper (1985)			x											16 parents			x					questionnaire re: school satisfaction			
Costello, Dulcan, & Kalas	x			x							x			x			x					x			
Cullinan, Epstein, & Sabornie (1992)	x				x						x			x			x						x	x	x
Dalton, Bolding, & Forman (1990)		x		x								x						x				x		x	
Dalton, Forman, Daul, & Bolding (1986)	x			x							x	x					x					x		x	
Dickson, Heffron, & Parker (1990)	x				x						x			x			x					x		x	
Doan & Petti (1989)	x							x							x			x				x			
Duchnowski, Johnson, Hall, Kutash, & Friedman (1992)	x				x						x		x							x	x	x		x	x
Dydyk, French, Gertsman, Morrison, & O'Neill (1989)	x				x				x				x				x					x		x	

Epstein, Foley, & Cullinan (1992)			x										191 teachers 2 times		x			survey re: types of treatment programs				
Forness, Barnes, & Mourdaunt (1983)	x				x					x		x				x		x	x			x
Fuchs, Fuchs, Fernstrom, & Hohn (1991)	x				x					x	x					x		x	x			x
Gabel, Finn, & Ahmad (1988)	x			x						x		x				x			x		x	
Gossett, Barnhart, Lewis, & Phillips (1980)			x					x		x			x			x			x		x	
Greenberg & Mayer (1972)			x			x						x				x			x		x	
Grizenko, Papineau, & Sayegh (1993)	x			x						x	x				x			x	x		x	x
Guterman, Hodges, Blythe, & Bronson (1989)	x				x				x		x					x		questionnaire re: client satisfaction; cost analysis; goal attainment ratings				
Harris & Kierstead (1985)	x											x					x		x		x	
Harris, King, Reifler, & Rosenberg (1984)	x			x					x			x				x		x	x			x
Haslum (1988)	x			x						x				x	x			x	x		x	x
Herrera, Lifson, Hartmann, & Solomon (1974)	x						x			x		x				x			x			
Hodges & Plow (1990)	x			x						x		x			x			x	x		x	x
Hutchinson, Tess, Gleckman, & Spence (1992)	x				x					x			x		x				x		x	
Inamdar, Darrell, Brown, & Lewis (1986)	x				x					x			x			x			x			
Jaffa & Dezsery (1989)	x				x					x			x		x				x		x	
King & Pittman (1971)		x					x			x	x					x			x	x	x	
Larsson, Bohlin, & Stenbacka (1986)	x			x									x			x			x	x	x	
Laslett (1982)		x						x		x		x				x			x		x	
Levy (1969)		x						x		x		x				x			x		x	x

(Continued)

TABLE 4.2
(Continued)

Citation	*Type of Study:* Quantitative	Qualitative	Combination	*Ages of Subjects:* 0–12 Years	Children and Teens	13–19 Years	Older Teen, Adults	Full Range	*Gender Studied:* Male	Female	Both	*Total Ns of Studies:* 30 or less	31–100	101–450	451–850	+4,000 & +14,000	*Type of Setting or Change:* Single Setting	Single with Change	Multiple Settings	Multiple with Change	*Dependent Measures:* Academic	Social/Psychological	Medical	Familial	Cognitive
Lewis, Lewis, Shanok, Klatskin, & Osborne (1980)	x				x						x		x					x				x		x	x
Lund (1989)	x				x								x				x					x			
Marsden, McDermott, & Minor (1977)	x												x				x				questionnaire re: institutional characteristics & procedures				
Mattison & Gamble (1992)	x			x					x				x						x			x			
Mattison, Humphrey, Kales, Handford, et al. (1986)	x				x						x			x				x			x	x	x	x	x
Mattison, Humphrey, Kales, & Wallace (1986)	x			x					x				x				x					x		x	x
Mattison, Morales, & Bauer (1992)	x			x					x					x				x			x	x		x	x
McClure, Ferguson, Boodoosingh, Turgay, & Stavrakaki (1989)	x				x						x			x					x			x			
McDavid (1987)			x												x		x				survey re: assessment, instruction, & services				
Mikkelson, Bereika, & McKenzie (1993)	x							x			x			x						x		x		x	

Moore & O'Conner (1991)	x		x				x		x			x					x	x	x	
Munson, Klein, & Delafield (1989)	x									33 professionals		x						questionnaire re: treatment modality		
Myers, Burket, Lyles, Stone, & Kemph (1990)	x			x		x		x				x					x		x	x
Myles & Simpson (1992)	x									194 teachers		x						vignettes & questions		
Ney, Adam, Hanton, & Brindad (1988)	x	x					x			x		x					x	x	x	
Parmalee et al. (1991)	x		x				x		x			x					x			
Pfeiffer & Naglieri (1984)	x									60 professionals			x					psychological reports & a placement scale		
Prentice-Dunn, Wilson, & Spivey (1985)	x							x				x						questionnaire re: program characteristics		
Quinton & Rutter (1976)	x	x					x			x			x				x	x	x	
Ravenel et al.	x		x							x				x				survey re: problems & needs		
Ricciuti, Morton, Behar, & Delaney (1986)	x	x					x			x		x					x	x		
Rosenblatt & Attkisson (1992)	x									3 counties		x					x			
Rosenblatt & Attkisson (1993)	x									3 counties				x				expenditures & utilization of settings		
Rosenblatt, Attkisson, & Fernandez (1992)	x									3 counties		x						expenditures of group homes		
Roth & Nicholson (1988)	x		x				x		x				x			x	x		x	x
Sack, Mason, & Collins (1987)	x	x					x		x								x		x	x
Shanok et al.	x			x	x				x						x		x		x	
Silver et al.	x		x				x				x			x		x	x		x	x
Sindelar, King, Cartland, Wilson, & Meisel (1985)	x									x				x			x			

(Continued)

TABLE 4.2
(Continued)

	Type of Study			*Ages of Subjects*					*Gender Studied*			*Total Ns of Studies*					*Type of Setting or Change*				*Dependent Measures*				
Citation	*Quantitative*	*Qualitative*	*Combination*	*0–12 Years*	*Children and Teens*	*13–19 Years*	*Older Teen, Adults*	*Full Range*	*Male*	*Female*	*Both*	*30 or less*	*31–100*	*101–450*	*451–850*	*+4,000 & +14,000*	*Single Setting*	*Single with Change*	*Multiple Settings*	*Multiple with Change*	*Academic*	*Social/Psychological*	*Medical*	*Familial*	*Cognitive*
Stotsky, Browne, & Lister (1987)	x										x				x				x			x		x	x
Swan, Brown, & Jacob (1987)	x				x						x			x				x			type of placement				
Tarico, Low, Trupin, & Forsyth-Stephens (1989)			x		x						x		x									x			
Trickett, Leone, Fink, & Braaten (1993)	x							x			x				x				x		rating of classroom environment				
Webb & Maddox (1986)	x																	x			data on impact, satisfaction, & use of procedures				
Wells & Whittington (1990)	x				x						x			x				x				x			x
Wells, Wyatt, & Hobfoll (1991)	x						x				x		x					x				x		x	
Westendorp, Brink, Roberson, & Oritz (1986)	x					x					x			x				x			x	x			
Wright, Pillard, & Cleven (1990)	x							x			x										definitional variables, severity, etiology, & deviation from norm				

TABLE 4.3
Labels Used in Research Studies

Adjustment disorder	Mood disordered
Affective disturbance	Neurotic
Antisocial	Obsessive/compulsive
Anxiety disorder	Oppositional defiant
Anxious	Organic brain syndrome
Attention deficit disorder	Organic brain damage
Autistic	Panic disordered
Behavior(ally) disordered	Paranoid
Behaviorally handicapped	Personality disorder
Behaviorally disturbed	Psychiatric problems
Character disordered	Psychiatrically hospitalized
Conduct disordered	Psychiatrically disturbed
Convulsive disorder	Psychoneurotic
Delinquent	Psychotic
Depressive, depressed	Reading retarded
Developmental disorder	Schizophrenic
Developmentally delayed	School refusal
Deviant	Separation anxiety disorder
Disturbed	Seriously emotionally disturbed
Dysthymic disorder	Severely handicapped
Emotional difficulties	Severely emotionally disturbed
Emotionally disturbed	Severely disturbed
Exceptional	Socially disturbed
High risk	Sociopathic personality
Hyperactive, hyperkinetic	Sociopathic
Impulsive	Specific learning disabled
Inpatients	Suicidal
Juvenile offender	Symptomatic
Learning disabled	Thought disturbed
Learning handicapped	Transient situational disorder
Maladjusted	Transitional behavior
Manic-depressive	Personality disorder
Mentally handicapped	Troubled
Mild personality disorder	Undersocialized
Moderately disordered	

Table 4.4 shows the characteristics of each of the 85 articles classified as research literature. This table allows study-by-study comparisons and provides the details of the data summarized in Table 4.2.

Type of Study. We classified 73 (86%) of the research studies as quantitative because they reported numerical data (i.e., percentages or frequencies) or used either descriptive statistics (e.g., means, variances, percentages, or correlations) or inferential statistics (i.e., tests used to generalize from sample data to populations too large to observe completely; Smith & Glass, 1987) in their method and discussion sections. Quantitative methods included tests of statistical significance of the difference between groups, such as *t* tests and analysis of

TABLE 4.4
Summary of Study Characteristics (85 Research Studies)

		Number of Studies	*% of Total (% of Those Reporting)*	
Type of study	Quantitative	73		86%
	Qualitative	6		7%
	Combination	6		7%
Ages of subjects	0–12 (Child)	21		25% (32%)
	Child and Teen	30		35% (46%)
	13–19 (Teen)	4		5% (6%)
	Teen and Adult	3		4% (5%)
	Full Range	7		8% (11%)
Gender studied	Male (5,652 total)	9		11% (16%)
	Female (1,922 total)	1		1% (2%)
	Both	46		54% (71%)
Number of subjects	30 or Less	15		18% (19%)
	31 to 100	31		36% (38%)
	101 to 450	23		27% (28%)
	451 to 850	10		12% (12%)
	+4,000 or +14,000	1 each		2% (3%)
Types of placement settings and changes	Single Setting	34		40% (41%)
	Single with Change	32		38% (39%)
	Multiple Setting	13		15% (16%)
	Multiple w/Change	3		4% (4%)
Dependent measures[a]	Academic	16		19%
	Social/Psychological	63		74%
	Medical	9		11%
	Familial	42		49%
	Cognitive	26		31%
	Academic: WRAT-R	4	(20%)	
Measures used most often	Social/Psychological:			
	DSM-III Diagnostic Criteria	10	(22%)	
	CBCL	12	(26%)	
	RBPC	4	(9%)	
	Medical: Clinic Records	4	(50%)	
	Familial: Hollingshead et al. SES	4	(29%)	
	Cognitive: WISC-R	9	(53%)	
Labels used most often[b]	Emotionally Disturbed	25		30% (33%)
	Conduct Disordered	23		27% (29%)
	Behavior(ally) Disordered	21		24% (26%)
	Schizophrenic	16		19% (20%)
	Psychotic	14		16% (18%)
	Severely Emotionally	11		13% (14%)
	Disturbed	10		12% (13%)
	Seriously Emotionally	8		9% (10%)
	Disturbed			
	Delinquent			

[a]Totals not equal to 100% because studies used multiple types of measures.
[b]Totals not equal to 100% because studies used multiple labels.

variance (ANOVA), and tests of the degree of relationship among variables, such as regression and factor analysis.

Of the 73 studies classified as quantitative, 63 (86%) used inferential statistics or a combination of inferential and descriptive statistics. Most of the remaining 10 studies (14%) that reported only descriptive statistics were program descriptions or evaluations (Guterman, Hodges, Blythe, & Bronson, 1989; Harris & Kierstead, 1985; Mikkelson, Bereika, & McKenzie, 1993; Moore & O'Conner, 1991; Rosenblatt & Attkisson, 1992; Webb & Maddox, 1986). Other descriptive studies examined characteristics of clients using particular services (Burns, 1991; Doan & Petti, 1989), factors associated with admission to psychiatric hospitalization (Dalton, Forman, Daul, & Bolding, 1986), and quantity and types of laboratory tests used with inpatients (Ricciuti, Morton, Behar, & Delaney, 1986).

Qualitative research typically yields data in the form of words, pictures, and graphs rather than numbers and statistics (Miles & Huberman, 1984; Smith & Glass, 1987). However, at times qualitative researchers may generate numerical data to "suggest trends in a setting" or to "provide descriptive information . . . about the population served" by a particular program (Bogdan & Biklen, 1992, pp. 147–148). Qualitative data are primarily obtained through observations, interviews, and collection of existing documents. Case studies or histories in which detailed examinations of individual subjects are provided are common in the social sciences, and interviews are used to "gather descriptive data in the subjects' own words so that the researcher can develop insights on how subjects interpret some pieces of the world" (Bogdan & Biklen, 1992, p. 96).

We classified only six of the studies as qualitative research. Barker (1968) used the case histories of six children to summarize advantages and disadvantages of differing treatments. Telephone or personal interviews were conducted to determine who would benefit from transferring to regular schools (Askew & Thomas, 1987), and to assess stability of symptoms and remission (King & Pittman, 1971), satisfaction with programs (Laslett, 1982), and outcomes of the treatment of former patients (Dalton, Bolding, & Forman, 1990; Levy, 1969). Several studies combined qualitative and quantitative methods to describe subjects and interpret findings: Cooper (1985) used a survey to elicit views held by a group of parents and applied qualitative data analysis to reduce the amount of information into smaller categories for explanation; Epstein, Foley, and Cullinan (1992) applied both logical categorization of information and factor analysis to interpret data provided by teachers about program and student characteristics; Gossett, Barnhart, Lewis, and Phillips (1980) assessed long-term outcomes of former patients with interviews, surveys, case histories, and rating forms; Greenberg and Mayer (1972) used frequency counts and percentages in addition to case histories to describe a population of children served by a group home; McDavid (1987) evaluated a special education program based on existing documents, interviews, surveys, and site records; and Tarico, Low, Trupin, and Forsyth-Stephens (1989) quantified interview data and used standardized checklists to identify unmet needs and barriers to intervention.

Age of Subjects. Across the 63 research studies reporting ages, subjects ranged in age from less than 1 to 41 years old. We sorted the age ranges represented by each study according to a five-category classification system: children (0–12 years); teenagers (13–19 years); a combination of children and teenagers; a combination of teenagers and adults (adults = age 20 or older); and the full range from children to adults. Studies including the full age range were primarily longitudinal or follow-up studies (Gossett et al., 1980; Laslett, 1982; Levy, 1969; Mikkelson et al., 1993). The majority of studies reporting age (50 studies, 79%) examined subjects who were classified as children or teenagers.

Gender of Subjects. Only 56 (66%) of the 85 research studies clearly identified the gender of their subjects. Although most of the studies reporting gender included both males and females, the number of males across all studies (5,652) outnumbered the number of females across all studies (1,922) by 2.9:1. Considering that males with emotional or behavioral disorders outnumber females with such disorders by a ratio of about 4:1 or 5:1 (Kauffman, 1993), it is not surprising that fewer girls than boys were included in the studies we reviewed.

Total Sample Size. Most of the 85 research studies provided clear statements regarding the number of subjects. Although the majority of studies were concerned with subjects exhibiting emotional or behavioral disorders (described by a variety of labels), 9 (11%) examined the opinions or contributions of people providing services to individuals with those disorders, including teachers, other professionals, and parents. A series of evaluations was conducted by Rosenblatt and Attkisson (1992, 1993) and Rosenblatt, Attkisson, and Fernandez (1992) to assess different aspects of programs in three California counties. In cases like this, *subjects* are described in Table 4.2 as "staff members," "teachers," "counties," and so on. This accounts for some of the blank cells in Table 4.2 regarding age and gender of subjects.

Type of Setting or Placement Change Studied. "Setting" refers to the primary placement described or evaluated or the placement from which subjects were selected for study. Most of the studies (47 studies, 55%) did not deal with placement changes; instead, they focused on a single setting (e.g., a psychiatric hospital) or investigated aspects of a variety of settings (i.e., multiple settings). The remainder of the studies—excepting three in which the setting could not be clearly identified—dealt with changes from or to more restrictive environments.

Single settings investigated in the 85 research studies included hospitals (18 studies, 21%), residential schools or group homes (6 studies, 7%), regular schools (4 studies, 5%), day or alternative schools (2 studies, 2%), and an intensive family therapy unit (1 study, 1%). Aspects of multiple settings, including correctional facilities and other alternatives such as foster care in addition to those already listed, were investigated in 13 studies (15%). There were almost as many combinations of setting changes (either single setting to single setting, single setting to multiple settings, multiple settings to a single setting, or multiple settings to multiple settings) as there were studies addressing placement changes directly. These changes included hospitals to regular schools (3 studies, 3%), hospitals to various (multiple) settings (7 studies, 8%), residential settings to multiple settings (4 studies, 5%), and day or alternative settings to regular schools (5 studies, 6%).

Dependent Measures. Although Table 4.2 shows that almost all of the studies used multiple measures to describe and evaluate subjects, many of the measures were nonstandardized and difficult to define for coding purposes. Initially, we coded only those measures that were clearly described or standardized, such as the Wide Range Achievement Test-Revised (WRAT-R) as an academic measure, or the Child Behavior Checklist (CBCL) as a social or psychological measure. Later, we determined that this system was not comprehensive, so we recoded the articles with a broader definition of *measures*. We decided that different dependent measures would be checked in Table 4.2 if a study indicated that some method was used to gather information about any of the areas of interest (academic, social or psychological, medical, familial, or cognitive). Even with this modification, 15 of the studies (18%) could not be classified according to those areas. Those studies are indicated in Table 4.2 if their particular method of gathering data was acknowledged in the method section of the article.

Academic measures ranged from locally developed criterion measures and school records to common standardized tests such as the Woodcock–Johnson (WJ) and the Peabody Individual Achievement Test (PIAT). Twelve different standardized tests were used in the 16 studies (19%) reporting academic data.

Nearly 60 different measures were used in 63 studies reporting social or psychological data. These included *DSM-III* diagnostic criteria, the CBCL, the Minnesota Multiphasic Personality Inventory (MMPI), the Vineland Adaptive Scales, the Hare Self-Esteem Scale, the Beck Depression Inventory, and the Revised Behavior Problem Checklist, to name only a few. It is not surprising that this area would be the primary interest of those studying individuals with emotional or behavioral disorders, but the range of tests and methods used to gather data is disconcerting. The range of instruments may legitimately reflect the many aspects of such complex disorders, including self-esteem, social skills problems, depression, hyperactivity, violence, and negative or noncompliant behavior, but it makes comparison of the characteristics of subjects in different studies extremely difficult, at best. However, it is likely that in a more restricted review of the literature—one on studies of depression in children with emotional or behavioral disorders, for example—there would be less variation in the measures used.

Medical information was gathered by several methods in 8 (9%) of the 85 research studies. Clinic records were the primary source of information in half of these 8 studies, but some standardized forms, such as the Adolescent Health Inventory, were used as well. In other cases, families were simply questioned about the medical history of an individual included as a subject.

Family histories were investigated primarily by questioning the parents of study subjects, as well as the subjects themselves. Standardized measures were used in only 10 (24%) of the 42 studies reporting familial data, and included the Family Adaptability and Cohesion Evaluation Scale, the General Scale of the Family Assessment Measure, and the Family History Research Diagnostic Criteria.

Only 26 (31%) of the 85 research studies referred to cognitive data, with 14 (54%) of those indicating actual tests used. An unspecified IQ measure was reported in 5 studies (19% of those reporting cognitive data). The majority of studies reporting specific measures (17 studies, 64% of those reporting cognitive data) used the WISC-R. Other tests included the Bender Gestalt, the Slosson Intelligence Test, and the Stanford Binet.

Professional Literature

Table 4.5 shows the characteristics of each of the 85 articles classified as nonresearch professional literature. The categories for Table 4.5 were developed from a review of the nonresearch articles in our database. Several themes emerged from our review of this literature, and we selected those occurring most frequently as column headings; other readers undertaking the same task may have classified these articles differently. An explanation of column headings follows. An x in a column indicates that the study shown in that row had the characteristic shown in the column. Note that to receive a mark in a column, an article had to provide sufficient emphasis on that topic; for example, the comment that "further research is needed" was not enough to merit placement in the "research needs" column.

Legal. Articles having an x in this column emphasized legal proceedings concerning the placement of students with emotional or behavioral disorders.

Program Description. Articles marked in this category described a program or programs for children and youth with emotional or behavioral disorders, paying particular attention to the process by which students are placed in the program.

Review of Research or Literature. The articles marked in this category reviewed research or literature concerning some aspect of the placement process for children and youth with emotional or behavioral disorders.

Issues. An x in this column indicates that the article is about the placement process in general or contains discussion of several aspects of the process. Some articles marked by an x in this column highlighted issues not represented among those listed. Issues marked "a" through "i" were as follows: (a) rights

TABLE 4.5
Characteristics of the Nonresearch Professional Articles

Citation	*Legal*	*Program Descrip.*	*Review of Res or Lit*	*Issues*	*Historical Review*	*Cases*	*Research Needs*	*Other*
A.W.M.C. Working Party on Residential Resources (1984)	x			b, c				
"Appropriateness of Private Residential" (1985)	x			h				
Armstrong & Evans (1992)		x						
Armstrong, Grosser, & Palma (1992)				f				manual
Burns & Friedman (1988)			x				x	
Burns & Friedman (1990)			x				x	
Cheney & Sampson (1990)		x						
Cocozza & Melick (1977)				a				
Curry (1991)			x				x	
Duchnowski & Friedman (1990)				f, x	x		x	
Eaton (1967)				b, c		x		
Farley (1985)				b, c, d				
Goldfine et al. (1985)			x	h				
Goldman (1988)		x		f	x			
Grosenick et al. (1982)				e		x		
Grubb & Thompson (1982)				f				Theor. Model
Hamm (1989)		x				x		
Institute of Medicine (1989)							x	

(Continued)

TABLE 4.5
(Continued)

Citation	*Legal*	*Program Descrip.*	*Review of Res or Lit*	*Issues*	*Historical Review*	*Cases*	*Research Needs*	*Other*
Jaffe (1986)				b, c	x			
Jenson, Hawkins, & Catalano (1986)				d, g				
Jenson & Whittaker (1987)				d				
Johns (1982)		x		f, h				
Kester (1966)				h				
Laneve (1982)		x						
Laufer (1986)			x	d, f				
LeCroy (1984)			x	d				
Macmillan & Kavale (1986)				c				
Maddox & Edgar (1988)				f				
Matek (1964)				c, h				
McCauley (1984)				e, h				
Melton (1982)			x	a, d				
Miskimins (1990)		x						Theor. Model
Morrissette (1989)				f				
Noel (1982)		x			x			
Noshpitz (1962)								Theor. Model
One Hundredth Congress (1987)				x				
Paul (1977)				x				

Priestly (1987)				h			
Quay (1986)			x	h			x
Schneider (1985)	x			f			
Simon (1986)			x				x
Smith (1987)	x						
Smollar & Conelli (1990)		x		h			
Steinberg & Knitzer (1992)				x			x
Streitmatter & Santa Cruz (1982)				f			
Stilwell (1991)				h			
Stone (1979)				h, x	x		
Stroul (1988)		x	x				
Toman (1986)		x		h			
Tuma (1989)				f			
Van Den Brink (1984)		x		h			
Voineskos (1976)		x		h			
Walker & Bullis (1991)				i, x			
Webb (1988)				h			
Weintrob (1975)				h			
Weithorn (1988)					x		
Wells (1991a)				d, g, h		x	
Wells (1991b)			x	c			
Wilson & Lyman (1983)			x	h	x		
Wood (1985)	x						
Wood, Johnson, & Jenkins (1986)	x						
Zimet & Farley (1985)		x		h			

of patients, clients, or students; (b) referral practices in the placement process; (c) assessment practices in the placement process; (d) family and the placement process; (e) disciplinary exclusion of students with emotional or behavioral disorders; (f) integration of services/interagency collaboration; (g) community and the placement process; (h) role and/or efficacy of specific kinds of placements (i.e., residential, hospital, day program); (i) client characteristics.

Historical Review. Articles marked in this column contained a long-term perspective on some issue pertaining to the placement of children and youth with emotional or behavioral disorders, such as the use of residential facilities.

Cases. The articles marked in this column used a case or cases in which a student's placement is the central issue to highlight concerns about the placement process.

Research Needs. The authors of articles marked in this column pointed out the need for research on the placement process and often provide detailed suggestions for those considering conducting a study of this topic.

Other. Two types of articles are noted in this column. One is a manual from the state of New York containing guidelines for providing mental health services to children and youth with emotional or behavioral disorders, including a section on placement decisions. Other articles provided a theoretical model for making placement decisions based on the authors' understanding of research and current practices in this area.

Observations on the Nonresearch Articles. The articles represented in Table 4.5 cover a tremendous range of topics and take a wide variety of forms. In addition, they were written by professionals from many disciplines and appeared in 29 different journals. Finally, in the "issues" column, if all issues had been coded to appear in the table, over 30 issues would have been noted. We believe these are important indicators of the complexity of the placement process.

The most frequently discussed issue was the role or efficacy of specific types of placement, usually residential or hospital placement. These articles often advocated a certain type of placement, such as a residential school. Clearly, there is no consensus on the appropriate uses of various placement options. For example, professionals across and within disciplines do not agree on the criteria that must be met for a child to be sent to a residential school.

Not surprisingly, the next most common issue concerned interagency collaboration or the integration of services—a glaring weakness in services to children and youth with emotional or behavioral disorders. People have developed elaborate systems to improve the integration of services and devoted many pages to lamenting the current status of interagency collaboration, but little progress seems to have been made in getting different agencies serving children to work in close concert.

Finally, many of these articles note the dearth of research on all aspects of the placement process. It seems that we are operating with a minimum of empirically derived support for our placement practices.

COMMON VIEWPOINTS AND CONTROVERSIES

We examined all of the articles in the database—both research and nonresearch—for references to the major issues included on the coding form (interagency collaboration, administration, programming, laws and policies, ethics, and subject-specific issues). For example, we printed all references to interagency collaboration, along with their citations, and noted the different topics. We counted each occurrence of a numbered topic to indicate which points recurred most frequently in the database.

Interagency Collaboration

We found reference to 21 different topics regarding interagency collaboration, with the need for better coordination of services for transition between settings cited most frequently (12 times). Dalton et al. (1990) noted that a united effort among the legal, social service, education, and health care delivery systems is needed to provide appropriate therapy during transitions because "each move (from one facility to another) involves a severing of important relationships developed during the previous placement," and "special alliance-building therapeutic work is necessary at the next level of care to manage the psychological regression that accompanies each move" (p. 62). Laufer (1986) indicated that there is poor communication between social workers in the community and institutional social workers because they are not familiar with the particulars of each others' settings, and Streitmatter and Santa Cruz (1982) lamented that "Too often a child simply appeared in a public school classroom, with only minimal information exchanging hands between the referring and receiving agencies" (p. 16).

Other frequently cited topics included the following:

1. different threats to interagency collaboration, such as ambiguity over who provides what services (Burns & Friedman, 1988; Crittenden, 1992; Edwards, 1987; Jaffe, 1986; Maddox & Edgar, 1988; Stilwell, 1991; Stone, 1979; Webb & Maddox, 1986) and problems with operating institutions at a state level with almost no obligation to coordinate services (Ravenel et al., 1982);
2. descriptions of interagency collaboration and explanations of its importance (Duchnowski & Friedman, 1990; Goldman, 1988; Greenberg & Mayer,

1972; Grubb & Thompson, 1982; Maddox & Edgar, 1988; Miskimins, 1990; Stone, 1979; Tuma, 1989);

3. descriptions of people involved in collaboration, and their roles (Brassard & Barnes, 1987; Clarke, Schaefer, Burchard, & Welkowitz, 1992; Forness, Barnes, & Mordaunt, 1983; Lewis, Lewis, Shanok, Klatskin, & Osborne, 1980; Morrissette, 1989; Zimet & Farley, 1985);
4. the importance of parental involvement in planning and treatment (Crittenden, 1992; Dettlebach, 1955; Grubb & Thompson, 1982; Laneve, 1982; Moore & O'Conner, 1991); and
5. specific examples of collaboration (Dydyk, French, Gertsman, Morrison, & O'Neill, 1989; Fuchs, Fuchs, Fernstrom, & Hohn, 1991; Grizenko, Papineau, & Sayegh, 1993; Hamm, 1989).

Crittenden (1992) warned:

> Changes in services threaten existing boundaries between agencies [and] may be viewed as an encroachment on another's territory. . . . [The] complexities of interdisciplinary relationships, particularly the interdependencies among agencies, can make change difficult to conceive or implement. (p. 31)

Administrative Issues

Of the 22 topics categorized under administrative issues, references to the need for program goals and plans to be clearly stated occurred most frequently (11 times). Epstein et al. (1992) conducted a national survey of educational programs for adolescents with serious emotional disturbance and found that they could account for only about 25% of the variance among programs, probably because "many of the persons who create programs for adolescents with SED have no particular plan in mind, but simply amalgamate an unsystematic collection of program features with little justification or forethought" (p. 208). Emphasizing that administrative organization is not synonymous with an educational program, McCauley (1984) explained that a "school" is an administrative organization with certain objectives, and "programming" refers to instructional and curriculum practices that should be evaluated to assist in "formulating objectives, revising or modifying program components, critiquing curricula and instructional practices, and establishing a feedback mechanism" (p. 110).

Four other topics relating to administrative issues recurred with notable frequency:

1. public schools are the primary source of referrals to different programs (Doan & Petti, 1989; Gabel, Finn, & Ahmad, 1988; Goldman, 1988; Grizenko et al., 1993; Harris, King, Reifler, & Rosenberg, 1984; Riciutti et al., 1986);

2. there is tremendous variation in criteria for admissions to different programs (Apsler & Bassuk, 1983; Beitchman & Dielman, 1982; Laneve, 1982; Maluccio & Marlow, 1972; Weithorn, 1988);
3. administrators should appreciate the need to develop transitions to new settings to prevent regression (Duchnowski, Johnson, Hall, Kutash, & Friedman, 1992; Friedman & Street, 1985; Maddox & Edgar, 1988; Morrissette, 1989; Streitmatter & Santa Cruz, 1982); and
4. there is a need for well-trained and educated staff (Goldman, 1988; Grizenko et al., 1993; LeCroy, 1984; Wells & Whittington, 1990).

According to Miskimins (1990), administrators should always make decisions from a patient-centered approach, understanding that:

> There sometimes has to be a compromise in those situations where not everyone can be pleased . . . the "bottom line" must always be "what is best for the patient." Occasionally, staff job satisfaction, community linkages, or whatever, must be compromised [after seeking a negotiated settlement in times of conflict]. (p. 877)

Programming Issues

This area was the one most often noted on the coding forms for the database. In reference to programming issues, 27 different topics were mentioned, but the topic receiving by far the most coverage (39 references) was related to specific treatments or characteristics of programs. Although it is beyond the scope of this review to compare specific programs, some general findings are of interest. According to the Institute of Medicine (1989), children and families often require a combination of interventions such as behavioral and psychological therapies, family therapy, special education, and medication, and there is a "growing body of evidence" to support "the effectiveness of many treatments used in clinical care. In general, conventional treatments are demonstrably better than no treatment" (p. 202). Saxe, Cross, and Silverman (1986) supported these conclusions, adding specifically that "behavioral treatment is clearly effective for phobias, . . . cognitive-behavioral therapy is effective for a range of disorders involving self-control (except aggressive behavior), . . . group therapy . . . with delinquent adolescents, and family therapy for children with conduct disorders and psychophysiological disorders" (p. 9). However, in their review of types of interventions, Macmillan and Kavale (1986) concluded: "Educational programs do not adhere rigidly to the tenets of theoretical models but rather take a more pragmatic approach based upon an eclectic combination of intervention strategies derived from the theoretical models" (p. 59). They warned that few truly theoretical models "have derived their continued popularity on proof of efficacy or cost benefit," and that intervention models should be judged based on replicability, efficiency, breadth, and effectiveness (p. 59).

Five other programming issues were referred to frequently in the database:

1. an emphasis on a family systems approach to treatment, and parental involvement (Armstrong & Evans, 1992; Armstrong, Grosser, & Palma, 1992; Barker, 1988; Dettlebach, 1955; Duchnowski & Friedman, 1990; Dydyk et al., 1989; Edwards, 1987; Farley, 1985; Guterman et al., 1989; Jenson & Whittaker, 1987; Ney, Adam, Hanton, & Brindad, 1988; Wells, Wyatt, & Hobfoll, 1991; Zimet & Farley, 1985);
2. the need for clear program rationales, goals, and objectives (Barker, 1988; Dalton & Forman, 1987; Dalton et al., 1986; Easson, 1969; Stone, 1979; Wells, 1991b);
3. the importance of effective methods for the assessment of clients (Alessi & Magen, 1988; Dickson, Heffron, & Parker, 1990; Eaton, 1967; Gossett et al., 1980; Matek, 1964; Ney et al., 1988; Pfeiffer & Naglieri, 1984; Smith, Wood, & Grimes, 1988; Trickett, Leone, Fink, & Braaten, 1993);
4. the need for program evaluations (Barker, 1988; Durkin & Durkin, 1975; Gossett et al., 1980; Grubb & Thompson, 1982; Laslett, 1982; Levy, 1969; Moore & O'Conner, 1991; Stone, 1979); and
5. the level of training and understanding needed by program personnel (Barker, 1988; Brassard & Barnes, 1987; Costello, Dulcan, & Kalas, 1991; Mikkelson et al., 1993; Small, Kennedy, & Bender, 1991; Smith et al., 1988; Stone, 1979; Wilson & Lyman, 1983).

We hasten to note that these arguments have varying degrees of intuitive appeal, but that they are only arguments, not proven facts.

Subject-Specific Issues

Most of the information in the database classified as "subject-specific" consisted of demographic characteristics like race, gender, age, family structure, and socioeconomic status. In addition, there were many references to subjects' particular problems, or principle diagnoses. This information has been summarized in Table 4.6, which includes only articles reporting more than subjects' ages and gender (because most others were included in Table 4.2).

Several more substantive issues in the database concerned subjects. These included the following:

1. information on how subjects were selected for inclusion in studies or programs (Askew & Thomas, 1987; Barker, 1988; Cullinan, Epstein, & Sabornie, 1992; Fuchs et al., 1991; Harris & Kierstead, 1985; Harris et al., 1984; Hodges & Plow, 1990; Mattison & Gamble, 1992; Mikkelson et al., 1993);

TABLE 4.6
Subject-Specific Issues

Citation	Diagnois/Problem	*Gender*		*Race*			*SES*			*Family*					*Family Mental*	
		M	*F*	*Wh*	*AA*	*Hs*	*L*	*M*	*H*	*2*	*1*	*0*	*Age*	*IQ*	*Illness*	*History of Abuse*
Beitchman & Dielman (1982)	psychoneurosis and personality disorder			maj.						X			4–12			
Cheek & Wolcott (1968)	26% organic brain damage			82%	18%											
Coleman et al. (1992)	64% conduct disorder, 16% major depression, 10% oppositional/defiant	29	10	67%	25%	8%	x	x	x				13–18	<avg.		
Dalton et al. (1986)		72%	28%	61%									avg. 4.5	30 to 115	72%	56%
Dickson et al. (1990)	39% affective disturbance, 42% behavioral disturbance			95%	5%					34% 12%	23%		14–17			
Gabel et al. (1988)	27% suidical, 37% severe assaultive or destructive			13		–39–	maj.								50%	50%
Herrera et al. (1974)		equal #		100%			40% 5%	55%					14–17	avg. 115		38%
Hodges & Plow (1990)		50	26	64%	36%		66%							avg. 97.5		
Hutchinson et al. (1992)				maj.												60%
King & Pittman (1971)	psychotic or SED												14–19			
Laneve (1982)		5:1									–maj–					30%
Mattison, Humphrey, Kales, & Wallace (1986)	demonstrated severe behavior problems			90%	10%					42% 22%	36%		avg. 9	72–126 avg. 97		
Mattison, Humphrey, Kales, Hanford, et al. (1986)	behavior cannot be managed in the classroom	86%	14%	89%	11%								avg. 11.4	avg. 95.7		

(Continued)

TABLE 4.6
(Continued)

Citation	Diagnois/Problem	Gender		Race			SES			Family			Age	IQ	Family Mental Illness	History of Abuse
		M	*F*	*Wh*	*AA*	*Hs*	*L*	*M*	*H*	*2*	*1*	*0*				
Mattison et al. (1992)	unresponsive to classroom intervention	100%		89%	11%								avg. 8.7			
Moore & O'Conner (1991)	40% conduct disorder	72%	28%										avg. 12.4			
Myers et al. (1990)				60%	33%	7%	maj.				–80%–		avg. 15.3			
Ney et al. (1988)		73%	27%				maj.						maj. 11 & 12			
Parmalee et al. (1991)	60% suicidal	64%	36%	78%	22%					17%		72%	avg. 12.2			
Ravenel et al. (1982)	68% dangerous histories	73%	27%	72%									avg. 14.4			33%
Ricciuti et al. (1986)		71%	29%	34% 15%	51%		85%						avg. 9.2			
Rosenblatt & Attkisson (1992)	22% mood disorders, 20% adjustment disorder, 37% disruptive behavior			62%		22%							42% 15–20			
Roth & Nicholson (1988)	conduct disorder			22%	53%								avg. 12.5			
Sack et al. (1987)				81%	11%								avg. 6			20%
Silver et al. (1992)		75%	25%	71%	22%	5%							avg. 13.11			33%
Small et al. (1991)																56%
Swan et al. (1987)		2.5:1		56%	44%											
Tarico et al. (1989)				71%	–29%–											
Wells & Whittington (1990)	psychotic			75%			50%									

2. from where subjects admitted to different settings come, or from where they were referred (Beitchman & Dielman, 1982; Cheek & Wolcott, 1969; Coleman, Pfeiffer, & Oakland, 1992; Connolly, 1987; Dickson et al., 1990; Inamdar, Darrell, Brown, & Lewis, 1986; King & Pittman, 1971; Moore & O'Conner, 1991; Rosenblatt & Attkisson, 1992; Roth & Nicholson, 1988);
3. general characteristics of subjects, which are more broad than the demographic characteristics referred to earlier (Doan & Petti, 1989; Goldman, 1988; Inamdar et al., 1986; Jensen & Whittaker, 1987; Levy, 1969);
4. prevalence of emotional or behavioral disorders in different locations (Armstrong et al., 1992; Laneve, 1982; Mattison, Morales, & Bauer, 1992; Weintrob, 1975); and
5. differences between subjects according to treatment settings (Cheek & Wolcott, 1968; Silver et al., 1992; Trickett et al., 1993; Zimet & Farley, 1985).

According to Doan and Petti (1989), youth who are characterized as having emotional or behavioral disorders tend to live at home, are relatively impoverished, and most commonly have externalizing or disruptive disorders. Goldman (1988) found that the majority of clients who use crisis intervention services are adolescents, and that there are increasing numbers who have been sexually or physically abused and who have parents addicted to drugs or alcohol. In a review of literature on gender and incidence of violent crimes, Inamdar et al. (1986) revealed the disturbing trend that the proportion of "more violent" girls almost equals the proportion of "more violent" boys and is on the rise.

Legal and Policy Issues

Many of the references to legal or policy issues in the database concerned specific court rulings or laws and are given the coverage they deserve in a later chapter (see chap. 12, this volume). Provisions of specific programs, such as the Child and Adolescent Service System Program (CASSP), are described in many references as well. However, several more general issues relating to laws and policies were included in the database. The most notable of those is the emphasis placed on family systems of therapy and policies in favor of community-based programs. Armstrong and Evans (1992) suggested that "the emphasis on supporting families has been related to a change in the orientation of children's mental health services from viewing parents as clients in need of treatment to viewing them as allies or partners in the treatment of their children" (p. 63). But Wells (1991b) warned that current policies favoring placement in the least restrictive setting in community-based and family-focused programs have limited utility because they fail to address criteria for placement and are too vague.

Another topic given equal weight in the literature deals with funding policies and insurance companies. Many authors lamented the lack of health insurance coverage for people placed in less restrictive settings, such as day care centers and other community-based programs (Burns & Friedman, 1990; Dalton & Forman, 1987; Goldfine et al., 1985; Jenson, Hawkins, & Catalano, 1986). Voineskos (1976) suggested that advocates have oversold the community-based system of care because too often clients' release to a community is prompted by political pressure and economics rather than as a treatment plan, and funds saved are not used for development in the community. Along the same lines, Burns and Friedman (1988) stated that certain lessons have been learned—or should have been—from experience, including the lesson that "expected savings from decreased use of inpatient settings must be available for care in the community at the time that a new policy is implemented" (p. 88).

Several other issues occurred frequently in the database. These included the following:

1. criteria, or the lack of adequate criteria, for placement in different settings (Armstrong et al., 1992; A.W.M.C. Working Party on Residential Resources, 1984; Barack, 1986; Barker, 1988; Friedman & Street, 1985; Maluccio & Marlow, 1972; Small et al., 1991; Stotsky, Browne, & Lister, 1987; Wells, 1991b);
2. the use of official definitions of emotional or behavioral disorders in making placement and policy decisions (Cheney & Sampson, 1990; Mattison et al., 1992; Smith et al., 1988; Wright, Pillard, & Cleven, 1990); and
3. calls for more research on the factors on which policymaking is based (Cheek & Wolcott, 1969; Duchnowski & Friedman, 1990; Institute of Medicine, 1989; Maluccio & Marlow, 1972).

Ethical Issues

Only 1 of the 25 topics related to ethical issues occurred more than once or twice—the fear, suspicion, or conclusion that placement and programming decisions are not based on the real needs of children (A.W.M.C. Working Party on Residential Resources, 1984; Doan & Petti, 1989; Kester, 1966; Maluccio & Marlow, 1972; McCauley, 1984). The A.W.M.C. Working Party on Residential Resources (1984) observed:

> There is greater readiness to move children from one provision to another on grounds which do not appear to be specifically related to meeting the special needs of these children. Apart from anything else, this is of particular concern because of the unsettling and damaging effects it will have on children whose greatest needs are often the stability and security of a long term placement. (p. 21)

Kester (1966) noted that residential placement was, in most cases,

> more a decision of desperation than of deliberation . . . undertaken in response to the insistence of either the family or society that the child be removed from the community. The welfare of the child is seldom the deciding impetus behind the decision, although it is invariably stated as if it were. (p. 340)

Ethical issues referenced twice in the database were as follows:

1. the potential stigma associated with psychiatric treatment (Alexson & Sinclair, 1986; Forness et al., 1983);
2. issues of confidentiality, particularly in small communities (Brassard & Barnes, 1987; Morrisette, 1989);
3. inappropriate assessment (Cheney & Sampson, 1990; Marsden, McDermott, & Minor, 1977); and
4. placement of youth with serious mental health problems in correctional facilities rather than hospitals (Cohen et al., 1990; Shanok et al., 1983).

Another ethical issue discussed was the overuse of psychotropic drugs (Herrera, Lifson, Hartman, & Solomon, 1974).

Setting-Specific Issues

Regular School. Most of the information from the database specifically referring to regular school placement for children with emotional or behavioral disorders could be divided into two categories: (a) aspects of the programs, including costs, staff, and services; and (b) effects on students in the programs. Although Stotsky et al. (1987) concluded that "the public schools could successfully manage students with severe psychoeducational problems, previously thought to be unmanageable within public school settings" (p. 240), Clarke et al. (1992) cautioned that "studies comparing the educational and clinical effectiveness of mainstreaming with other special education strategies for behavioral disordered children are uncommon" (p. 244). Despite the lack of clear evidence for the effectiveness of mainstreaming programs, there appears to be a trend toward placing children with more serious emotional or behavioral disorders in less restrictive settings, including the regular classroom (Cullinan et al., 1992).

Most of the program aspects were described by writers who viewed regular classroom placement as the preferred setting for students with emotional or behavioral disorders. Askew and Thomas (1987) and Paul (1977) cited problems with discontinuity of curricula between regular classrooms and other settings, arguing that the regular classroom tends to have a more academically challenging and diverse curriculum. Grubb and Thompson (1982) emphasized the advantage of using a team concept in a regular school with staff already in the education system. Seip and McCoy (1982) argued that trained teachers do not require a segregated location to provide quality instruction and that regular education teachers can benefit from the opportunity to work with students with disabilities. Furthermore, Wilson and Lyman (1983) proposed that the home environment is usually less affected in mainstreaming situations than in more restrictive settings. However, Steinberg and Knitzer (1992) raised important concerns, including the question of what, if any, mental health services students receive in regular classroom settings. Walker and Bullis (1991) and Noel (1982) questioned the degree to which public schools are actually providing a full range of services to students. According to Walker and Bullis, "Public schools' record of effectively accommodating students with behavior disorders . . . is close to abysmal" and "most school districts have not developed and do not use an adequate continuum of services and placements" (p. 80).

Several writers expressed concern about the potential negative effects that being mainstreamed into a regular classroom might have on students with emotional or behavioral disorders. Parents may fear that their child will experience "psychologically defeating failure" from being placed in an environment where success may not be possible (Paul, 1977, p. 21), and an overwhelming amount of stimulation in regular classrooms can cause distractibility and may threaten students' success (Streitmatter & Santa Cruz, 1982). However, Seip and McCoy (1982) argued that regular classroom placement provides students having emotional or behavioral disorders with more opportunities to interact with nonhandicapped peers in positive ways, and Sindelar, King, Cartland, Wilson, and Meisel (1985) suggested that special placement may foster more anxious behavior and rule breaking than would occur in a regular classroom, where students are exposed to positive role models.

Day or Alternative Schools and Partial Hospitalization. References to day or alternative settings included 10 different definitions of this placement option. Many of the definitions had elements in common, including the functions of day treatment centers that may include the following:

1. providing support to children and families as an alternative to inpatient or residential treatment (Johns, 1982; Tuma, 1989; Voineskos, 1976);
2. a transition between inpatient treatment and return to public school (Johns, 1982; Tuma, 1989; Voineskos, 1976; Zimet & Farley, 1985);
3. preparation for residential treatment (Johns, 1982);
4. supportive treatment, such as an after-school group (Johns, 1982); (d) short-term crisis intervention (Johns, 1982); and
5. rehabilitation of long-term inpatients (Voineskos, 1976; Zimet & Farley, 1985).

Others emphasized that day-treatment programs should be composed of both therapeutic and educational components (Armstrong et al., 1992; Saxe et al.,

1986; Trickett et al., 1993; Voineskos, 1976). Armstrong et al. (1992) provided the most comprehensive definition when they stated that day-treatment programs

> are highly structured, intensive, non-residential mental health programs that offer a blend of clinical intervention and special education to children and adolescents, as well as social and clinical support to their families [in a] therapeutic environment that facilitates the coordinated delivery of mental health and education services. (p. 18)

In recent years, the term *partial hospitalization*, rather than *day treatment* has become popular, resulting in some confusion. Saxe et al. (1986) stated that "partial hospitalization is the use of a psychiatric hospital setting for less than 24-hour-a-day care for given patients. . . . In effect, this is day treatment applied in a psychiatric hospital setting" (p. 84). According to Doan and Petti (1989), there is no clear distinction between special or private day schools for students with emotional or behavioral disorders and partial hospital programs with an educational component, but Burns and Friedman (1988) pointed out that programs called "partial hospitalization" are beginning to attract third-party payment, making it an attractive alternative to families who may not be able to afford other day-treatment programs.

Many advantages and disadvantages of day treatment are listed in the literature on treatment settings. Day treatment offers at least the following advantages: (a) It preserves placement in a community location and helps maintain links to family and peer groups (Grizenko et al., 1993; Wilson & Lyman, 1983); (b) there is an opportunity for day schools to provide more intensive services than are available at regular schools (Harris et al., 1984; Weithorn, 1988); and (c) day schools are able to provide consistency in highly protective environments, which makes a nonthreatening atmosphere and academic instruction easier to achieve than in public schools (Streitmatter & Santa Cruz, 1982). Potential disadvantages of a day treatment model include: (a) The curriculum may be less academically challenging and diverse, making it difficult for students when they are ready for the transition back to regular schools (Askew & Thomas, 1987); (b) the benefits of day school are sometimes undermined when students have to spend their nights and weekends with dysfunctional families where parents "can undo in a weekend what took a week in school to build up" (Hamm, 1989, p. 14); (c) there can be a problem with insurance companies determining the length of stay for patients (Mikkelson et al., 1993); and (d) "day treatment classes may experience more disruptions and more mobility among students than in residential or regular education classes" (Trickett et al., 1993, p. 193).

Residential School. Seip and McCoy (1982) defined a residential institution as one in which children receive "total care within a self-contained community . . . the children may or may not attend school, depending upon the severity of their behavior," and the institution is usually a "private, not-for-profit program specifically structured to meet the needs of a certain target group," housing 20 to 100 residents and providing "a comprehensive therapeutic educational program within its own setting" (p. 115). The A.W.M.C. Working Party on Residential Resources (1984) lauded residential programs for their capacity "to provide a totality of experiences emotionally, socially, and educationally in a planned and comprehensive fashion" (p. 23), and acknowledged that there

> will always be a number of children who will not respond to programs of integration provided in the ordinary school system . . . who will not be able to remain with their families . . . [and who] cannot manage without the personal support and understanding that only very specialized residential programs make available. (p. 21)

Other proponents of residential centers noted advantages: (a) With adequate staffing and resources they provide safe, humane care and multiple opportunities for reestablishing connections with families (Small et al., 1991); (b) they remove children and adolescents from their homes and the stresses of their interactions with their parents while providing intensive treatment (Weintrob, 1975); and (c) they "provide substantial benefits to many adolescents who would spend most of their youth in institutions" if there were no residential treatment option (Weithorn, 1988, p. 796).

Combining the criticisms of residential treatment put forth by its many opponents results in a daunting list of potential drawbacks. Barker (1988) noted several disadvantages of residential schools supported by other writers: (a) They bring the child into potentially harmful contact with other troubled children; (b) children can become institutionalized and overdependent on treatment centers (Durkin & Durkin, 1975; Kester, 1966; Stone, 1979); (c) children may learn dysfunctional behaviors from other disturbed children who are in treatment with them (Stone, 1979); and (d) separation can be a damaging experience for families (Jenson & Whittaker, 1987; Smollar & Condelli, 1990; Stone, 1979). Many other disadvantages are suggested in the literature as well. Similar to the situation with day treatment, the gains of the residential treatment center experience may not be maintained when children and adolescents return to dysfunctional families (Burns & Friedman, 1988; Easson, 1969; Kester, 1966). Edwards (1987) described residential centers as a "neutral environment," and suggested that the lower level of closeness experienced with staff at residential facilities does not prepare a child fully for the intimacy of family living. According to Jaffe (1986), the "lack of continuity and constant breaking of relationships with the children in care" is a serious problem in institutional placement (p. 134). LeCroy (1984) pointed out the necessity of dealing with the problem of high staff turnover rates. Silver et al. (1992) claimed that

> a significant proportion of school-aged children are placed into residential care each year. . . . These children are being served in one of the most restrictive envi-

> ronments available to children, an environment that is extremely costly, with little empirical evidence to support its use over less restrictive settings such as day treatment. (pp. 44–45)

However, others have concluded that available research on treatment settings does offer evidence to "support the potential effectiveness of a system of services ranging from outpatient community-based care to intensive residential-based care" (Saxe et al., 1986, p. 9), and Matek (1964) noted that "variation makes it all the more difficult to describe the advantages or disadvantages of one kind of facility over another" (p. 346). Despite its many detractors, residential placement is a "desirable part of many plans for treatment" (Kester, 1966, p. 340). For children with

> histories of poverty, overcrowding, parental rejection or abuse, removal from the family situation to a residential school can be therapeutic in itself. A residential school can provide good food, clean clothing, opportunities for constructive leisure, and freedom from . . . victimisation . . . within a framework of compassionate controls by qualified staff. (Priestly, 1987, p. 35)

Psychiatric Hospital. Many issues concerning hospitalization were noted, but the need for posthospital placement support was cited most often. Writers seemed to agree that psychiatric hospitalization alone is not successful as remediation unless clients receive aftercare services, especially when children are returning to home situations that cannot provide enough structure and support to sustain progress (Dalton et al., 1990; Johns, 1982; Ney et al., 1988; Pfeiffer & Strzelecki, 1990; Quinton & Rutter, 1976). Although many writers agreed that community-based systems should be attempted first and the goal should be to place or move patients into community-based systems as soon as possible (Barber, Allen, & Coyne, 1992; Saxe et al., 1986), many also agreed that "some children and adolescents need hospitalization for extended periods, and . . . to deprive them of such treatment at a critical juncture of their illness could entail high social, economic, and human costs" (Barber et al., 1992, p. 458; see also Barker, 1988; Saxe et al., 1986).

As with the other treatment settings, there are many advantages and disadvantages of hospitalization cited in the literature on placement issues. Most of the references concern psychological treatment issues, but there are several references to hospital school programs as well. Although Friedman (1982) stated that the hospital school experience can be a rewarding and accepting learning situation because of small class sizes, Haslum (1988) contended that the "hospital school service operates in conditions which are less than ideal educationally. Access to children can be restricted by their condition and the treatments they receive," and educational support is "dependent on appropriate contact with the children's school teachers" (p. 289). Morrisette (1989) and Wilson and Lyman (1983) noted that academic time in inpatient classrooms tends to be very limited because of intensive therapeutic work.

No single advantage or disadvantage to hospitalization was referred to more than once or twice in the database, but numerous different potential disadvantages and advantages were pointed out. Some writers indicated that psychiatric hospitalization stigmatizes children and may lead to lowered expectations (Alexson & Sinclair, 1986; Morrisette, 1989). According to Bloom and Hopewell (1982), the longer an adolescent is hospitalized, the less likely he or she is to be successfully reintegrated into the community, and Zimet and Farley (1985) noted that extended hospitalization may encourage dependency on the setting. Other problems with hospitalization included: (a) An environment without family and friends is likely to be frightening to a child (Haslum, 1988); (b) there is too much staff turnover (Weintrob, 1975; Zimet & Farley, 1985); and (c) there is extreme dissimilarity from the natural environment with few opportunities for patients to "engage in such normal activities as room cleaning, snacking, or going outside" (Wilson & Lyman, 1983). Advantages to hospitalization include: (a) It may reduce the suffering of both the patient and the family and shorten the duration of serious problems, and (b) it may prevent multiple treatment failures and emergency hospitalization (Costello et al., 1991).

Although the majority of references included under the "hospital costs and benefits" heading of our database indicated negative results of hospitalization (Burns & Friedman, 1988; Goldfine et al., 1985; Grizenko et al., 1993; Herrera et al., 1974), others claimed that specialized psychiatric hospitalization with aftercare yields positive results (Pfeiffer & Strzelecki, 1990; Zimmerman, 1990). However, Saxe et al. (1986) rightly emphasized that questions about the effectiveness of hospitalization "are difficult to answer because of the lack of systematic research. . . . The lack of methodologically sound evidence for the effectiveness . . . does not necessarily mean that these treatment settings are inappropriate—only that there is no solid evidence one way or the other" (p. 9).

AREAS IN NEED OF INVESTIGATION

One of the most striking features of the research literature on placement is the lack of any consistent markers used to define either the populations of children and youth being studied or the characteristics of the placement options being researched. An immediate need is common agreement among researchers about the definition of variables to be studied. The needed agreement involves (a) consistently detailed descriptions of the children and youth placed, (b) consistently detailed descriptions of the treatment delivered in the placement, and (c) the critical outcome measures. Until researchers attain a reasonable level of consistency across studies in what is measured, aggregation of results across studies will have little meaning.

Relatively little of the available literature consists of reliable data. The literature is, in fact, characterized by strong opinions based on few data. We suspect that decisions about placement are typically made on questionable grounds, but even here we must plead ignorance of just how these decisions are in fact made. More study of the decision process is warranted. We suspect that selection biases operate in studies comparing children and youth in more versus less restrictive settings (cf. Bloom & Hopewell, 1982). If this is the case, then differing outcomes for placements differing in restrictiveness are not attributable to placement per se. Nevertheless, fervid opinions but few reliable data are available to address the issue of selection bias in placement studies. We suspect that students in few placement options are systematically or effectively prepared to move to another placement, yet we have little reliable evidence to indicate what steps are taken to facilitate students' movement from one place to another. In short, we can think of no issue in the educational placement of students with emotional or behavioral disorders that does not need much more thorough investigation. The most critical need is for sustained, programmatic research to overcome the patchwork quality of the studies that characterizes the field to date.

ACKNOWLEDGMENTS

Preparation of this manuscript was supported in part by Grant #H237A10002 from the U.S. Department of Education, Office of Special Education Programs. Opinions expressed herein do not necessarily represent those of the Department of Education.

REFERENCES

Alessi, N., & Magen, J. (1988). Panic disorder in psychiatrically hospitalized children. *American Journal of Psychiatry, 145,* 1450–1452.

Alexson, J., & Sinclair, E. (1986). Psychiatric diagnosis and school placement: A comparison between inpatients and outpatients. *Child Psychiatry and Human Development, 16,* 194–205.

Appropriateness of private residential placements. (1985). *Mental and Physical Disability Law Reporter, 9,* 49–52.

Apsler, R., & Bassuk, E. (1983). Differences among clinicians in the decision to admit. *Archives of General Psychiatry, 40,* 1133–1137.

Armstrong, M., & Evans, M. (1992). Three intensive community-based programs for children and youth with serious emotional disturbance and their families. *Journal of Child and Family Studies, 1,* 61–74.

Armstrong, M., Grosser, R., & Palma, P. (1992). *At the crossroads: Expanding community-based care for children and families* (The New York State plan for children and families mental health services). New York: New York Office of Mental Health.

Askew, H., & Thomas, D. (1987). But I wouldn't want to go back. *British Journal of Special Education, 14,* 6–9.

A.W.M.C. Working Party on Residential Resources. (1984). Residential provision for maladjusted and emotionally disturbed children. *Maladjustment and Therapeutic Education, 2,* 20–29.

Balla, D., Lewis, D., Shanok, S., Snell, L., & Henisz, J. (1974). Subsequent psychiatric treatment and hospitalization in a delinquent population. *Archives of General Psychiatry, 30*, 243–245.

Barack, R. (1986). Hospitalization of emotionally disturbed children: Who gets hospitalized and why. *American Journal of Orthopsychiatry, 56*, 317–319.

Barber, C. C., Allen, J. G., & Coyne, L. (1992). Optimal length of stay in child and adolescent psychiatric hospitalization: A study of clinical opinion. *American Journal of Orthopsychiatry, 62*, 458–463.

Barker, P. (1968). The inpatient treatment of school refusal. *British Journal of Medical Psychology, 41*, 381–387.

Barker, P. (1988). The future of residential treatment for children. In C. Schaefer & A. Swanson (Eds.), *Children in residential care: Critical issues in treatment* (pp. 1–16). New York: Van Nostrand Reinhold.

Beitchman, J., & Dielman, T. (1982). Predicting hospitalization in child psychiatry: The influence of diagnosis and demographic variables. *Clinical Child Psychology, 11*, 116–122.

Bergquist, C. (1982). A methodology for validating placement of children in exceptional child programs. *Exceptional Children, 49*, 269–270.

Bloom, R., & Hopewell, L. (1982). Psychiatric hospitalization of adolescents and successful mainstream reentry. *Exceptional Children, 48*, 352–357.

Bogdan, R., & Biklen, S. (1992). *Qualitative research for education: An introduction to theory and methods*. Boston: Allyn & Bacon.

Brassard, M., & Barnes, S. (1987). Serving emotionally disturbed students in rural settings: A case of service delivery problems and alternative solutions. *School Psychology Review, 3*, 391–397.

Burns, B. (1991). Mental health service use by adolescents in the 1970s and 1980s. In A. Algarin & R. Friedman (Eds.), *A system of care for children's mental health: Building a research base, 3rd annual conference proceedings* (pp. 3–19). Tampa: Florida Mental Health Institute.

Burns, B., & Friedman, R. (1988). The research base for child mental health services and policy: How solid is the foundation? In P. Greenbaum, R. Friedman, A. Duchnowski, K. Kutash, & S. Silver (Eds.), *Proceedings of the first annual conference on children's mental health services and policy: Building a research base* (pp. 7–13). Tampa: Florida Mental Health Institute.

Burns, B., & Friedman, R. (1990). Examining the research base for child mental health services and policy. *The Journal of Mental Health Administration, 17*, 87–98.

Cheek, F., & Wolcott, R. (1969). Hospitalized disturbed children: Demographic family background and behavioral characteristics. *Psychiatry Quarterly Supplement, 42*, 349–370.

Cheney, C., & Sampson, K. (1990). Issues in the identification and service delivery for students with conduct disorders: The "Nevada Solution." *Behavioral Disorders, 15*, 174–179.

Christ, A., Adler, A., Merling, B., & Gershansky, I. (1981). Brooklyn Kings County child psychiatric study, 1957–1977: A longitudinal comparison of court-remanded and psychiatrically admitted children. *Journal of the American Academy of Child Psychiatry, 20*, 777–791.

Clarke, R., Schaefer, M., Burchard, J., & Welkowitz, J. (1992). Wrapping community-based mental health services around children with a severe behavioral disorder: An evaluation of Project Wraparound. *Journal of Child and Family Studies, 1*, 241–261.

Cocozza, J., & Melick, M. (1977). The right to refuse treatment: A broad view. *Bulletin of the American Academy of Psychiatry and the Law, 5*, 1–7.

Cohen, R., Parmelee, D., Irwin, L., Weisz, J., Howard, P., Purcell, P., & Best, A. (1990). Characteristics of children and adolescents in a psychiatric hospital and a corrections facility. *Journal of the American Academy of Child and Adolescent Psychiatry, 29*, 909–913.

Coleman, M., Pfeiffer, S., & Oakland, T. (1992). Aggression replacement training with behaviorally disordered adolescents. *Behavioral Disorders, 18*, 54–66.

Connolly, J. A. (1987). Sociometric status among emotionally disturbed adolescents in a residential treatment program. *Journal of Adolescent Research, 2*, 411–421.

Cooper, P. (1985). The perceptions of parents of a residential school for pupils with behavioral and emotional difficulties. *Maladjustment and Therapeutic Education, 3*, 21–29.

Costello, A., Dulcan, M., & Kalas, R. (1991). A checklist of hospitalization criteria for use with children. *Hospital & Community Psychiatry, 42*, 823–828.

Crittenden, P. M. (1992). The social ecology of treatment: Case study of a service system for maltreated children. *American Journal of Orthopsychiatry, 62*, 22–34.

Cullinan, D., Epstein, M., & Sabornie, E. (1992). Selected characteristics of a national sample of seriously emotionally disturbed adolescents. *Behavioral Disorders, 17*, 273–280.

Curry, J. F. (1991). Outcome research on residential treatment: Implications and suggested directions. *American Orthopsychiatric Association, 61*, 348–356.

Dalton, R., Bolding D., & Forman, M. A. (1990). Psychiatric hospitalization of preschool children: A follow-up study. *Child Psychiatry and Human Development, 21*, 57–64.

Dalton, R., & Forman, M. A. (1987). Conflicts of interest associated with the psychiatric hospitalization of children. *American Journal of Orthopsychiatry, 57*, 12–14.

Dalton, R., Forman, M. A., Daul, G. C., & Bolding, D. (1986). Psychiatric hospitalization of preschool children: Admission factors and discharge implications. *Journal of the American Academy of Child and Adolescent Psychiatry, 26*, 308–312.

Dettelbach, M. H. (1955). The role of residential treatment for children. *American Journal of Orthopsychiatry, 25*, 669–674.

Dickson, L., Heffron, W., & Parker, C. (1990). Children from disrupted and adoptive homes on an inpatient unit. *American Journal of Orthopsychiatry, 60*, 594–602.

Doan, R., & Petti, T. (1989). Clinical and demographic characteristics of child and adolescent partial hospital patients. *American Academy of Child and Adolescent Psychiatry, 28*, 66–69.

Duchnowski, A., & Friedman, R. (1990). Children's mental health: Challenges for the nineties. *The Journal of Mental Health Administration, 17*, 3–12.

Duchnowski, A., Johnson, M., Hall, K., Kutash, K., & Friedman, R. (1992). The alternatives to residential treatment study: Initial findings. *Journal of Emotional and Behavioral Disorders, 1*, 17–26.

Durkin, R., & Durkin, A. (1975). Evaluating residential treatment programs for disturbed children. In M. Guttentag & E. L. Struening (Eds.), *Handbook of evaluation research* (Vol. 2, pp. 275–339). Newbury Park, CA: Sage.

Dydyk, B., French, G., Gertsman, C., Morrison, C., & O'Neill, I. (1989). Admitting whole families: An alternative to residential care. *Canadian Journal of Psychiatry, 34*, 694–699.

Easson, W. (1969). *The severely disturbed adolescent: Inpatient, residential, and hospital treatment* (pp. 224–239). Toledo, OH: International Universities Press.

Eaton, L. (1967). Hospitalizing the emotionally disturbed child. *Postgraduate Medicine, 41*, 399–406.

Edwards, J. (1987). Continuity and orchestration of after-care services to disturbed children: From residential treatment to adoptive placement. *Residential Treatment for Children & Youth, 4*, 53–67.

Epstein, M., Foley, R., & Cullinan, D. (1992). National survey of educational programs for adolescents with serious emotional disturbance. *Behavioral Disorders, 17*, 202–210.

Farley, J. (1985). Preparing the family to make the decision about residential placement for an adolescent. *Hospital and Community Psychiatry, 36*, 662–664.

Forness, S., Barnes, T., & Mordaunt, J. (1983). Brief psychiatric hospitalization: A study of its effect on special education placement. In R. Rutherford (Ed.), *Severe behavior disorders of children and youth* (Vol. 6, pp. 66–75). Reston, VA: Council for Exceptional Children.

Friedman, N. (1982). An educational program for the hospitalized, emotionally disturbed child. In L. Hoffman (Ed.), *The evaluation and care of severely disturbed children and their families* (pp. 75–78). New York: Spectrum.

Friedman, R. M., & Street, S. (1985). Admission and discharge criteria for children's mental health services: A review of the issues and options. *Journal of Clinical Child Psychiatry, 14*, 229–235.

Fuchs, D., Fuchs, L., Fernstrom, P., & Hohn, M. (1991). Toward a responsible reintegration of behaviorally disordered students. *Behavioral Disorders, 16*, 133–147.

Gabel, S., Finn, M., & Ahmad, A. (1988). Day treatment outcome with severely disturbed children. *Journal of the American Academy of Child and Adolescent Psychiatry, 27*, 479–482.

Goldfine, P., Heath, G., Hardesty, V., Berman, H., Gordon, B., & Lind, N. (1985). Alternatives to psychiatric hospitalization for children. *Psychiatric Clinics of North America, 8*, 527–535.

Goldman, S. (1988). *Series on community-based services for children and adolescents who are severely emotionally disturbed: Vol. II. Crisis services* (pp. 12–54). Washington, DC: Georgetown University Child Development Center.

Gossett, J. T., Barnhart, F. D., Lewis, J. M., & Phillips, V. A. (1980). Follow-up of adolescents treated in a psychiatric hospital: Measurement of outcome. *Southern Medical Journal, 73*, 459–466.

Greenberg, A., & Mayer, M. (1972). Group home care as an adjunct to residential treatment. *Child Welfare, 51*, 423–435.

Grizenko, N., Papineau, D., & Sayegh, L. (1993). Effectiveness of a multimodal day treatment program for children with disruptive behavior problems. *Journal of the American Academy of Child and Adolescent Psychiatry, 32*, 127–134.

Grosenick, J., Huntze, S., Kochan, B., Peterson, R., Robertshaw, S., & Wood. F. (1982). *Disciplinary exclusion of seriously emotionally disturbed children from public schools: Monograph 7*. Des Moines, IA: Midwest Regional Resource Center, Drake University.

Grubb, R., & Thompson, M. (1982). Delivering related services to the emotionally disturbed: A field-based perspective. In N. G. Haring & M. Noel (Eds.), *Progress or change: Issues in educating the emotionally disturbed* (pp. 85–97). Seattle, WA: University of Washington.

Guterman, N. B., Hodges, V. G., Blythe, B. J., & Bronson, D. E. (1989). Aftercare service development for children in residential treatment. *Child & Youth Care Quarterly, 18*, 119–130.

Hamm, J. (1989). Intensive day treatment provides an alternative to residential care. *Children Today, 18*, 11–15.

Harris, J., King, S., Reifler, J., & Rosenberg, L. (1984). Emotional and learning disorders in 6–12 year old boys attending special schools. *Journal of the American Academy of Child Psychiatry, 23*, 431–437.

Harris, W., & Kierstead, J. (1985). *The education of behaviorally handicapped students in Maine.* Augusta: Maine State Department of Educational and Cultural Services.

Haslum, M. (1988). Length of preschool hospitalization, multiple admissions and later educational attainment and behavior. *Child: Care, Health, and Development, 14*, 275–291.

Herrera, E., Lifson, B., Hartmann, E., & Solomon, M. (1974). A 10-year follow-up of 55 hospitalized adolescents. *American Journal of Psychiatry, 131*, 769–774.

Hodges, K., & Plow, J. (1990). Intellectual ability and achievement in psychiatrically hospitalized children with conduct, anxiety, and affective disorders. *Journal of Consulting and Clinical Psychology, 58*, 589–595.

Hutchinson, R., Tess, D., Gleckman, A., & Spence, W. (1992). Psycho-social characteristics of institutionalized adolescents: Resilient or at risk? *Adolescence, 27*, 339–356.

Inamdar, S., Darrell, E., Brown, A., & Lewis, D. (1986). Trends in violence among psychiatrically hospitalized adolescents: 1969 and 1979 compared. *Journal of the American Academy of Child Psychiatry, 25*, 704–707.

Institute of Medicine. (1989). *Research on children and adolescents with mental, behavioral, and developmental disorders: Mobilizing a national initiative.* Washington, DC: National Academy Press.

Jaffa, T., & Dezsery, A. M. (1989). Reasons for admission to an adolescent unit. *Journal of Adolescence, 12*, 187–195.

Jaffe, E. D. (1986). Trends in residential and community care for dependent children and youth in Israel: A policy perspective. *Child and Youth, 7*, 123–141.

Jenson, J. M., Hawkins, J. D., & Catalano, R. F. (1986). Social support in aftercare services for troubled youth. *Children & Youth Services Review, 8*, 323–347.

Jenson, J. M., & Whittaker, J. K. (1987). Parental involvement in children's residential treatment: From preplacement to aftercare. *Children & Youth Services Review, 9*, 81–100.

Johns, C. (1982). The day treatment program. In L. Hoffman (Ed.), *The evaluation and care of severely disturbed children and their families* (pp. 97–100). New York: Spectrum.

Kauffman, J. M. (1993). *Characteristics of emotional and behavioral disorders of children and youth* (5th ed.). Columbus, OH: Merrill/Macmillan.

Kester, B. (1966). Indications for residential treatment of children. *Child Welfare, 45*, 338–340.

King, L. J., & Pittman, G. D. (1971). A follow-up of 65 adolescent schizophrenia patients. *Diseases of the Nervous System, 32*, 328–334.

Laneve, R. (1982). Pathways to success: Working with seriously emotionally disturbed students in a public school setting. In N. G. Haring & M. Noel (Eds.), *Progress or change: Issues in educating the emotionally disturbed* (pp. 29–59). Seattle: University of Washington.

Larsson, G., Bohlin, A., & Stenbacka, M. (1986). Prognosis of children admitted to institutional care during infancy. *Child Abuse & Neglect, 10*, 361–368.

Laslett, R. (1982). Leavers from three residential schools for maladjusted children. *Educational Review, 34*, 125–137.

Laufer, Z. (1986). Institutional placement: An interim stage or an end in itself? The role of parents in the continuum of care. *Child and Youth Services, 7*, 33–50.

LeCroy, C. W. (1984). Residential treatment services: A review of some current trends. *Child Care Quarterly, 13*, 83–97.

Levy, E. Z. (1969). Long-term follow-up of former inpatients at the Children's Hospital of the Menninger Clinic. *American Journal of Psychiatry, 125*, 47–53.

Lewis, M., Lewis, D. O., Shanock, S. S., Klatskin, E., & Osborne, J. R. (1980). The undoing of residential treatment: A follow-up study of 51 adolescents. *Journal of the American Academy of Child Psychiatry, 19*, 160–171.

Lund, R. (1989). Self-esteem and long-term placement in day schools for children with emotional and behavioral difficulties. *Maladjustment and Therapeutic Education, 7*, 55–57.

Macmillan, D., & Kavale, K. (1986). Educational intervention. In H. C. Quay & J. S. Werry (Eds.), *Psychopathological disorders of childhood* (pp. 583–621). New York: Wiley.

Maddox, M., & Edgar, E. (1988). Maneuvering through the maze: Transition planning for human service agency clients. In P. Dugan & H. Kaney (Eds.), *California transition: Resources and information for transition* (pp. 69–77). Sacramento: California Department of Education.

Maluccio, A., & Marlow, W. (1972). Residential treatment of emotionally disturbed children: A review of the literature. *Social Service Review, 46*, 230–250.

Marsden, G., McDermott, J., & Minor, D. (1977). Selection of children for residential treatment. *Journal of the American Academy of Child Psychiatry, 28*, 427–438.

Matek, O. (1964). Differential diagnosis for differential placement of children. *Child Welfare, 43*, 340–348.

Mattison, R., & Gamble, A. (1992). Severity of socially and emotionally disturbed boys' dysfunction at school and home: Comparison with psychiatric and general population boys. *Behavioral Disorders, 17*, 219–224.

Mattison, R. E., Humphrey, F. J., Kales, S. N., & Wallace, D. J. (1986). An objective evaluation of special class placement of elementary school boys with behavior problems. *Journal of Abnormal Child Psychology, 14*, 251–262.

Mattison, R., Humphrey, F., Kales, S., Handford, H. A., Finkenbinder, R., & Hernit, R. (1986). Psychiatric background and diagnosis of children evaluated for special class placement. *Journal of the American Academy of Child Psychiatry, 25*, 514–520.

Mattison, R., Morales, J., & Bauer, M. (1992). Distinguishing characteristics of elementary schoolboys recommended for SED placement. *Behavioral Disorders, 17*(2), 104–114.

McCauley, R. (1984). Alternative school programming for behavior disordered children. In J. Grosenick & S. Huntz (Eds.), *Positive alternatives to the disciplinary exclusion of behaviorally disordered students. National needs analysis in behavior disorders* (pp. 89–113). Washington, DC: Office of Special Education and Rehabilitative Services.

McClure, G., Ferguson, H. B., Boodoosingh, L., Turgay, A., & Stavrakaki, C. (1989). The frequency and severity of psychiatric disorders in special education and psychiatric programs. *Behavioral Disorders, 14*, 117–126.

McDavid, J. (1987). *Special education annual program evaluation* (Rep. No. 473). San Diego, CA: San Diego City Schools.

Melton, G. B. (1982). Children's rights: Where are the children? *American Journal of Orthopsychiatry, 52*, 530–538.

Mikkelson, F., Bereika, G., & McKenzie, J. (1993). Short-term, family-based residential treatment: An alternative to psychiatric hospitalization for children. *American Journal of Orthopsychiatry, 63*, 28–33.

Miles, M., & Huberman, A. M. (1984). *Qualitative data analysis: A sourcebook of new methods.* Newbury Park, CA: Sage.

Miskimins, R. W. (1990). A theoretical model for the practice of residential treatment. *Adolescence, 25*, 878–890.

Moore, L., & O'Conner, T. (1991). A psychiatric residential centre for children and adolescents: A pilot study of its patient's characteristics and improvement while resident. *Child: Care, Health, and Development, 17*, 235–242.

Morrissette, P. (1989). Re-entry of the inpatient client to the regular classroom: Transitional considerations for the school counselor. *Guidance and Counseling, 4*, 12–18.

Munson, R. F., Klein, R., & Delafield, D. (1989). Treatments of adolescents in a residential facility: A study of three approaches. *Adolescence, 24*, 817–820.

Myers, W., Burket, R., Lyles, W., Stone, L., & Kemph, J. (1990). DSM-III diagnosis and offenses in committed female juvenile delinquents. *Bulletin of the American Academy of Psychiatry and the Law, 18*, 47–54.

Myles, B. S., & Simpson, R. L. (1992). General educators' mainstreaming preferences that facilitate acceptance of students with behavioral disorders and learning disabilities. *Behavioral Disorders, 17*, 305–315.

Ney, P., Adam, R., Hanton, B., & Brindad, E. (1988). The effectiveness of a child psychiatric unit: A follow-up study. *Canadian Journal of Psychiatry, 33*, 793–799.

Noel, M. (1982). Public school programs for the emotionally disturbed: An overview. In N. G. Haring & M. Noel (Eds.), *Progress or change: Issues in educating the emotionally disturbed* (pp. 1–26). Seattle: University of Washington.

Noshpitz, J. (1962). Notes on the theory of residential treatment. *Journal of American Academy of Child Psychiatry, 1*, 284–296.

One Hundredth Congress. (1987). *Children's mental health: Promising responses to neglected problems* (Hearing before the select committee on children, youths, and families, House of Representatives). Washington, DC: U.S. Government Printing Office.

Parmalee, D., Cohen, R., Best, A., Brunk, M., Cassell, S., Dyson, F., Nemil, M., Purcell, P., & Reid, S. (1991). A study of children and youth admitted to two psychiatric hospitals: Issues of access to a continuum of care. In A. Algarin & R. Friedman (Eds.), *A system of care for children's mental health: Building a research base* (pp. 75–88). Tampa: Florida Mental Health Institute.

Paul, J. (1977). Mainstreaming emotionally disturbed children. In A. Pappanikou & J. Paul (Eds.), *Mainstreaming emotionally disturbed children* (pp. 1–17). Syracuse, NY: Syracuse University Press.

Pfeiffer, S., & Naglieri, J. (1984). Special education placement decisions as a function of professional role and handicapping condition. *Psychology in the Schools, 21*, 61–65.

Pfeiffer, S. I., & Strzelecki, S. C. (1990). Inpatient psychiatric treatment of children and adolescents: A review of outcome studies. *Journal of American Academy of Child and Adolescent Psychiatry, 29*, 847–853.

Prentice-Dunn, S., Wilson, D., & Spivey, C. (1985). Assessing the cost of behaviorally oriented residential treatment: Predictive program factors. *Child Welfare, 64*, 137–142.

Priestly, P. (1987). The future of residential schools for the maladjusted. *Maladjustment and Therapeutic Education, 5*, 30–38.

Quay, H. C. (1986). Residential treatment. In H. C. Quay & J. S. Werry (Eds.), *Psychopathological disorders of childhood* (pp. 558–582). New York: Wiley.

Quinton, D., & Rutter, M. (1976). Early hospital admissions and later disturbances of behavior: An attempted replication of Douglas' findings. *Developmental Medicine and Child Neurology, 18*, 447–459.

Ravenel, L., Fraser, J., McAbee, T., Leath, M., Bowers, L., Ross, P., & Mengedoht, H. (1982). *Filling in the cracks: A study of the problems and needs of severely emotionally handicapped children and adolescents and of mentally/emotionally handicapped adults in South Carolina.* Columbia: South Carolina Developmental Disabilities Council.

Ricciuti, A., Morton, R., Behar, D., & Delaney, M. (1986). Medical findings in child psychiatric inpatients. *Journal of the American Academy of Child and Adolescent Psychiatry, 26*, 554–555.

Rosenblatt, A., & Attkisson, C. (1992). Integrating systems of care in California for youth with severe emotional disturbance I: A descriptive overview of the California AB377 evaluation project. *Journal of Child and Family Studies, 1*, 93–113.

Rosenblatt, A., & Attkisson, C. (1993). Integrating systems of care in California for youth with severe emotional disturbance III: Answers that lead to questions about out-of-home placements and the AB377 evaluation project. *Journal of Child and Family Studies, 2*, 119–141.

Rosenblatt, A., Attkisson, C., & Fernandez, A. (1992). Integrating systems of care in CA for youth with severe emotional disturbance II: Initial group home expenditure and utilization findings from the CA AB377 evalaluation project. *Journal of Child and Family Studies, 1*, 263–286.

Roth, H., & Nicholson, C. L. (1988). Profile differences between successfully and unsuccessfully mainstreamed violent and assaultive youth. *Diagnostique, 13*, 130–138.

Sack, W. H., Mason, R., & Collins, R. (1987). A long-term follow-up study of a children's psychiatric day treatment center. *Child Psychiatry and Human Development, 18*(1), 58–68.

Saxe, L., Cross, T., & Silverman, N. (1986). *Children's mental health: Problems and services; a background paper.* Washington, DC: Office of Technology Assessment.

Schneider, E. (1985). Expanding public school placement options for emotionally disturbed students—one district's efforts. *Journal of Clinical Child Psychology, 14*, 239–245.

Seip, J., & McCoy, D. (1982). Alternative living arrangements for the severely behavior disordered. In N. G. Haring & M. Noel (Eds.), *Progress or change: Issues in educating the emotionally disturbed* (pp. 111–136). Seattle: University of Washington.

Shanok, S., Malani, S., Ninan, O., Guggenheim, P., Weinstein, H., & Lewis, D. (1983). A comparison of delinquent and nondelinquent adolescent psychiatric inpatients. *American Journal of Psychiatry, 140*, 582–585.

Silver, S., Duchnowski, A., Kutash, K., Friedman, R., Eisen, M., Prange, M., Brandenburg, N., & Greenbaum, P. (1992). A comparison of children with serious emotional disturbance served in residential and school settings. *Journal of Child and Family Studies, 1*, 43–59.

Simon, J. I. (1986). Day hospital treatment for borderline adolescents. *Adolescence, 21*, 561–572.

Sindelar, P. T., King, M. C., Cartland, D., Wilson, R. J., & Meisel, C. J. (1985). Deviant behavior in learning disabled and behaviorally disordered students as a function of level and placement. *Behavioral Disorders, 10*, 105–112.

Small, R., Kennedy, K., & Bender, B. (1991). Critical issues for practice in residential treatment: The view from within. *American Journal of Orthopsychiatry, 61*, 327–337.

Smith, C., Wood, F., & Grimes, J. (1988). Issues in the identification and placement of behaviorally disordered students. In M. C. Wang, M. C. Reynolds, & H. J. Walberg (Eds.), *Handbook of special education: Research and practice* (Vol. 2, pp. 95–123). New York: Pergamon.

Smith, M., & Glass, G. (1987). *Research and evaluation in education and the social sciences.* Englewood Cliffs, NJ: Prentice-Hall.

Smith, O. (1987). Four courts decide EAHCA cases. *Mental and Physical Disability Law Reporter, 11*, 40–42.

Smollar, J., & Condelli, L. (1990). Residential placement of youth: Pathways, alternatives and unresolved issues. *Children Today, 19*, 4–8.

Steinberg, A., & Knitzer, J. (1992). Classrooms for emotionally and behaviorally disturbed students: Facing the challenge. *Behavioral Disorders, 17*, 145–156.

Stilwell, B. (1991). Lessons from the difficult child: The impact of the severely emotionally disturbed child on the residential school. *RE:view, 23*, 17–28.

Stone, L. (1979). Residential treatment. In J. D. Noshpitz (Ed.), *Basic handbook of child psychiatry* (Vol. 3, pp. 231–262). New York: Basic Books.

Stotsky, B. A., Browne, T. H., & Lister, B. (1987). Differences among emotionally disturbed children in three treatment and school settings: Discriminate function and multiple regression analysis. *Child Psychiatry and Human Development, 17*, 235–241.

Streitmatter, J., & Santa Cruz, R. (1982). Mainstreaming the institutional exceptional child. *Pointer, 27*, 14–16.

Stroul, B. (1988). *Series on community-based services for children and adolescents who are severely emotionally disturbed: Vol. 1. Home-based services.* Washington, DC: Georgetown University Child Development Center.

Swan, W., Brown, C., & Jacob, R. (1987). Types of service delivery models used in the reintegration of severely emotionally disturbed/behaviorally disordered students. *Behavioral Disorders, 12*, 99–103.

Tarico, V., Low, B., Trupin, E., Forsyth-Stephens, A. (1989). Children's mental health services: A parent perspective. *Community Mental Health Journal, 25*, 313–325.

Toman, M. (1986). Information paper 17: Residential special education in Scotland for children with emotional, social, and behavioral difficulties. *Scottish Educational Review, 18*, 54–59.

Trickett, E., Leone, P., Fink, C., & Braaten, S. (1993). The perceived environment of special education classrooms for adolescents: A revision of the classroom environment scale. *Exceptional Children, 59*, 411–420.

Tuma, J. (1989). Mental health services for children. *American Psychologist, 44*, 188–199.

Van Den Brink, S. (1984). Expanding the options for disturbed youth and their families. *Children Today, 13*, 32–35.

Voineskos, G. (1976). Part-time hospitalization programs: The neglected field of community psychiatry. *Canadian Medical Association Journal, 114*, 320–324.

Walker, H., & Bullis, M. (1991). Behavior disorders and the social context of regular class integration: A conceptual dilemma? In J. W. Lloyd, N. N. Singh, & A. C. Repp (Eds.), *The regular education initiative: Alternative perspectives on concepts, issues, and models* (pp. 75–93). Sycamore, IL: Sycamore.

Webb, D. (1988). Specialized foster care as an alternative therapeutic out of home placement model. *Journal of Clinical Child Psychology, 17*, 34–43.

Webb, S., & Maddox, M. E. (1986). The juvenile corrections interagency transition model: Moving students from institutions into community schools. *Remedial and Special Education, 7*, 56–61.

Weintrob, A. (1975). Long-term treatment of the severely disturbed adolescent: Residential treatment versus hospitalization. *Journal of the American Academy of Child Psychiatry, 14*, 436–450.

Weithorn, L. (1988). Mental hospitalization of troublesome youth: An analysis of skyrocketing admissions rates. *Stanford Law Review, 40*, 773–838.

Wells, K. (1991a). Eagerly awaiting a home: Severely emotionally disturbed youth lost in our systems of care—a personal reflection. *Child & Youth Care Forum, 20*, 7–17.

Wells, K. (1991b). Placement of emotionally disturbed children in residential treatment: A review of placement criteria. *American Journal of Orthopsychiatry, 61*, 339–347.

Wells, K., & Whittington, D. (1990). Prior services used by youths referred to mental health facilities: A closer look. *Children and Youth Services Review, 12*, 243–256.

Wells, K., Wyatt, E., & Hobfoll, S. (1991). Factors associated with adaptation of youths discharged from residential treatment. *Children and Youth Services Review, 134*, 199–216.

Westendorp, F., Brink, K. L., Roberson, M. K., & Ortiz, I. E. (1986). Variables which differentiate placement of adolescents into juvenile justice or mental health systems. *Adolescence, 21*, 23–37.

Wilson, D., & Lyman, R. (1983). Residential treatment of emotionally disturbed children. In C. Walker & M. Roberts (Eds.), *Handbook of clinical child psychology* (pp. 1069–1088). New York: Wiley.

Wood, F. (1985). Issues in the identification and placement of behaviorally disordered students. *Behavioral Disorders, 10*, 219–228.

Wood, F. H., Johnson, J. L., & Jenkins, J. R. (1986). The Lora case: Nonbiased referral, assessment, and placement procedures. *Exceptional Children, 52*, 323–331.

Wright, D., Pillard, E., & Cleven, C. (1990). The influence of state definitions of behavior disorders on the number of children served under PL 94-142. *Remedial and Special Education, 11*(5), 17–22.

Zimet, S., & Farley, G. (1985). Day treatment for children in the United States. *Journal of the American Academy of Child Psychiatry, 24*, 732–738.

Zimmerman, D. (1990). Notes on the history of adolescent inpatient and residential treatment. *Adolescence, 25*, 9–38.

CHAPTER

5

Educational Placements of Students with Emotional and Behavioral Disorders: What Do They Indicate?

R. Kenton Denny*
Kansas University Affiliated Program

Phillip L. Gunter
Valdosta State University

Richard E. Shores
C. Robert Campbell
Kansas University Affiliated Program

The instructional and systemic challenges presented by children and youth with emotional and behavioral disturbances (EBD) continue to foster debate about the most appropriate structure and content for service delivery. Indicated by the continued discussion of issues related to inclusion (CCBD, 1992; NASBE, 1991), attempts to define "exemplary practices and programs" (Peacock Hill Working Group, 1991), and data on the outcomes of special education (Neel, Meadows, Levine, & Edgar, 1988; Wagner, 1993; Wagner, D'Amico, Marder, Newman, & Blackorby, 1992), there is consensus regarding the need to examine the practice and process of special education for students with EBD.

Placement issues lie at the center of a long-standing and ongoing debate regarding the nature of placements and the extent to which varying locations produce the outcomes desired for children with disabilities (Hallahan, Keller, McKinney, Lloyd, & Bryan, 1988; Tucker, 1989; Vergason & Anderegg, 1989; Wang, Reynolds, & Walberg, 1989). The importance of placement as an issue is that placement for the receipt of specialized curriculum, instruction, and related services, in part defines special education (P.L. 101-476). In this chapter we present a discussion of the significance given the physical location of educational service delivery for students with EBD.

---

*R. Kenton Denny is now at Louisiana State University and C. Robert Campbell is now at Valdosta State University.

WHAT ARE INDICATORS?

The term *indicator* has been defined as a "statistic of direct normative interest which facilitates concise, comprehensive, and balanced judgments about the conditions of major aspects of society" (U.S.D.H.E.W., 1969, p. 69). Shavelson (1989) defined an *indicator* as "an individual or composite statistic that relates to a basic construct in education and is useful in a policy context" (p. 5). The purpose of an indicator is to provide information regarding the current functioning of a system for the purpose of predicting the future functioning of that system. Rockwell (1989) provided several characteristics or criteria for a measure to serve as an indicator. These included timeliness of reporting, the potential to facilitate decision making, a future orientation, collectability across time, validity, reliability, and accuracy. An indicator should have the potential to be reported within a time frame that makes the data current enough to be relevant; provide information that is useful not only to policymakers but also others involved in the system, such as administrators, parents, and teachers; be broad enough to anticipate and encompass changing situations so as not to become useless over time; be capable of being collected often, so that a context is provided from one measurement to the next; and possess adequate measurement properties of validity, reliability, and accuracy (Rockwell, 1989).

McCollum and Turnbull (1989) contended that indicators may be measures of inputs, processes, or outcomes with the utility of each limited by collection procedures and reliability across reporters. Individual indicators exclusive of other data and/or context are insufficient for prediction (McCollum & Turnbull, 1989; Shavelson, 1989). With the current emphasis on the development of general education accountability systems (e.g., America 2000), indicators of system and individual performance are of great concern to policymakers and educators. In the education of students with disabilities, issues of accountability are not new. Child counts and placement data have been used for years to indicate the provision of special education and related services. Indicators of appropriate education and least restrictive environment (LRE), including placement, continue to be major areas in need of further development.

Placement as an Accountability Measure

In 1975, as part of the Education of the Handicapped Act, Congress mandated that the Department of Education provide an annual report on the implementation of the act (Part B, Section 618, P.L. 94-142). This "annual report" has various reporting requirements, among them the number of children receiving special education and related services and their placements (i.e., where they would receive their education). Potential placements ranged from general education classrooms to residential facilities based on the cascade of service delivery options described by Deno (1973). The number of children and their placements were intended to be "indicators" of the extent to which children and youth with disabilities were being identified and served under the new law.

The Office of Special Education and Rehabilitation Services has compiled this information for 15 years. The Fourteenth Annual Report to Congress (U.S. Department of Education, 1992) reported that 4,437,630 students were served during the 1989–90 school year under P.L. 101-476 (Part B) and P.L. 89-313 (State Operated Programs). Students identified as serious emotionally disturbed (SED) are most frequently placed within a separate class setting (37.1%), followed by resource room settings (28.5%) and regular class placements (14.9%). The most recent data indicate that this pattern of placement changes very little from year to year. For example, since the 1985–86 school year, the placement of students with SED into separate classes has increased 1%, from 36.1% to 37.1% (U.S. Department of Education, 1992). During the same time period, the placement of students with SED into regular class and resource room settings decreased .6%, from 44.1% to 43.5%. Since 1977, when national placement data were first available, the percentage of students with SED served in regular schools (regular classes, resource rooms, and separate classes) has decreased 4.2%.

Placement data do not appear to have all the qualities of an indicator described by Rockwell (1989), McCollum and Turnbull (1989), or Shavelson (1989). Whether placement data serve as an indicator depends largely on the purpose for which we wish the indicator to serve (McCollum & Turnbull, 1989). Placement data on a national level do not appear to meet the requirements of timeliness as indicated by the 2-year delay in reporting (data in the most recent report is approximately 2 academic years behind publication date). Placement data do appear to be a collectible measure across time, as evidenced in successive annual reports. Placement data, as currently collected, have limited utility for future orientation when taken in isolation of other measures (e.g., Haring et al., 1992). Placement data have been utilized as an indicator of process when attempts have been made to link placement with outcomes (cf. the review on individual outcomes in this chapter) and as an outcome indicator for compliance with LRE requirements (cf. Danielson & Bellamy, 1989; Haring et al., 1992). However, little attention has been given to placement as an outcome measure of the responsiveness of a system (i.e., state education agency, local education agency, school building) to the often changing needs of children with disabilities.

Certainly, our current notions and utilization of placement data would not fulfill all of the characteristics just mentioned. We treat placement as a cumulative static statistic (e.g., number of children in a given setting) rather than change scores that would indicate trends, directionality, and movement. To state that a certain percentage of children with EBD are served in self-contained classes yields less information than the number of students moving from self-contained classes to resource arrangements, the number moving to segregated special schools, or the number that are stable and successful or unsuccessful. This chapter highlights the need for a more dynamic indicator system (Rockwell, 1989; Shavelson, 1989) that includes placement.

Placement as an Indicator of Least Restrictive Environment

Little data exist to shed light on the relationship of placement, instructional and related services provided, and the outcomes obtained by students with EBD. Placement is generally considered as a point in time sample; that is, the number of students receiving special education services is reported on December 1 of each year by each state. We know that on that date a certain number of students in a given category of disability are receiving services in a given environment (e.g., resource room, self-contained class, etc.). Although this type of census data may be useful to funding agencies, it falls short of serving as an indicator. As previously stated, an indicator should provide a sensitive measure of change in the social phenomenon being studied. *Sensitivity* refers to the indicator's ability to reflect change for the purpose of forecasting as well as evaluation.

Danielson and Bellamy (1989) examined placement figures for each state submitted to the Office of Special Education Programs. They found significant differences between an individual state's reliance on particular types of placement options and stability across time in a state's use of segregated educational settings. States varied by as much as a factor of 25 in their use of particular placement options (segregated vs. integrated). Much of the change in placement rates across time was attributed to the growth in the population receiving special education and related services as opposed to movement of students along the continuum of placement options. Although criticized for methodological problems (Blackman, 1989; U.S. Department of Education, 1990) and interpretation of the data in regard to LRE requirements (Blackman, 1989; Tucker, 1989), the study provided an incentive to investigate placements and placement statistics.

McLaughlin and Owings (1992) examined the relationship between state-level variables, demographic variables, identification rates, and cumulative placement rates for students with learning, emotional, and multiple disabilities. Utilizing data samples from 1976, 1980, and 1983, which included data gathered as part of the OSERS Annual Report, McLaughlin and Owings examined the correlation between state factors and cumulative placement rates. Their findings indicate that certain factors, such as financial status and population density, correlated with measures of placement. States with higher per-capita income tended to have higher placement rates overall as well as to utilize more restrictive settings through which to deliver services. However, the extent to which these rates reflect a state's responsiveness to the needs of children as opposed to a policy orientation remains obscured.

Haring et al. (1992) conducted a survey of three states regarding the placements of students with severe disabilities. Their conclusions indicated that placement figures as a measure of LRE were potentially flawed. In one state, the reinterpretation of integrated setting (excluding separate wings or annexes within regular schools) resulted in a change of 31% from the data reported in the Danielson and Bellamy (1989) figures. They further suggested that as the emphasis has changed from accountability (e.g., child count to ensure children are identified and receive services) to service enhancement, the nature of the statistical indicators must also change to reflect measures of services or support provided rather than physical placement.

Placement as an Indicator Related to Individual Outcomes

Recently, Stanford Research Institute (Wagner, 1993; Wagner et al., 1992) reported on the National Longitudinal Transition Study (NLTS) of Special Education Students, a 5-year follow-along study of students with disabilities receiving special education services. The data associated with children and youth experiencing serious emotional disturbance present a disturbing picture of outcomes. Wagner (1993) indicated that (a) two thirds of youth identified as SED cannot pass competency exams for their grade level, (b) these students have the lowest grade point average of all identified disability groups, (c) 43.9% failed one or more courses in their most recent school year, (d) 54.7% do not successfully complete high school, (e) almost 60% are not employed within 2 years of exiting school, with over 50% unemployed 3–5 years after exiting school, and (f) 57.6% had been arrested within 5 years of exiting school.

Neel et al. (1988) reported a follow-up study of 160 students who were labeled as behavior disordered in the state of Washington. Their findings were similar to the NLTS study in that students labeled as behavior disordered were more likely to be unemployed and underemployed, as indicated by salaries compared to working nondisabled students. The majority of students did not access social service systems and were less likely to be engaged in postschool education or training programs than students not identified as disabled. The results of these studies and others (Hasazi, Gordon, & Roe, 1985; Mithaug, Horiuchi, & Fanning, 1985) indicate a similar picture of outcomes for students with EBD.

Although we can agree that these outcomes are unacceptable, research related to service delivery (Grosenick, 1989; Grosenick & Huntze, 1980; Knitzer, Steinberg, & Fleisch, 1990) in general, and placement specifically, is limited. Additionally, research on placement and outcomes for students with EBD has been limited and plagued by a number of methodological problems (Quay, 1979). These problems include lack of or insufficient descriptions of subject characteristics, instructional or behavior change procedures, limited behavioral targets, and insufficient procedures to demonstrate experimental control. Recent information (Duchnowski, Johnson, Hall, Kutash, & Friedman, 1993) indicates that little has changed since Quay's (1979) observations. Nevertheless, extant findings show considerable commonality, whether the movement was being made from the most restrictive (residential treatment programs) or less restrictive (short-term special class placement, resource rooms) special programs.

Quay (1979) reviewed the results of residential treatment programs for emotionally disturbed and delinquent children and youth. The programs reviewed included the Herman Adler Zone Facility at the University of Illinois, Achievement Place at the University of Kansas, and Project Re-ED at Peabody College. Programs were reviewed in terms of both in-program change and the postprogram adjustment of residents in community and school. Quay concluded that the programs reviewed had provided considerable evidence for in-program behavior change. However, the results with respect to lasting postprogram effects were disappointing.

Recidivism of institutionalized students may be viewed as an indication of the treatment effects on the success of placement changes. The majority of studies investigating recidivism have been conducted with adolescents identified as juvenile delinquents. In an early study, Glueck and Glueck (1950) followed 1,000 adolescents identified as juvenile delinquents for three 5-year periods. After the initial 5-year period, 80% of the subjects had been rearrested. Similar high rates of recidivism were reported in other studies with delinquent boys (e.g., Schepses, 1955). In addition to these findings, researchers have reported high rates of exiting school before graduation among juvenile delinquents who returned to public school settings after incarceration in correction institutions. Greenstone (1961) reported that 45% of returnees had dropped out after the first year of school. Satten, Novotny, Ginsparg, and Averill (1970) reported that although two thirds of a group of delinquent boys returned to school after release from a juvenile correctional facility, the majority of the subjects quickly dropped out of school.

Although researchers have focused on follow-up studies of juvenile delinquents, much less follow-up data has been reported on adolescent students labeled as behaviorally disordered or emotionally disturbed. This is somewhat surprising, given the fact that these individuals often exhibit antisocial behaviors similar to those displayed by juvenile delinquents. Those follow-up studies that have investigated these individuals were most often studies of students treated in residential or other facilities outside the public school setting. For example, Bloom and Hopewell (1982) followed a group of 88 adolescents who were released from a state mental hospital. These subjects were diagnosed as having a variety of psychopathological disorders. Results show that 43% of the adolescents were reinstitutionalized within 6 months of discharge. Variables that were significant in discriminating recidivists from nonrecidivists included educational and vocational placement, length of hospitalization, family structure, hospitalization of a family member, and living arrangement at the time of discharge. The majority of adolescents who were successful were placed in public educational programs. Successful adolescents also had been hospitalized for shorter periods of time and were less likely to have been in the custody of human resource agencies. Shorter periods of hospitalization may reflect significant subject differences within the population (i.e., degree of psychopathology), and custody status may well reflect an important ecological variable identified later by Lewis (1988).

Leone, Fitzmartin, Stetson, and Foster (1986) collected data on students who were previously enrolled in a program that consisted of residential and day-care treatment. Program administrators identified two groups of students as being successful or unsuccessful "leavers" of the program. Leone et al. defined successful students as those who consistently exhibited positive prosocial behaviors while in treatment. These students were subsequently reintegrated into regular public school programs or graduated from high school. The unsuccessful program "leavers" were those students who ran away, were placed in more restrictive hospital settings, were removed from the facility by their parents, or were removed from the facility under court order for delinquent acts in the community. Multiple regression analysis revealed that the best predictors of treatment outcome were treatment in the day program (vs. the residential program) and absenteeism. If students attended school during treatment and were enrolled in the day-care program rather than the residential program, they were more likely to be successful after discharge. Academic performance counted for very little of the variance. Absenteeism appeared to be a very strong factor in predicting successful treatment (cf. Zigmond & Kerr, 1985).

Schneider and Byrne (1984) conducted one of the few studies to investigate students who were transitioned from special education to regular education. Their sample included 129 children who were transferred from self-contained special education classes to regular classes. Nine months after the transfer, Schneider and Byrne administered a four-item Likert-type scale, which assessed social and emotional adjustment to the students' classroom teachers and collected data on the IQ and achievement of the students. They found that students who were enrolled for longer periods or exited the program early were less well adjusted. In addition, junior and senior high students who were reintegrated had far greater difficulty in being successful than did the students who were younger.

Swan, Brown, and Jacob (1987) reported on the reintegration of 385 students identified as seriously emotionally disturbed or behavior disordered from the Georgia Psycho-Educational Centers network to various public school placements. Of the high school age group contained in their sample, 24 (43%) were placed directly back into the regular education setting, 14 (25%) were placed into resource settings, and 18 (32%) were placed into self-contained, special education settings. An additional 30 students were placed in homebound, postsecondary, or employment settings, but data was not provided on the success or failure of these placements. Although notable for tracking placements within the continuum, the study does not give the much-needed information on the longer term student success or failure rate, nor the critical environmental descriptions related to successful adjustment.

Of the studies reviewed, only Leone et al. (1986) evaluated changes that might have occurred within the environments to which the children returned. Lewis (1982) concluded, after a review of several follow-up studies, that the amount of improvement made by a child in residential treatment did not determine the degree of successful adjustment he or she experienced when returning to home and community. He stated that ecological factors were deemed as important in maintaining or suppressing gains made during residential treatment. Lewis (1988) reported a pilot study in which he related changes in the children's ecology to being successful or unsuccessful. Results indicated that the students who were successfully reintegrated into the community had greater support from families, more appropriate interactions with the staff during treatment, and stronger plans for management by families and staff after discharge than did the unsuccessful students.

The literature suggests that students who are successful in transferring into regular education from more restrictive settings, as opposed to those who are unsuccessful, have fewer absences, are less aggressive, have stronger support from their families, and, in general, meet the expectations of their communities. Those students who are unsuccessful (recidivist) drop out of school or often revert to patterns of behavior that may have shown improvement while they were in the special placement. The majority of the studies address individual variables with little attention given to the setting characteristics of environments to which the students were returned.

Placement as a Measure of System Responsiveness

By strictly interpreting the definition of *special education* as the delivery of services rather than placement, we might be tempted to assume that states and districts that use the full continuum of placements are being responsive to the unique needs of students. Indeed, little data exist to refute this argument. Studies such as that of McLaughlin and Owings (1992), indicating differential rates of placements into restrictive settings based on financial data, however, lead us to question the certainty of this assumption.

In a recent study, Shores, Jack, et al. (1993) observed students with EBD and their teachers in integrated and segregated classroom placements. Based on their observations, it appears only minimal differences in instructional behavior (e.g., teacher mands, praise, etc.) and student behavior (e.g., disruption, aggression, compliance, noncompliance) existed. Gunter et al. (1993) and Jack et al. (1994) replicated these results in subsequent investigations of teachers' use of behavior management strategies.

Denny, Epstein, and Rose (1992) examined the instructional interactions of students identified as behavior disordered in secondary vocational education classes. They found few significant differences in instructional behavior of teachers toward students identified as EBD and students not identified for special education. More disturbing were the low levels of teacher engagement and teacher praise in the vocational classes.

These studies raise the issue of whether particular placements are indicative of specially designed instruction for students with EBD. These studies and others examining placement and the use of placement data (Gerber, 1984; Gerber & Levine-Donelson, 1989; Haring et al., 1992; Kauffman, Cullinan, & Epstein,

1987; McLaughlin & Owings, 1992) point to the need to develop more sensitive and composite indicators. Haring et al. (1992) and Neel et al. (1988) called for the development of measurements that reflect services provided and student characteristics as more sensitive measures of system responsiveness. Questions remain concerning what setting characteristics (including placement) and ecological factors (Hobbs, 1965; Kerr & Zigmond, 1986; Prieto & Rutherford, 1977; Rhodes & Tracy, 1972) in combination with student variables predict the success or failure of students with EBD.

A DESCRIPTIVE STUDY OF SECONDARY STUDENTS WITH EBD

Because of the growing concern and debate regarding placement issues and the disturbing outcomes for students with EBD, we, at the Kansas University Affiliated Program at Parsons, have begun a program of research to better understand issues related to placement and placement patterns. We are studying the variables that may affect the outcome of transition or placement. In a demographic study, we have collected descriptive data regarding general placements (e.g., general education program, self-contained special classroom in a special school, self-contained special classroom in a general education setting, and resource room and general classroom setting combined) of students with EBD. This study had two general purposes: The first was to use school records to document and describe the current status and placement of students with EBD in urban and rural districts in Kansas; the second was to obtain preliminary information on variables that are potentially relevant to the transition process through record review and teacher, family, and student interviews. Beyond the descriptive implications of the placement data, we used lag sequential analysis (Bakeman & Gottman, 1986) to determine the probability of student movement from one placement category to another. Lag sequential analysis procedures produce a conditional probability (CP) of events in sequence (Bakeman & Gottman, 1986).

Current Status of Students

One urban district, two suburban districts, and two rural special education cooperatives agreed to participate in the study. We asked participating school districts to identify all students between the ages of 14 and 21 years labeled as serious emotionally or behavior disordered and having current individualized education plans (IEPs) for the 1991–92 school year. Students were to have reached at least their 14th birthday during the 1991–92 school year. The placement analysis was based on the review of 226 records meeting the selection criteria.

We designed a survey containing questions regarding the demographic and placement history of each student. In addition, we included information regarding each student's current educational placement, attendance, and critical incidents.

Placement was scored according to the federal categories, with a notable exception: Resource programs were separated into two categories indicating whether the student received services for greater or less than a half day. This was done to attempt a more sensitive measure of placement changes than allowed for under one category. For the purposes of this chapter, we present only descriptive data regarding individual student characteristics (i.e., home status and placement histories).

Three undergraduate observers and a doctorate-level observer collected information and reliability data. Prior to beginning the archival searches, we trained each data collector to use the survey instrument to review student education records. Given that each district had forms and filing procedures that varied widely, we placed emphasis on various places within each record (e.g., staffing reports, IEP, evaluation reports, etc.) that might contain the desired information. If the information could not be found, data collectors requested assistance from school personnel in locating the information. If information could not be located, the observers entered a code for "could not determine." Whenever possible, the record's stated placement was used. In cases in which the placement information was not specific (i.e., placement was not specified by category but a description was provided, such as "special education for 2 hours per day"), project staff made a determination (i.e., "special education for 2 hours per day" was entered as "resource less than one half day").

On 20% of the surveys, a second data collector reviewed the identical record and compared entries with the primary reviewer. Disagreements were scored when the two records differed substantively (e.g., different placements, sequence of placements, test scores differed, or placement dates varied by more than 1 month). Disagreements were reviewed by both data collectors, and the record was reviewed to determine the correct entry. In cases for which the data collectors could not reach consensus, the primary investigator reviewed the record and determined the most appropriate entry. Mean initial agreement on placements was .87 (range of 0–1). It should be noted that the most frequent problems involved the classification of nonschool placements, such as hospitalizations, treatment programs, and special schools, and the determination of the extent of resource placements (i.e., "resource less than or greater than one half day"). Hospitalization data were included as part of the placement history when the placement and dates of placements were included in the students' records. Descriptions of critical incidents contained the date and reported reasons for transitions involving hospitalizations. "Resource greater than one half day" was determined to mean that the student participated in four or more periods of special education; "resource less than one half day" indicated daily attendance in special education for three or fewer periods; "regular education with support" was scored when students did not receive daily special education services or met on an as-needed basis with counselors and special education personnel. Data collectors scored the placement of "regular education" when the student returned to regular classes but had a current IEP.

Table 5.1 presents the distribution of students by age during the 1991–92 school year. Students aged 14 to 17 accounted for approximately 85% of the sample. The average age of the students was 15.5 years, with a range of 13.25 to 19.25 years. Males ($n = 190$) constituted approximately 84% of the population.

Of the 226 students, 152 (67.3%) had been receiving special education services for 5 years or longer, either as behavior disordered (63%) or as learning disabled (4.31%). Seventy-four students (32.7%) were initially identified for special education services between September 1, 1987 and January 1, 1992.

Almost all students were identified as within normal ranges of intelligence, either by intelligence tests or by staffing reports. The most frequently employed measure of intelligence was the WISC-R. Full-range scores were provided in 193 records (85.3%) and ranged from 62 to 130, with a mean score of 96.3.

Additional measures were taken on the students' current "home" status by identifying the primary caretaker. We were able to determine home status on 202 students (89.3%). Eighty-three (36.7%) students resided at home with natural parents, 79 (34.9%) students lived in a single-parent home, 17 (7.5%) students resided in homes with a remarried parent and stepparent, 14 (6.1%) students resided in foster care or other type of guardian arrangement, and 9 (4.4 %) students lived with other family members (e.g., grandparents, aunts).

Table 5.2 illustrates the last placement identification for each student during the 1991–92 school year. The placement status for each student was identified by examining the placement indicated on the IEP and attempting to identify any placement change through record entry such as quarterly progress reports, semester grade reports, or other format. For example, the IEP could indicate that the student was placed in resource for less than one half day during the current school year with the most recent semester or quarter report indicating that the student withdrew, had been hospitalized, and so forth. The most recent information was included as the current placement.

As Table 5.2 indicates, the most prevalent placements for the population was resource for less than one half day. Approximately 56% of the population was served for up to three periods per day in special education. The second most

TABLE 5.1
Number of Students by Age (10/1/91)

Age	*Number of Students*
13	18
14	38
15	55
16	56
17	42
18	13
19	4

TABLE 5.2
Current Placement Status of Students During the 1991–92 School Year (n = 226)

Placement Category	*Number*	*Percentage*
Homebound	1	0.44
Hospital or treatment center	1	0.44
Separate school	24	10.62
Separate class	29	12.83
Resource > 1/2 day	22	9.73
Resource < 1/2 day	127	56.19
Regular education with support	1	0.44
Regular education	3	1.33
Exit	18	7.96

prevalent placements were self-contained classes and separate schools, accounting for slightly over 20% of the student placements. Almost 8% of the sample exited during the 1991–92 school year.

A Sequential Analysis of Placements

Following the analysis of current year placements, we constructed a placement history for each student for the previous 5 years. We identified and arranged placements in chronological order from IEPs, staffing reports, critical incident reports, and social histories. All references to placements were included in a review of a student's history. Only placement histories having sufficient information for chronological order of placements were included for analysis.

We constructed an overall movement pattern by categorizing each placement as upward (i.e., to a less restrictive setting), downward (i.e., to a more restrictive setting) or no change (i.e., to a different but equivalent program level, or no movement). The number of placement changes for the 5-year period ranged from 0 to 7, with a mean of 1.7 placement changes. Approximately 22% of the students remained in the same category of placement for the 5-year period. Of the students, 9% were initially placed during the time period reviewed and did not change category of placement during the remaining time period. Of the placement changes (aggregated across subjects) made during 1987–92, 41.7% represented an upward movement (i.e., to less restrictive settings), and 56% moved to more restrictive settings. Exits accounted for 2.3% of total placement changes.

We then conducted a sequential analysis of placements, presented as conditional probabilities of a particular placement preceding or following a placement category. Each student's record was coded in sequence and the data analyzed using an adaptation of the MOOSES observation program developed by Tapp, Wehby, and Ellis (1993). The program computes CPs on interaction data and describes the data in terms of the probability of a given event in sequence (Bakeman & Gottman, 1986). The CPs represent the proportion of a placement meeting the condition (e.g., preceding or following a particular placement) of the total instances of that placement. For the purposes of this analysis, the data were treated as an individual file, with each placement recorded as an event. This allowed for the analysis of placement changes of the entire sample. Tables 5.3, 5.4, and 5.5 illustrate the three preceding placements and three subsequent placements for each category of placement.

Homebound placements are presented in Table 5.3. The most frequent placements that immediately preceded homebound placement (shown as Placement 1 to the left of placement options) were separate school placement (CP = .26), hospital or treatment center placement (CP = .21), and self-contained class placement (CP = .21). The most frequent placements that followed homebound placement (shown as Placement 1 to the right of placement options) were hospital or treatment center placement (CP = .52), separate school placement (CP = .15), and resource less than one half day (CP = .15).

Table 5.4 presents the prior and subsequent placements to placement within a hospital or treatment center. The most frequent placements prior to placement within a hospital or treatment center were resource less than one half day (CP = .194), separate school (CP = .138), and homebound (CP = .138). The most frequent placements made after placement into a hospital or treatment center were separate schools (CP = .236), resource less than one half day (CP = .194), and placement into regular education (CP = .111) and resource greater than one half day (CP = .111).

Table 5.5 presents prior and subsequent placements to placement in a separate school. Placement in a hospital or treatment center preceded placement into

TABLE 5.3
Conditional Probabilities of Preceding and Subsequent Placements to Homebound Placement (n = 19)

Preceding Placements				Subsequent Placements		
Placement 3	Placement 2	Placement 1		Placement 1	Placement 2	Placement 3
	.052		**Homebound**		.052	
.105	.21	.21	**Hospital/treatment center**	.526	.052	.105
	.052	.263	**Separate school**	.157	.263	.105
.157	.052	.21	**Self-contained class**		.105	
		.052	**Resource > ½ day**	.105	.052	
	.105	.157	**Resource < ½ day**	.157	.105	.052
			Regular education support		.052	
	.052		**Regular education**			
.052	.052	.052	**Initial placement**			
			Current placement			
			Exit		.052	
			Label change			

TABLE 5.4
Conditional Probabilities of Preceding and Subsequent Placements
to Hospital and Treatment Center Placement (n = 72)

Preceding Placements				Subsequent Placements		
Placement 3	Placement 2	Placement 1		Placement 1	Placement 2	Placement 3
.027	.013	.138	Homebound	.055	.055	.027
.097	.18	.097	Hospital/treatment center	.097	.18	.097
.069	.111	.138	Separate school	.236	.125	.069
.013	.069	.069	Self-contained class	.069	.113	.027
.027		.041	Resource > ½ day	.111	.069	.027
.013	.013	.194	Resource < ½ day	.194	.083	.055
.027	.027		Regular education support	.013	.013	
.013	.027	.027	Regular education	.111		
.013	.083	.125	Initial placement			.013
			Current placement			
			Exit	.069		
			Label change			

TABLE 5.5
Conditional Probabilities of Preceding and Subsequent Placements
to Separate School Placement (n = 65)

Preceding Placements				Subsequent Placements		
Placement 3	Placement 2	Placement 1		Placement 1	Placement 2	Placement 3
.03	.076	.046	Homebound	.076	.015	
.076	.138	.261	Hospital/treatment center	.153	.123	.076
.046	.076	.015	Separate school	.015	.076	.046
.03	.076	.03	Self-contained class	.092		
		.107	Resource > ½ day	.076	.015	.03
.061	.046	.153	Resource < ½ day	.20	.03	
.03	.03	.061	Regular education support	.03		
.03		.03	Regular education	.015		
.03	.061	.015	Initial placement			
			Current placement			
			Exit	.015	.076	.03
.015	.015		Label change			

TABLE 5.6
Conditional Probabilities of Preceding and Subsequent Placements to Separate Class Placement (n = 86)

Preceding Placements: Placement 3	Preceding Placements: Placement 2	Preceding Placements: Placement 1		Subsequent Placements: Placement 1	Subsequent Placements: Placement 2	Subsequent Placements: Placement 3
	.025		**Homebound**	.051	.012	.038
.025	.012	.064	**Hospital/treatment center**	.064	.064	.012
		.076	**Separate school**	.025	.064	.025
.025	.076	.012	**Self-contained class**	.012	.076	.025
	.025	.012	**Resource > ½ day**	.051	.076	
.012		.166	**Resource < ½ day**	.358	.038	.064
.012		.012	**Regular education support**			
		.025	**Regular education**	.012	.012	
.025	.115	.153	**Initial placement**			
			Current placement			
		.012	**Exit**	.038	.012	.025
	.012	.064	**Label change**			

separate school in 26.1% of the cases. The combined categories of resource room also accounted for 26% of the cases. This would indicate an equal probability that a placement into a separate school was a movement from a more restrictive setting or a movement from a less restrictive setting. The highest probability placement subsequent to placement into a separate school was placement into the combined resource settings (CP = .276), followed by placement into a hospital or treatment center (CP = .15).

Table 5.6 provides the conditional probabilities of placements to and from a separate class within a regular school setting. The most frequently occurring placement that preceded placement into a separate class was resource less than one half day (CP = .166). Separate class placement was the initial placement subsequent to identification as behavior disordered in 12 cases, yielding a conditional probability of .153. The highest conditional probability of a placement subsequent to placement in a separate class was the combination of resource settings (CP = .409). The probability of exiting school from a separate class setting was .038. Movement to a more restrictive setting (e.g., separate school, hospital or treatment center, or homebound) had a conditional probability of .14, whereas movement from a separate class to a less restrictive setting (e.g., combined resource, regular education with support, or regular education) had a conditional probability of .421. The probability that a student moved to a more restrictive setting as the second placement subsequent to separate class placement was .120. The probability that a student moved to a less restrictive placement as the second placement subsequent to separate class placement was .126. The probability of exiting as a second placement subsequent to separate class was .038.

TABLE 5.7
Conditional Probabilities of Preceding and Subsequent Placements
to Resource Greater Than One Half Day Placement (n = 48)

Preceding Placements				Subsequent Placements		
Placement 3	Placement 2	Placement 1		Placement 1	Placement 2	Placement 3
.02	.02	.041	Homebound	.02		
.041	.104	.166	Hospital/treatment center	.062		.041
.041	.02	.104	Separate school	.145		
	.02	.083	Self-contained class	.02	.041	
	.145		Resource > ½ day		.145	
.083	.041	.229	Resource < ½ day	.312	.02	.02
		.02	Regular education support			
	.02	.02	Regular education			
.02	.083	.166	Initial placement			
			Current placement			
			Exit			
	.041	.02	Label change			

Table 5.7 presents the conditional probabilities of placements preceding and subsequent placement into resource settings for greater than one half day. The highest probability of preceding placement to resource greater than one half day was resource less than one half day (CP = .229). The probability that the preceding placement was movement from a more restrictive setting (e.g., separate class, separate school, hospital or treatment center, or homebound) was .394. The probability that movement was from a less restrictive setting was .435. This figure includes 16.6% of the placements that were initial placements for special education services. The highest probability placement subsequent to placement in resource for greater than one half day was resource for less than one half day (CP = .312). The probability that placement subsequent to placement in resource for greater than one half day was to a more restrictive setting (separate class, separate school, hospital, treatment center, homebound) was .247, whereas all of the placements to less restrictive settings were to resource for less than one half day.

Table 5.8 presents the conditional probabilities for placements preceding and subsequent to resource for less than one half day. The most frequent placements preceding placement into resource for less than one half day were an initial placement into special education (CP = .208) and separate class placement (CP = .142). The probability of placement to a more restrictive setting subsequent to placement in resource for less than one half day was 256, whereas movement to less restrictive settings was .03. The probability of exits from resource for less than one half day was .055.

TABLE 5.8
Conditional Probabilities of Preceding and Subsequent Placements to Resource Less Than One Half Day Placement (n = 197)

Preceding Placements				Subsequent Placements		
Placement 3	Placement 2	Placement 1		Placement 1	Placement 2	Placement 3
	.01	.015	Homebound	.015	.01	
.02	.03	.071	Hospital/treatment center	.071	.005	.005
	.01	.065	Separate school	.05	.015	.02
.025	.015	.142	Self-contained class	.065		.005
.005	.005	.076	Resource > ½ day	.055	.01	.02
.015	.147		Resource < ½ day		.147	.015
	.005	.01	Regular education support	.01		
.005	.015	.035	Regular education	.02	.005	
.076	.04	.208	Initial placement			
			Current placement			
		.005	Exit	.055	.01	.01
.005	.005	.025	Label change			

Table 5.9 presents the conditional probabilities for placements into regular education with support. The most probable placements preceding placement into regular education with support were separate class, resource less than one half day, and an initial placement into special education services (CP = .181). The most frequent placement subsequent to placement in regular education with support was placement into a separate school with a conditional probability of .363. There is an equal probability of .181 that placement into regular education with support will be followed by placement into resource for less than one half day or placement into regular education.

Table 5.10 presents the conditional probabilities for preceding and subsequent placements to regular education without support. Placements from hospital or treatment centers (CP = .47) and resource rooms for less than one half day (CP = .235) accounted for the majority of placements preceding placement into regular education settings. For placements following placement in regular education, the most frequent placement was resource less than one half day (CP = .411), and equal probabilities of .117 for hospitalization, separate school, and self-contained class.

Table 5.11 presents the conditional probabilities for initial placements for special education services. Initial placements were scored for those students who were receiving services during the 1991–92 school year yet had not received services during the 1987–88 school year. As might be expected, the majority of initial placements was placement into resource for less than one half day (CP = .539) and placement into separate classes (CP = .157). Approximately 40.7% of the

TABLE 5.9
Conditional Probabilities of Preceding and Subsequent Placements
to Regular Education with Support (n = 11)

Preceding Placements				**Subsequent Placements**		
Placement 3	**Placement 2**	**Placement 1**		**Placement 1**	**Placement 2**	**Placement 3**
	.09		**Homebound**			
	.09	.09	**Hospital/treatment center**		.181	.181
		.181	**Separate school**	.363	.181	.181
			Self-contained class	.09		.09
			Resource > ½ day	.09		
		.181	**Resource < ½ day**	.181	.09	
	.09		**Regular education support**		.09	
		.09	**Regular education**	.181		
.09	.09	.181	**Initial placement**			
			Current placement			
			Exit			
			Label change			

TABLE 5.10
Conditional Probabilities of Preceding and Subsequent Placements
to Regular Education Placement (n = 17)

Preceding Placements				**Subsequent Placements**		
Placement 3	**Placement 2**	**Placement 1**		**Placement 1**	**Placement 2**	**Placement 3**
			Homebound		.058	
.058		.47	**Hospital/treatment center**	.117	.117	.058
		.058	**Separate school**	.117		.117
	.058	.058	**Self-contained class**	.117	.058	
			Resource > ½ day	.058	.176	
	.058	.235	**Resource < ½ day**	.411		.058
		.117	**Regular education support**	.058		
	.058		**Regular education**		.058	
.058	.529		**Initial placement**			
			Current placement			
			Exit		.058	
		.058	**Label change**			

TABLE 5.11
Conditional Probabilities of Subsequent Placements
to Initial Placements ($n = 76$)

Preceding Placements				Subsequent Placements		
Placement 3	Placement 2	Placement 1		Placement 1	Placement 2	Placement 3
			Homebound		.013	.013
			Hospital/treatment center	.118	.078	.013
			Separate school	.013	.052	.026
			Self-contained class	.157	.118	.026
			Resource > ½ day	.105	.052	.013
			Resource < ½ day	.539	.105	.197
			Regular education support	.026	.013	.013
			Regular education		.018	.013
			Initial placement			
			Current placement			
			Exit		.039	.039
			Label change	.026		

initial placements were not followed by change in placement. For placements following the initial placement (Placement 2), the most probable placements were placement into separate class (CP = .118) and resource for less than one half day (CP = .105).

Table 5.12 presents the conditional probabilities of preceding and subsequent placements to school exit. Exit was preceded by resource room for less than one half day placement in 55% of the cases. Exit was preceded by hospital or treatment center placements in 25% of the instances. Subsequent placements indicate that in two instances students exited and returned to school.

Discussion

The demographic data and current placement data were intended to provide an initial description of where students with EBD in participating districts were placed, and their movement to other placements. Several findings are interesting given current national data. First, it appears that resource settings are utilized to a greater extent than would be expected from the national figures. Combined resource categories accounted for 65% of the current placements, compared with a national average of only 28.5%. Conversely, the use of segregated environments (separate schools, separate classes, hospital or treatment center) accounted for only 24.3% of the current placements, compared with 51% nationally. One explanation is that the placement profile for students with EBD may change dramatically during the secondary years. It is logical given low levels of school

TABLE 5.12
Conditional Probabilities of Preceding and Subsequent Placements to School Exit ($n = 20$)

Preceding Placements				Subsequent Placements		
Placement 3	Placement 2	Placement 1		Placement 1	Placement 2	Placement 3
	.05		Homebound			
		.25	Hospital/treatment center			
.10	.25	.05	Separate school			
.10	.05	.15	Self-contained class	.05		
			Resource > ½ day			
.10	.10	.55	Resource < ½ day	.05		
			Regular education support			
	.05		Regular education			
.15	.15		Initial placement			
			Current placement			
	.05		Exit		.05	
			Label change			

completion (Wagner & Shaver, 1989) that our placement data reflects a school age population heavily impacted by attrition. Current efforts include additional recruiting efforts from rural areas as well as continuing to follow current students.

The sequential analysis presents several movements of particular interest. The exit category represents the preceding placements for students within the population who exited the system during the 1991–92 school year. Twenty exits occurred, representing 18 students (2 students exited, returned, and then re-exited). Ten students left school without graduating, which would be considered an "unsuccessful" transition. However, 5 students successfully completed school and graduated with diplomas. Three students were in a pattern of nonattendance that would indicate they were not in school and yet had not formally withdrawn. One student returned to a resource setting and subsequently re-exited. One student returned to a self-contained class after exiting. Little is known regarding the subsequent success or failure of students returning to school following school exit. The data on school exits is not suprising given the outcome data reported earlier. Parents and teachers of several of the successful exiters have agreed to be interviewed and to provide information regarding perceptions of variables impacting successful exit.

Approximately 17% of the placements involving regular education were placement back into regular education without support (Table 5.10). Although these would be considered successful placements, over half were placements into regular education from hospital or treatment centers prior to being identified as behaviorally disordered. Critical incident reports indicate that three of the remaining seven placements involved the removal from special education at the request of the parent and not an indication of a student's improvement. Although efforts were made to identify parents and students requesting decertification and determine reasons related to the request, none of these students and parents agreed to participate in the subsequent, more detailed analysis of movements.

Further discussion is limited due to the incomplete status of the project. However, several aspects are worth noting with conclusions awaiting the completion of analysis. Although, the prevalence of hospitalization is not surprising (Duchnowski et al., 1993; Stephens, Lakin, Brauen, & O'Rielly, 1990), it remains a recurrent and disturbing figure in our population. Hospitalization, as reported, was scored as a critical incident and placed within the sequence of placements for our analysis. In no records reviewed was hospitalization an educational placement documented as part of the IEP process. A total of 70 hospitalization or treatment center placements occurred; 19 students had multiple hospitalizations within the previous 5 years (Range 2–7). The most frequent occurring placement pattern involved placement of students who were hospitalized or in a treatment center back into their previous placement. Current research efforts include the verification of hospitalizations and reasons associated with hospitalizations via parent and school personnel interviews. Additional data is being sought as to the initiator of hospital placement and perceived impact on the students' subsequent educational placements. These data raise interesting questions regarding issues of classification. For example, what policy and procedural factors impact the ability of a school system to be responsive to students "at risk" of developing emotional or behavioral disturbances as evidenced by hospitalization prior to being classified as EBD? Another issue involves the need for systems of communication between schools and hospital or treatment programs that might facilitate differential programming, including placement changes.

Integration of parent, teacher, and student interviews, and limited direct observations in classrooms, will provide a more complete picture of the relationship of individual and ecological variables to movement patterns. It is hoped that potentially powerful ecological variables associated with successful and unsuccessful secondary student transitions will be identified.

SUMMARY AND CONCLUSIONS

Placement has long been used as a systemic indicator at the national level. For example, any Annual Report to Congress on the Implementation of IDEA (P.L. 101-476, formerly P.L. 94-142) contains placement data on students receiving services under IDEA by disability category, age, funding, and various other variables. Although no one is asserting that placement data should be used as an indicator of service quality, some have used these data as a global measure of systems moving to less or more restrictive educational environments (e.g.,

Danielson & Bellamy, 1989). This use has and will continue to be scrutinized (Haring et al., 1992; Lipsky & Gartner, 1989; McLaughlin & Owings, 1992)

In this chapter, we illustrate that measures of placement may be enhanced when not viewed as a static measure. A child count indicating that the number of students with EBD receiving services in separate schools increases or decreases from one year to the next does not adequately illustrate the variety of movements that students experience, especially students identified as EBD. Certainly, placements for these students are not static. Attempts to track changes and ecological variables related to these movements appear warranted.

Several implications may be seen. First, as already mentioned, there exists a need for continuing "educational archeology" (H. M. Walker, personal communication, 1992). The review of extant databases offers a host of research opportunities with potential for identifying meaningful relationships for the design of systems as well as improving our understanding of program indicators (e.g., McLaughlin & Owings, 1992). Researchers and program evaluators should be encouraged to pursue the improvement and analysis of data collected by educational systems. Certainly, these data will continue to be used for accountability purposes, but the potential for these data to be part of an integrated and ongoing system evaluation should not be overlooked. Walker, Block-Pedego, Todis, and Severson (1991) developed the School Archival Record System (S.A.R.S.) for the systematic review of student records. The S.A.R.S. identifies elements such as discipline contacts, absences, negative comments, and so forth contained in school records. Walker and his colleagues found these elements to have relatively strong relationships with subsequent school completion. Variables such as negative comments, low academic achievement, number of schools attended, and referrals to outside agencies predicted school dropout when collapsed across Grades 7 through 10. Walker et al. (1991) reported that these variables identified 94% of students who drop out in Grades 11 and 12. Perhaps the formalized system of record review illustrated by S.A.R.S. will promote our investigation of the wealth of information hidden in the files of our students.

Second, there is a need to expand our notion of transition. Transitions during the secondary years prior to exiting school occur and may well be powerful variables in determining success. These data must not be construed to indicate that schools are being responsive or unresponsive to the changing needs of students. School responsiveness may not be indicated by the school's formalized recordkeeping system and a cumulative, static measure of placement. Schools need to be responsive to the changes that occur within students' lives. The need for a more responsive system of services is echoed on a national level (Council for Exceptional Children, 1991) and constitutes an integral part of the developing national research and program agenda for students identified as seriously emotionally disturbed (Chesapeake Institute, 1994; Coutinho & Denny, 1994).

Researchers will continue to argue the validity and reliability of placement data on a national level. Indicators cannot set goals and priorities, and they cannot replace individual program evaluation. However, these data will continue to be a much-needed indication of our provision of a free and appropriate education to children and youth with disabilities, including those with EBD. There is a pressing need to expand our system of indicators to encompass composite measures that reflect place, nature of instruction, and services provided, as well as outcomes. As these measures are approximated across time, we may be better positioned to answer questions of what works and how we are doing. Perhaps, if we view placement data within the dynamic context offered by Rockwell (1989), we will persist in our efforts to improve and understand its potential as a much-needed indicator among many.

ACKNOWLEDGMENT

The research reported in this chapter was supported by Grant No. H158P10033 from the U.S. Department of Education, Office of Special Education Programs. The views represented herein do not necessarily represent the policy of the Department of Education nor should the endorsement of the federal government be assumed.

REFERENCES

Bakeman, R., & Gottman, J. M. (1986). *Observing interaction: An introduction to sequential analysis.* New York: Cambridge University Press.

Blackman, H. P. (1989). Special education placement: Is it what you know or where you live? *Exceptional Children, 55*, 459–462.

Bloom, R. B., & Hopewell, L. R. (1982). Psychiatric hospitalization of adolescents and successful mainstream reentry. *Exceptional Children, 48*, 352–357.

Chesapeake Institute. (1994, May). *National agenda for achieving better results for children and youth with serious emotional disturbance.* Washington, DC: Author.

Council for Children with Behavioral Disorders (CCBD). (1992, June). Position statement: Inclusion. *CCBD Newsletter.* Reston, VA: Author.

Council for Exceptional Children (1991). *Electronic town meeting on students with serious emotional disturbance: Developing an agenda for innovation and development* [Film]. Reston, VA: ERIC Clearinghouse.

Coutinho, M. J., & Denny, R. K. (1994). *National leadership initiatives for children and youth with serious emotional disturbance.* Manuscript submitted for review.

Danielson, L. J., & Bellamy, G. T. (1989). State variation in placement of children with handicaps in segregated environments. *Exceptional Children, 55*, 448–455.

Denny, R. K., Epstein, M., & Rose, E. (1992). Direct observation of adolescents with serious emotional disturbance and their non-handicapped peers in mainstream vocational education classrooms. *Behavioral Disorders, 18*, 33–41.

Deno, E. N. (1973). *Instructional alternatives for exceptional children.* Reston, VA: Council for Exceptional Children.

Duchnowski, A. J., Johnson, M. K., Hall, K. S., Kutash, K., & Friedman, R. M. (1993). The alternatives to residential treatment study: Initial findings. *Journal of Emotional and Behavioral Disorders, 1*, 17–26.

Gerber, M. M. (1984). The Department of Education's Sixth Annual Report to Congress on P.L. 94-142: Is Congress getting the full story? *Exceptional Children, 51*, 209–224.

Gerber, M. M., & Levine-Donelson, D. (1989). Educating all children: Ten years later. *Exceptional Children, 56*, 17–29.

Glueck, S., & Glueck, E. T. (1950). *Juvenile delinquents grown up*. New York: The Commonwealth Fund.

Greenstone, S. M. (1961). Getting the returnee back to school. *Crime and Delinquency, 7*, 249–254.

Grosenick, J. K. (1989). Current issues in the delivery of services to seriously emotionally disturbed students. In S. Bratten, F. Wood, & G. Worbel (Eds.), *Celebrating the past preparing for the future: 40 years of serving students with emotional and behavioral disorders*. Minneapolis, MN: Minnesota Council for Children with Behavioral Disorders and Minnesota Educators of Emotionally/Behaviorally Disordered.

Grosenick, J. K., & Huntze, S. (1980). *National needs analysis in behavior disorders: Adolescent behavior disorders*. Columbia: University of Missouri, Department of Special Education.

Gunter, P. L., Jack, S. L., Shores, R. E., Carrell, D., & Flowers, J. (1993). Lag sequential analysis as a tool for functional analysis of student disruptive behavior in classrooms. *Journal of Emotional and Behavioral Disorders, 1*, 138–148, 198.

Hallahan, D. P., Keller, C. E., McKinney, J. D., Lloyd, J. W., & Bryan, T. (1988). Examining the research base of the regular education initiative: Efficacy studies and the Adaptive Learning Environments Model. *Journal of Learning Disabilities, 21*, 29–35.

Haring, K., Faron-Davis, F., Goetz, L., Karasoff, P., Sailor, W., & Zeph, L. (1992). LRE and the placement of students with severe disabilities. *Journal for the Association for Persons with Severe Handicaps, 17*, 145–153.

Hasazi, S. B., Gordon, L. R., & Roe, C. A. (1985). Factors associated with the employment status of handicapped youth exiting high school from 1979 to 1983. *Exceptional Children, 51*, 455–469.

Hobbs, N. (1966). Helping disturbed children: Psychological and ecological strategies. *American Psychologist, 21*, 1105–1115.

Jack, S. L., Shores, R. E., Denny, R. K., Gunter, P. L., DeBriere, T., & DePaepe, P. (1994). *An analysis of the effects of teachers' use of classroom management strategies on types of classroom interactions*. Manuscript submitted for review.

Kauffman, J. M., Cullinan, D., & Epstein, M. H. (1987). Characteristics of students placed in special programs for the seriously emotionally disturbed. *Behavioral Disorders, 12*, 175–184.

Kerr, M. M., & Zigmond, N. (1986). What do high school teachers want? A study of expectations and standards. *Education and Treatment of Children, 9*, 239–249.

Knitzer, J., Steinberg, Z., & Fleisch, B. (1990). *At the school house door: An examination of programs and policies for children with emotional and behavioral problems*. New York: Bank Street College of Education.

Leone, P. E., Fitzmartin, R., Stetson, F., & Foster, J. (1986). A retrospective follow-up of behaviorally disordered adolescents: Identifying predictors of treatment outcome. *Behavioral Disorders, 11*, 87–97.

Lewis, W. W. (1982). Ecological factors in successful residential treatment. *Behavioral Disorders, 7*, 149–156.

Lewis, W. W. (1988). The role of ecological variables in residential treatment. *Behavioral Disorders, 13*, 98–107.

Lipsky, D. K., & Gartner, A. (1989). The current situation. In D. K. Lipsky & A. Gartner (Eds.), *Beyond separate education: Quality education for all*. Baltimore, MD: Paul H. Brookes.

McCollum, H., & Turnbull, B. J. (1989). *Educational indicators*. Washington, DC: Washington Consulting Group, National Center for Education Statistics.

McLaughlin, M. J., & Owings, M. F. (1992). Relationships among states' fiscal and demographic data and the implementation of P.L. 94-142. *Exceptional Children, 59*, 247–261.

Mithaug, D. E., Horiuchi, C. N., & Fanning, P. N. (1985). A report on the Colorado statewide follow-up survey of special education students. *Exceptional Children, 51*, 397–404.

National Association of State Boards of Education (NASBE). (1991). *Winners all: A call for inclusive schools*. Alexandria, VA: Author.

Neel, R. S., Meadows, N., Levine, P., & Edgar, E. B. (1988). What happens after special education: A statewide follow-up study of secondary students who have behavioral disorders. *Behavioral Disorders, 13*, 209–216.

Peacock Hill Working Group. (1991). Problems and promises in special education and related services for children and youth with emotional or behavioral disorders. *Behavioral Disorders, 16*, 299–313.

Prieto, A. G., & Rutherford, R. B. (1977). An ecological assessment technique for behavioral disordered and learning disabled children. *Behavioral Disorders, 2*, 169–175.

Quay, H. C. (1979). Residential treatment. In H. C. Quay & J. S. Werry (Eds.), *Psychopathological disorders of childhood* (2nd ed.). New York: Wiley.

Rockwell, C. R. (1989). *Lessons from the history of the social indicators movement*. Washington, DC: Social Science Research Council, Washington Consulting Group.

Rhodes, W. C., & Tracy, M. L. (1972). *A study of child variance: Conceptual models* (Conceptual Project of Emotional Disturbance, Institute for the Study of Mental Retardation and Related Disabilities). Ann Arbor: University of Michigan.

Satten, J., Novotny, E. S., Ginsparg, S. L., & Averill, S. (1970). Ego disorganization and recidivism in delinquent boys. *Bulletin Menninger Clinic, 34*, 270–283.

Schepses, E. (1955). The academic school experience of the training school student. *Federal Probation, 19*, 48–51.

Schneider, B. H., & Byrne, B. M. (1984). Predictors of successful transition from self-contained special education to regular class settings. *Psychology in the Schools, 21*, 375–380.

Shavelson, R. J. (1989). The design of educational indicator systems: An overview. In R. J. Shavelson, L. M. McDonnell, & J. Oakes (Eds.), *Indicators for monitoring mathematics and science education*. Santa Monica, CA: Rand Corporation.

Shores, R. E., Jack, S. L., Gunter, P. L., Ellis, D. N., DeBriere, T., & Wehby, J. (1993). Classroom interactions of children with severe behavior disorders. *Journal of Emotional and Behavioral Disorders, 1*, 27–39.

Stephens, S. A., Lakin, K. C., Brauen, M., & O'Rielly, F. (1990). *The study of programs of instruction for handicapped children and youth in day and residential facilities*. Washington, DC : U.S. Department of Education and Mathmatical Policy Research.

Swan, W. W., Brown, C. L., & Jacob, R. T. (1987). Types of service delivery models used in the reintegration of severely emotionally disturbed/behaviorally disordered students. *Behavioral Disorders, 12*, 99–103.

Tapp, J. T., Wehby, J. H., & Ellis, D. N. (1993). *A multiple option observation system for experimental studies: MOOSES*. Unpublished manuscript, Vanderbilt University, Nashville, TN.

Tucker, J. A. (1989). Less required energy: A response to Danielson and Bellamy. *Exceptional Children, 55*, 453–458.

U.S. Department of Education. (1990). *Twelfth annual report to congress on the implementation of the education of the handicapped act*. Washington, DC: Office of Special Education Programs, U.S. Government Printing Office.

U.S. Department of Education. (1992). *Fourteenth Annual Report to Congress on the Implementation of the Individuals with Disabilities Education Act*. Washington, DC: Office of Special Education Programs, U.S. Government Printing Office.

U.S. Department of Health, Education, & Welfare (U.S.D.H.E.W.). (1969). *Toward a social report*. Washington, DC: U.S. Government Printing Office.

Vergason, G. A., & Anderegg, M. L. (1989). Save the baby! A response to "Integrating the children of the second system." *Phi Delta Kappan, 71*, 61–63.

Wagner, M. (1993). *Trends in post-school outcomes of youth with disabilities.* Menlo Park, CA: SRI.

Wagner, M., D'Amico, R. Marder, C., Newman, L., & Blackorby, J. (1992). *What happens next? Trends in the post school outcomes of youth with disabilities.* Menlo Park, CA: SRI.

Wagner, M., & Shaver, D. M. (1989). *Educational programs and achievements of secondary special education students: Findings from the National Longitudinal Transition Study.* Menlo Park, CA: SRI.

Walker, H. M., Block-Pedego, A., Todis, B., & Severson, H. (1991). *School Archival Records Search* (SARS). Longmont, CO: Sopris West.

Wang, M. C., Reynolds, M. C., & Walberg, H. J. (1989). Integrating the children of the second system. *Phi Delta Kappan, 70,* 248–251.

Zigmond, N., & Kerr, M. M. (1985, April). *Managing the mainstream: A contrast of the behaviors of learning disabled students who pass their assigned mainstream courses and those who fail.* Paper presented at meeting of the American Education Research Association, Chicago.

CHAPTER

6

Teachers of Students with Emotional or Behavioral Disorders: Who They Are and How They View Their Jobs

Nancy Clark-Chiarelli
Judith D. Singer
Harvard University

The U.S. public school teaching force includes approximately 30,000 teachers whose primary responsibility it is to serve the nearly 400,000 students labeled as "seriously emotionally disturbed" (Office of Special Education and Rehabilitative Services [OSERS], 1991). During the past 15 years, the demand for these teachers has increased as the number of students identified as having emotional or behavioral disorders has grown (OSERS, 1991; Smith-Davis, Burke, & Noel, 1984). Small-scale studies suggest that teachers of students with emotional and behavioral disorders may have an even higher rate of attrition than other special educators (Lauritzen & Friedman, 1991; Lawrenson & McKinnon, 1982), a finding particularly disturbing in light of the fact that special educators, as a group, have a somewhat higher attrition rate than regular educators (Boe, Bobbit, & Cook, 1993). To add to what has been painted as a rather grim portrait, the research literature characterizes teachers of students with emotional and behavioral disorders as particularly susceptible to stress and burnout (Johnson, Gold, & Vickers, 1982; Lauritzen & Friedman, 1991; Zabel & Zabel, 1982). Lauritzen and Friedman (1991) characterized the need for competent teachers to work with students with emotional and behavioral disorders as "education's greatest challenge."

But is there rigorous scientific evidence to support these claims? What do we actually know about the people who teach students with emotional and behavioral disorders? A critical review of the literature suggests that many of the ominous forecasts and reports of stress, burnout, and disillusionment are based on nothing more than anecdotal evidence. Yet, to understand the motivations of this group of special educators, to set informed policy that will support their professional development, and to understand more clearly what life is actually like for people who serve these students day in and day out, we need better evidence—generalizable evidence—about their professional lives.

In this chapter we summarize the available evidence on two core questions: Who are America's teachers of students with emotional and behavioral disorders and how do they view their job, and how do their working conditions and attitudes toward teaching compare to those of other special educators? The evidence we present comes from two distinct sources: previous research on teachers of students with emotional and behavioral disorders, and our ongoing work on the special education work force based on data collected by the National Center for Education Statistics (NCES) as part of the 1987–88 Schools and Staffing Survey (SASS). Taken together, these sources provide a clear portrait of teachers of students with emotional and behavioral disorders, a portrait that suggests broad similarities with teachers in the other special education specialties and striking differences unique to this particular field.

WHAT DO WE KNOW ABOUT AMERICA'S TEACHERS OF STUDENTS WITH EMOTIONAL OR BEHAVIORAL DISORDERS?

In the nearly 20 years following the enactment in 1975 of the Education for All Handicapped Children Act (known since 1990 as the Individuals with Disabilities Act), there has been increasing interest in understanding who America's special educators are and what their work lives are like. Although few studies have focused exclusively on teachers of students with emotional or behavioral disorders, there is now a sizable body of evidence on the special education work force as a whole. In this section, we briefly summarize previous research on seven specific topics: teacher demographics; teacher preparation and qualifications; teacher career paths; school working conditions; instructional settings; teacher autonomy and support; and job rewards, satisfaction, and commitment.

Teacher Demographics

Most national studies of teachers either group all special educators into a single category (e.g., Choy et al., 1993) or set aside special educators altogether (Murnane, Singer, Willett, Olsen, & Kemple, 1991), thereby making it difficult to provide a detailed description of the group of teachers who serve students with emotional or behavioral disorders. Two recent studies, however, do provide some insight. McManus and Kauffman (1991) conducted a national survey of teachers of students with emotional and behavioral disorders using lists provided by the Council for Children with Behavioral Disorders. They found that the average teacher of these students was a woman, 37 years of age. Two thirds had master's degrees; the average length of teaching experience was over 7 years in the area of emotional or behavioral disorders and nearly 5 years with other types of students. Three fourths of the teachers taught in urban or suburban schools.

Another source of evidence is a recent study of special educators in Virginia (Cross & Billingsley, 1994). Cross and Billingsley found that teachers of students with emotional and behavioral disorders differed demographically from other special educators in two important ways. First, there were more men in this special education field than there were in all other special education fields (12% vs. 4%). Second, these teachers tended to be somewhat younger and more racially and ethnically diverse; 22% of the teachers of students with emotional or behavioral disorders were African Americans, versus 17% in other areas of special education.

Although both these excellent studies are based on probability samples from well-defined target populations, we must be careful not to use them to draw a national portrait of all teachers who serve emotionally and behaviorally disordered students. The problem concerns their sampling frames. The first study was drawn from a nationwide membership list; the second, from a single state. As a result, as we later show, even these seemingly straightforward demographic characterizations do not fully describe the entire group of teachers serving students with emotional and behavioral disorders.

Teacher Preparation and Qualifications

The U.S. public school teaching force has been the subject of growing criticism. Every year, another report decries the declining quality of our nation's teachers. Study after study asserts that teaching as a field fails to attract and retain the best and the brightest (Carnegie Forum on Education and the Economy, 1986; Schlechty & Vance, 1981). It is clear that as measured by standardized tests, students entering careers in education rank at the bottom in verbal and quantitative aptitudes. And within special education, there is concern that our newly minted special educators lack the skills necessary for being successful in the classroom. For example, state educational administrators surveyed by McLaughlin, Valdivieso, Spence, and Fuller (1988) reported that new special education recruits lacked knowledge in areas such as understanding state rules and regulations, eligibility criteria, and due process guarantees, as well as in writing individualized educational plans, working on teams, and teaching cross-categorical groups of students.

Special education has been especially hard hit, in part due to the continual shortage of qualified special educators. Although the severity of personnel shortages varies according to handicapping condition, grade level, and locale (Lauritzen & Friedman, 1991; Schofer & Duncan, 1986; Smith-Davis, Burke, & Noel, 1984), it is also clear that the problem has been particularly acute for teachers of students with behavioral problems (Lauritzen, 1990).

In many instances, the solution to a local teacher shortage has been to issue emergency licenses. To many, emergency licensure is equated with a reduction in teacher qualification and is of particular concern as shortages place increasing demand on what is perceived as a shrinking supply of qualified special educators (Sattler & Sattler, 1985). It is important to note, however, that the percentage of special education personnel with less than "full" certification varies widely from state to state. For example, Schofer and Duncan (1986) found that "in one state, up to 90% of the special education personnel may not be fully certified; however, the percentage most frequently indicated was 10%" (p. 66). Previous research suggests that approximately one third of newly hired teachers of students with emotional or behavioral disorders have less than full certification (Lauritzen & Friedman, 1991; Lawrenson & McKinnon, 1982).

Teacher Career Paths

In many ways, the career paths of special educators appear to be quite similar to the career path of regular educators (Singer, 1993a). Special educators are most likely to leave during their early years on the job, when they first confront the daily demands of classroom life; teachers who survive this initial risky period typically remain in the classroom for many years to come. Singer's analysis of Michigan and North Carolina special educator data suggests that 12% and 13% of beginning special educators leave after their first year of teaching, respectively. After this initial year, attrition continues so that by the end of 5 years, only an estimated 57% of newly hired special educators were still teaching in the states.

Who is especially likely to leave? Singer (1993a) found that the average length of stay in special education for teachers of students with emotional or behavioral disorders was 6.8 years for those in elementary schools and 5.5 years for those in secondary schools, figures that place these special educators near the average career durations for special educators as a whole. In their work in Minnesota, Lauritzen and Friedman (1991) reported that these teachers in small districts have a higher attrition rate than those in larger districts. Other research suggests that more able teachers—of any specialty—are more likely to leave the special education work force than less able teachers, as measured by standardized testing. Frank and Keith (1984) reported that attrition among high verbal and mid-verbal ability was substantially greater than for special educators with low ability by their fifth year of teaching. Similarly, Singer (1993a) found a strong relationship between scores on the National Teacher Examination (NTE) and the length of time special educators remained in teaching: The higher a teacher's score, the more likely a teacher was to leave.

Extrinsic rewards, such as salary, also affect the retention of special educators. As reported by Singer (1993a), teachers in North Carolina and Michigan who received comparatively higher salaries were more likely to remain teaching in the state. Although higher salaries may be associated with teacher retention, it would appear that the relationship between the two is complex. In her analysis of longitudinal data of 14,489 teachers, Heyns (1988) found that some of the most advantaged schools, on average, have the lowest rates of retention. Although lower salaries may "push" some teachers out of the profession, the "pull" toward competing career options, particularly for the most capable teachers, should be considered as well. A serious shortcoming of Heyns' analysis, however, is that she did not control for district characteristics.

Some special educators make a different switch—they continue to be teachers, but do so as regular educators. The loss of special education personnel to regular education is of particular concern (Billingsley & Cross, 1991). Chandler (1983) argued that many special education teachers transfer to regular education because they burn out in the special education settings. Platt and Olson (1990) maintained that the issue is caseload. But whatever the reason, there is empirical evidence to document the movement. Lauritzen (1990) found that in Wisconsin, the probability of a teacher transferring from special education to regular education is 25 times higher than the probability that the reverse will occur. Data from Kansas (McKnab, 1989) suggests a rate 20 times greater; in Washington, 13 times (Schrag, 1989). Schrag argued that many newly hired special education teachers in Washington transfer to regular education when a position opens up, so that special education is used by some merely as a way to get one's foot in the door (Schrag, as cited in Lauritzen & Friedman, 1991).

Some teachers who transfer to regular education consider returning to special education. In their study of teachers who transferred to regular education, for example, Billingsley and Cross (1991) found that 14% said they would return to special education within the next 1 to 3 years if a position opened up, and 50% reported that they might eventually return.

And many special educators who leave the schools do, ultimately, return. The phenomenon of female teachers leaving in order to raise a family and then returning to the work force has been known for years (Lortie, 1975), but recent data suggests that the number of older women entering the teaching force is increasing (Murnane et al., 1991; Singer, 1993b). Thus, a career interruption is not unusual and may not signal a permanent exit from teaching. In her analysis of data from Michigan, Singer (1993b) found that of the special educators who were hired between 1972 and 1981 and who stopped teaching by 1983, 35% returned to teaching by 1985.

Working Conditions

A recurrent theme in much of the literature on the work lives of special educators is that adverse working conditions—both role related and student related—create stress and job burnout. A myriad of adverse working conditions have been identified:

- overabundance of paperwork (e.g., Bensky et al., 1980; Chandler, 1983; Dangel, Bunch, & Coopman, 1987; Lauritzen & Friedman, 1991; Olson & Matuskey, 1982; Platt & Olson, 1990),
- litigation (Johnson et al., 1982),

- inadequate policies (Billingsley & Cross, 1991; Fimian & Santoro, 1983),
- excessive pupil–teacher ratios (Algozzine, Hendrickson, Gable, & White, 1993; Bensky et al., 1980; Billingsley & Cross, 1991; Fimian & Santoro, 1983; Olson & Matuskey, 1982; Platt & Olson, 1990),
- inadequate planning time (Fimian & Santoro, 1983; Olson & Matuskey, 1982),
- lack of advancement and growth opportunities (Dangel et al., 1987; Fimian & Santoro, 1983; Platt & Olson, 1990),
- lack of recognition (Fimian & Santoro, 1983),
- loneliness and isolation (Chandler, 1983; Fimian & Santoro, 1983; McManus & Kauffman, 1991; Schrag, 1989),
- conflict between a teacher's perception of role and others' expectations (Bensky et al., 1980; Billingsley & Cross, 1992; Crane & Iwanicki, 1986),
- stress of working with special needs students (e.g., Billingsley & Cross, 1991; Byrne, 1991),
- student disciplinary problems and apathy (Fimian & Santoro, 1983; Johnson et al., 1982; Olson & Matuskey, 1982), and
- a lack of acceptance of students with disabilities by regular education teachers (Johnson et al., 1982).

By definition, special educators work with those students whose academic, physical, and emotional needs lie outside what is considered "typical." As a result, it might seem logical to expect that these issues confronting special educators are atypical as well. Yet many of the issues just identified differ little from those as problematic for general educators. Many teachers, both special and regular education alike, feel isolated. Many are dismayed at problems of student discipline, student apathy, and student disrespect. Many perceive a conflict between their own perceptions of their roles and others' expectations. In fact, the few studies that have directly compared regular and special educators' levels of stress and burnout find few, if any, differences (for one of the best studies, see Byrne, 1991).

But research within the special education work force suggests that the work experiences of teachers of students with emotional or behavioral disorders may be different. Several studies have found that these teachers (and consulting teachers) report higher levels of stress (Cross & Billingsley, 1994; Johnson et al., 1982; Lauritzen & Friedman, 1991; Zabel & Zabel, 1982). Other issues raised by teachers of students with emotional or behavioral disorders include insufficient and inappropriate supervisory service, insufficient psychological service, fear of physical attacks, verbal threats, and other potential violence by students as sources of stress more than teachers of students with learning disabilities or mental retardation (Johnson et al., 1982) experience.

Instructional Settings

In their nationwide survey, McManus and Kauffman (1991) found that three fourths of the teachers of students with emotional or behavioral disorders taught in regular public schools. One third taught in self-contained classrooms and, on average, maintained a caseload of 12 students. The mean caseload for resource room teachers was 19 students. On average, teachers with resource room programs had significantly more students integrated into the classroom on a half-time basis than teachers with self-contained programs. Three fourths of the resource rooms tended to be located next to regular classrooms, in comparison to one half of self-contained rooms. On the other hand, nearly one third of the self-contained classrooms were located on a separate campus. Approximately half the teachers (in both self-contained and resource room settings) reported having 30 minutes to 1 hour of planning time per day. Over half of the teachers also reported spending more than 3 hours per week in planning and paperwork outside of class. Both resource room and self-contained teachers reported moderate satisfaction with most aspects of their working conditions. The most problematic area was parent participation; the least problematic area was the quality of support from other special education colleagues.

Does the instructional setting make a difference in terms of burnout or stress? On this issue there is little consistent evidence. Bensky et al. (1980) reported that teachers in self-contained classes experience less stress than those in resource rooms or regular classes, although Crane and Iwanicki (1986) revealed that they experience significantly higher levels of burnout. Teachers of students with emotional or behavioral disorders working in self-contained classrooms are reported to experience more verbal and physical threats and deal with more disruptive behaviors than resource room teachers do, although there is great variability (McManus & Kauffman, 1991). In more restrictive settings, such as special education schools, lower levels of satisfaction are reported (Billingsley & Cross, 1991). But these studies do not reveal whether the problem is the setting itself or the students who get assigned to these particular settings.

Teacher Autonomy, Decision Making, and Support

Autonomy is an important factor in promoting a teacher's sense of efficacy (Johnson, 1990; Rosenholtz, 1989). But when autonomy becomes isolation, it can be a double-edged sword. As the only person in a building responsible for providing a particular service, many special educators experience a high degree of autonomy, perhaps more than they would like. McManus and Kauffman (1991) documented the isolation experienced by many teachers of students with emotional or behavioral disorders. For individual students, special educators' decisions may be important ones. But many special educators express dismay at their isolation from the decision-making processes within the mainstream of general education (Platt & Olson, 1990).

Support is another factor that affects teachers' views of their jobs. Many decry the lack of support for special education professionals. Administrators (e.g., Billingsley & Cross, 1991; Fimian, 1986; Fimian & Santoro, 1983; Johnson et al., 1982; Lawrenson & McKinnon, 1982; Platt & Olson, 1990), parents (e.g., Platt & Olson, 1990), and the central office (Billingsley & Cross, 1991) have all been cited as problematic in this regard. Researchers have also documented the positive, often stress-mediating, role that well-placed support can have (e.g., Breton & Donaldson, 1991; Fimian, 1986; Lawrenson & McKinnon, 1982; McManus & Kauffman, 1991; Schetz & Billingsley, 1992). Some focus on support from colleagues (Fimian, 1986; Lawrenson & McKinnon, 1982; McManus & Kauffman, 1991; Zabel & Zabel, 1982) and supervisors (Breton & Donaldson, 1991; Fimian, 1986; Lawrenson & McKinnon, 1982; McManus & Kauffman, 1991; Zabel & Zabel, 1982), whereas others cite parent support (McManus & Kauffman, 1991; Zabel & Zabel, 1982) as a mediator of job-related stress.

Work Rewards, Satisfaction, and Commitment

Teachers' perceptions of the rewards they receive in helping children learn have been described by many researchers (Johnson, 1990; Lortie, 1975). Johnson (1986) found that most teachers in her sample were still enthusiastic about teaching and still experiencing the reward of feeling as though they were making a difference. In their survey of teachers of students with emotional or behavioral disorders, McManus and Kauffman (1991) found that "Although teachers tended to describe themselves as feeling tired and worn out . . . , they tended to rate themselves as maintaining considerable enthusiasm for teaching and having a positive attitude toward their job" (pp. 253–254). Yet when asked to reflect on the past year, more than two thirds of these teachers considered leaving their current job, nearly one half considered switching to regular education, and one half of the self-contained and two thirds of the resource room teachers considered leaving teaching altogether.

In contrast, Billingsley and Cross (1991) found that 87% of 286 former special educators who had transferred to regular education reported being satisfied or being very satisfied with instructional aspects of special education, whereas 60% reported being somewhat dissatisfied or very dissatisfied with the noninstructional aspects. Lawrenson and McKinnon (1982) found that the major source of satisfaction for teachers of students emotional or behavioral disorders was positive, productive relationships with students. Similarly, the vast majority of former teachers of students with learning disabilities surveyed by Dangel et al. (1987) reported that they felt they could still gain personal satisfaction from teaching learning disabled students.

What Remains to Be Learned?

Although there is a growing body of research on teachers of students with emotional or behavioral disorders, much of the evidence is based on studies suffering from one or more of the following three shortcomings:

- Indirect data sources: Many important perspectives relevant to the issue of special educator attrition and retention remain unrepresented. It is only recently, for example, that researchers have studied job commitment by interviewing special educators themselves. Instead, much of the information to date has come from administrators or those in teacher education.
- Small samples of limited generalizability: Small samples and samples drawn from schools with similar profiles limit generalizability and may underestimate the variation in the population of special educators nationwide. Many studies include teachers in only one state or serving one disability group. Few studies have sufficient data to allow generalizations across groups and grade levels.
- Lack of comparison groups: A lack of appropriate comparison groups permeates the special education research base. Many researchers describe the work experience of teachers of students with emotional or behavioral disorders but fail to provide any benchmark for comparison. As Billingsley (1993) noted in her recent review of the literature on special educator attrition and retention, remarkably little is known about the special education work force in general, and about teachers of students with emotional or behavioral disorders in particular.

It is for this reason that we searched for another source of information about the nation's special education teaching force. We were particularly interested in a data source that would contain information from the teachers themselves, provide data on a variety of measures, be gathered from a probability sample of teachers selected using rigorous methodological principles, and include special educators in a wide variety of subspecialties. One such source, on which we have begun extensive analyses, is the first annual SASS conducted in 1987–88 by the NCES. In the remainder of this chapter, we provide preliminary findings from our research, findings that focus directly on the work lives of a national sample of teachers of students with emotional or behavioral disorders.

THE SCHOOLS AND STAFFING SURVEY

The first national SASS was conducted during the 1987–88 school year using a nationally representative sample of teachers, school administrators, schools, and local education agencies (LEAs). The SASS is actually an integrated set of four surveys: The Teacher Demand and Shortage Survey, The School Administrator Survey, The School Survey, and The Teacher Survey. Our research has focused exclusively on public school teachers, who in SASS were selected according to a stratified, multistage cluster sampling scheme. All U.S. public schools were placed into one of 153 strata defined by cross-classifying the 50 states and the District of Columbia by three grade levels (elementary, secondary, and combined). Within each strata, a sample of schools was selected, and within each school, an average sample of four, eight, and six teachers was randomly selected from elementary, secondary, and combined schools respectively. The final public school sample is comprised of 5,594 LEAs, 9,317 schools, and 56,242 teachers. Further details about the study design are available from NCES.

Analytic Sample

The results presented herein are based on data collected from the 3,848 full-time special educators who were surveyed as part of the SASS. Of these, 404 identified their primary teaching assignment as providing services to students identified as emotionally disturbed. The remaining 3,444 special educators in the sample served students identified as learning disabled ($N = 1{,}712$); mentally retarded ($N = 1{,}013$); speech, vision, and hearing impaired ($N = 248$); or "other" ($N = 471$).

We restricted our analyses to data describing full-time public school teachers. We did so for several reasons. First, by definition, the duties and responsibilities of part-time teachers are reduced due to their part-time status. The extent to which these teachers participate in the various aspects of the school and special education program may vary considerably depending on district, school, and teacher characteristics. One must also question the degree to which the work experiences of part-timers differ from full-timers. For example, most part-time teachers will not be primarily responsible for educational plans, nor will they serve as liaisons. Second, although a study of differences between part-time and full-time teachers would no doubt be appropriate and useful, the fact that most of the part-time special educators are teachers of students with speech, hearing, and visual impairments prohibits a clear analysis of this differential. Results from such an analysis would be difficult to interpret: Are differences observed attributable to part-time teaching status or being a teacher of the speech, hearing, or visually impaired? Third, as the number of part-time teachers of the emotionally disturbed was quite small ($n = 16$), our decision resulted in only a minor diminution of our focal sample. We should note, however, that our analytic sample does include itinerant and long-term substitutes. In small districts, or those with geographically dispersed schools, many special educators must serve more than one school. In addition, we felt that it was prudent to retain the small number of long-term substitutes, as it has been speculated that districts facing shortages in special educators may use long-term substitutes to fill positions.

Analytic Approach

When analyzing data from a stratified multistage cluster sample, researchers must take specific steps to account for (a) the oversampling of certain individuals and (b) the potential underestimation of the variance (standard error) compared to simple random sampling of the same size (Kalton, 1983). In SASS, a stratified random sample of schools was selected, and within each school a stratified random sample of teachers was selected. Because new teachers were oversampled, and because the building-level clustering increases the likelihood that there may be less variance among teachers selected (Lee, Forthofer, & Lorimor, 1989), familiar statistical procedures for estimating quantities as seemingly straightforward as means and standard errors may be incorrect. To estimate parameters and their standard errors appropriately, we therefore used a specialized statistical program (WESVAR) for all the analyses reported herein. All estimated means, percentages, and standard errors, therefore, generalize back to the entire U.S. population of special educators.

A NEW NATIONAL PORTRAIT OF TEACHERS OF STUDENTS WITH EMOTIONAL OR BEHAVIORAL DISORDERS

In many ways, teachers of students with emotional and behavioral disorders resemble those of other special educators. As shown in Table 6.1, in both groups nearly half are age 35 or younger; three fourths are married; over half have children. As other studies of the public school teaching force have found, the vast majority of special educators are Whites of non-Hispanic origin. Only 10% of special educators—both teachers of students with emotional or behavioral disorders and all other teachers—were African American, and far fewer were either Hispanic, Asian, or Native American. Given the racial composition of the special education student population—and the population of students with emotional or behavioral disorders in particular—this lack of diversity in the teaching force will remain a major policy issue in the years ahead.

But there is one striking difference between the demographic composition of the group of teachers who serve students with emotional or behavioral disorders and those who serve all other special education students. Although the majority of teachers in both groups are female, there are far more men in this subspecialty of special education than in the other subspecialties (24% vs. 14%). This representation of men is in stark contrast to that reported in previous studies of teachers of students with emotional or behavioral disorders. For example, in their national survey, McManus and Kauffman (1991) estimated that men comprised only 3% of the group; in their Virginia study, Cross and Billingsley (1994) offered an estimate of 12%. Given that the present study's estimate is based on a national

TABLE 6.1
Demographics of Special Education Teaching Force, by Subject Specialty

	ED Teachers		*All Others*	
Characteristic	%	*SE (%)*	%	*SE (%)*
Gender				
Female	76	(2.55)	86	(.67)
Male	24	(2.55)	14	(.67)
Age				
<31 years	24	(2.57)	21	(.78)
31–35	22	(2.76)	22	(1.05)
36–40	21	(2.36)	23	(.95)
41–45	16	(2.04)	13	(.81)
46–50	7	(1.37)	8	(.64)
>50	9	(1.52)	12	(1.68)
Marital status				
Single, no children	24	(2.65)	22	(.83)
Married, no children	22	(2.92)	21	(.82)
Single, with children	8	(1.24)	10	(.71)
Married, with children	46	(2.05)	47	(1.03)
Race				
White	85	(2.35)	87	(.75)
African American	10	(1.97)	10	(.62)
Hispanic	2	(.93)	2	(.30)
Asian	1	(.76)	1	(.19)
Native American	1	(.76)	1	(.23)

probability sample and, therefore, describes the national picture (within the limits of sampling variation), this simple demographic result highlights the danger in extrapolating from locally conducted studies and from studies of members of professional organizations.

Academic Preparation, Certification, and Perceived Competence

The issue of teacher quality lies at the heart of the issues of teacher preparation, certification, and perceived competence. Government analysts, school administrators, parents, and the tax-paying public would all like better data describing the qualifications of the teacher work force. But as researchers into the teacher work force have noted, it is incredibly difficult to measure the quality of the teaching force (e.g., National Academy of Sciences, 1992). Hence, researchers rely on indirect measures that may, or may not, be correlated with quality—teacher preparation, certification, and self-reported competence.

As shown in Table 6.2, on average, the two groups of special educators—those teaching students with emotional or behavioral disorders and all others—have nearly identical academic preparation: 44% have a master's degree, 11% have an advanced degree beyond the master's, and the remaining 45% have only a bachelor's degree. Data not reported here reveal that approximately 40% of both groups participated in at least one continuing education program during the previous academic year. Given the pay incentives associated with degree attainment and the frequent requirements for continuing education, this high level of academic qualification and continuing involvement with training should come as no surprise.

There are, however, two striking findings about the qualifications of teachers of students with emotional or behavioral disorders. First, there is a large percentage of teachers who are not certified in their primary teaching assignment. Although it is certainly distressing that only 70% of all other special educators have a regular certificate in their primary teaching assignment, it is even more distressing that the same is true for only 57% of teachers of students with emotional or behavioral disorders. Nearly 25% of these teachers chose not to specify their type of certification (casting some doubt on the certainty of their certification), another 10% have only temporary certification in the field, 6% have only probationary certification, and 3% are not certified in this field. Two percent are not certified at all. It is clear that districts experiencing difficulties hiring qualified teachers for students with emotional disorders have hired many teachers with less than full certification.

These findings about certification would be ameliorated if the teachers themselves reported that they nevertheless felt qualified to be teaching their students. But in this regard, the characterization of teachers serving students with emotional or behavioral disorders is even more problematic. Although 66% reported that they are currently teaching in the field in which they feel best qualified and another 7% reported that this field is their second best qualified field, 27% reported that this field is neither their best nor their second best qualified field. Teachers teaching out of field is a problem in other areas of special education as well, but in the area of emotional or behavioral disorders a staggering one in four teachers reported not feeling qualified to serve his or her students.

Teaching Experience

Teachers of students with emotional or behavioral disorders have fewer years of experience than their colleagues teaching other students with special needs (see Table 6.2). Nearly one third have been teaching for 5 years or less; nearly two thirds have been teaching in their current school for 5 years or less. Among other special education fields, only 21% of teachers have 5 or fewer years of teaching

TABLE 6.2
Preparation, Qualifications, and Experience of Special Education Teaching Force, by Subject Specialty

Characteristic	ED Teachers %	ED Teachers SE (%)	All Others %	All Others SE (%)
Highest degree				
None	0	(0.00)	<1	(.03)
BA	45	(3.49)	45	(.94)
MA	44	(2.89)	44	(.90)
>MA	11	(2.14)	11	(.62)
Certification in primary teaching assignment				
Regular	57	(2.49)	70	(.92)
Probationary	6	(1.46)	2	(.32)
Temporary	10	(2.00)	6	(.51)
Unknown type	24	(2.20)	19	(.70)
None	3	(1.38)	3	(.35)
Certification in any area				
Regular	60	(2.42)	71	(.91)
Probationary	6	(1.47)	2	(.32)
Temporary	8	(2.11)	5	(.49)
Unknown type	25	(2.33)	19	(.73)
None	2	(.69)	2	(.27)
Teaching emotionally/behaviorally disordered students is best qualified field				
Not best qualified	27	(2.47)	18	(.83)
Best qualified	66	(3.15)	75	(.84)
Second best qualified	7	(1.58)	7	(.49)
Total years of teaching experience				
1–5	31	(2.64)	21	(.77)
6–10	25	(2.34)	29	(.97)
11–15	25	(2.45)	25	(.86)
16–20	13	(2.04)	14	(.70)
Over 20	6	(1.32)	10	(.59)
Years teaching in this school				
1–5	64	(2.54)	52	(.81)
6–10	20	(2.60)	28	(.67)
11–15	11	(2.20)	12	(.69)
16–20	3	(1.01)	5	(.45)
Over 20	1	(.85)	2	(.28)
Teaching spell				
First	70	(3.05)	66	(1.12)
Second	20	(2.53)	24	(1.01)
Third or more	10	(1.64)	10	(.51)
Teaching last year				
Teaching here	75	(2.54)	83	(.65)
Teaching elsewhere	13	(1.66)	10	(.64)
Not teaching	12	(2.32)	7	(.56)

experience and almost half have been teaching in their present school for more than 5 years.

The group of teachers serving students with emotional or behavioral disorders appears to be as mobile as all other special educators. Half the teachers in both groups have previously taught in a different field. The most common previous field is elementary education or another field of special education. Approximately one third of the teachers in both groups have had at least one break in service. There is, however, a small difference in how they describe what they were doing in the previous academic year. Although 83% of the teachers of other special education students reported that in the previous year they were teaching in their present school, only 75% of the teachers of students with emotional and behavioral disorders reported the same. This difference, exceeding the limits of sampling variation, may provide some evidence concerning the issue of turnover among this group of special educators. Without an adequate follow-up into the future, however, it is difficult to compare the attrition rates of these two groups.

Characteristics of Classes and Schools

One particular advantage of the SASS as a data source for studying teachers' careers is the detailed information it provides on teachers' classes and schools. One must take care, however, to remember that the findings concerning class and school characteristics generalize to the teaching force, not to the student body. Thus, for example, when we report (as we do in Table 6.3) that an estimated 73% of the teachers serve students in self-contained settings, this does not imply that 73% of the *students* are served in self-contained settings.

As shown in Table 6.3, teachers of students with emotional or behavioral disorders provide services in self-contained classes far more often than other special educators (73% vs. 45%). They are, therefore, far less likely to be working in a team-teaching situation (only 15% of the teachers reported this as their primary working arrangement) or in resource rooms (only 12%). Other special educators are far more evenly split among these instructional settings.

Data not tabled here reveal wide variation in the numbers of students served. Caseloads for these teachers ranged from a low of 1 to a high of over 100. Across all teachers of students with emotional or behavioral disorders, the average caseload is 10.5 students. Approximately one fourth of the teachers of students with emotional and behavioral disorders also reported a secondary teaching assignment. For two thirds of these teachers, it is serving students with learning disabilities.

Teachers of students with emotional or behavioral disorders work in a variety of school settings. Like their colleagues serving other types of special education students, they cover a variety of grades and school types. Yet despite this similarity, it is worth highlighting two particular characteristics of the distribution of settings in which these teachers work. First, in comparison to their colleagues

TABLE 6.3
Classroom and School Characteristics of Special Education Teaching Force, by Subject Specialty

	ED Teachers		*All Others*	
Characteristic	*%*	*SE (%)*	*%*	*SE (%)*
Setting				
Self-contained	73	(2.59)	45	(1.14)
Departmentalized/team teaching	15	(1.63)	22	(.89)
Pull-out	12	(2.19)	33	(.99)
Grade level				
Elementary	35	(3.18)	48	(.85)
Junior high school	28	(3.06)	19	(.96)
Senior high school	22	(2.13)	22	(.79)
Combination	7	(1.14)	5	(.47)
Other	8	(1.94)	6	(.55)
School type				
Regular	74	(2.76)	84	(1.01)
Magnet	6	(1.14)	6	(.61)
Special education	16	(2.24)	6	(.55)
Alternative	1	(.23)	1	(.17)
Technical	<1	(.26)	<1	(.13)
Other	3	(1.17)	3	(.73)
Location				
Rural	10	(1.86)	24	(.93)
Small city	26	(3.07)	26	(1.06)
Suburban	33	(3.13)	30	(1.04)
Urban	31	(3.27)	19	(.90)
Other	0	(0.00)	<1	(.10)
Socioeconomic status of school (SES)				
Low SES	26	(3.68)	23	(1.14)
Medium low SES	20	(2.50)	21	(.93)
Medium high SES	18	(2.03)	24	(.95)
High SES	37	(3.52)	32	(1.02)

serving other special education students, those serving students with emotional or behavioral disorders are less likely to work in elementary schools (35% vs. 48%). Second, they are more likely than their colleagues to be working in separate special education schools. Whereas only 6% of those special educators serving all other specialties work in separate schools, 16% of the teachers of students with emotional or behavioral disorders do so. This larger proportion of teachers in separate schools may have implications for the degree of isolation that these special educators may feel.

A further difference between teachers of students with emotional or behavioral disorders and other special educators is their geographic distribution. Although many teachers in both groups work in rural, small city, suburban, and urban settings, teachers in this group are far more likely to be working in urban schools (31% vs. 19%) and far less likely to be working in rural schools (10% vs. 24%). This geographic differential is not simply an artifact of variation in socioeconomic status, which does not differ systematically across the two teacher groups; rather, it probably reflects a disproportionate identification of children with emotional or behavioral disorders in urban schools.

Attitudes Toward Teaching and Working Conditions

The SASS includes many items that tap teachers' opinions about their jobs and working conditions. Table 6.4 presents the distribution of responses to 15 questions concerning teachers' relationships with authority, peers, and parents. Within

TABLE 6.4
Attitudes and Beliefs of Teachers of Emotionally Disturbed Students Toward Peers, Authority, and Parents, by Percentage of Teachers of ED Students

	Percentage Who:			
Attitudes and Beliefs	*Strongly Agree*	*Somewhat Agree*	*Somewhat Disagree*	*Strongly Disagree*
Relationship with authority				
Principal enforces school rules	52	32	10	6
Principal gets resources	52	28	16	4
Principal informs staff of expectations	48	35	12	5
Principal knows kind of school he or she wants	44	36	16	5
Administration is supportive and encouraging	38	38	18	6
School goals and priorities are clear	37	42	16	5
Teachers are fairly evaluated	31	53	11	6
Staff is recognized for a job well done	23	45	21	11
Teachers participate in important decisions	16	40	27	17
Principal talks to teachers about teaching	12	35	32	21
Relationship with peers				
Courses coordinated with other teachers	45	45	8	2
Lots of cooperation among staff	29	46	19	6
Colleagues share beliefs about school mission	23	60	13	4
Consistent rules for student behavior	19	38	28	15
Relationship with parents				
Parents are supportive	10	28	29	33

these three substantive groups, we have sorted the items by the degree to which the teachers of students with emotional and behavioral disorders endorsed the statement.

First examine the items concerning the principal. Teachers agree most emphatically with statements that describe their principal as a manager—as an individual who enforces rules, gets resources, and informs staff about expectations. Items that describe principals as instructional coaches and teachers as participators in the decision-making process receive less endorsement. For example, over half the teachers of students with emotional or behavioral disorders disagreed with the statement that their "principal talks to teachers about teaching," and nearly half disagreed with the statement that "teachers participate in important decisions." It is clear that for many teachers of students with emotional or behavioral disorders, the principal is a manager who does not involve them in the decision-making processes of the school.

Relationships with colleagues appear reasonably satisfactory. Only 10% of these teachers reported that their courses are not coordinated with colleagues; only 25% reported that there is not a lot of cooperation among staff. If there is an area in which these teachers reported an inconsistency with their peers, it is the matter of consistently enforcing rules about student behavior. An estimated 43% disagreed with the statement "rules for student behavior are consistently enforced by teachers in this school, even for students who are not in their classes." Given the student population that these teachers serve, it is probably not surprising that they find their peers to be most inconsistent in this regard.

Parents, however, are clearly problematic for teachers of students with emotional or behavioral disorders. Almost two thirds disagreed with the statement "I receive a great deal of support from parents for the work I do;" one third disagreed strongly. To place this finding in context, consider that of the 15 items in Table 6.4, it is for the item concerning parents with which these teachers reported the most dissatisfaction. Indeed, in comparison to data not reported here on general educators, it is clear that these teachers feel far less support from their students' parents than they would like.

Another perspective on these teachers' work lives can be obtained by examining their responses to a series of items that asked them about how much control they had over their classroom and how much control teachers in their school had over school governance (see Table 6.5). Teachers of students with emotional or behavioral disorders reported having a great deal of control over many aspects of classroom life. Nearly 90% reported having a great deal of control over the amount of homework assigned and teaching techniques; approximately 75% reported having a similar amount of control over discipline, content, skills, texts, and materials.

But when it comes to school policy—on issues ranging from curriculum and discipline to decisions concerning the grouping of students—teachers of students with emotional or behavioral disorders reported that they (and their colleagues)

TABLE 6.5
Perceptions of Teacher Influence and Help, by Percentage of Teachers of ED Students

	Percentage With Each Level of Control		
	Great Deal	*Some*	*None*
Teachers' control in school			
Teachers' influence in curriculum	38	40	22
Teachers' influence in discipline	34	43	24
Teachers' influence in planning inservices	34	37	29
Teachers' influence in grouping decisions	29	36	35
Teacher's control in own classroom			
Teacher's control over amount of homework	89	9	2
Teacher's control over teaching techniques	88	9	3
Teacher's control over discipline	71	22	7
Teacher's control over content and skills	67	27	6
Teacher's control over texts and materials	66	22	12

have far less control. Of particular concern is their response to the items concerning "setting policy on grouping students in classes by ability," which may serve as an indicator of the degree to which teachers perceive that they influence major instructional policy. Over one third reported that teachers in their school had no actual influence over this important placement decision.

Teachers were also asked to rate the severity—in their school—of 12 specific problems that teachers might face. As shown in Table 6.6, the problem these teachers identified as most serious was the verbal abuse of teachers, followed by student absenteeism, drug abuse, and physical conflicts between students. Far lower percentages of teachers reported actual violent crimes as problematic. It is worth reiterating, however, that this survey was conducted during the 1987–88 school year. Given the recent increases in violent crime in schools, these rankings may differ considerably under the present social climate.

How do these perceptions and attitudes toward teaching compare to those reported by other special educators? Rather than compare responses on an item-by-item basis, we created six scales using the items presented in the SASS questionnaire. (A detailed description of the procedures for variable development is available from the authors.) As shown in Table 6.7, the six scales are: ATTADMIN (comprised of the 10 items in Table 6.4 that describe the teacher's attitude towards the school's administrators and principal); ATTSTAFF (comprised of the 4 items in Table 6.4 that describe the teacher's attitude toward his or her colleagues); STUDPROB (comprised of the 6 items on the student problem checklist in Table 6.6 that do not involve violent behavior); VIOLENCE (comprised of the 6 items on the student problem checklist in Table 6.6 that *do* involve

TABLE 6.6
Perceived Student Problems, by Percentage of Teachers of ED Students

	Percentage Who Rate the Problem as:			
Problem	*Serious*	*Moderate*	*Minor*	*No Problem*
Verbal abuse of teacher	22	27	36	15
Student absenteeism	17	36	31	16
Drug abuse	15	19	31	34
Physical conflicts between students	13	29	42	16
Student tardiness	13	27	36	24
Alcohol use	12	20	28	40
Students cutting class	8	15	30	47
Vandalism	5	17	49	29
Teenage pregnancy	5	13	28	54
Robbery/theft	4	17	52	27
Weapons	4	12	37	47
Physical abuse of teachers	4	9	30	57

TABLE 6.7
Scales of Attitudes and Beliefs of Special Education Teaching Force, by Subject Specialty

	ED Teachers		*All Others*	
Attitude/Belief Scale	*M*	*SE (mean)*	*M*	*SE (mean)*
ATTADMIN	2.0	(.03)	2.0	(.01)
ATTSTAFF	2.01	(.04)	1.91	(.01)
STUDPROB	2.90	(.05)	3.07	(.01)
VIOLENCE	2.96	(.05)	3.21	(.01)
OWNCNTL	4.99	(.05)	5.11	(.02)
TCHRCNTL	3.60	(.08)	3.5	(.03)

violent behavior); TCHRCNTL (comprised of 4 items in Table 6.5 that describe the general control that teachers in the school have); and OWNCNTL (comprised of the 5 items in Table 6.5 that describe the specific control that this teacher has over his or her own classroom).

Using these six measures, we compared the responses of teachers of students with emotional or behavioral disorders to other special educators. Although the observed differences between the estimated means for the two groups of special educators with regard to their attitudes toward the administration (ATTADMIN) or teacher control over schoolwide decisions (TCHRCNTL) were well within the limits of sampling variation, we did find statistically significant differences ($p < .05$) on the remaining four measures. In each case, teachers of students with emotional or behavioral disorders gave responses that were less positive: They had fewer positive words for their colleagues (ATTSTAFF), reported that they had less control over their classroom (OWNCNTL), and identified more student problems of both a nonviolent (STUDPROB) and violent (VIOLENT) nature. These comparisons reveal that teachers of students with emotional or behavioral disorders are indeed different in many regards from their colleagues who serve all other special education students.

IMPLICATIONS

What have we learned about teachers of students with emotional or behavioral disorders? What implications does this evidence have for administrators and policymakers concerned with the work lives of these educators? Rather than recapitulate our findings, we highlight the three specific areas we believe are most worthy of attention.

These data provide some of the first nationally generalizable information on the qualifications of teachers providing educational services to students with emotional or behavioral disorders. On this count, the news is not good. Many of these teachers have advanced degrees, but far too few are actually certified to be serving the types of students that they do. Although provisional and temporary certification are a problem throughout special education, the data presented here show that the problem is especially severe among those serving students with emotional or behavioral disorders. A staggering 43% of these teachers report not holding permanent regular certification in the field of emotional or behavioral disorders. Yes, a school district may occasionally have to resort to hiring teachers with less than full certification, but this should not be true in 4 out of 10 instances. We need to develop policies to increase the number of teachers who are qualified to work with these students.

Will this need remain if we move away from a categorical system? We believe that it will. Our belief stems from our finding concerning these teachers' self-reported assessment of their qualifications for working with students who have emotional or behavioral disorders. More than 25% of the teachers whose primary assignment was to work with students with emotional or behavioral disorders reported that this was not the field in which they were best qualified or second best qualified. Although this is not an admission of incompetence, it does suggest that certification alone is not the issue. Even without the labels, these teachers would continue to report that they are not best qualified to be working with these students. The need for better training and preparation is clear. We need more teachers to work with these students, and those that we need must be better trained.

A second issue is the role that administrators play in the lives of teachers of students with emotional or behavioral disorders. More often than not, these special educators see their principals as managers, not coaches. Although the characterization of their principals is no different from the characterization offered by colleagues in other special education fields, it is also clearly not entirely satisfactory. Too many teachers report that their principals do not talk to them about teaching. Too many report that they are not recognized for a job well done. Too many feel left out of the important decisions made in their schools. In fairness to recent efforts at school reform, these data were collected several years ago, before some of the more innovative initiatives took hold. Yet it seems clear that these teachers' relationships with their building-level administrators need rethinking and rebuilding.

Finally, we would like to draw attention to an area of concern that we touched on only lightly: parents. In their survey of teachers of students with emotional or behavioral disorders, McManus and Kauffman (1991) found that lack of support from parents was a particular concern. So, too, we found that nearly two thirds of the teachers of these students reported that parents are not supportive of their efforts. This percentage is vastly different from that found among regular educators. It is not clear whether parents of these students have become disenfranchised from the system, have been forced to become adversaries in the hopes of receiving better services for their children, or whether they have simply become apathetic and nonparticipatory. But for whatever reason, the concern must be addressed. Teachers need parents to support their efforts. If they are in conflict, then the children will lose out.

REFERENCES

Algozzine, B., Hendrickson, J. M., Gable, R. A., & White, R. (1993). Caseloads of teachers of students with behavioral disorders. *Behavioral Disorders, 13*, 103–109.

Bensky, J. M., Shaw, S. F., Gouse, A. S., Bates, H., Dixon, B., & Beane, W. E. (1980). Public law 94-142 and stress: A problem for educators. *Exceptional Children, 47*, 24–29.

Billingsley, B. S. (1993). Teacher retention and attrition in special and general education: Research findings and issues. *The Journal of Special Education, 27*, 137–174.

Billingsley, B. S., & Cross, L. H. (1991). Teachers' decisions to transfer from special education to general education. *The Journal of Special Education, 24*, 496–511.

Billingsley, B. S., & Cross, L. H. (1992). Predictors of commitment, job satisfaction, and intent to stay in teaching: A comparison of general and special educators. *The Journal of Special Education, 25*, 453–471.

Boe, E. E., Bobbit, S. E., & Cook, L. H. (1993, May). *Whither didst thou go? Retention, reassignment, migration, and attrition of special and general education teachers in national perspective.* Paper presented at the Meeting of the Council for Exceptional Children, San Antonio, TX.

Breton, W. A., & Donaldson, G. A. (1991). Too little, too late? The supervision of Maine resource room teachers. *The Journal of Special Education, 25*, 114–125.

Byrne, B. M. (1991). Burnout: Investigating the impact of background variables for elementary, intermediate, secondary, and university educators. *Teaching and Teacher Education, 7*, 197–209.

Carnegie Forum on Education and the Economy: Task Force on Teaching as a Profession. (1986). *A nation prepared: Teachers for the 21st century.* New York: Author.

Chandler, H. N. (1983). The loneliness of the special education teacher. *The Journal of Learning Disabilities, 16*, 126–127.

Choy, S. P., Bobbitt, S. A., Henke, R. R., Medrich, E. A., Horn, L. J., & Lieberman, J. (1993). *America's teachers: Profile of a profession.* Washington, DC: National Center for Education Statistics.

Crane, S. J., & Iwanicki, E. F. (1986). Perceived role conflict, role ambiguity, and burnout among special education teachers. *Remedial and Special Education, 7*(2), 24–31.

Cross, L. H. & Billingsley, B. S. (1994). Testing a model of special educators' intent to stay in teaching. *Exceptional Children, 60*, 411–421.

Dangel, H. L., Bunch, A. W., & Coopman, M. P. (1987). Attrition among teachers of learning disabled students. *Learning Disabilities Focus, 2*, 80–86.

Fimian, M. J. (1986). Social support and occupational stress in special education. *Exceptional Children, 52*, 436–442.

Fimian, M. J., & Santoro, T. M. (1983). Sources and manifestations of occupational stress as reported by full-time special education teachers. *Exceptional Children, 49*, 540–543.

Frank, A. R., & Keith, T. Z. (1984). Academic abilities of persons entering and remaining in special education. *Exceptional Children, 51*, 76–77.

Heyns, B. (1988). Educational defectors: A first look at teacher attrition in the NLS-72. *Educational Researcher, 17*(3), 24–32.

Johnson, A. B., Gold, V., & Vickers, L. L. (1982). Stress on teachers of the learning disabled, behavior disordered and educable mentally retarded. *Psychology in the Schools, 19*, 552–557.

Johnson, S. M. (1986). Incentives for teachers: What motivates, what matters. *Educational Adminstration Quarterly, 22*(3), 54–79.

Johnson, S. M. (1990). *Teachers at work: Achieving success in our schools*. New York: Basic Books.

Kalton, G. (1983). *Introduction to survey sampling*. Beverly Hills, CA: Sage.

Lauritzen, P. (1990). *Wisconsin teachers supply and demand: An examination of data and trends*. Madison, WI: Department of Public Instruction.

Laurtizen, P., & Friedman, S. J. (1991). Teachers for children with emotional/behavioral disorders: Education's greatest challenge? *Preventing School Failure, 35*(2), 11–15.

Lawrenson, G. M., & McKinnon, A. J. (1982). A survey of classroom teachers of the emotionally disturbed: Attrition and burnout factors. *Behavioral Disorders, 8*, 41–49.

Lee, E. S., Forthofer, R. N., & Lorimor, R. J. (1989). *Analyzing complex survey data*. Beverly Hills, CA: Sage.

Lortie, D. (1975). *Schoolteacher: A sociological study*. Chicago: University of Chicago Press.

McKnab, L. (1989). *Attrition of special education personnel in Kansas for 1988–89*. Unpublished report, Emporia State Univeristy, Division of Psychology and Special Education, Emporia, KS.

McLaughlin, M. J., Valdivieso, C. H., Spence, K. L., & Fuller, B. C. (1988). Special education teacher preparation: A synthesis of four research studies. *Exceptional Children, 55*, 215–221.

McManus, M. E., & Kauffman, J. M. (1991). Working conditions of teachers of students with behavioral disorders: A national survey. *Behavioral Disorders, 16*, 247–259.

Murnane, R. J., Singer, J. D., Willett, J. B, Olsen, R. J., & Kemple, J. J. (1991). *Who will teach? Policies that matter*. Cambridge, MA: Harvard Unversity Press.

National Academy of Science. (1992). *Teacher supply, demand, and quality: Policy issues, models, and data bases*. Washington, DC: National Academy Press.

Office of Special Education and Rehabilitative Services. (1991). *Thirteenth Annual Report to Congress on the Implementation of PL 94-142*. Washington, DC: U.S. Department of Education.

Olson, J., & Matuskey, P. V. (1982). Causes of burnout in SLD teachers. *Journal of Learning Disabilities, 15*, 97–99.

Platt, J. M., & Olson, J. (1990). Why teachers are leaving special education. *Teacher Education and Special Education, 13*, 192–196.

Rosenholtz, S. J. (1989). Workplace conditions that affect teacher quality and commitment: Implications for teacher induction programs. *The Elementary School Journal, 89*, 421–439.

Sattler, E. L., & Sattler, J. L. (1985). Economic realities of special education. *Teacher Education and Special Education, 8*, 98–103.

Schetz, K. F., & Billingsley, B. S. (1992). Speech-language pathologists' perceptions of adminstrative support and non-support. *Language, Speech, and Hearing Services in Schools, 23*, 153–158.

Schlechty, P. C., & Vance, V. S. (1981). Do academically_able teachers leave education? The North Carolina case. *Phi Delta Kappan, 63*, 106–117.

Schofer, R. C., & Duncan, J. R. (1986). A study of certain personnel preparation factors in special education. *The Journal of Special Education, 20*, 61–68.

Schrag, J. A. (1989). *The adequacy of current and projected special education personnel supply in Washington state*. Olympia, WA: Division of Special Services and Support Programs.

Singer, J. D. (1993a). Are special educators' career paths special? Results from a 13-year longitudinal study. *Exceptional Children, 59*, 262–279.

Singer, J. D. (1993b). Once is not enough: Former special educators who return to teaching. *Exceptional Children, 60*, 58–72.

Smith-Davis, J., Burke, P. J., & Noel, M. (1984). *Personnel to educate the handicapped in America: Supply and demand from a programmatic viewpoint*. College Park, MD: University of Maryland, Institute for the Study of Exceptional Children and Youth.

Zabel, R. J., & Zabel, M. K. (1982). Factors in burnout among teachers of exceptional children. *Exceptional Children, 49*, 261–263.

CHAPTER

7

Teachers' Participation in Decisions About Placement of Students with Emotional or Behavioral Disorders

John Wills Lloyd
Kerri F. Martin
James M. Kauffman
University of Virginia

Students identified as having emotional or behavioral disorders and requiring special education are frequently placed in settings seen as more restrictive than their home schools and regular classes (Forness, 1989). In a national study of education of students with disabilities in separate facilities, Stephens, Lakin, Brauen, and O'Reilly reported that "by far, the largest group of residential facility students were those with emotional disturbance (52 percent)" (1990, p. I.46; see also chap. 3, this volume).

Some of these children and youth are moved into or out of such more restrictive environments on the recommendations of professionals other than educators, sometimes by professionals working entirely outside the realm of education. For example, physicians, psychologists, and counselors, whether in private practice or employed by public agencies, may refer children and youth to day and residential facilities. But some students are placed in such facilities primarily on the recommendation of educators as a result of changes in their individualized education programs (IEPs).

Teachers are by law supposed to play an important role in the development and implementation of IEPs. Thus, to understand issues in the placement of children and youth in more and less restrictive environments, it is important to understand teachers' views of these placements and their participation in making placement recommendations. In this chapter, we review the professional and research literature regarding teachers' decisions about placements. How do teachers view alternative placements? What is the rationale for teachers' participation in placement decisions? To what extent are teachers thought to participate in placement decisions, and to what extent do they actually participate in placement decisions? How much influence do teachers have on placement decisions, and what factors affect their influence?

TEACHERS' VIEWS OF PLACEMENTS

As any casual visitor to a teachers' lounge probably knows, teachers have quite diverse opinions about the appropriateness of placements of students who need special education services. In the same way that advocates of various positions about many other issues differ, teachers disagree about the advisability of placing students with problems in more or less restrictive environments. Some teachers may argue strongly for placing students in regular classrooms, considering them the least-restrictive alternative and, therefore, the most beneficial for individuals with disabilities. Others may argue passionately that consideration of the needs of other students in regular classrooms, as well as the welfare of students with special needs, makes alternative placements of many students with disabilities preferable.

Teachers' views of appropriate placement are apparently different from the views of administrators and psychologists, depending on the problems students manifest. Pfeiffer and Naglieri (1984) compared the placement recommendations of three groups—special education teachers, school administrators, and school psychologists—to whom they gave brief case descriptions of students exhibiting various types of problems. The researchers then rated the restrictiveness of the placements recommended by the three groups. Although they reported no statistical analyses of placement recommendation by type of problem, they reported analyses showing that there were no significant differences among the three professional groups in the overall restrictiveness of the placements they recommended. They did find, however, a significant interaction between type of handicapping condition and professional group; administrators and psychologists, but not teachers, recommended substantially less restrictive placements for a case with less severe problems (Pfeiffer and Naglieri labeled this case "learning disabled") than they did for either the case with the lowest IQ or the case with "significant 'conduct and personality' problems" (p. 63). These data may be interpreted as suggesting that teachers are less likely than administrators or psychologists to base placement decisions on the types or severity of problems manifested by students.

Other research has shown that teachers' views of appropriate placement are, in fact, quite varied or heterogeneous, not merely different from those of other professionals working in the schools (i.e., administrators and psychologists). For example, Martin, Lloyd, Kauffman, and Coyne (in press) reported the results of intensive interviews with 14 regular and special education teachers about their views of placement decisions. The teacher informants provided highly varied perspectives on topics related to serving students with emotional or behavioral disorders in regular education settings, as illustrated in Table 7.1.

We should not be surprised to find considerable variance in teachers' opinions, for they are simply opinions, not truths. However, we probably would benefit from a better understanding of teachers' opinions about placement alternatives, as their opinions may influence their recommendations about placements. We need to know how teachers' opinions about placements are formed, how they change over time, and what influence they exert on placement decisions. Regardless of their opinions, teachers must be among the group of people who determine placement if they are to have influence on placement decisions.

WHY TEACHERS SHOULD PARTICIPATE IN DECIDING PLACEMENTS

Arguably, teachers should be one of the primary sources of information used in determining the placement of students in more and less restrictive environments. Teachers' experiences in such environments and the students who are assigned to them should provide an important basis for understanding the benefits and

TABLE 7.1
Divergent Views About Issues Related to Placement, Expressed by Teachers

Topic	*One View*	*Another View*
Views about different settings	*Teacher of a certain class:* I think part of the problem is that we've held back on self-containing these children who have emotional problems because we haven't liked what has gone on in self-contained programs—because we think we know that they won't get any better, they'll probably just maintain their inappropriate behavior now they're with a bunch of other kids who are acting this way and they can feed off each other and learn "new and improved" bizarre behavior and we've held back.	*Different teacher in xyz area* (about a problem student): The EMH classroom is not an appropriate placement. He's not integrated with any of his peers, which he really needs. He needs to learn the social skills, he needs to get along with his peers. You know, he's hitting kids, he's hitting teachers, I mean, the most appropriate placement is where he's at so he'll stay, but everybody's angry about it.
Views about restrictiveness	*Susan* (about special ed. teachers' feelings about sending students to more restrictive placements): It's a failure mentality, too. It's like we have to send this kid out because we haven't been able to fix his problem here, so you're kind of a little edgy on that too. And it's not necessarily that we feel like it's our fault, but then again we didn't fix it.	*Linda:* I think also, to me, a restrictive setting is really dealing with the behaviors on more of a regular full-time basis. Whereas in a classroom setting you try, at least I think so, one is trying to get them to the point where they can integrate into some of the other less restrictive classrooms, like an LD classroom.

limitations of more restrictive environments. Furthermore, their expertise should carry considerable weight in making decisions about placements into or out of the programs provided in these environments. The importance of teachers' participation in decisions about placement is recognized in federal regulations governing special education, and other education professionals emphasize the critical nature of teachers' participation.

By law, teachers must participate in decisions about placement of students with emotional or behavioral disorders (see chap. 12, this volume). Teachers' participation was an original component of efforts to bring sense to the provision of educational programs for students with disabilities. We should hasten to note, too, that decisions about placement are, by law, to occur during the planning of educational programs, not during evaluations of eligibility. Bateman (1992) illustrated the relationship among decisions about eligibility and placement clearly by referring to legs of a triangle (see Fig. 7.1). As shown in the figure, the first order of business is determining whether a student is eligible for services; this decision must be made without reference to whether those services are available. Later, at the time of the development of the individualized education plan, the specific services must be described and only then is the place in which the services will be delivered to be specified.

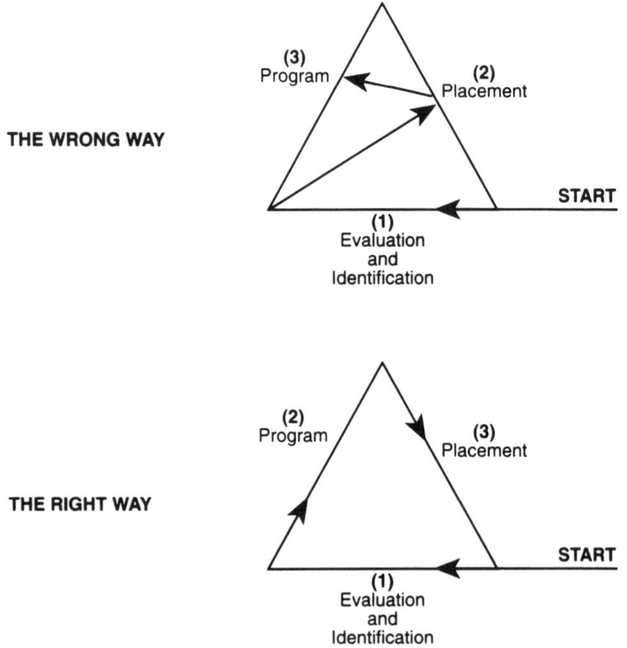

FIG. 7.1. The three steps in the process of providing an appropriate public education (from Bateman, 1992).1

The rationale for stipulating that teachers participate in placement decisions should, then, be patently obvious. Such decisions are made at the time of planning an educational program, and it would be hard to contend that there is any group whose members are more appropriately qualified to contribute to those decisions than are teachers. Few, if any, adults other than teachers have a more intimate understanding of the educational needs of an individual with emotional or behavioral disorders. To be sure, psychologists may have opinions about the characteristics of individual students, but these are usually based only on brief contact during testing or observation; despite their laudable efforts to deliver direct services (e.g., Sheridan & Kratochwill, 1991), psychologists and counselors rarely spend as many hours each day with individual students as do teachers. Administrators may see students with emotional or behavioral disorders whenever they are sent to the office for disciplinary reasons, but these contacts may be as infrequent as those of psychologists and counselors. Perhaps the only adults who spend as much time with a student with emotional or behavioral disorders as do teachers are the students' own parents or guardians (and their participation in the placement decision phase of an individual education plan is stipulated in law as well); as much as parents may contribute to placement decisions about their child, they do not have the broad perspective about students' behavior that is common to teachers, who may see 10 to 150 students per day.

PROFESSIONALS' VIEWS OF WHETHER TEACHERS SHOULD PARTICIPATE

Our discussion to this point suggests that we should expect to see teachers participating as members of any team charged with making decisions about the placement of students with emotional or behavioral disorders. Such an expectation is consistent with the views held by special education administrators about teachers' roles in such decisions. In a survey of directors of special education for local education agencies (LEAs), Poland, Thurlow, Ysseldyke, and Mirkin (1982) asked their informants what educators should be included on a team of four people charged with making placement decisions (parents were assumed to be a fifth member of the team). The special education administrators identified regular education teachers (80%) and special education teachers (72%) as appropriate members of the team more often than any other groups, including psychologists (64%) and administrators (51%). Poland et al. noted that "these four professionals are the same four professionals mentioned most frequently as participating in placement team decisions" (p. 176).

An important observation here is that as many as one in five administrators did not include regular education teachers and as many as one in four did not include special education teachers on their ideal teams for making placement decisions. To be sure, the data from the Poland et al. (1981) study are dated, and we can hope that this accounts for the inappropriate absence of teachers from administrators' ideal placement decision teams. However, there surely are other reasons that administrators may exclude teachers. One possible reason is that teachers may advocate more restrictive placements than do administrators (Pfeiffer & Naglieri, 1984), thus making recommendations that come into conflict with other factors (e.g., cost of placements) to which administrators give greater emphasis.

DO TEACHERS PARTICIPATE IN PLACEMENT DECISIONS?

That we ask this question implies an answer other than "yes." Despite the legal stipulation that teachers *must* participate and the consensual (if not unanimous) view that they *should* participate, teachers are not always included in teams making placement decisions.

The participants in placement teams reported by Poland et al. (1982) differed from the composition of the ideal team described by LEA administrators in their study. Comparison of the actual participation (as reported by administrators) by special education teachers (85%), regular education teachers (78%), psychologists (81%), and administrators (89%) with the LEA administrators' ideal team membership reveals percentages bordering on statistical significance, $\chi^2(3, N = 97) = 5.51, p < .10$. Examining the percentages reveals that psychologists and administrators (probably school principals) participate in making placement decisions more frequently than the LEA administrators think that they should.

Further data about teachers' participation in placement decisions were provided by Vacc et al. (1985), who observed interactions during IEP conferences for 47 students. They found that special education teachers were present at all of the conferences and that regular classroom teachers were present at about 25% of the meetings. In fact, Vacc et al. reported that only 6 of the 47 meetings were in compliance with rules and regulations regarding participants.

Placement was discussed at nearly all of the meetings, but placement was the topic of discussion for only about 7% of the time. Integration plans were discussed at 41 of the 47 meetings and were the topic of discussion for about 5% of the time.

Vacc et al. noted that approximately 33% of parents' participation involved passive responding (e.g., head nodding), but only 3% of special education teachers' responses were passive. Whereas parents and both regular and special education teachers devoted a plurality of their discussion to children's academic and social functioning, they devoted less than 10% of their discussion to placement. Regular class teachers were the only group for which Vacc et al. reported percentages of discussion devoted to placement and integration, and these topics were discussed infrequently.

The results reported by Poland et al. (1981) and Vacc et al. (1985) obviously can not be considered conclusive. First, practices presumably have changed since the studies were conducted. For example, perhaps replication of Poland et al. (1981) would reveal more or fewer LEA administrators saying that teachers participate in placement teams. Second, we do not know to what extent the reports from LEA administrators represented reality. Even those district-level administrators who work overtime are unlikely to be able to collect precise data about participation in IEP meetings. To be sure, we ought to be able to get a more complete look at the composition of placement teams by examining compliance data, as suggested by the Vacc et al. (1985) report. Such studies would help to clarify which teachers (those with regular classroom or special classroom assignments) participate in placement decisions and the extent of their participation. However, even if teachers are attending team meetings and participating, they may not have much actual influence on placement decisions.

TEACHERS' INFLUENCE ON PLACEMENT DECISIONS

How much influence do teachers have on placement decisions? When asked who was involved in making the decision to reintegrate students, the teachers responding to a survey by Smith, White, and Peterson (1979) most frequently cited special education teachers (91%), regular classroom teachers (70%), and principals (63%); parents (57%), the students themselves (54%), special education consultants (54%), and psychologists (49%) were less likely to be involved; and social workers (30%), counselors (25%), mental health workers (8%), representatives of other schools (4%), and special education settings (3%) were least likely to be involved.

These data indicate that Smith et al.'s informants saw themselves as participating in the placement decisions when students were to be reintegrated into regular classrooms (see also Peterson, Smith, White, & Zabel, 1980). Because of the way the question was asked, however, it is not clear to what extent the teachers saw themselves as influential in the decisions. Nevertheless, the high percentage of teachers indicating that they were involved implies substantial influence.

Two observations about these findings are important. First, the data from the Smith et al. (1979) report are dated and specific to one state; teachers' roles in making placement decisions may have changed since the time Smith et al. conducted their survey or may be different in different states. (Compare this sample with the discussion of samples in chap. 6, this volume.) Second, Smith et al. specifically asked about reintegration; teachers' participation in and views about placement decisions may differ according to whether a student is moving into or out of a special education setting.

Participants in meetings convened to develop individualized education programs consider special education teachers to have the most influence in those meetings (Gilliam, 1979; Gilliam & Coleman, 1981). In the Gilliam study, the "survey was made of 130 participants at 27 educational planning committee meetings [and was] . . . conducted in three medium sized school districts . . . in southeastern Michigan" (p. 466). In the Gilliam and Coleman studies, "the survey, conducted in three school districts in southeastern Michigan, included 130 participants at 27 IEP meetings" (p. 642). Unfortunately, the brief reports of these studies do not reveal what positions those participants held. Given that they were present at IEP meetings, however, one must suspect that the participants included teachers, parents, and perhaps school psychologists and administrators.

However, Clark-Chiarelli and Singer (chap. 6, this volume) examined data from the School and Staffing Survey (SASS) and reported that nearly half of the teachers of students with emotional or behavioral disorders believed that their principals did not allow them to participate in important decisions. Similarly, they reported that fewer than one in three teachers of students with emotional or behavioral disorders believed they had great influence on decisions about grouping students, and nearly an equal proportion believed that they had no influence in these decisions.

The results of the Poland et al. (1982) study imply that administrators such as principals may have greater influence in placement decisions than do teachers. Surely, it is appropriate for principals to influence placements in their schools. But, to the extent that this is true, it may be that teachers have less influence in decisions about placements, deferring to the more powerful positions held by psychologists and administrators. Perhaps the influence of teachers in placement decisions is moderated by whether a student is moving into or out of a more restrictive placement.

Indeed, Martin et al. (in press) reported that the teachers they interviewed felt they had little influence in placement decisions. Teachers told Martin et al. that new students essentially appeared unannounced at their classroom doors, or that students who had been receiving services in outside settings for a limited time, such as residential schools or hospitals, sometimes unexpectedly reappeared in their classrooms with no information forthcoming from the outside agency. Perhaps even more disturbing was the claim made by some teachers that they were often left out of the decision-making process because decisions were made informally, outside of meetings. The teachers who were interviewed suggested several factors that they thought influence how decisions of where to place students are sometimes made, including consideration of placements for which insurance companies will pay; overutilization of existing, easily accessible facilities and services; responding to what they perceived as popular trends (e.g., inclusion) rather than considering the educational needs of individual students; and responding to pressure from others (e.g., parents, court or hospital officials) who may not understand students' educational needs as well as their teachers do.

WHAT FACTORS AFFECT TEACHERS' INFLUENCE ON PLACEMENT DECISIONS?

Presumably, teachers have greater influence on placement decisions under some conditions than they have under other conditions. What do we know about those conditions, about the factors that affect teachers' influence? In their interviews with teachers, Martin et al. identified at least two bases for the theme of teachers feeling that did not have influence on placement decisions.

Teachers reported that they had limited knowledge about placement options. One teacher said that her school division was planning a major shift in approach to placements, but she had not been consulted about it. Another highly experienced secondary school teacher, charged with participating in decisions about placements, said she simply was unfamiliar with the characteristics of the more restrictive placements used by her school district.

Teachers reported that overloaded schedules made it impossible for them to participate. A regular education teacher said that she may get invited to an IEP meeting if her view meshes with the view of the psychologist, social worker, and resource teacher. Another said that she does not even get to participate in meetings. Other teachers complained that IEP meetings were scheduled for times when it was impossible for them to attend.

Although these teachers stopped short of claiming an outright conspiracy to exclude them from the decisions about placing students with disabilities in less restrictive settings, there is an implication that teachers think placement decisions are made without their advice or consent. Movement of students into less restrictive placements are unlikely to succeed under such conditions.

However, the variance in reintegration efforts is not affected solely by receiving teachers' participation in the process. Rock, Rosenberg, and Carran (1993) examined variables affecting rates of reintegration of students with emotional or behavioral disorders. They studied teachers in separate schools or special wings of schools devoted exclusively to students with severe levels of disorder. After accounting for the proportion of variance attributable to other factors (i.e., program orientation toward reintegration, program demographics, and teachers' demographic characteristics), Rock et al. reported that teachers' attitudes and opinions about reintegration did not significantly contribute to the probability of reintegration.

However, among the variables that Rock et al. (1993) reported as explaining the greatest proportion of the variance in rate of reintegration were two relevant to our discussion here. They found that special education teachers who have opportunities to become familiar with the expectations for students in mainstream classes and who are able to influence the choice of mainstream classes where their students will be placed are likely to have higher rates of reintegration. These results stand in contrast to other data (Clark-Chiarelli & Singer, this volume; Martin et al., in press) indicating that teachers say they have little influence on placement decisions and are unfamiliar with placement alternatives.

The findings of Rock et al. (1993) are consistent with other evidence. When Smith, White, and Peterson (1979) surveyed 76 teachers in Iowa about the reintegration of students with emotional or behavioral disorders, they found that fewer than one in three teachers (30%) reported that they had time set aside to plan reintegration of students and that fewer than one in seven teachers (13%) said that regular education teachers had received inservice training prior to reintegration efforts. Given these results, we can integrate the disparate findings. Teachers who are more familiar with alternative placements, particularly those who have sufficient time to plan (including planning efforts to move students from one setting to another), are more likely to see themselves as informed and able to contribute to making placement decisions. Differences in teachers' views of their own potency may, indeed, have to do with how much opportunity they have to make informed contributions to the process.

Zabel, Peterson, Smith, and White (1982) surveyed teachers of students with emotional or behavioral disorders and other teachers who were likely to have students with such disorders in their classes. They asked responding teachers which of 15 types of information were available to and used by them in planning programs for these students. Zabel et al. (1982) reported that teachers had substantially more information available to them when they were making decisions about reintegrating students than when they were deciding to place them in more restrictive settings. Whereas teachers reported that all 15 types of information studied by Zabel et al. were available upon reintegration, only two thirds (10) of those sources of information were available when making outplacements.

Probably more important, Zabel et al. (1982) examined the views of teachers about the usefulness of the data available to them. Although teachers considered any information useful, they considered some data more useful than others. Their opinions about utility are particularly important when considered in conjunction with the information available to teachers. The correlation between the information teachers considered available and the information they considered useful was not significant, $r_s < .50$, regardless whether the data were available at the time of decisions regarding placement into more or less restrictive settings. Apparently, the data available to teachers for making placement decisions are not the data they consider useful in making educational decisions.

In summary, teachers are more likely to participate in placement decisions and to have influence on them under several conditions: When they have sufficient, useful, information available to them regarding placement alternatives; when they have opportunities to participate, taking their schedules into consideration; when they are familiar with the expectations for students in different settings; and when they are able to set aside time for planning for the movement of students (i.e., reintegration of students coming from more restrictive environments, or movement of students into more restrictive environments).

DISCUSSION

Studies of teachers and placement decisions reveal some surprising findings. The unexpected or counterintuitive findings center on the extent to which teachers participate in placement decisions and their views about how placement decisions are made. In this chapter we examined this research in order to identify problems in policy and practice and gaps in our knowledge base about placement decisions. Our conclusions focus on these areas.

Problems in Policy and Practice

Federal policy, and many state and local policies as well, are intended to encourage, if not mandate, the participation of teachers in educational placement decisions. Nevertheless, research suggests widespread ignorance or circumvention of these policies. One of the great challenges of special and general education is to implement current policies in ways that achieve the intent of special education law—determination of students' programs and placements by a team of professionals and parents, with substantial weight being given to the judgments of teachers who have worked or will be working with the students day to day. Achieving this goal may require a pervasive change in perceptions of teachers' roles in the identification of and amelioration of disabilities such that teachers' professional judgment is taken more seriously and given more weight in eligibility and placement decisions (cf. Bateman & Chard, chap. 12, this volume; Gerber & Semmel, 1984).

An issue of policy and practice needing particular attention is the articulation of placement decisions involving public schools and other agencies serving students with emotional or behavioral disorders. As Denny et al. (chap. 5, this volume), Lakin and Stephens (chap. 3, this volume) and others (e.g., Martin et al., in press) have indicated, students are often placed in residential or hospital settings directly from regular or special classrooms or returned directly from residential or hospital settings to regular or special classrooms, with little communication between teachers and mental health personnel. Movement along the continuum of alternative placements envisioned by special educators and ensconced in federal special education laws and regulations is often sudden and unanticipated by teachers. To be sure, such moves may often be made on the basis of recommendations by people (e.g., physicians) outside the schools. Still, much more needs to be done to build a system of care and educational support for students with emotional or behavioral disorders that provides smooth, informed transitions from one placement to another.

Research Needs

Only fragmentary and mostly dated data are available regarding the questions we posed at the beginning of this chapter. A variety of research strategies will be needed to provide the information necessary to answer questions about the role of teachers in placement decisions. Studies of the records of meetings in which placements are determined could provide useful information about teachers' involvement, and extant databases from compliance studies could provide the sources for such studies. But these records may not include important documentation (cf. Hallenbeck, Kauffman, & Lloyd, 1993); thus additional work is probably warranted. Further qualitative studies extending those of Martin et al. (in press), in which teachers and others are interviewed regarding their participation in placement decisions, would be useful in revealing perceptions and subjective reports of team participants. The strategy of participant observation, in which the researcher attends actual meetings and records the decision-making process, could add immeasurably to our knowledge of teachers' participation and influence. Finally, we note that current studies from various regions of the nation are needed, as substantial changes may occur over time and great differences in policies and procedures may be seen in different schools.

REFERENCES

Bateman, B. (1992). *Better IEPs.* Creswell, OR: Otter Ink Press.

Forness, S. R. (1989). *Statement of the National Mental Health and Special Education Coalition to the Senate Subcommittee on the Handicapped Regarding the Reauthorization of the Education of the Handicapped Act.* Los Angeles: National Mental Health and Special Education Coalition, Neuropsychiatric Institute and Hospital, University of California at Los Angeles.

Gerber, M. M., & Semmel, M. I. (1984). Teacher as imperfect test: Reconceptualizing the referral process. *Educational Psychologist, 19,* 137–148.

Gilliam, J. E. (1979). Contributions of status rankings of educational planning committee participants. *Exceptional Children, 45,* 466–468.

Gilliam, J. E., & Coleman, M. C. (1981). Contributions of status rankings of educational planning committee participants. *Exceptional Children, 47,* 642–644.

Hallenbeck, B. A., Kauffman, J. M., & Lloyd, J. W. (1993). When, how, and why educational placement decisions are made: Two case studies. *Journal of Emotional and Behavioral Disorders, 1,* 109–117.

Martin, K. F., Lloyd, J. W., Kauffman, J. M., & Coyne, M. (in press). Teachers' perceptions of educational placement decisions for pupils with emotional or behavioral disorders. *Behavioral Disorders.*

Peterson, R. L., Smith, C. R., White, M. A., & Zabel, R. (1980). *Practices used in the reintegration of behavior disordered children in three midwestern states.* Paper presented at the National Topical Conference on Seriously Emotionally Disturbed Children, Minneapolis, MN. (ERIC Document Reproduction Service No. ED 201 122)

Pfeiffer, S. I., & Naglieri, J. A. (1984). Special education placement decisions as a function of professional role and handicapping condition. *Psychology in the Schools, 21,* 61–65.

Poland, S. F., Thurlow, M. L., Ysseldyke, J. E., & Mirkin, P. K. (1982). Current psychoeducational assessment and decision-making practices as reported by directors of special education. *Journal of School Psychology, 20,* 171–179.

Rock, E. E., Rosenberg, M. S., & Carran, D. T. (1993). *Variables affecting the reintegration rate of students with serious emotional disturbance.* Unpublished manuscript, Johns Hopkins University, Baltimore, MD.

Sheridan, S. M., & Kratochwill, T. R. (1991). Behavioral consultation in educational settings. In J. W. Lloyd, N. N. Singh, & A. C. Repp (Eds.), *The regular education initiative: Alternative perspectives on concepts, issues, and models* (pp. 193–210). Sycamore, IL: Sycamore Press.

Smith, C. R., White, M., & Peterson, R. (1979). *Iowa study: Preliminary report: Reintegration of emotionally disabled pupils.* Des Moines, IA: Special Education Division, Department of Public Instruction.

Stephens, S. A., Lakin, K. C., Brauen, M., & O'Reilly, F. (1990). *The study of programs of instruction for handicapped children and youth in day and residential facilities: Vol. I. Overview*. Washington, DC: U.S. Department of Education and Mathematics Policy Research Center.

Vacc, N. A., Vallecorsa, A. L., Parker, A., Bonner, S., Lester, C., Richardson, S., & Yates, C. (1985). Parents' and educators' participation in IEP conferences. *Education and Treatment of Children, 8*, 153–162.

Zabel, R. H., Peterson, R. L., Smith, C. R., & White, M. A. (1982). Availability and usefulness of assessment information for emotionally disabled students. *School Psychology Review, 11*, 433–437.

CHAPTER

8

Parent Participation in and Perception of Placement Decisions

Albert Duchnowski
Kathleen Berg
Krista Kutash
University of South Florida

If this book had been written 10 years earlier, the probability is very high that this chapter would not have been included. The conventional wisdom, at that time, held that parents were probably major contributors to the emotional disorders of their children, their perceptions of placements were affected by their own problems, and they rarely attended meetings anyway, even when invited. During the mid-1980s, the role of the family of children who have behavioral or emotional disorders began a significant transformation. It is still developing, and we are not sure how it will finally take shape. We are sure, however, that the potential contribution of families to the overall treatment of their children, including placement decisions, is powerful and underutilized.

At this time, it is very difficult to present a systematic review of how parents perceive and participate in the placement decisions for their children. As Winton and Bailey (1993) pointed out, "Because a family centered approach is so new, there is not a lengthy history or tradition related to gathering family information. In fact, this is an area in which professionals are searching for measures, strategies, and guidelines" (p. 215). Further, the entire field of study that encompasses children who have emotional and behavioral disorders and their families is frequently characterized as having a paucity of research when compared to other disability groups (Burns & Friedman, 1990). For example, Halpern (1993) reviewed all follow-up studies of postsecondary outcomes of students with disabilities published between 1975 and 1990. Of the 41 studies found, only 4 specifically examined children with emotional and behavioral disorders.

In terms of data about families, two brief examples further illustrate the lack of empirical information. Over a decade ago, systematic research was being done with parents of children who had learning disabilities (McKinney & Hocutt, 1982). Likewise, in the field of developmental disabilities, the extensive work of the Turnbulls with parents is very well known (see, e.g., Turnbull & Turnbull, 1982). In each of these cases, surveys of parents, analyses of their attitudes, and programs to increase family involvement were conducted. Several researchers have been involved in these initiatives, which have encompassed several years. Such an information base does not exist about parents of children who have emotional and behavioral disorders. However, there is the beginning of such a literature, and we plan to present and summarize the current state of the art. The sources of this information vary, with some empirical data, some that is anecdotal, and some information from parent advocacy groups. Our purpose is to give the reader an up-to-date summary of what we know about how parents perceive the placement process and how they participate. We conclude with a discussion of new efforts that are leading the way to enhanced participation by families.

WHAT DO WE KNOW?

The first point that should be examined is whether parent involvement makes any difference in the outcomes for children. Although there is not an overwhelming amount of data to support the positive effect of parents being knowledgeable and involved, several studies are supportive. James Comer extensively examined the positive influence of parents being involved in all aspects of their child's education. Although his early work focused on children who had behavioral disorders and low achievement, he has expanded his model to encompass the whole school and all children, including those with disabilities. After many years and several studies investigating the issue, he concluded that parent involvement is essential for effective schooling of all children (Comer & Haynes, 1991).

More specifically, Sheridan and Kratochwill (1992) found that consulting with parents, eliciting their input, and sharing information can sustain treatment effects for children with behavioral disorders. Further, they found that there were positive changes in the home environment when such an approach was used. Friesen, Koren, and Koroloff (1992) reviewed studies evaluating the effects of parent involvement in decision making. Among the few reports they found were studies by Williams (1988) and Byalin (1990), in which length of placement in restrictive residential settings was significantly reduced as a result of improving the involvement of families in treatment team decision making.

Admittedly, the available evidence is slim. A conclusion seems to be emerging, however, that parent involvement in the decision-making process affecting the educational placement of their children can lead to improved outcomes. Successful outcomes can be enhanced by this involvement, and these outcomes may even extend to improved conditions in the home.

HOW DO PARENTS FEEL?

Again, there are few studies that answer this question directly, but some data do exist. In general, parents of children who have emotional and behavioral disorders are not satisfied with the quality of involvement they have with professionals who make decisions about their children (Friesen, Koren, & Koroloff, 1992). They feel very strongly about wanting choices in how they can be involved and how information about potential placement of their children is shared (Bailey & Blasco, 1991). Further, parents do not like the traditional methods of assessment and information sharing in staff meetings (Summers et al., 1990). They want a more unstructured, conversational approach to what they view as a cold, clinical process. They even suggest that some meetings could take place at home. Several perceptions that parents have of the process are described in the few studies that exist. Some of the studies are empirical and have data that support a basis for these perceptions.

Parents Feel Blamed

Probably the most common feeling that parents have when their child is being placed in a program for children with emotional or behavioral disorders is that they are perceived by professionals as being at fault (Friesen, Koren, & Koroloff, 1992; Friesen & Koroloff, 1990). Whether the message is subtle or more obvious, parents often see the decision to place a child as an attempt by professionals to "undo" the harm that parents have caused. The basis for this attitude of parent blaming by professionals is not difficult to find when the types of materials used to train professionals are examined. We conducted an informal review of the current leading textbooks for preparing teachers of children who have emotional and behavioral disorders and found little support for including families as allies and much about "familial causes of emotional disorders in children." The point we wish to make here is not to be critical of the authors of the textbooks but rather to illuminate the imbalance in the type of information currently available. Part of the problem is the lag in incorporating new information into the most recently published textbooks.

Beginning with Freud (see, e.g., Freud, 1952), Kanner (1943), and perhaps most dramatically, Bettleheim (1967), a series of unsubstantiated, psychodynamic hypotheses were advanced that linked parental behaviors and characteristics with subsequent emotional disorders in their children. These hypotheses were either based on poor science or no science at all (see Friesen & Koroloff, 1990; Schreibman, 1988, for a thorough review of this literature). In spite of overwhelming evidence to the contrary, we are still too often presenting professionals in training with the stereotype of parents who cause emotional disorders in their children. Although there certainly are indications that some parents engage in behaviors that have negative consequences for their child's mental health, too often parents are broadly categorized and implicated. Currently, the field does not have enough training material to offer an alternative to students. For example, the literature that describes strengths-based assessment of families is growing, but it has not reached a level necessary to have a broad impact on the curriculum at universities or in practice.

Parents Are Confused

The information presented to parents during placement meetings is technical and complicated. In addition, the context of the meeting is usually not relaxed, but rather emotionally charged. Such a situation does not enhance understanding on the part of the parents. Williams and Hartlage (1988) examined the degree to which parents understood the diagnostic information presented to them at meetings for placement in classes for children with learning and behavioral disorders. They administered a questionnaire about the diagnostic information to the parents and the diagnostician. There was only 47% agreement between the diagnostician and the parents immediately after the meeting, and this dropped to 44% agreement one week later. This finding supports the frequent anecdotal reports of parents that they do not understand the information being imparted at placement meetings and that professionals use technical jargon much too frequently.

In the summer of 1991, the Office of Special Education Programs (OSEP) and the Council for Exceptional Children held a series of "electronic town meetings" with parents of children who have emotional or behavioral disorders. One of the messages from parents who participated in this meeting was that they want "family-friendly information," by which they meant information in a format that they could understand. This lack of understanding contributes to the general discomfort that parents have in the meeting and leads to an overall lack of involvement in the decision-making process, even when they are present at meetings (Nyberg, 1990).

Parents Feel Patronized and Not Involved

In spite of the guidelines and procedures of the Individuals with Disabilities Education Act (IDEA), parents of children who have emotional and behavioral disorders, in general, do not feel part of the process that places their children in special programs, either in school or in more restrictive residential settings. A few studies have investigated the perceptions and feelings that parents have when they participate in placement decision making. The results are consistent with the reports from family advocacy groups as well as the OSEP town meetings: Parents feel that they are not taken seriously by professionals and that their impressions are not given the same weight as those of teachers and other support personnel (Sonnenschein, 1981). A division develops between the experts and the parents, and parents report feeling stripped of any expertise concerning the complexities of the behavior and emotions of their children (Gallagher & Gallagher, 1985).

Parents also feel that the meeting is "canned," and that they are only invited to give their signature to a plan that has already been determined (Singer & Butler, 1987; Strickland, 1993). There are rarely discussions of alternatives to placement or issues related to least restrictive environment. In an investigation of the decision-making process of Family Service Planning Teams in Florida, Nyberg (1990) and his colleagues found that an informal process developed in these meetings, in which consensus was reached. The parents were given a formal opportunity to agree or disagree with this consensus in only 23% of the observed cases. During informal interviews with parents, it was found that parents often had valuable insights about proposed interventions, but admitted they often agreed to plans that they did not fully understand.

Evidence of parents' perceptions of noninvolvement comes also from results of the National Adolescent and Child Treatment Study (NACTS), conducted by the Center for Children's Mental Health (see Silver et al., 1992). As part of this 7-year longitudinal study of children with serious emotional and behavioral disorders and their families, 534 parents were asked about their perceptions of the needs within the system that cared for their children. The perceived need for more parent involvement in the process was the second most endorsed item, with an expressed need for improved program quality being first (Lardieri, Gaertner, & Green, 1993).

The studies reviewed above reveal a pattern of parents feeling guilty and blamed for the emotional disorders of their children. They do not feel valued by professionals when they express their impressions of the situation, and, more often than not, agree with what they perceive to be an already developed plan that they do not fully understand.

Parents Feel Their Perceptions of Their Child Are Discounted

The perceptions that parents have of the placement process can push the parent–professional relationship to its limit. It can be further exacerbated by the different perceptions of the child's behavior held by parents and teachers. A frequent comment by parents at a placement meeting is that their child does not behave at home the same way teachers describe them as behaving at school. In the past, this type of parent comment was easily dismissed as defensiveness and denial, contributing to the parents' feelings of belittlement described previously. However, there is now a substantial body of empirical evidence that indicates that the source of information about a child is an important factor in assessing the child's behavior (Achenbach, McConaughy, & Howell, 1987).

Although the issues surrounding assessment are discussed in other chapters, we summarize briefly some of the findings describing parent and teacher perceptions of children's behavior as they relate to parents' perceptions of the placement process. As referenced earlier, much of the work in this area has been done by Achenbach and his colleagues (see, e.g., Achenbach, 1985). Briefly, what they have found is that the agreement in behavior ratings differs, depending on the source and situation. For example, two parents and two teachers may have relatively high correlations between their ratings of a child's behavior. In fact, the average correlation in such cases is around .60. On the other hand, the correlations of ratings between a parent and a teacher average around .28 (Achenbach, McConaughy, & Howell, 1987). As Achenbach and his colleagues pointed out, this does not mean that instruments such as behavior checklists that ask both parents and teachers to rate a child's behavior are unreliable or invalid. The results indicate that different informants, in different situations, observe different kinds of behavior, and that these different sources must be taken into account during placement decisions (McConaughy, 1993).

Another type of investigation of the different perspectives of parents and teachers was conducted by Kutash (1991). She examined the relationship among social skills, adaptive functioning, and emotional competence rated by parents and teachers, when applied to children identified as seriously emotionally disturbed. Her findings indicated that teachers do not differentiate between social skills and emotional competence in children who have serious emotional disorders. That is, they rate these as a single factor. Parents, on the other hand, differentiate between these factors and see their children as having various strengths and weaknesses on these domains that are not necessarily correlated.

There is, then, empirical support for the observation previously mentioned that parents often see a different type of behavior at home than teachers see in school. The dismissal of this observation by professionals is unwarranted. The task currently facing the field is to make multisource assessment of children suspected of having emotional or behavioral disorders standard practice, and for parent observations to be treated as valid information critical to the decision-making process.

Parents Feel They Are Treated Without Cultural Sensitivity

A special perception exists for those parents who are members of ethnic and cultural minorities. Solid data are even more scarce in this area, but there is a growing consensus that for parents of color the guilt, confusion, and lack of involvement described earlier is magnified by an overall impression held by these parents that the system is not sensitive to their ethnic and cultural traditions and values (National Mental Health Association, 1989). In an investigation of children of color who have emotional disorders, Cross, Bazron, Dennis, and Isaacs (1989) concluded that children and families of color are the poorest served group, in that they are either served in the most restrictive environments or not served at all. The issues surrounding cultural diversity are fully described in chapter 10 of this text; our purpose here is to validate the issue as a serious concern from the perspective of the perceptions of parents.

One of the forums in which parents of color may express their feelings and concerns is the Mental Health and Special Education Coalition (National Mental

Health Association, 1989). This coalition of families, professionals, and advocacy groups has studied and addressed several issues related to services for children with emotional and behavioral disorders, including the issue of cultural diversity. The coalition reported finding

> patterns of under- and overrepresentation of some groups of ethnically diverse students in programs for children with serious emotional disturbance, inappropriate placements, services in conflict with the values and perceptions of particular cultural groups, low rates of parental involvement, and the ethnic mismatches of children and service providers.... (National Mental Health Association, 1989, p. 7)

The challenges presented to professionals and the service system are formidable. The facts emerging from various studies as well as the perceptions of families of color point to a need for systematic investigation of these issues and the development of innovative corrective measures.

LACK OF PARTICIPATION

Given the perceptions of families described earlier, it is not surprising that they have a low rate of participation in placement decisions. In fact, compared to other disabilities, families of children who have emotional and behavioral disorders have the lowest attendance rate at placement meetings (Palfrey, Walker, Butler, & Singer, 1989; Singer & Butler, 1987). In a study of Family Service Planning Teams in Florida, Nyberg (1990) found that only 31% of families attended meetings to make decisions about their children with emotional and behavioral problems.

The studies cited earlier have identified several factors that contribute to low attendance rates for this group of parents. In addition to the negative perceptions held by parents, there are practical and logistical barriers to attendance. This group of families tends to be the lowest socioeconomically when compared to other disabilities. As a result, the effects of other barriers, such as transportation, can be exacerbated for these families. There is a very high number of single-parent households in this group, with almost half of identified children living in such a family constellation (Silver et al., 1992). When the pressures and responsibilities fall on one parent, time becomes a scarce resource. When all of these factors are taken into account, the diminished participation of families is understandable.

NEW DIRECTIONS

The picture that has emerged from this review is not positive. As we pointed out in our opening section, however, the empirical data contribute only one part to the patchwork of information about parents, their feelings and perceptions, and their participation in the decision-making process that affects their children as well as themselves. The awareness of these conditions for families has resulted in an identifiable movement that is essentially a coalition of families and professionals in the major caregiving systems—education, mental health, child welfare—as well as advocacy groups. As a result of this continuing movement, a new perception by parents is emerging, one in which they see their child and themselves as having many strengths but also in need of support that goes beyond the special education system. They look for a collaborative, integrated system of care that can supply that support, and one that will recognize them as allies in the treatment of their children. Except in a few communities, this service system does not fully exist, so parents must participate in the decision-making process as case managers and advocates for their child. Not all parents are ready for these roles, of course, but when they are, positive things can happen. As an example, we would like to share the following case study of parent participation. The behaviors and diagnosis of the child are not the critical issues—they are the context. This is the story of the second author of this chapter and her family.

MATHIEU'S STORY

At the age of 4, Matt was more than ready for preschool "work," so we enrolled him in a private Montessori preschool. His language skills, which seemed to disappear when he turned 2, had returned stronger than ever, but socially he started having a difficult time. He could not or would not listen to and follow directions. Matt had trouble playing with the other children. He preferred watching, choosing one of the older, calmer kids to mimic, or just being alone and exploring, usually places he was not supposed to be. Matt became more and more "hyper," and his inquisitiveness was becoming impulsive and at times dangerous. By the time Matt was 5½ and ready for first grade, it became evident that he was going to need a more structured setting, so we enrolled him in the local public school.

Between the ages of 5 and 6, Matt's emotional behavior began deteriorating. He was having a lot of behavior problems in school and was prone to temper tantrums and self-destruction. Decision making and concentrating were becoming more and more difficult for Matt. Because of this, we tried transferring him to a local public school, hoping a little more structure and consistency would help him out. We were lucky to have a school with warm, caring teachers and a school psychologist and principal who took the time to find out what Matt needed and what they could do to help him. The school psychologist did not want to label Matt but knew he needed some extra help. He often had Matt come to visit him (unofficially) and tried to help Matt understand some of the things that were going on in the classroom and on the playground. He worked with Matt's teacher on classroom strategies, like having Matt sit near the teacher so that he could concentrate, writing down his assignments to help with follow through, letting him do some of his work orally, and so forth. The principal knew Matt had trouble with transition times, so she would often go to lunch and recess with him and allow Matt to come find her when he felt totally overwhelmed. But the problems continued. Although doing well academically, Matt continued to have problems (even with the interventions) with following directions, remembering school rules, and pretty much anything to do with transitions.

Eventually, we took Matt to a child psychiatrist. After numerous tests, he diagnosed Matt as schizophrenic. Years later I have realized that this was a catch-all diagnosis and the doctor probably did not know what was wrong with Matt. Matt was admitted to a children's unit at a psychiatric hospital. After 2½ months of tests, various medications, and behavior modification programs, we were able to take Matt home. He was 1 month away from his eighth birthday and on enough medication to slow down an average adult. Matt was discharged with an "at-risk" status and no transition plan. He was just supposed to "drop back" into second grade.

Although Matt continued at his old school, any changes, such as a substitute teacher, special assemblies, even going to a new chapter in a book, would cause him to lose his very shaky hold on self-control. There were times when Matt had to be physically restrained to prevent him from banging his head into walls and tearing at his hair and skin. The tantrum episodes became more and more frequent, with Matt causing serious injuries to himself. Finally, his behavior problems escalated at school, leading to frequent in-house suspensions. Matt's teachers all tried hard, but they admitted they were losing him. Not yet 9 years old, Matt was placed on an inpatient unit with 14- to 17-year-olds, who were there for such things as substance abuse, aggressive behavior, running away, and clinical depression.

Realizing this program was destroying my son, I fired his doctor and found a very good residential center. Although Matt did better, the staff felt that he needed a locked unit. This would have to be out of state at a new center, because California did not have locked units for children. We found a warm, caring staff and observed a program with under 20 children in a very concrete, consistent environment. Matt did well.

This time the transition home went a little smoother. I met with the people from our local Special Education Consortium and explained Matt's needs, both academic and therapeutic. We put together an individualized education plan that included all the documentation from the residential center. Our district was able to implement all of the strategies recommended by the transition team, namely, a small special day class on a regular school campus and a private day treatment program at a local hospital. Matt was on the elementary school campus in the morning and then bused to the hospital for the "mental health" component of his day. Our local school district contracted and paid for the hospital program.

As Matt approached puberty, he was faced with several other challenges beyond the usual stressors of that stage of life. A new school, fears about seventh grade, an awareness that he was "different," and a move to the Adolescent Day Program were all too much. Then, in late October 1989, Matt was once again hospitalized, and things went from bad to worse. From February until April, Matt was admitted and discharged, between psychiatric hospitals and the residential treatment center, eight times! Our son was in constant turmoil and pain, so we brought him home to see if we could put *something* together for him.

We enrolled him in the day treatment program at a nearby hospital. Matt's doctor was convinced he needed to have a very thorough diagnostic workup done, and we fully agreed. We had a book full of psychiatric workups, all with different "professional conclusions" as to what Matt's problems were, but no recent look at his educational and medical needs. Matt's doctor and numerous others kept recommending the University of California at Los Angeles (UCLA). We tried it, and it turned out to be very helpful. UCLA's program "made sense" to Matt. It was very concrete, structured, and safe. New tests were done, all medication was discontinued, a specific program was put together. Through it all Matt stayed strong and was successful. In September 1990, Matt was formally diagnosed with autism, infantile onset. Matt's capabilities are what kept professionals from seeing his true disability for so many years. My son, who could mimic the behavior of others so completely that it became "his" behavior, had spent the last 6½ years developing, growing, and learning in acute care psychiatric facilities.

With Matt's discharge from UCLA came the knowledge that we had a lot of work ahead of us. Matt needed structured social skills classes, independent living skills, social language/speech therapy, small classes to address his academic needs, and lots of therapy to deal with his many learned behaviors.

Unfortunately, we could not find a program in California that could implement the plan developed at UCLA. Finally, in the summer of 1991, we found a possibility in a residential center in Florida. Matt could go into their Steps Towards Independent Living Program, and the Navy agreed to transfer our family to Florida. We worked hard for 10 months getting the staff to focus on Matt's academics and helping him develop social skills. Every time they tried to go back to a traditional program, my husband and I reminded them that Matt is autistic and needed a logical, concrete program. Every time they put Matt in for a special diploma, we reminded them that Matt's goal was to go to college and that he was fully capable of obtaining a regular diploma. We made sure the correct assessments were done and that a functional transition plan was created. Our family worked as a team in making sure everyone understood that the goal was not for Matt to move to a group home but to *come home* and attend his neighborhood high school. After nearly 10 months in the residential center, Matt came home, stronger and more in control. He came home to a part-time job at the University of South Florida, doing odd clerical jobs and very proud of his title of Consumer Consultant at the Research and Training Center for Children's Mental Health. He came home to attend 10th grade at his neighborhood high school.

The odds were definitely against Matt, because the idea was that he should be placed according to his diagnosis or label. Our job, once again, was to advocate that Matt was entitled to attend his local high school. We knew it would take some added supports, like being staffed into the resource room for children with emotional handicaps, having key adults always available to help Matt process a lot of the new "teenage stuff" he would encounter, and modified regular classes (tests in his emotionally handicapped class). However, it would be the most appropriate placement when compared to a classroom for adolescents who are seriously emotionally disabled or a class for teenagers who are autistic (and nonverbal). With a letter from Matt (asking for a chance), strong documentation from UCLA as to Matt's strengths and needs, and a high school staff that believed in his abilities, we were able to help Matt attain his dream of being a "regular" kid.

The pitfalls still trip us up at times. Matt's difficulties seem to be cyclical, and we find him in need of stronger supports in the late winter and early spring. But, for today, Matt is home, he is happy, and he is living his dream to be a "normal" kid, girlfriend and all!

A LOOK FORWARD: PARENTS AS ALLIES

The use of a case study can never satisfy all readers or illustrate all the points that need to be made. In this case, we do not read about feelings of blame or transportation problems, but the confusion and frustration are there. We do see a parent on the cutting edge of participation as an equal partner in the decision-making process concerning her son. We do see a parent who has mastered the role of advocate and case manager. How can more parents learn to participate at this level?

In 1984, the National Institute of Mental Health (NIMH) began the Child and Adolescent Service System Program (CASSP) as an impetus to improve services for children, with a special emphasis on developing family support (Knitzer, 1993). In that same year, the National Institute of Disability and Rehabilitation Research cofunded, along with NIMH, two centers with the mission of improving services for children and their families (one at Portland State University, the other at the University of South Florida). The CASSP projects and the efforts of the centers, particularly the Families as Allies Program at Portland State (McManus & Friesen, 1986), led to a new conceptualization of the role of families. Advocacy for children and families experienced a renewed vigor (Friedman, Duchnowski, & Henderson, 1989), and new organizations such as the Child and Adolescent Network of the National Alliance for the Mentally Ill (NAMI-CAN) and the Federation of Families for Children's Mental Health were developed.

All of these activities, and the efforts of many people and organizations, have contributed to developing a context in which the knowledge level and participation described in this case study can be fostered in the majority of, if not all, parents. In many states and local communities, exemplary programs have developed in which special education and mental health systems have linked with parents and other agencies to provide an integrated system of care (Boyd, 1992; Nelson & Pearson, 1991). As these programs expand to other communities, the impact of the parent movement will also expand. Parents will then assume their role as equal participants with professionals.

REFERENCES

Achenbach, T. M. (1985). *Assessment and taxonomy of child and adolescent psychopathology.* Beverly Hills, CA: Sage.

Achenbach, T. M., McConaughy, S. H., & Howell, C. T. (1987). Child/adolescent behavioral and emotional problems: Implications of cross-informant correlations for situational specificity. *Psychological Bulletin, 101*, 213–232.

Bailey, D. B., & Blasco, P. M. (1991). Parent's perspective and written survey of family needs. *Journal of Early Intervention, 14*(3), 196–203.

Bettleheim, B. (1967). *The empty fortress.* New York: Free Press.

Boyd, L. A. (1992). *Integrating systems of care for children and families: An overview of values, methods and characteristics of developing models, with examples and recommendations.* Tampa: Florida Mental Health Institute, University of South Florida.

Burns, B. J., & Friedman, R. M. (1990). Examining the research base for child mental health services and policy. *Journal of Mental Health Administration, 17*, 87–98.

Byalin, K. (1990). Parent empowerment: A treatment strategy for hospitalized adolescents. *Hospital and Community Psychiatry, 41*, 89–90.

Comer, J., & Haynes, N. M. (1991). Parent involvement in schools: An ecological approach. *Elementary School Journal, 91*(3), 271–277.

Cross, T., Bazron, B., Dennis, K., & Isaacs, M. (1989). *Toward a culturally competent system of care.* Washington, DC: CASSP Technical Assistance Center, Georgetown University.

Freud, S. (1952). Recommendations to physicians. In *Standard edition of the complete works of Sigmund Freud* (Vol. 12). London, England: Hogarth Press.

Friedman, R. M., Duchnowski, A. J., & Henderson, E. L. (Eds.). (1989). *Advocacy on behalf of children with serious emotional problems.* Springfield, IL: Thomas.

Friesen, B., Koren, P., & Koroloff, N. (1992). How parents view professional behaviors: A cross-professional analysis. *Journal of Child and Family Studies, 1*(2), 209–232.

Friesen, B., & Koroloff, N. (1990). Family-centered services: Implications for mental health administration and research. *Journal of Mental Health Administration, 17*, 13–25.

Gallagher, J. J., & Gallagher, G. G. (1985). Family adaptations to a handicapped child and assorted professionals. In H. R. Turnbull & A. P. Turnbull (Eds.), *Parents speak out* (2nd ed., pp. 233–242). Columbus, OH: Merrill.

Halpern, A. S. (1993). Quality of life as a conceptual framework for evaluating transition outcomes. *Exceptional Children, 59*, 486–498.

Kanner, L. (1943). Autistic disturbances of affective contact. *Nervous Child, 2*, 217–250.

Knitzer, J. (1993). Children's mental health policy: Challenging the future. *Journal of Emotional and Behavioral Disorders, 1*, 8–16.

Kutash, K. (1991). *A construct validation study of the Social Skills Ratings System with children and adolescents who have serious emotional disturbances: A multitrait multimethod approach.* Unpublished doctoral dissertation, University of South Florida, Tampa.

Lardieri, S., Gaertner, C., & Green, J. (1993, March). *Reports from parents on improving services for youth with emotional or behavioral problems.* Paper presented at fifth annual Research Conference, A System of Care for Children's Mental Health, Tampa, FL.

McConaughy, S. H. (1993). Evaluating behavioral and emotional disorders with the CBCL, TRF, and YSR cross-informant scales. *Journal of Emotional and Behavioral Disorders, 1*, 40–52.

McKinney, J. D., & Hocutt, U. M. (1982). Public school involvement of parents of learning-disabled children and average achievers. *Exceptional Education Quarterly, 3*(2), 64–73.

McManus, M., & Friesen, B. (1986). *Families as allies: Conference proceedings.* Portland, OR: Research and Training Center to Improve Services for Seriously Emotionally Disturbed Children and Their Families, Portland State University.

National Mental Health Association. (1989). *Children in need of mental health care* (Draft proposal). Alexandria, VA: Author.

Nelson, M., & Pearson, C. (1991). *Integrating services for children and youth with emotional/behavioral disabilities.* Reston, VA: Council for Exceptional Children.

Nyberg, T. C. (1990). *Family service planning teams: An initial survey.* Tampa: Florida Mental Health Institute, University of South Florida.

Palfrey, J. S., Walker, D., Butler, J., & Singer, J. (1989). Patterns of responses in families of chronically disabled children: An assessment in five metropolitan school districts. *American Journal of Orthopsychiatry, 59*, 94–104.

Schreibman, L. (1988). *Autism.* Newbury Park, CA: Sage.

Sheridan, S., & Kratochwill, T. (1992). Behavioral parent–teacher consultation: Conceptual and research considerations. *Journal of School Psychology, 30*(2), 117–139.

Silver, S. E., Duchnowski, A. J., Kutash, K., Friedman, R. M., Eisen, M., Prange, M. E., Brandenburg, N. A., & Greenbaum, P. E. (1992). A comparison of children with serious emotional disturbance served in residential and school settings. *Journal of Child and Family Studies, 1*, 43–59.

Singer, J. D., & Butler, J. A. (1987). The Education for All Handicapped Children Act: Schools as agents of social reform. *Harvard Educational Review, 57*(2), 125–152.

Sonnenschein, P. (1981). Parents and professionals: An uneasy relationship. *Teaching Exceptional Children, 14*(2), 62–65.

Strickland, B. (1993). Parents and the education system. In J. L. Paul & R. J. Simeonsson (Eds.), *Children with special needs: Family, culture, and society* (pp. 231–255). Fort Worth, TX: Harcourt, Brace, Jovanovich.

Summers, J., Dell'Oliver, C., Turnbull, A., Benson, H., Santelli, E., Campbell, M., & Siegel-Causey, E. (1990). Examining the IFSP process: What are family and practioner preferences? *Topics in Early Childhood Special Education, 10*(1), 79–99.

Turnbull, A., & Turnbull, H. R. (1982). Parent involvement in the education of handicapped children: A critique. *Mental Retardation, 20*(3), 115–122.

Williams, B. (1988). Parents and patients: Members of an interdisciplinary team on an adolescent inpatient unit. *Clinical Social Work Journal, 16*, 78–91.

Williams, B., & Hartlage, L. (1988). Diagnostician–parent communication. *School Psychology International, 9*(3), 229–233.

Winton, P. J., & Bailey, D. B. (1993). Communicating with families: Examining practices and facilitating change. In J. L. Paul & R. J. Simeonsson (Eds.), *Children with special needs: Family, culture, and society* (pp. 210–230). Fort Worth, TX: Harcourt, Brace, Jovanovich.

CHAPTER

9

MENTAL HEALTH SYSTEM INVOLVEMENT IN SED PLACEMENT DECISIONS

Richard E. Mattison
Washington University

Steven R. Forness
University of California, Los Angeles

The process of placing students with serious emotional disturbance (SED) in special education programs has been the subject of much recent scrutiny, leading to the development of more specific SED criteria than provided by Public Law 94-142 (Forness & Knitzer, 1992). Simultaneously, the actual SED evaluation process has also been reviewed, and found to be lacking in standardization (McGinnis, Kiraly, & Smith, 1984; Reiher, 1992).

As this reassessment of SED continues, another question appears timely—what role should a consultant child psychiatrist or psychologist have in the SED evaluation process? What functions should such a consultant perform that complement and supplement the work of school evaluation teams, rather than duplicating educators' efforts as a costly redundancy? Further, in addition to placement planning, what role can a child psychiatrist or psychologist serve in the initial comprehensive treatment planning for SED students (as proper placement is typically only one part of these pupils' needs)?

One approach to answering this consultation question could be based on understanding which objective characteristics of students recommended for SED placement distinguish them from other students who have behavioral and/or emotional problems in school but require less intensive classroom intervention. In particular, are there "noneducational" characteristics that are beyond the expertise of school evaluation teams but need to be considered at the time of SED evaluation, and for which consultants can provide assistance? These characteristics may well also lead to a determination of other related treatment needs that, although they may not be within the scope of responsibility of the school, may nonetheless be important for a complete program of comprehensive treatment, part of which may need to be delivered in the mental health system.

OVERVIEW OF A MODEL FOR SED PLACEMENT CONSULTATION BY CHILD PSYCHIATRISTS AND PSYCHOLOGISTS

Before defining the most efficacious role for a child psychiatrist or psychologist consulting during the evaluation of a student for SED placement, the actual consultation process must first be understood. Then the question must be posed concerning which information gained through such a consultation is truly important to a school team for the final placement decision.

The format for SED consultation is in need of standardization. Therefore, Mattison (1993) recently outlined extensively one model for the SED consultation process. The procedure is based on the comprehensive evaluation of a new child and family, which is typically practiced by child psychiatrists and psychologists. However, this method as practiced in school situations has a slightly different focus and depends on much more input from school personnel who know the child than is usually available to a child psychiatrist or psychologist in an office or clinic setting.

An overview of the model is as follows. The consultation is most efficiently done in the school setting, where staff who know the student are readily available to provide information to the consultant, and vice versa. The initial step is the consultant's review of the most pertinent existing materials, such as the school psychologist's recent psychoeducational evaluation, teacher behavioral checklists, and other key evaluations that have been performed in the school or community. This preliminary database then allows the consultant to ask more pertinent questions during the next step, the initial meeting with the school staff. At such time the educators can concisely state their concerns, which the psychiatrist or psychologist can clarify with further questioning. Thus, the consultant is more fully informed about issues before proceeding to the next step, the separate interviews of the student and the parent(s).

Although the child psychiatrist or psychologist is, at this point, quite aware of the student's school problems, the interviews should not focus entirely on those issues—the interview of the pupil should be a standard mental status examination including questioning for specific symptoms, both those that might be predicted from the school history as well as those that may not be as apparent to school personnel because they may occur outside the school setting (e.g., sleep disturbances in childhood depression). The interview of the parent should also be comprehensive: current and past problems of the child at home, treatment history, developmental and medical history, and family history (the medical, educational, and psychiatric background of the parents, quality of the marriage, parenting practices, occurrence of stressors such as abuse, and a brief survey of pertinent family genetic information).

As a next step after these interviews, the consultant should summarize findings to the evaluation team as well as outline the diagnostic formulation. All information for the student can then be considered and discussed by the team, leading to decision-making about SED placement, ideally along with comprehensive treatment planning. The final recommended step in this model is for the consultant and one school staff person (who will subsequently be working with the student and family) to meet with the student and parent to share the team's decisions, answer questions, and commence arrangements toward the team's treatment plan.

This model generates much information that might prove valuable to a school team considering a student for SED placement, as well as planning a comprehensive treatment program for both school and home. However, what of this information gathered by a consultant is the most important for the placement process, rather than just interesting or poignant?

METHOD FOR A STUDY OF NONEDUCATIONAL CHARACTERISTICS OF SED STUDENTS

Before determining SED placement criteria that consultants can help school teams address, we must first understand what criteria may truly distinguish SED students. Unfortunately, the literature has described little information concerning objective characteristics for SED students. Potentially important noneducational characteristics, such as type and severity of psychiatric diagnoses and family stressor background, have been neglected. To summarize the limited past work, overt patterns of externalizing or internalizing behavior disorders were thought predominant and more pertinent to school intervention programs. There was also a trend for families of SED students not to be as completely included in the placement or treatment process, or for such families to be considered too fragile for such involvement because of their own presumed psychopathology.

Therefore, over the past decade, one group of researchers (headed by Mattison) in a semirural area of south central Pennsylvania has closely investigated over 300 students recommended for SED evaluation. They wished to understand what characteristics of students and their families were influencing the decision to recommend SED placement. In this section we briefly describe the method employed in this project, because the results will serve to help answer the main focus of this chapter—what should the role of a child psychiatrist or psychologist be in the SED evaluation process?

Consecutive students (primarily White) were evaluated, for the first time, because of their serious behavioral and emotional problems in school that had not responded to intervention by school staff. They were initially referred by their teachers and principals. Multidisciplinary teams then evaluated the pupils according to the standard procedure of the school district unit that provided special education services (including SED classes) for the area. First, a school psychologist conducted a psychoeducational evaluation, which included educational history, intelligence testing (usually the WISC-R), and achievement testing. Next, a consultant child psychiatrist performed a thorough evaluation (similar to the model consultation described earlier in this chapter) that included separate interviews with the student and a parent (usually the mother) based on a semistructured psychiatric interview known as the Kiddie-SADS-E (Puig-Antich, Orvaschel, Tabrizi, & Chambers, 1980), history of psychiatric illness in the natural parents using the Family History–Research Diagnostic Criteria (Endicott, Andreasen, & Spitzer, 1975), history of substantiated or reportable abuse, and information on prior or current mental health services. Finally, these data were used by the consultant and an accompanying resident trainee in child psychiatry together to determine *DSM-III* diagnoses (American Psychiatric Association, 1980).

A recommendation for SED placement was then decided during a meeting of a multidisciplinary team (MDT) that considered all this information. The MDT consisted of the student's teacher(s), the testing school psychologist, the child psychiatric consultant, and an SED social worker and administrator. SED placement criteria were those mandated in PL 94-142. The pupil's parent(s) had to approve each step of the evaluation process.

Thus, data were gradually accumulated and have been reported on for students recommended for SED placement from four different groups: girls aged 6 through 11 and 12 through 16 years (Mattison, Morales, & Bauer, 1991), and boys aged 6 through 11 (Mattison & Gamble, 1992; Mattison, Morales, & Bauer, 1992) and 12 through 16 years (Mattison, Morales, & Bauer, 1993). Thus, many objective characteristics of SED students have been more clearly identified, along with indication of those variables with the most differentiating value. We summarize these reports in the remaining sections of this chapter and discuss their implications for defining the consultation role of a child psychiatrist or psychologist.

FACTORS THAT MAY DETERMINE SED PLACEMENT

Severity of Disorder

How ill are students who present for SED evaluation, and can the expertise of a child psychiatrist or psychologist help school teams determine the degree of severity and the level of intervention that may be necessary? The recent research with the Pennsylvania SED students shows that students recommended for SED placement have serious and global psychopathology, which distinguishes them from students evaluated but not recommended for SED classrooms. Clinically, ratings by child psychiatrists on the *DSM-III* Axis V scale (level of adaptive functioning) have shown mean scores ranging from 5.2 to 5.6 (poor to very poor;

on a 7-point scale with 7 as the worst score) for all age–gender groups of new SED pupils. Thus, they were in general judged by the clinicians to have moderate to marked impairment in social relationships, school functioning, or both.

As other indices of severity, during the evaluation process of the Pennsylvania SED students, teachers and parents completed behavior checklists, generally the Teacher Report Form (TRF) and the parent Child Behavior Checklist (CBCL) of Achenbach and Edelbrock (1983, 1986). Tables 9.1 and 9.2 present mean *T* scores for the SED students on the total score for both instruments. The total problem scores for both age groups of boys on the TRF (another teacher checklist without *T* scores was used with the girls) and for all age–gender groups on the CBCL were near or above a mean *T* score of 70. Thus, the magnitude of the behavioral or emotional problems of these students entering SED classes was not only severe, that is, 2 standard deviations above the mean (or in the upper 2% of deviance), but also global in that scores were similar for both teacher and parent ratings. These findings seem consistent with the clinician ratings, which were determined without knowledge of any checklist scores.

Tables 9.1 and 9.2 also show that externalizing problems were severe in both environments, more so than internalizing problems. However, the levels of internalizing psychopathology (mean *T* scores ranging from 63 to 68) were clearly in the clinical range, probably indicative of the complex presentation that is common in SED students (Pullis, 1991).

TABLE 9.1
Teacher TRF Ratings for SED Boys

	Mean T Scores	
Scales	*Elementary (n = 97)*	*Secondary (n = 59)*
Internalizing	63.6	68.7
Externalizing	73.6	73.7
Total problems	71.4	73.5

TABLE 9.2
Parent CBCL Ratings for SED Students

	Mean T Scores			
	Elementary		*Secondary*	
Scales	*Boys (n = 97)*	*Girls (n = 15)*	*Boys (n = 59)*	*Girls (n = 14)*
Internalizing	64.7	68.1	65.6	64.9
Externalizing	69.3	72.9	69.1	68.6
Total problems	69.1	72.3	69.0	71.0

TRF and CBCL scores for the Pennsylvania SED boys aged 6 through 11 years have also been compared to two psychiatric groups of boys from the same geographic area: boys entering outpatient and inpatient treatment (Mattison & Gamble, 1992). The SED boys were most similar to the inpatient boys on the TRF; indeed, their scores were generally higher than those for boys at the outset of psychiatric hospitalization. The TRF scores of both the SED and inpatient groups indicated significantly more severe levels of pathology than the scores of the outpatient boys on all scales. On the parent CBCL, the scores of the SED boys were quite similar to the scores of the outpatient group, whereas the scores for the inpatient boys were the highest and generally significantly greater than the scores of both other groups. Thus, SED and inpatient pupils may look similarly dysfunctional in school, with home functioning as one pertinent determinant of the final level of intervention.

In summary, students recommended for SED placement have obvious and severe problems, both at school and home. Therefore, the information that child psychiatrists and psychologists routinely obtain in assessing and planning treatment for youth with serious psychiatric illness could well serve school teams evaluating students for possible SED placement. Further, teams are often faced with students for whom the proper question is not whether they need SED placement, but rather whether they need wraparound services (Nelson & Pearson, 1991), acute psychiatric hospitalization, or even long-term residential care. Important for such decision making is not only knowledge of the history and severity of the student's psychopathology in school, but also information about the history and severity of the symptomatology in the home and neighborhood environments. A consultant can perhaps more readily assess these variables and, thus, help the team decide what level of intervention is required in both school situations and related mental health services.

Psychiatric Diagnosis

The determination of a student's special education classification is one diagnostic step that occurs during the SED evaluation process. A parallel diagnostic step is the determination of which specific psychiatric disorder(s) is present, a role that can be well performed by a consultant based on a comprehensive evaluation of the student and family. This latter process could be quite significant in determining eligibility for related services as well as for coordination of a comprehensive process of overall treatment planning.

Also, much recent debate about the use of psychiatric diagnosis has focused on conduct disorder, that is, whether a student with this diagnosis should not receive SED programming because the disorder is a possible exclusionary criterion under current guidelines (Forness, 1992a). The discussion of this controversy could be furthered by better understanding the specific diagnoses for students entering SED classrooms.

Table 9.3 lists the principal *DSM-III* Axis I diagnoses for the four age–gender groups of Pennsylvania students recommended for SED placement. Externalizing disorders (attention deficit disorder or conduct/oppositional disorder) predominated in all age–gender groups (62.7%–79%) except the adolescent girls; attention deficit disorder was more common than conduct/oppositional disorder in each of these three groups. Except for the elementary school boys, internalizing disorders (especially depressive disorders) were diagnosed in 30% or more of the pupils, including 55.0% of the secondary school girls. The only significant difference in diagnoses between an SED group and the non-SED comparison group was a greater percentage of conduct/oppositional disorders in the grade school boys.

Multiple disorders were common. Excluding the older girls, majorities of the age–gender groups (59.3%–63.0%) had more than one diagnosis. Also, comorbidity was significantly greater in these three groups than in comparison groups.

What from this information applies to the conduct disorder controversy? First, conduct/oppositional disorder is relatively common among SED students (approximately 20%–30%), but usually is not the most frequent externalizing disorder. Second, type of diagnosis, including conduct disorder, generally is not a distinguishing factor for SED placement. Finally, and of most diagnostic importance, the principal *DSM-III* Axis I diagnosis of an SED student is often associated with another diagnosis, and this comorbidity serves as a common distinguishing factor. Thus, conduct disorder as a principal diagnosis may often have a comorbid diagnosis, or when not a principal diagnosis may often be a comorbid diagnosis. For example, among the younger SED boys, the most common dual diagnosis was attention deficit disorder and conduct/oppositional disorder (21.0%), and, overall, a mix of an externalizing disorder and an internalizing disorder occurred

TABLE 9.3
Principal *DSM-III* Axis I Diagnoses of SED Students

	Diagnoses (%)			
	Elementary		*Secondary*	
DSM-III Categories	*Boys (n = 100)*	*Girls (n = 16)*	*Boys (n = 59)*	*Girls (n = 20)*
Externalizing disorders:	(79.0)*	(68.8)	(62.7)	(35.0)
ADD	47.0	50.0	32.2	10.0
Conduct/oppositional	32.0*	18.8	30.5	25.0
Internalizing disorders:	(17.0)	(31.3)	(30.5)	(55.0)
Depressive	12.0	18.8	28.8	50.0
Anxiety	5.0	12.5	1.7	5.0
Other disorders	4.0	0.0	6.8	10.0
Multiple disorders	63.0*	62.5*	59.3*	35.0

*Significantly greater than students evaluated for SED placement but recommended for other non-SED educational intervention, for example, a learning disability resource room.

in 39.0% of these boys. Thus, the diagnostic issue of conduct disorder in SED students is complex, indicating that much of the debate to exclude conduct disorder may be oversimplified. These findings are also indeed similar to those found in other studies of children or youth with SED (Forness, 1992b) and to those recently reported in a major longitudinal study of 812 students with SED in both school and residential settings (Silver et al., 1992).

The previous discussion illuminates what diagnostic role can be served by a consultant child psychiatrist or psychologist. Much as the training of these professionals prepares them to work with the most seriously ill youth, their background also exposes them to children and adolescents with complicated clinical pictures. Thus, the frequent comorbidity of SED students is within their expertise and represents an area in which they can greatly assist school evaluation teams during SED placement discussion.

Family Stressor Background

In their basic evaluations of children, child psychiatrists and psychologists acquire extensive family histories, often more than typically is able to be established for potential SED students by school personnel alone. Could this expertise benefit the placement process, that is, should family factors play a part in the SED decision making of school teams?

Specific family factors were investigated during the evaluation of the Pennsylvania SED students: socioeconomic status (Hollingshead 7-level; 7 = lowest level), employment status of parents in the home, marriage of the natural parents (intact or broken), presence of past or present psychiatric illness in the natural parents (with *Family History—Research Diagnostic Criteria*), and experience of abuse (substantiated or reportable). Table 9.4 presents the results for the four age–gender groups of SED students. The average socioeconomic level was in the clerical–skilled manual labor range (Hollingshead 4–5), and parent unemployment was only a noteworthy factor for the adolescent girls. A majority of all age–gender groups (approximately 60% or more) lived in a broken home, and over 80% of each group had at least one natural parent with a psychiatric illness. At least 60% of each group had experienced abuse (physical rather than sexual abuse being the most common in each group). In addition to the large percentages of these groups who had experienced each stressor, the experience of multiple stressors (i.e., the five listed in Table 9.4, along with an SES rating at the lowest level of 7) was common, with a range of 2.2 to 2.8.

Specific stressors did significantly differentiate the students recommended for SED placement from students evaluated but referred for other non-SED intervention in school (Table 9.4). The rates of abuse were significantly greater in all age–gender groups, and SES rankings were lower in all groups except the younger girls. The high percentages of parental psychiatric illness distinguished

TABLE 9.4
Family Stressor Background of SED Students

	Elementary		*Secondary*	
	Boys (n = 100)	*Girls (n = 16)*	*Boys (n = 59)*	*Girls (n = 20)*
Mean SES	5.0*	4.9	5.0*	5.4*
No employed parent	12.1%	0.0%	10.3%	30.0%
Broken home	71.0%*	62.5%	58.6%	65.0%
Parental psychiatric disorder	86.2%*	81.2%	84.2%	90.0%*
Abuse	61.0%*	75.0%*	63.8%*	60.0%*
Number of multiple stressors	2.4*	2.3*	2.2*	2.8*

*Significantly greater than students evaluated for SED placement but recommended for other non-SED educational intervention, for example, a learning resource room.

the younger boys and the older girls. Coming from a broken home only differentiated the grade school boys, and parental unemployment did not distinguish any group. The occurrence of multiple stressors significantly differentiated all four groups.

Thus, the family stressors that could prove helpful in SED placement decisions are abuse experience, low socioeconomic status, and parental psychiatric illness, along with the presence of multiple stressors. Indeed, as further evidence, the family variables listed in Table 9.4 were investigated with other variables (using logistic regression analysis) to determine factors that helped to identify accurately SED boys aged 6 through 11 years (Mattison, Morales, & Bauer, 1992). A combination proved superior to any single factor, and this combination included the family stressors of SES and abuse experience.

Therefore, family factors are emerging that appear to influence school teams to recommend SED placement (along with other nonfamily factors). The presence of such stressors can perhaps more readily be ascertained by a consultant child psychiatrist or psychologist, because inquiry about these family variables is part of the routine evaluation performed by these professionals and may be too sensitive for routine inquiry by school professionals.

In addition to the consultant establishing what family stressors are present, knowledge of such information should greatly assist school personnel toward more accurate understanding of a student. For example, a common family profile is a natural father with antisocial and alcohol abuse disorders, who has been physically abusive to both the wife and the student. Divorce has occurred and the single-parent mother frequently struggles with ongoing depression. Such background information should affect SED personnel's treatment of a student with temper and socializing problems, as their etiology could be considerably related to the exposure to an alcoholic, abusive parent rather than to other factors that might produce those problematic behaviors.

ADDITIONAL CONSULTANT ROLES AT TIME OF SED PLANNING

Treatment Planning

The focus of this chapter is to define a proper role for a consultant child psychiatrist or psychologist in the SED placement process. Findings indicate that a consultant can help to determine severity of a student's psychopathology, diagnoses, and family stressors, factors that particularly warrant team discussion during the process of reaching a placement decision. However, as part of the placement determination, treatment planning for the student and family also must occur, a step in which the consultant can prove very useful to a school team, not only in the design of the comprehensive intervention plan but also in the initiation of its execution.

As we discussed in the section on diagnosis, the diagnoses of SED students are varied and often multiple. Thus, SED staffs must be able to handle very different externalizing and internalizing psychiatric diagnoses, as well as comorbid presentations. Educators appear to be increasingly interested in the information associated with current *DSM* psychiatric diagnoses, particularly in reference to multimodality treatments (Kauffman et al., 1991). Such knowledge can help in their more complete understanding of a student's problems, assist in their selection of classroom intervention techniques, and encourage their collaboration with community resources.

Thus, at the time of treatment planning during the placement process, a consultant child psychiatrist or psychologist can help translate psychiatric diagnoses into meaningful and useful information for the educators who will be caring for the student. Most SED classrooms provide individual planning for each student in addition to the general classroom behavioral plan that all students must follow. A new SED student may present an array of problems; the SED teacher's knowledge of the pupil's specific diagnoses can help determine prioritization of those problems as well as selection of specific behavioral or related techniques for initial intervention. For example, the common secondary behavioral problems of a boy with dysthymia (chronic depression) will require firm structure, but the primary intervention plan must emphasize much positive reinforcement and create situations to ensure success for the student.

Even if the psychiatric diagnosis(es) of an SED student does not imply specific intervention approaches in the classroom, it may nonetheless indicate what treatment should be sought in the community, and at what level of intervention (i.e., from once-a-week outpatient care to intensive wraparound services). For example, in the case of the boy with dysthymia, he might require further assessment for a trial of an antidepressant medication, cognitive–behavioral therapy to reverse his self-reinforcing negative approach to life, parent training to change their negative style toward him, and/or family therapy to relieve stress that only maintains or deepens his depression. The consultant can lead the treatment discussion and help determine proper community resources. Further, the consultant can help explain to the family what therapeutic steps must be taken in addition to school intervention, and can help arrange community resources.

Such active participation by the consultant might help ensure achievement of the full treatment plan. Currently, SED students typically receive no or limited services from community mental health resources (Steinberg & Knitzer, 1992) (the treatment background of the Pennsylvania SED students was consistent with this finding; only 8.5%–20.0% of the pupils in all the age–gender groups were receiving therapy at the time of their evaluation for SED placement, and only 9.0%–15.0% were receiving any medication). However, communication with a community resource by the consultant followed by a copy of the consultation report may improve the chances of proper intervention by the community resource. This step may also catalyze the beginning of collaboration between the community professional and SED personnel. Improved school–agency interaction is becoming imperative with the increase in wraparound programs designed to integrate services for the most needy students and their families (Nelson & Pearson, 1991).

Finally, in addition to determination of a student's psychiatric diagnoses to achieve an appropriate treatment plan, the family's needs must also be entered into the treatment equation. The consultant's knowledge of the family can assist with this step. However, possibly more important, the consultant's interaction with the family can begin a working relationship between the family and the SED staff. This collaboration is, needless to say, vitally important. Given the complex treatment needs of most SED students and their families, if the family does not participate in seeking community intervention or in working with the SED program, school progress for that SED student may very well be slowed if not limited.

Education of SED Teams

School teams evaluating students for SED placement are confronted with children and adolescents who have complex clinical pictures, are seriously dysfunctional in most environments, and have stressful family backgrounds. Previously in this chapter we defined roles for consultant child psychiatrists and psychologists to assist school teams in the placement decision making, as well as during accompanying treatment planning. In addition to this active phase, a final role can prove quite helpful to school staff—education. That is, consultants can expand the knowledge base of team members to allow them to evaluate potential SED pupils more critically and to plan more precisely for their needs in school. Several authors have recently emphasized this need for education of school staff who work with SED students (Shapiro, 1991; Smith, Wood, & Grimes, 1988; Steinberg & Knitzer, 1992).

Educational literature, for example, special issues of the *School Psychology Review* (Teeter, 1991) and the *Journal of Learning Disabilities* ("Attention Deficit Disorder," 1991) devoted to attention deficit–hyperactivity disorder, is increasingly addressing the issue of psychiatric diagnoses and their relationship to school planning. Thus, school personnel are desirous of learning more about current classification. Consultants should be ready not only to explain diagnostic criteria, but also share what knowledge may be established (or not established) about the etiology, natural history, complications, and differential diagnosis for a disorder. As school personnel gain more basic understanding of psychiatric diagnoses, this will undoubtedly help their understanding and consideration of difficult SED students.

Related to this, as SED staff learn more about current psychiatric diagnoses, some of that accruing knowledge will include treatment techniques. As educators understand how children with a particular diagnosis benefit from intervention with specifically described individual therapy, pharmacotherapy, or family therapy, such findings may influence their selection and development of specific classroom strategies. Knowledge of prognostic variables can also be useful in shaping a staff's approach to a student.

Working with families can be uncomfortable for educators, who often have little training in this important additional need of SED students. Not only can consultants help school teams understand family issues facing a potential SED student and thereby help incorporate those needs into an initial treatment plan, but they can also teach and model communicative and therapeutic interactions with families. This education can begin during the feedback process, when a consultant with a school staff member can openly discuss family issues and needs and establish the school person as the family's liaison (not their adversary from whom crucial information and needs should be hidden because it will be held against the parents).

The consultant can also educate school teams on community resources and facilitate interaction. The latter step can often occur at the end of the team's treatment planning, with the consultant volunteering to call a resource while helping the team decide which members will participate in other necessary community arrangements. Collaboration is frequently required by community resources, another service that a consultant can improve by encouraging community professionals to attend team discussions of SED students who become their patients.

These educational services by a consultant are case oriented. Consulting child psychiatrists and psychologists may also help educate school personnel through inservice lectures on topics that are currently very relevant to school personnel (e.g., substance abuse, suicide, physical abuse, living with a parent with a psychiatric disorder, and sexual diseases). Material from the field of child psychiatry or psychology can supplement what school staff may have already learned from their own training or professional publications. Finally, any consultant should keep abreast of the SED literature, both articles that appear in the educational literature (e.g., the journals *Behavioral Disorders, Journal of Emotional and Behavioral Disorders*, and *Remedial and Special Education*) as well as those that appear in the child psychiatry or psychology publications. Consultants will then be in a position to refer pertinent articles to school staff, especially if school professionals have limited access to such journals. Such efforts by a consultant may help to solidify the working relationship with educators.

CONCLUSIONS

In this chapter we have sought to describe how consulting child psychiatrists and psychologists can best assist school teams who are evaluating students for SED placement. We presented a consultation model that is largely based on how child psychiatrists and psychologists routinely assess children and their families. We reviewed results from an extensive study of objective characteristics of SED students, which identified important distinguishing variables: serious global dysfunction, complex diagnostic pictures, and family stressors such as abuse and parental psychiatric illness. Thus, the consultation model we described can provide unique information to school teams about students with SED.

The need for substantial knowledge about these factors may become much more important because they represent some of the criteria included in the proposed definition of "emotional or behavioral disorder" (EBD), that is, revised specific criteria offered to replace the current imprecise federal definition of SED (Forness & Knitzer, 1992). These new criteria require evidence for serious dysfunction across settings, with the possibility of a wide range of coexisting psychiatric diagnoses. Thus, information gained from a consultation may further help school teams determine whether a student fulfills the guidelines of the probable future definition of SED.

In addition to defining a consultant's placement role, we addressed two other roles that are integral to the placement process: initial treatment planning and education of school SED staff. The treatment of SED students leaves much to be desired, particularly in regard to collaboration between educators and mental health professionals (Shapiro, 1991; Smith et al., 1988; Steinberg & Knitzer, 1992). Thus, current child psychiatry and psychology knowledge conveyed during consultations should prove useful to special educators as they develop their methods of understanding and treating SED students. Active participation by the consultant in the initial treatment planning can lead to more frequent realization of the comprehensive intervention through related services that is usually necessary, as well as promotion of increased collaboration between school staff and community professionals.

Indeed, the driving principle behind SED consultation by child psychiatrists and psychologists should be collaboration. SED students and their families typically require complex treatment interventions by school and community professionals, best delivered by a coordinated effort. Not surprisingly, this principle is receiving increased emphasis, both through the promotion of integrated, wraparound programs (Nelson & Pearson, 1991) as well as the call for research that will develop such comprehensive care to more effective levels for students in SED classrooms (Kauffman et al., 1991).

REFERENCES

Achenbach, T. M., & Edelbrock, C. (1983). *Manual for the child behavior checklist and revised child behavior profile.* Burlington: University of Vermont, Department of Psychiatry.

Achenbach, T. M., & Edelbrock, C. (1986). *Manual for the teacher's report form and the teacher version of the child behavior profile.* Burlington: University of Vermont, Department of Psychiatry.

American Psychiatric Association. (1980). *Diagnostic and statistical manual of mental disorders* (3rd ed.). Washington, DC: Author.

Attention deficit disorder (Special issues). (1991). *Journal of Learning Disabilities, 24* (2 and 4).

Endicott, J., Andreason, N., & Spitzer, R. L. (1975). *Family history-research diagnostic criteria.* New York: New York State Psychiatric Research, Biometrics Research.

Forness, S. (1992a). Broadening the cultural–organizational perspective in exclusion of youth with social maladjustment. *Remedial and Special Education, 13*, 55–59.

Forness, S. R. (1992b). Legalism versus professionalism in diagnosing SED in the public schools. *School Psychology Review, 21*, 29–34.

Forness, S. R., & Knitzer, J. (1992). A new proposed definition and terminology to replace "serious emotional disturbance" in Individuals with Disabilities Education Act. *School Psychology Review, 21*, 12–20.

Kauffman, J., Lloyd, J., Cooke, L., Cullinan, D., Epstein, M., Forness, S., Hallahan, D., Nelson, C. M., Polsgrove, L., Strain, P., Sabornie, E., & Walker, H. (1991). Problems and promises in special education and related services for children with emotional and behavioral disorders. *Behavioral Disorders, 16*, 299–313.

Mattison, R. E. (1993). A model for SED case evaluation. In G. K. Fritz, R. E. Mattison, B. Nurcombe, & A. Spirito, *Child and adolescent mental health consultation in hospitals, schools, and courts* (pp. 109–130). Washington, DC: American Psychiatric Press.

Mattison, R. E., & Gamble, A. D. (1992). Severity of socially and emotionally disturbed boys' dysfunction at school and home: Comparison with psychiatric and general population boys. *Behavioral Disorders, 17*, 219–224.

Mattison, R. E., Morales, J., & Bauer, M. A. (1991). Elementary and secondary socially and/or emotionally disturbed girls: Characteristics and identification. *Journal of School Psychology, 29*, 121–134.

Mattison, R. E., Morales, J., & Bauer, M. A. (1992). Distinguishing characteristics of elementary schoolboys recommended for SED placement. *Behavioral Disorders, 17*, 107–114.

Mattison, R. E., Morales, J., & Bauer, M. A. (1993). Adolescent schoolboys in SED classes: Implications for child psychiatry. *Journal of the American Academy of Child and Adolescent Psychiatry, 32*, 1223–1228.

McGinnis, E., Kiraly, J., & Smith, C. R. (1984). The types of data used in identifying public school students as behaviorally disordered. *Behavioral Disorders, 9*, 239–246.

Nelson, C. M., & Pearson, C. A. (1991). *Integrating services for children and youth with emotional and behavioral disorders.* Reston, VA: Council for Exceptional Children.

Puig-Antich, J., Orvaschel, H., Tabrizi, M. A., & Chambers, W. (1980). *The schedule for affective disorders and schizophrenia for schoolage children—epidemiologic version (Kiddie-SADS-E).* New York: New York State Psychiatric Institute and Yale University School of Medicine.

Pullis, M. (1991). Practical considerations of excluding conduct disordered students: An empirical analysis. *Behavioral Disorders, 17*, 9–22.

Reiher, T. C. (1992). Identified deficits and their congruence to the IEP for behaviorally disordered students. *Behavioral Disorders, 17*, 167–177.

Shapiro, E. S. (1991). Training school psychologists for service delivery to children with severe emotional disturbance. *School Psychology Review, 20*, 485–497.

Silver, S. E., Duchnowski, A., Kutash, K., Friedman, R., Eisen, M., Prange, M., Brandenburg, N., & Greenbaum, P. (1992). A comparison of children with serious emotional disturbance served in residential and school settings. *Journal of Child and Family Studies, 1*, 43–59.

Smith, C. R., Wood, F. H., & Grimes, J. (1988). Issues in the identification and placement of behaviorally disordered students. In M. C. Wang, M. C. Reynolds, & H. J. Walberg (Eds.), *Handbook of special education: Research and practice: Vol. 2. Mildly handicapped conditions* (pp. 95–123). New York: Pergamon.

Steinberg, Z., & Knitzer, J. (1992). Classrooms for emotionally and behaviorally disturbed students: Facing the challenge. *Behavioral Disorders, 17*, 145–156.

Teeter, P. A. (Ed.). (1991). Attention-deficit hyperactivity disorders in children: Clinical and treatment issues [Special issue]. *School Psychology Review, 20*(2).

PART

III

Special Problems and Options

CHAPTER

10

SERVING CULTURALLY DIVERSE STUDENTS[1] WITH EMOTIONAL OR BEHAVIORAL DISORDERS: BROADENING CURRENT PERSPECTIVES

Stanley C. Trent
Michigan State University

Alfredo J. Artiles
University of California, Los Angeles

Currently, much controversy surrounds the practices that are used to place culturally diverse children into programs for the emotionally or behaviorally disordered. Moreover, critics of placement practices also contend that the services provided to these students (e.g., instructional and behavioral interventions) are inappropriate and ineffective. However, an examination of these placement and instructional practices before and since the enactment of the Education for All Handicapped Children Act (EHCA, 1975) reveals that this is not a recent occurrence within the field of special education.[1]

During the years that preceded the enactment of this law, many individuals and advocacy groups found it problematic that minority and poor children were disproportionately placed into special education programs—particularly programs for children with mental retardation (Dunn, 1968; Hilliard, 1984; Mercer, 1973, 1979; Mercer & Lewis, 1978). These advocates purported that programs for the mentally retarded served to maintain segregated classrooms within integrated schools and failed to provide low-income African-American, Hispanic, Native

[1]The term *culturally diverse children* is used with different connotations in the research literature depending on the context in which it is presented. Typically, ethnicity, race, language, and socioeconomic status (SES) are variables associated with the term. Often, the term is equated with the constructs *children of color* and *minority children.* However, there is no consensus to date as to how to define or differentiate these terms. Thus, we use these terms interchangeably throughout the chapter.

American, and other minority students with an education that would prepare them to become productive, self-sufficient citizens. In fact, in 1968, in what has become a frequent citation, Dunn commented that, "the overwhelming evidence is that our present and past practices have their major justification in removing pressures on regular teachers and pupils, at the expense of the socioculturally deprived slow learning pupils themselves" (p. 6).

Even though the prevalence rate for children with emotional or behavior disorders is significantly below the rates for other disabilities, many educators and advocacy groups contend that disproportionate numbers of minority children are placed into these programs (Council for Children with Behavior Disorders [CCBD], 1987; Chinn & Hughes, 1987; Smith, Wood, & Grimes, 1987). For example, Chinn and Hughes (1987) determined that in 1984, the representation of African-American children in programs for the behaviorally disordered was twice the level expected based on the percentage of African-American children in the general school population. Even though representation of other minority children appears to be consistent with their representation in the total population, there are other factors that cause great concerns on the part of parents and others who advocate for these children. For example, although mental health advocates and policymakers have proposed more comprehensive service delivery models in this field (Rogler, Cortes, & Malgady, 1991; Stokols, 1992), national mental health policy has been criticized for its inherent flaws (e.g., reactive rather than proactive) and lack of effectiveness (Kiesler, 1992). More specifically, Cross, Bazron, Dennis, and Isaacs (1989) found discontinuities in the way that children of color with emotional or behavioral disorders (e.g., African-American, Asian-American, Hispanic-American, Native American) are treated within the mental health system as compared to their Anglo-American counterparts. According to these authors:

> In short, if you are a racial minority of color, you will probably not get your needs met in the present system. Yet, you are more likely to be diagnosed seriously emotionally disturbed than your Caucasian counterpart. When you do make it into the system, you will experience more restrictive interventions. Cultural traits, behaviors, and beliefs will likely be interpreted as dysfunctions to be overcome. (p. 4)

In light of such evidence, we might ask: Why do we continually find ourselves struggling with these inequities as we attempt to serve children of color with special educational needs? Is the disproportionate labeling of African-American students into the emotional or behavioral disorders category warranted? If not, do we need to develop more guidelines related to assessment that would decrease this disproportionality? How can we improve the quality of services for children of color with emotional or behavioral disorders within schools, mental health, and other agencies?

As we grapple with these questions, we have concluded that there are no clear-cut, easy answers. Moreover, we believe that in our efforts to create environments where prevention, equitable and fair placement practices, and improved interventions become the major focuses of service providers, we must begin to examine this complex problem from a multidisciplinary perspective. Hence, in keeping with the focus of this book, in this chapter we present factors identified by experts in the areas of special education, sociology, educational anthropology and psychology, and educational policy analysis that, in totality, provide a comprehensive perspective on how minority children who live in poverty may be more susceptible to develop emotional or behavioral disorders than their White and middle-class counterparts. For the convenience of this chapter, we first present these factors separately. Then we discuss how they overlap and interact to create the problems previously stated. Finally, we provide general recommendations that will facilitate the establishment of more culturally competent systems of care for this group of children. It is our hope that this discussion will help to broaden the perspectives of those who advocate for and serve this population of students.

SPECIAL EDUCATION: INAPPROPRIATE REFERRAL AND ASSESSMENT PRACTICES

Perhaps at the forefront of the discourse on the placement of minority students into programs for the emotionally and behaviorally disordered are special educators and special education advocacy groups. These individuals and groups purport that biased referral practices and inappropriate assessment procedures have resulted in inappropriate and disproportionate placements of minority children into special education programs—including programs for children with emotional or behavioral disorders (Chinn & Hughes, 1987; Cummins, 1986, 1989; Duffey, Salvia, Tucker, & Ysseldyke, 1981; Executive Committee of The Council for Children with Behavioral Disorders, 1989; Forness, 1988; Galagan, 1985; Hilliard, 1990; Sugai, 1988; Sugai & Maheady, 1988; Tomlinson, Acker, Conter, & Lindborg, 1977). According to a report issued by CCBD (1989):

> We argue that problems inherent in the assessment of culturally diverse children are linked inextricably to larger conceptual and procedural shortcomings within our existing norm-referenced assessment approach. Furthermore, we suggest that efforts to improve assessment practices for culturally diverse learners by simply altering "surface level" facets of the existing norm-references systems are insufficient. (p. 263)

Sugai (1988) provided information that verifies claims of inadequacy of norm-referenced procedures in assessing the needs of minority children who are being considered for placement into programs for children with emotional or behavioral disorders. He contended that many of the standardized instruments used to assess the behavior of students are not related to instruction, and that such instruments fail "to evaluate the effect of individual biases and values on educational decision making" (p. 6).

Sugai stated further that when assessing whether a child has an emotional or behavioral disorder, norm-referenced procedures fail to consider "the major factors that contribute to determinations of normalcy and deviancy" (p. 4). Sugai referred to these factors as predisposing factors (e.g., biological or genetic factors), behaviors, precipitating factors (antecedent conditions) and contributing factors (e.g., consequence conditions). Sugai concluded that "The outcomes associated with a failure to consider predisposing, precipitating, and contributing factors and failure to change school contributions to deviancy can be dramatic for the culturally different student" (p. 5). These outcomes include lowered expectations on the part of teachers and increased referrals of minority students for special education. The following vignette identifies how the traditional referral and assessment practices outlined by Sugai might result in inappropriate recommendations and placements for any child, and how the added factor of minority status might further exacerbate the problem.

> Susan Harris, a third-grade teacher at Jacobson Elementary School, headed straight to the office after afternoon bus duty to obtain a referral form from the coordinator of special education. Susan decided to forgo her intentions to review her plans for the culminating social studies activity scheduled for the next day; she could do this at home tonight. Right now, the only thing she could think about was starting the process for getting Trevor Timmons out of her classroom and into a special education class where he belonged. Susan breathed heavily as she rushed to her classroom with the "pink form" and Trevor's cumulative folder. After entering her classroom, she went to her desk immediately and began to pull the information that she would need from the cumulative folder.
>
> "I've had it up to here with this kid," she thought as she spotted the personal data information that she needed to include on the referral form. "Trevor is disrupting what is otherwise a well-behaved class. I simply can't continue to allow him to jeopardize the learning and the safety of the other students. There are no ifs, ands, or buts about it. He has to be removed from this class before he hurts someone. He has to go. I'm just not set up to deal with his serious problems."
>
> In only a few minutes, Susan had transferred the necessary data to the referral form. She was now ready to write the required narrative that outlined specifically the reasons for the referral to the child study team. For a moment, she reflected on her experiences with Trevor and then she began to write her narrative. She noticed the limited space provided on the front of the form and the statement in parentheses that read, "Please use reverse side of this page if additional space is required." Susan raised her eyebrows and shook her head as she began to write, for she was certain that in addition to using the back of the referral form, she would also have to attach additional sheets. Following is her final report.
>
> 11/3
>
> "Since Trevor transferred to Jacobson at the beginning of the year, he has been involved in one calamitous situation after another. Just one week into the school year, he brought a cigarette lighter to school and set the contents of the bathroom

trash can on fire. When I asked him why he would do such a thing, he shrugged his shoulders and stated that he was flickering the lighter in the bathroom during break and some of the other boys dared him to light the paper towels in the trash can. He said he had to show them that he wasn't afraid. 'So I lit it,' he volunteered. Neither a referral to the office nor a telephone call home to his mother seemed to spark any improvement in Trevor's behavior. Instead, things just seemed to continue to go downhill after this incident. Trevor has started to provoke other students in one way or another almost every day. One day when he thought I wasn't looking, I saw him stick out his foot and trip another student as he walked to the pencil sharpener. When I confronted him, he denied the whole thing. I took him out in the hallway and tried to reason with him. I could not get him to even look at me. He just held his head down and refused to say anything. He just shut down. Several times, I have seen him punch other students on the shoulder or in the chest. A few times, parents have contacted me to indicate that their children are afraid of Trevor.

"In no way does Trevor display any respect for authority. One of our standing classroom rules is that students should raise their hands and be acknowledged before responding to a question. Trevor blatantly ignores this rule. He blurts out answers and then looks at me with this devious smirk on his face. Some days when he behaves in this way, I'll put him in time out in the corner of the classroom and he'll just sit there and tap his fingers or a pencil on the desktop or make animal noises that disrupt what's going on in the class. He never completes homework assignments and always gives as an excuse that he forgets to take his books home or he doesn't have a quiet place to study. When I ask him about his assignments, most of the time he just shrugs his shoulders and spouts out something like, 'I can't do any studying with all that noise in my house. I need some quiet so I can concentrate.' In actuality, I suspect that part of Trevor's reaction to homework and classwork assignments is his poor general functioning in the third-grade curriculum. He struggles in every subject except science. I think this is because our new curriculum emphasizes a hands-on, experiential approach. Any task that requires reading is extremely difficult for Trevor. Math skills are somewhat more developed, but Trevor has not yet mastered his math facts and has great difficulty solving application problems.

"Today something happened that really lets me know just how serious Trevor's problems are. I had just put the students into their cooperative learning groups and given them instructions to finish their art projects for social studies. It seems that Trevor was upset because he wanted to paint the poster for the group and Bobbie insisted that this was his responsibility. Bobbie was right, of course, but for Trevor, it's going to be his way, or no way at all. I was writing some vocabulary words on the board to prepare for reading and I had my back turned to the class. I heard this loud, clanging noise. Someone was knocking over desks, tables, and chairs in the back section of the room. It sounded like we were in the middle of an earthquake. I turned and saw Trevor and Bobbie scuffling on the floor. Spilled paint was all over the other students in the group, the table, the overturned chairs, and the floor. Trevor was on top of Bobbie screaming, 'If I can't paint the damn poster, nobody's goin' to!' Jessica, one of the students in the group, was crying and others were screaming at the top of their lungs trying to describe to me what had just happened. I had to send a student across the hall for Clarice, my team member, to come over

> and help me restore order to this chaos. It took the two of us to pull Trevor off of Bobbie and get him down to the office.
>
> "I think these reasons verify the need for Trevor to be evaluated for placement into a special education class. His behaviors are so uncontrollable and inappropriate that he just doesn't fit in with the rest of my students. I believe that he needs someone to really work with him on learning appropriate social skills and controlling his potentially dangerous outbursts. With 30 other students in my classroom, I just can't give him all of the individualized attention that he needs."
>
> Approximately two months after Susan's screening meeting with the child study team, Trevor was found eligible for placement into a self-contained classroom for students with emotional or behavior disorders. Based on the results from norm-referenced testing (e.g., educational evaluation, psychological evaluation, sociological evaluation) and a medical report, tentative long- and short-term objectives were also developed for the IEP during this eligibility meeting. All persons present at the meeting—including Trevor's mother—agreed with the decision to place Trevor. One week after the eligibility meeting, Trevor started in his special class placement.

There are some educators who, after reading this case report, would conclude that Susan's referral to the child study team, the assessment process, and Trevor's subsequent placement into a special education program were appropriate and justifiable. After all, as Susan indicated, Trevor was jeopardizing the safety of himself and others in the classroom. However, there are others who might question the appropriateness and legitimacy of the referral and subsequent placement. Some opponents would be concerned about Susan's state of mind when she made the referral. She was extremely upset and angry with Trevor. She completed the form hastily and she did not present the information in a cohesive, sequential manner. Susan made a recommendation for special education in her referral prior to the initiation of any type of assessment. She did not examine her behaviors. She did not report antecedent conditions in the classroom that might have triggered some of Trevor's inappropriate behaviors. Finally, based on the suspect information presented by Susan, a multidisciplinary team used mostly norm-referenced tools to make a decision about Trevor's placement. There are special educators and special education advocacy groups who would consider this process to be inappropriate and inadequate for any child who is experiencing learning and behavior problems—regardless of his or her race or ethnicity. According to W. Anderson (1988):

> Bias in assessment often plagues minority children who stand in need of psychological evaluation, but some forms of bias are problematic in the assessment of all children regardless of their cultural or ethnic backgrounds. For example, all children to varying degrees run the risk of misevaluation due to assessor bias in the assessment instruments being used. To some extent, all children may suffer from shortcomings inherent in diagnostic systems currently in use. Among these shortcomings, problems of reliability and validity figure prominently. (p. 193)

Citing the works of O'Leary and Johnson (1979), Nathan and Harris (1980), Greenberg (1977), and Spitzer and Fliess (1974), Anderson concluded further that, "the reliability of measures of personality and of psychopathologic diagnosis is comparatively low. Thus, assessment methodologies with low validity and reliability may lead to the misapplication of diagnostic labels to children" (p. 194). Based on this discussion, it is apparent that current procedures and practices used to identify all children for emotional or behavior disorders may need to be modified or reoperationaized (Hoover & Collier, 1985). Despite this realization, however, we assert that it would be erroneous to conclude that racial or class bias are never a part of the equation when special education placement is being considered.

Once again, we can use Trevor's case as an illustration. Could any combination of the following factors have affected the final decision of the child study team?

Trevor is not middle class and/or White.

He is Dianco Jones, an African-American student.

He is Juan Santos, a Mexican or Mexican-American student.

He is Running Wolf, a Native American student.

He is Lee Hwang, an Asian or Asian-American student.

He lives with four other siblings and a single parent in a high-poverty urban or rural area.

His primary language is one other than English.

Susan is an upper-middle-class White person and has never had any positive interactions with children of color or poor children.

Susan is an upper-middle-class person of color who has never interacted with poor children.

Our response to this question is yes. In fact, Smith, Wood, and Grimes (1987) supported this assertion in their discussion on the biasing effects of race, SES, and gender on the identification and placement of students with emotional or behavioral disorders (see also Reschly, 1987). Further, the research literature supports a relationship between student ethnicity/SES, teacher expectations/treatment, and pupil achievement level (Brophy & Good, 1986; Cooper, 1979; Cooper & Tom, 1984; Dusek & Joseph, 1983; Good, 1983; Irvine, 1990). Also, Ysseldyke, Algozzine, Richey, and Graden (1982) found that pupil's gender, appearance, and SES can be the basis for eligibility decisions.

We know also that the definition and perception of a deviant behavior might differ according to the culture in which it is observed (Achenbach et al., 1990; Weisz, Suwanlert, Chaiyasit, Weiss, Achenbach, & Walter, 1988; Weisz, Suwanlert, Chaiyasit, Weiss, Walter, & Anderson, 1988), or that teachers might perceive student behaviors differentially depending on the pupil's ethnic background

(Carlson & Stephens, 1986). Thus, we assert that modification of current referral and assessment practices alone will not reduce the problem of overrepresentation or improve the quality of services for these children. To deal with these issues adequately and fairly, we must examine factors that move beyond but interact with the problems that surround current assessment practices. Hence, we now turn to the fields of sociology, educational anthropology, and psychology.

Sociology: The Effects of External Stressors on Mental Health

Experts from the mental health field contend that external stressors experienced by many minority children—particularly minority children who live in poverty—place them more at risk than dominant culture children of developing emotional or behavioral disorders. For example, Isaacs (in Isaacs & Benjamin, 1991) identified several of these stressors. They include:

- Racism and discrimination.
- Mass media and the way in which ethnic minority groups are portrayed.
- The strain of acculturation and the migration experience.
- Legal constraints and strategies for circumvention, such as issues on American Indian reservations or those associated with refugee status.
- Language and communication pattern differences.
- Socioeconomic status, especially because ethnic minority groups are disproportionately represented among those defined as living in poverty.
- The American economy and the availability of employment opportunities.
- Geographic isolation and resource-poor environments; such environments include urban inner cities, rural areas, reservations, barrios, and other enclaves in which people of color are isolated from the mainstream.
- Inter- and intragroup conflicts and tensions.
- Assimilation and the loss of some of the most highly skilled/competent members of ethnic minority groups to the larger society. (p. 14)

Wilson (1987) provided documentation that validates the assertions of Isaacs. In his analysis of the plight of "the underclass," Wilson contended that the racial injustices and discrimination of the past do not explain totally the inequities that still exist in this country. However, Wilson espoused that there are other factors within American society that, when coupled with racial discrimination and prejudice, serve to create the devastation experienced by members of a growing underclass comprised mostly of racial and ethnic minorities. Although the primary focus of Wilson's analysis is the African-American underclass, he argued persuasively that many of the circumstances that have influenced the quality of life for African Americans now threaten to influence the lives of members of other minority groups in a similar manner (e.g., Hispanics, Asians, Native Americans).

For example, Wilson (1987), citing the work of Lieberson (1980), outlined how African Americans along with Japanese, Chinese, and other people of color were discriminated against more severely than Europeans who immigrated to this country at the turn of the century. However, he asserted that one reason for the increased discrimination and significantly less economic success among African Americans was the fact that larger numbers of them migrated to northern cities. According to Wilson (1987):

> The flow of migrants also made it much more difficult for blacks to follow the path of both the new Europeans and the Asian-Americans in overcoming the negative effects of discrimination by finding special occupational niches. Only a small part of a group's total work force can be absorbed in such specialties when the group's population increases rapidly or is a sizable proportion of the total population. Furthermore, the continuing flow of migrants had a harmful effect on the urban blacks who had arrived earlier. (p. 34)

Wilson also noted that this same phenomenon that occurred for African Americans is now occurring for other minorities. He documented that Hispanics are now showing increases in their rate of urban migration. He also noted that there is a significant increase in Asian immigration. Likewise, Snipp and Sandefur (1988) documented an increase in the migration of Native Americans to large urban areas. Wilson concluded that this migration and immigration may result in the same types of problems that plague inner-city African Americans (e.g., high unemployment, crime, female pregnancies, female-headed households, welfare dependency). In fact, he presented documentation illustrating that the increased immigration of Asians from South Korea and China is already creating problems for once-stable Chinatowns.

This devastation is exacerbated by the economic changes that have occurred in this country and the nature of the work force. The industrial age, which once motivated so many minorities to migrate to northern urban cities, is now over. Automation, along with a growing need for more workers with higher levels of education and skills, have caused a shrinkage in the demand for unskilled workers with little or no postsecondary education.

Added to this situation are factors that clearly distinguish poor minority children from their White counterparts. For example, Wilson indicated that the "vertically class-integrated inner-city community" that once characterized where poor African Americans lived no longer exists. He went on to explain that the vast majority of working-class and middle-class minority people have abandoned the inner-city neighborhood and have left behind a "depressed, unstable, and socially isolated inner-city community" (p. 58). Wilson also documented that

> whereas 68 percent of all poor whites lived in nonpoverty areas in the five large central cities in 1980, only 15 percent of poor blacks and 20 percent of poor Hispanics lived in such areas. And whereas only 7 percent of all poor whites live

> in the extreme poverty areas, 32 percent of all poor Hispanics and 39 percent of all blacks lived in such areas. (p. 58)

These new circumstances create significant stress for members of minority groups who live in neighborhoods racked by extreme poverty, and this stress is felt by children as well as parents. For example, McLoyd's (1990) review of the literature illustrated that these problems for parents include a range of psychoemotional stressors that negatively affect their relationships with their children. These include "forced relocation, entry of other family members into the labor market, and unwanted changes in marital and family relations" (p. 318). Consequently, these stressors result in increased feelings of depression and increased consumption of alcohol. Further, parents who live in extreme poverty report "more somatic complaints and eating and sleeping problems, and are at higher risk for neurosis, psychoticism, and suicide" (p. 319). Also, McLoyd found in her review of the literature that children in these "underclass" families were more prone to experience socioemotional problems such as "depression, loneliness, emotional sensitivity, social withdrawal, low self-esteem, and behavior problems" (p. 328). Conduct disorders and social maladjustment were also noted as problems that these children experience more frequently than their White counterparts. If Wilson's predictions prove accurate, we can expect to see increasing numbers of minority children (other than African-American children) become at risk for developing emotional or behavioral disorders.

EDUCATIONAL ANTHROPOLOGY AND PSYCHOLOGY: DISCONTINUITY BETWEEN HOME CULTURE AND SCHOOL CULTURE

Others who are concerned about the problems related to the quality of instruction and the placement of low-income minority children into programs for children with emotional or behavioral disorders believe that in addition to these external stressors, there are cultural differences that shape the behavior and cognitive styles of children, and oftentimes these behaviors and cognitive styles are in direct conflict with traditional schooling approaches in the United States. They believe also that these mismatches between home and school cause problems for culturally and linguistically different children (J. Anderson, 1988; Clark-Johnson, 1988; Hale-Benson, 1986; Jordan, 1985; Phinney, 1989; Ramirez, 1988; Shade, 1989; Spencer & Markstrom-Adams, 1990; Vogt, Jordan, & Tharp, 1987). According to J. Anderson (1988):

> There are many similarities in the world views and cognitive styles of certain groups of color that affect their fundamental perceptions of the world and how they choose to think about it and then interact with it. . . . Cultural and cognitive

> conflict often occur when a group is asked to perform in a manner and setting which in some ways is foreign to their style or does not capitalize on it. In many critical areas of human functioning and behavior, the world view of the dominant group is indifferent to or conflicts with the world view of other groups in the culture. (p. 6)

Sociopolitical theory provides a broad, comprehensive explanation of how this cultural and cognitive conflict translates into school failure for many minority children (McDermott, 1987a, 1987b). McDermott contended that their failure is an intricate phenomenon rooted in the very foundations of American culture: competition and evaluation. These "thematic forces" typify the daily classroom sorting routines that almost every teacher organizes in our schools. Class schedules are saturated with multiple situations where teachers and students confirm the stratification of our educational system in terms of winners and losers (McDermott & Goldman, 1983).

The situation becomes even more complex when we consider the presence of many students with significant cultural differences in the classrooms across this country. According to the National Clearinghouse for Professions in Special Education (1988), by the year 2000 over one third of the students in public schools will likely be ethnic and racial minorities. Right after the year 2000, it is expected that we will live in a nation where one of every three persons is non-White (Hodgkinson, 1988). Along with this cultural mix comes a myriad of different values, languages, perceptions, assumptions, gestures, turn-taking procedures, and many other elements involved in communication processes (McDermott & Goldman, 1983). Because of our inadequate education about cultural differences and our lack of acknowledgment about our own biases, the most likely consequence of such diversity is the development of communication gaps and misunderstandings.

However, the notion of cultural conflict and the school failure of minority children goes even beyond the influence of competitive cultural values and communication processes. The substance of McDermott's hypothesis refers to the presence of political differentials that permeate the negotiated social world of the classroom. Instances of such negotiations during the school day include the establishment of status, the political connotation given to the use of language and dialects, and the establishment of communicative code differences to reaffirm group adherence and cultural identity.

McDermott (1987a) stressed the notion of "mutually constructive interactions" to acquire different status (e.g., pariah or host status). As he contended, "from their respective vantage points, both the pariah and the host groups are correct. To the pariah group, host behavior is indeed oppressive. To the host group, pariah behavior is indeed inadequate. If we understand how the two groups find this out about each other, we will have located the central problem" (McDermott, 1987a, p. 178).

McDermott proposed further that the gap between pariah children and host teachers is broadened because of differences in the codes that they use to communicate within their own groups. These differences eventually become a distinctive mode of intergroup exchanges. For instance, these interaction patterns are established when the teacher attaches demeaning messages to the customary ways in which children use their own code for behaving and for reading and interpreting events in the environment. Examples provided by minority educators and researchers illustrate how these relationships exist between teachers and minority students. Irvine (1988) purported that three characteristics of African-American children cause problems for them in the school setting because they deviate substantially from the norms established by the dominant society: "(1) style or the manner of personal presentation, (2) use of Black English, and (3) cognition or the processes of knowing and perceiving" (p. 6). Ramirez and Castaneda (1974) developed the concept of "bicognition" and concluded that many Mexican-American and other minority children are considered to be behavior problems and fail in school because they come from homes where the cognitive style employed is different from the cognitive style that is favored and reinforced in most schools. After studying the family life of Native Americans, Pepper (1974) concluded that culture influences all aspects of learning, and that the cultural values established by Native American parents are in direct conflict with the values established by the dominant society.

Ogbu (1992) conducted research and drew conclusions that closely parallel the hypotheses and theories espoused by McDermott. He concluded that there are different types of minority status (autonomous minorities, e.g., Mormons and Jews; immigrant or voluntary minorities, e.g., Chinese and Punjabi Indians in the United States; and castelike or involuntary minorities, e.g., American Indians, African Americans, and early Mexican Americans).

Ogbu introduced the concept of primary and secondary cultural differences to explain the discrepancies between the adaptability of voluntary and involuntary minorities to a dominant or controlling culture. As Ogbu stated, "Primary cultural differences are differences that existed before two groups came in contact, such as before immigrant minorities came to the United States" (p. 8) (e.g., these immigrants often spoke a language other than English). In contrast, "Secondary cultural differences are differences that arose after two populations came into contact or after members of a given population began to participate in an institution controlled by members of another population" (p. 5) (e.g., cognitive style, interaction style, learning style).

Ogbu stated further that secondary cultural differences present extensive and persistent problems for involuntary or castelike minority students. For example, some involuntary minority students in the United States perceive adoption of dominant cultural values and behaviors as "acting White," and they ostracize and shun their same-race peers who accept such cultures and values. Hence, these children are immersed in the politics of everyday life, and they are working hard at constructing their identities and gaining status in the classroom. If the teacher frequently devalues or ignores these children's cultural backgrounds, they will often reject the teacher's messages as worthless. As a consequence, such children lose interest in learning, become inattentive, and a self-perpetuating cycle begins to emerge. Reciprocally, if the behaviors of the child are not consistent with the expectations and standards espoused by the teacher and the dominant culture as a whole, the child may be seen as behaviorally and/or academically deficient.

EDUCATIONAL POLICY ANALYSIS: AN HISTORICAL PERSPECTIVE

We agree with the assertions made by experts from different fields that there are several factors that contribute to the placement of low-income minority children into programs for children with emotional or behavioral disorders. We contend further that in order to grasp more fully how these factors interact to produce less than desired results, it is important to examine these interactions in relation to educational policy designed to protect the rights of underserved groups. Based on our analysis, we have concluded that much of the policy designed to bring about equity in the education for minority children—particularly minority children who live in poverty—often falls short of meeting this goal because policymakers and implementers seek to claim cause–effect relationships so that solutions may be derived in a so-called rational, sequential manner. In their failure to identify policy solutions that consider the previously mentioned complexities, policymakers develop policies that result in the perpetuation of those inequities and the injustices that they sought to remedy (Astuto & Clark, 1992; Bell, 1987; Weick, 1979). Clark (1989), for example, cited how this process is played out. He stated that "the rational, sequential characteristic of the bureaucratic paradigm demands a distinction between cause and effect" and that "managers are instructed not to 'think in circles' " (pp. 53–54). In essence, then, everything must be linked to linear causality. Oakes (1985) provided a reflective interpretation of the viewpoints expressed by Clark. She stated, to wit:

> Many school practices seem to be the natural way to conduct schooling, an integral part of the way schools are. As a result we don't tend to think critically about much of what goes on. I don't mean to imply that these ways of schooling are not taken seriously. To the contrary, I think they are taken so seriously that we can hardly conceive of any alternatives to them. We have deep-seated beliefs and long-held assumptions about the appropriateness of what we do in schools. These beliefs are so ingrained in our thinking and behavior—so much a part of the school culture—that we rarely submit them to careful scrutiny. We seldom think very much about where practices came from originally and to what problems in schools they were first seen as solutions. We rarely question the view of the world on

> which practices are based—what humans are like, what society is like, or even what schools are for. (pp. 5–6)

To deal with this human propensity to seek solutions to policy problems from a linear, rational standpoint, Weick (1979) encouraged policymakers and implementers to "complicate" themselves. He urged further that "Whatever additional ways we can find to complicate observers should also be adopted because the primary thrust of organizations is towards simplification, homogeneity, and crude registering of consequential events" (p. 261).

Hence, without complicating ourselves, without acknowledging and analyzing the multidimensionality and the complexity of social and educational issues and without examining problems from an historical perspective, we often develop educational policies that are difficult to translate into practice or inadequate to bring about desired outcomes. We believe that *Brown v. The Board of Education of Topeka Kansas* (1954) and EHCA provide us with a classic illustration of how two incompatible policies based on a simplistic, rational model overlapped and interacted with socioeconomic, sociocultural, and sociopolitical factors to create systems that failed to bring about widespread positive change in the education of minority children who are, in some cases, disproportionately at risk for being labeled emotionally or behaviorally disordered.

Brown and EHCA: An Incompatible Marriage

During the turbulent years prior to *Brown* (1954), civil rights activists, attorneys, and behavioral scientists used results from quantitative research to conclude that the self-esteem of African-American children suffered (the effect) when they attended segregated schools (the cause). For example, Akbar (1990) illustrated how the work of two social scientists (Clark & Clark, 1958) helped civil rights attorneys argue convincingly that African-American schools were inherently inferior to White schools. These researchers instructed African-American children to examine White and African-American dolls and select "Which doll is nice?" or "Which doll is bad?" About 60% of the children assigned positive characteristics to the White doll and negative characteristics to the African-American doll. Based on the findings of this study, it was only rational and logical to conclude that school integration would improve the "African-American child's self-concept, intellectual achievement, and overall social and psychological adjustment" (Akbar, 1990, p. 24).

This example illustrates clearly how the concept of independent and dependent measures were used by researchers, educators, and policymakers to conclude that it was necessary to proceed with deliberate haste in desegregating our nation's public schools. Policymakers did not "complicate themselves." They did not consider the fact that centuries of discrimination and segregation in all facets of American life contributed in a large degree to feelings of inferiority and low self-esteem among African-American children. They did not consider the devastating effects of the media, broadcasting, and literature that excluded African Americans as equal competitors in the race to gain and enjoy equal access and opportunity. Perhaps most unfortunate, they did not consider that there were components of segregated African-American schools that influenced African-American children positively (Bell, 1987).

Hence, policymakers concluded that African-American children would benefit optimally only if they were rescued from their deficient, segregated educational environments and placed into a superior setting—a setting that ironically upheld the same belief systems and values that permeated all other aspects of Euro-American life. As Akbar stated:

> No research was quoted to identify the pathological implications of the delusional system or of racism itself. If you assume that only African-Americans are being benefited by such a system, then implicit in such a conclusion is a perpetuation of precisely that system that you allegedly are seeking to correct. (p. 25)

Consequently, in situations in which integration did occur, African-American children lost the security that they felt in segregated schools. One reason for this loss of security was the treatment of African-American teachers and administrators during the desegregation process. Many African-American principals were demoted to assistant principal positions and were given far less authority or responsibility in their new assignments. Many African-American teachers lost their positions. According to Irvine (1988), those who maintained their jobs were scattered throughout school systems and many of the most competent African-American teachers were reassigned to predominantly White schools.

And so, when African-American children entered integrated schools, they were met generally by White administrators and teachers who were unprepared to deal with their cognitive styles, social values, beliefs, customs, and traditions. Because of the discontinuity that developed overnight between home and school cultures, these personnel began teaching African-American children with preconceived notions and stereotypical views about how they functioned.

By making this argument, we do not imply that segregated schools were the ideal program for minority children. The pivotal point in our argument is that the educational system embarked on a major restructuring endeavor without taking into consideration the complexities of the problems being addressed. A simplistic and linear solution was advanced (i.e., total and abrupt integration). Issues of inequality, lack of opportunities, prejudice, and racism that were present in the larger society started to emerge and to be reflected in "integrated" school settings. Among other things, this phenomenon resulted in a lowering of expectations for African-American children.

In a review of studies related to teacher expectations after desegregation, Irvine (1990) concluded that "Several studies indicate that white teachers have more negative attitudes and beliefs about black children than do black teachers regarding such variables as personality traits and characteristics, ability, language, behavior, and potential" (p. 509). Irvine and Irvine (1983) also determined that after desegregation

> black children in desegregated schools were found to be suspended for subjective rather than objective offenses. Subjective offenses require teacher personal judgment. Such offenses include disobedience, insubordination, disrespectful behavior, and dress code violation. Objective offenses include such behavior as use of alcohol, drugs, assault, and truancy. The point seems obvious that the achievement of black students in desegregated schools is profoundly influenced by the likelihood of suspension or expulsion resulting from teachers' subjective perceptions of what is appropriate and respectful behavior for black youngsters. (p. 415)

Ford (1992) reviewed the literature related to this topic and found similar results (see Smith, 1988). In summarizing Smith's work, Ford found that:

> African-American males (both upper middle class and lower class) receive lower ratings on measures of teacher expectations than do white students in general. Teachers exhibit such lowered expectations, both overtly and covertly, by being less interested in these students, being more critical of them, praising them less often, providing less and nonspecific feedback, and demonstrating less acceptance of and patience toward them. (p. 108)

The massive influx of poor immigrants from developing countries—especially from Latin America—made more acute the plight of minority children who attended public schools in the United States. Consequently, the discontinuities between school and home cultures and the lack of preparedness among White teachers and administrators created communication gaps and misunderstandings between these personnel and culturally diverse children, their families, and their communities (Irvine, 1990). During the 1970s, the enactment of EHCA further served to widen these gaps.

EHCA

The enactment of EHCA (1975), which occurred while many states and localities were still in the process of developing and implementing desegregation plans, once more afforded policymakers the opportunity to use a rational model to define and attack a policy problem. Once again, policymakers and implementers did not complicate themselves to determine how the interaction of these two policies would affect minority children (e.g., assessment, placement). This is obvious when one reviews the terminology and guidelines that were stipulated in this law. Some of these safeguards include:

> Testing and evaluation materials and procedures used to evaluate and place handicapped children shall be selected and administered so as not to be racially or culturally discriminatory (20 USC Section 1412(5)(c); 34 CFR Section 300.530(b)).
>
> Tests and other evaluation materials have been validated for the specific purpose for which they are used (34 CFR Section 300.532(a)(2)).
>
> Tests and other evaluation materials include those tailored to assess specific areas of educational need (34 CFR Section 300.532(b)).
>
> Evaluation and placement be based on a variety of sources, including aptitude and achievement tests, teacher recommendations, physical conditions, social or cultural backgrounds, and adaptive behavior (34 CFR Section 300.533(a)(1)).

On the one hand, we can see that EHCA provided many safeguards that were designed to protect the rights of minority children. On the other hand, however, even though these safeguards were included, and even though the phrase "other evaluation materials" was used to indicate a need for comprehensive assessment practices, implementers of EHCA have continuously overemphasized the use of a norm-referenced evaluation paradigm to find students eligible for special education programs.

Hence, policy advocates, policymakers, and educators sought to enact legislation that would provide equitable educational services for children who in some instances had been denied access to school because of a disability (e.g., mental retardation, learning disabilities, emotional or behavioral disorders). At the same time, they sought to provide equal educational opportunities in integrated settings for children who had been denied services and resources by virtue of their ethnicity or race. Unfortunately, they failed to examine history to determine the origins of special education in this country and for what purposes these services were established. For example, in examining the development of special education in the United States, it is obvious that in the decades prior to the enactment of EHCA a social order existed that overwhelmingly supported the segregation and exclusion of ethnic minorities from mainstream American society. Hence, special education programs were established for immigrant children who came from southern and eastern Europe at the turn of the century—"atypical students" who could not function in general education settings (Hendrick & MacMillan, 1989; MacMillan & Hendrick, 1993). According to MacMillan and Hendrick (1993):

> The social attitudes dominant in the early 1900s played an important role in shaping special education. Most prominent of these attitudes in the minds of educated Americans were the orthodox and reform varieties of social Darwinism. The orthodox form led its adherents to view new immigrants as hopelessly defective and to recommend various forms of segregation. When applied to persons with mental

> retardation, the treatments that followed were even more severe. The "eugenics scare" was fueled by publication of several investigations, especially those by Dugale in 1877 and Goddard in 1912, that purported to show that mild mental retardation ran in families of particular racial, national, and ethnic backgrounds and was inevitably manifested in criminality, immoral behavior, and the need for public assistance. (p. 29)

The subsequent widespread use and dependency on intelligence tests provided school personnel with a standardized, scientific approach to use for identifying children for remedial and special education programs. According to MacMillan and Hendrick (1993), this practice, coupled with less subtle policies designed to segregate students (e.g., adjustment of attendance boundaries), along with eventual differential funding patterns that motivated school systems to identify students for special education, all contributed to significant increases in special education enrollment among minority students by the late 1960s.

The overlap of these policies and the interactions that existed among many unconsidered sociopolitical and sociocultural factors contributed significantly to the circumstance in which we now find ourselves. We represent a group of professionals—working in different fields with no conceptual consensus about basic interrelated constructs—trying to determine how to serve equitably a group of children about whom we know very little. We contend that solutions to such a complex problem must also be complex in nature, and must incorporate a full range of interlocking, overlapping resources designed to improve educational services for minority children who are at risk for or who are already placed in programs for the emotionally or behaviorally disordered. In the following section, we provide a broad spectrum of recommendations that are in no way all encompassing, but will serve as a springboard toward the development of a more holistic and culturally competent system of care for this group of children.

RECOMMENDATIONS FOR RESHAPING CURRENT REFERRAL AND ASSESSMENT PRACTICES

To deal with issues related to the appropriateness of referral and assessment practices used to identify culturally diverse children with disabilities, educators have developed procedures that modify the traditional child study process and the norm-referenced approach. According to Gonzales (1989), some of these approaches include the development of culture-specific tests and local norms (Blanton, 1975; Chinn, 1984; Ortiz & Ball, 1972), the development of culture fair tests (Kaufman, 1986a; Raven, Court, & Raven, 1977, 1986), and pluralistic assessment (Mercer & Lewis, 1978).

Despite these attempts to provide for more equitable and fair referral and assessment practices for minority children, many critics have argued that these modified practices have not resulted in desired outcomes (Anderson, 1988; Bailey & Harbin, 1980; Chinn, 1984; Das, 1984; Sattler, 1988). In fact, primary reliance on a psychometric, norm-referenced approach to assessment has yielded information that is often not useful for instructional planning. Further, the pre–posttest design that characterizes norm-referenced procedures does not adequately help educators to monitor progress and to evaluate the effectiveness of their interventions (Marston, 1989). Hence, many educators now call for a drastic decrease in the administration of norm-referenced procedures and advocate for a functional assessment approach to identify the needs of children with "behavior problems" (Alessi, 1988; Galagan, 1985; Sugai, 1988, Sugai & Maheady, 1988).

Functional Assessment: A Nondiscriminatory Assessment Model

According to Sugai and Maheady (1988), a functional assessment approach recognizes that "student learning or failure occurs in an instructional context and is affected by student characteristics and environmental influences, specifically the quantity and quality of instruction received" (p. 29). Components of functional assessment include prereferral interventions, direct observation, and data-based or curriculum-based measurement.

Prereferral Interventions. Prereferral interventions (CCBD, 1989; Chalphant, VanDusen Pysh, & Moultrie, 1979; Graden, Casey, & Christenson, 1985) are one aspect of a functional assessment approach. Prereferral interventions, as described by CCBD (1989), are interventions that "provide direct assistance to regular educators to help them better accommodate hard-to-teach students" (p. 272). CCBD also stipulates that one very important part of a prereferral intervention is the establishment of "multidisciplinary teams consisting primarily of regular education teachers and related services personnel" (p. 272). Typically, a designated coordinator, other team members, and the referring teacher(s) work together to develop strategies that may allow for the continued placement of an at-risk child in a regular classroom setting. After initial assessment of defining and measuring baseline behaviors (done through observation and monitoring), the team meets to go through a systematic problem-solving strategy to select target behaviors and interventions. Next, the team identifies the responsibilities of those who will assist the referring teacher with the implementation of the agreed-on intervention. Selection of assistants include a broad array of individuals, including the parents of the child, ancillary school personnel, administrators, and personnel from agencies outside of the school setting. Finally, follow-up meetings are scheduled to monitor performance and make modifications when necessary.

Advocates of this approach believe that these teams will assist regular educators in teaching students whose behavior and/or learning problems do not warrant special education placement. Also, these same procedures can be used by special educators to monitor performance and progress in a more systematic, effective manner for children who do require services in programs for children with emotional or behavioral disorders.

Direct Observation. Another component of the functional assessment approach that is also a part of the prereferral model is direct observation. Supporters of this approach believe that it will also yield more benefits for children with emotional or behavioral disorders than do indirect measures of student behavior. For example, Alessi (1988), in his review of the literature on direct observation versus teacher/parent reports (e.g., interviews, behavioral checklists, and teacher/parent questionnaires), found that there was little agreement between the two types of measurement, and that the latter type rarely focuses on the behaviors that a child displays within the classroom. He concluded that direct observation approaches might provide teachers with more relevant information from which they can develop more appropriate instructional programs and behavioral interventions.

Regarding culturally and linguistically different children, direct observation—particularly when performed by external observers—may assist the teacher in discerning whether behaviors are inappropriate versus being characteristic of different cultural and ethnic norms. Further, contemporary notions of learning place a great deal of importance on classroom context and pupil mediating variables. In this vein, the context (e.g., teacher actions, classroom discourse)—the ways in which students make sense of classroom instruction and learn—are crucial to understand the intricate classroom milieu. Direct observation from a naturalistic perspective is the most suitable method to capture subtle classroom events that rating scales or reports will never tap.

Analysis and reflection about behaviors in this manner will allow teachers to be more sensitive to cultural differences and, therefore, focus more attention on how they can restructure the curriculum and instructional activities to accommodate the needs of different learners more appropriately. (For more information about direct observation approaches, see Patton, 1980; Swanson & Watson, 1989; Taylor, 1989.)

Curriculum-Based Measurement. Finally, supporters of the functional assessment model believe that a data-based assessment and evaluation approach will also result in the development of more effective instructional practices for minority students who are either at risk for placement or who are already placed in programs for children with emotional or behavioral disorders. Typically, teachers of students with emotional or behavioral disorders administer norm-referenced behavioral rating scales and achievement tests to these students, and derive behavioral objectives for the IEP based on the results. Unfortunately, as we have indicated previously, the contents of these instruments do not always measure student behaviors in the classroom or concepts taught in the school curriculum. Consequently, the IEP goals and objectives generated from these assessments often are inappropriate and unrelated to the needs of the child and the classroom setting.

On the other hand, data-based assessment and evaluation models, often referred to as *curriculum-based measurement* (CBM), serve a more functional purpose. According to Fuchs and Deno (1991) there are two prominent features of CBM or general outcome measurement. These include "(a) the assessment of proficiency on the global outcomes toward which the entire curriculum is directed, and (b) the reliance on a standardized, prescriptive measurement methodology that produces critical indicators of performance" (p. 493). Further, CBM allows teachers to "analyze the nature of a problem in an objective and unbiased fashion by emphasizing direct observation under prevailing response conditions" (Sugai, 1988, p. 10). This type of assessment is more beneficial to students who are suspected of having an emotional or behavioral disorder and those who have already been classified, because it allows educators to rely on more than just pre- and posttest measures to monitor student progress. Assessment is ongoing. Also, CBM allows teachers to determine whether a functional relationship exists between the behavior and performance of the student and the behavior and performance of the teacher. In other words, educators involved in the assessment and instructional process are better able to determine if the instructional approach being implemented is what is causing a change in the behavior of the student. In this way, teachers can make more sound judgments about the effectiveness of their interventions, and this will lead to the systematic development and implementation of alternative instructional and behavioral interventions that might be more effective.

Functional assessment represents a promising model that can help teachers to develop strategies that will prevent, in some cases, the need to place children into programs for children with emotional or behavioral disorders. Functional assessment may also provide more effective and appropriate interventions for children who are already enrolled in programs for the emotionally or behaviorally disordered. However, we cannot elevate this model as a panacea or a "quick fix" that will allow us to meet the needs of culturally diverse children more appropriately. Also, we cannot assume that the wide-scale implementation of a functional assessment model, without any regard for the sociocultural and socioeconomic factors that we have discussed in this chapter, will create long-lasting, widespread improvements in how children are referred, placed, and served in programs for the emotionally or behaviorally disordered. We cannot assume, for instance, that a multidisciplinary team that uses primarily informal and curriculum-based measurement will make fairer, more equitable decisions about minority children at risk for emotional or behavior disorders if such teams are not aware of these children's culture and background or about discontinuities that exist between the expectations and standards of the majority culture and that of a microculture. Nor can we assume that a model that ignores the external stressors that characterize the life of many minority students who live in poverty will bring about needed changes in how these children are identified and served. Based on these assertions, we now provide recommendations that illustrate how these factors must be addressed concurrently with restructured referral and assessment practices to create more effective instructional and behavioral interventions and improved related services for this group of children at both the prevention and classification levels.

Narrowing the Gap Between School and Home Cultures

As educators, educational researchers, anthropologists, and psychologists, we need to make distinctions between what we know, what we do not know, and what we need to know. We need to learn from research that has already been conducted to identify discontinuities between school and home cultures, study the results of such projects alongside existing theoretical conceptions about how children from different cultures learn and behave, and, finally, use this information to develop and extend our knowledge base (Ogbu, 1992). The work of Tharp and Gallimore (1988) and Jordan (1985) provides us with an exemplary illustration of how such a process might evolve.

In 1970, the Kamehameha Elementary Education Program (KEEP) was founded to improve the performance of underachieving Native Hawaiian children in language arts (Jordan, 1985). Perhaps one of the most interesting points about the development of the KEEP model was that—through anthropological and psychological perspectives and methods—researchers sought to identify the differences between the Hawaiian culture and the schools and how these differences affected the performance of low-income Hawaiian children who were not being successful in school. As Jordan (1985) stated:

> This work began with traditional anthropological and psychological perspectives and methodologies, but when the study of the lives of Hawaiian children at home led to looking at their lives in school, the magnitude of the educational problems faced by the children quickly became apparent. Efforts to unravel these problems became a research goal. At the end of five years of work in community and school, a fairly good understanding had been achieved of what was going wrong in classrooms in terms of mismatches between the expectations and demands of the school and the culture of children. (p. 107)

Researchers, anthropologists, psychologists, and educators used ethnography to unlock knowledge about actual discontinuities, and to also identify ways to make the educational program for these children more compatible with their home cultures. It is important to note here that in evaluating and redesigning the language arts curriculum, this multidisciplinary team of researchers and educators were careful to include culturally defined behavioral patterns into this new curriculum.

Jordan (1985) provided an example of how this iterative process emerged and was incorporated into the school day—and eventually became a part of the school culture:

> Most interactions between Hawaiian children and adults are mediated through a child group, rather than being one-to-one interactions. Because of this, and because of the definition of what constitutes respectful behavior toward adults of established authority, Hawaiian children tend to react by "shutting down," ceasing to respond in a one-to-one confrontation with a teacher. In many classroom situations, this kind of reaction is the opposite of what is desired. Therefore, KEEP teachers try to avoid direct, insistent questioning of individual children who have not volunteered a response. (p. 114)

This represents but one way that changes have occurred to accommodate the needs and respect the cultures of these children. At the same time, these children are exposed—in a sensitive manner—to other communicative styles that they will be expected to use in adult life as they interact and work with people from other cultures. The KEEP model has made a significant difference in the lives of these Native Hawaiian children. According to Jordan (1985), students in the program moved from typical mean scores at the 27th percentile in reading to mean scores at or above the 50th percentile on standardized tests. The results from this program support the belief that behavior is learned through one's culture and that discontinuities between one's culture and the school culture can adversely affect student performance, both academically and behaviorally. Also, this research informs us that we need to test empirically our notions and hypotheses about how other minority and poor children think, behave, and learn. We need to extend our current knowledge, which is largely based on intuitive conceptions and inconclusive, preliminary findings. For example, Hale-Benson (1986) synthesized research findings on how culture shapes cognition and behavior based on the work of many researchers and theorists (e.g., Abrahams, 1970; Cohen, 1969, Levine, 1977). These individuals have described the African-American child in a similar manner: Most African-American children are relational versus analytical learners; they are highly affective; they are global, holistic learners—to these students, the whole is greater than the sum of its parts. African-American students are differentiated as being emotional learners and their language is characterized by strong, colorful, metaphoric expressions. Meanings are derived through context, they are more inductive than deductive, and they are community oriented versus individualistic and competitive.

Although Hale-Benson (1986) used psychological, sociological, and anthropological literature to provide possible explanations for how African-American children learn, she also concluded that, to date, much of the work done in this area is inconclusive:

> This book should be regarded also as a statement of a problem—a working paper. It is not a finished, data-based theory. It is not a curriculum or a "how-to-teach-

> black-children kit." It is a progress report. It is an attempt to share the analysis of presently existing research literature that may create a framework for such a theory. (p. 5)

In reviewing the research literature on African-American, Mexican-American, and Native-American cognitive patterns, Shade (1989) formulated conclusions similar to those of Hale-Benson. Shade examined literature on sensory modality preference, cue selection, information retrieval and recognition, and information analysis and evaluation, and found that researchers have reported distinct differences in these areas between different groups. Still, like Hale-Benson, Shade was tentative with her findings. She concluded that:

> The evidence that these patterns exist, while sufficient to produce a strong intuitive argument, is really insufficient to produce the types of changes necessary in the teaching–learning process and in the assessment of skills. There is an overwhelming need for a cadre of scholars to examine these issues in the laboratories and in the field in an effort to support these propositions. (p. 110)

In our efforts to provide services to culturally different children who may be at risk for developing emotional or behavioral disorders due to the several factors that we have identified, the continuation of this type of research presents a promising approach to developing models that will meet their needs more adequately. However, as we strive to extend this line of research, we must also remember that strong partnerships between home and school will enhance the effectiveness of these research efforts. We now provide more specific information on this topic in the following section.

Improving Home–School Relations

Perhaps one of the most neglected areas in educational reform is that of home–school relations. This problem is especially magnified as we examine the relationships between low-income minority parents and school personnel. For example, Edwards (1990) reviewed the results of work undertaken by the National Education Association to identify the needs and concerns of African-Americans, Hispanics, Asians/Pacific Islanders, and Native Americans/Alaska Natives. Edwards compared and contrasted the responses made by each group and concluded that, like White Americans, minority parents "are deeply concerned with getting an effective and relevant education for their children. They want the educational system to reflect their values and way of life, and they feel they ought to influence and exercise control over their children's education" (p. 223).

Despite this desire for quality education for their children, many minority parents—particularly those who live in poverty—are not actively involved with schools and the educative process. One of the major reasons for this absence of parents in the schools is because of misconceptions and misperceptions on the part of school personnel. For example, Edwards (1990) found that, historically, minority parents have not been viewed positively by school personnel. Negative perceptions about minority parents have surfaced in the form of "poor literacy skills, language deficits, inability to implement suggestions, cultural distance between school and community, unwillingness or inability to attend meetings, and the inability to recognize their importance to their children's achievement" (p. 223). Investigations of these assumptions, however, have revealed different results. Investigators who have taken a culturally competent approach to examining this issue have found that problems such as limited access, limited knowledge, feelings of alienation, and logistical problems all influence the degree to which these minority parents actively participate in their children's education (for related readings, see Harry, 1992).

Needless to say, improving relationships between these two groups is no easy task. However, accomplishing such a goal is not impossible. Edwards documented several successful programs that have significantly involved minority parents in the education of their children. These include parent programs in literacy (see also Edwards, 1989; Saunders, Goldenberg, & Hamann, 1992; Tharp & Gallimore, 1988; Weisner, Gallimore, & Jordan, 1988); parent programs in bilingual education; programs involving parents as supporters, advisors, and interviewers; programs involving parents as tutors and workshop attendees; and parent programs addressing special concerns (e.g. multicultural education). Likewise, Delgado-Gaitan (1991) reported a successful experience in which Latino parents were empowered to become involved in the education of their children through the use of culturally responsive practices. These special initiatives inform us that it is imperative that this crucial area be developed and nurtured as we seek to communicate and work with minority parents whose children are at risk for developing or are already identified as emotionally or behaviorally disordered.

Prevention

As we work to achieve more appropriate curriculum and instructional strategies and improved relationships among parents, communities, and schools, we must also rely on the work of psychologists to mitigate the negative effects of external stressors on minority children who live in poverty. As we have stated previously, investigators have worked intensively to detect different types of stressors so that predictions can be made and preventive endeavors can be undertaken (Gelfand, Ficula, & Zarbatany, 1986). For example, researchers have found that the presence and number of stressors in a person's life increase his or her chances to display maladaptive reactions. Also, researchers have identified protective factors that enable high-risk individuals to circumvent a negative outcome (Pianta, 1989; Rutter, 1987). A significant contribution that developmental psychologists have made, as a result of their research on resilience, is that intervention and prevention efforts should be multimodal and must focus on multiple domains

(Cowen, Wyman, Work, & Parker, 1990). Still, there is a need for more research on the influence and interactions of various domains of stressors on children's development.

Recruiting and Retaining Minority Teachers and Educational Researchers

As the nation's student population becomes increasingly diverse, the teaching force and the community of researchers remain predominantly White. This discontinuity between the composition of the school population and the community of professionals/researchers is starting to gain some attention in the reform discourse. Unfortunately, it has not become a prominent issue in the preparation of teachers in the field of emotional or behavioral disorders.

Indeed, there is a need for more non-White educators and educational researchers. Although we must begin to teach nonminority teachers and administrators about teaching and learning from a multicultural perspective, it is also imperative that we begin to develop policy that will result in the recruitment and retention of teachers of color who can serve as "realistic role models" for minority children (Obiakor, 1992). The same argument is applicable for Caucasian students and professionals; that is, they need to see capable minority professionals offering meaningful insights into the education reform discourse.

Some university teacher education programs in special education have addressed this critical issue. For example, an interuniversity linkage program between Lincoln University and Pennsylvania State University was established to recruit African-American students into a master of education program and eventual employment as special educators. In another recruitment effort, Luetke-Stahlman (1983) randomly sent questionnaires with questions "concerned with demographic and personal information and with suggestions for successful recruitment of more African-American college students into the field of hearing impairment" (p. 851). Very helpful suggestions were provided by African-American respondents, which included (a) educators in hearing impairment should be sent to career days at high schools with large African-American enrollments, (b) send African-American people who are hearing impaired to these schools as well, (c) encourage African-American publications to address the needs of African-American people who are hearing impaired, (d) programs in hearing impairment should be established at African-American colleges, and (e) actively recruit African-American students for training at Gallaudet College.

Similarly, two major national efforts have been undertaken to train minority researchers and practitioners in special education. These are The Center for Minority Special Education at Hampton University and the Project Alliance 2000, housed at the University of New Mexico. A common goal of these projects is to promote the implementation of research studies that deal with special education and diversity issues.

Such efforts are commendable and should be well advertised and replicated to increase the numbers of minority individuals who could serve as regular educators and special educators—including the area of emotional or behavioral disorders. In addition, Irvine (1990) provided yet another perspective that should be considered by policymakers as they attempt to reverse the negative affects produced by the dwindling supply of minority teachers. Although Irvine focused on the recruitment and retention of African-American teachers, her recommendation is certainly applicable to increasing the number of teachers from any underrepresented group. Irvine recommended insightfully that in order to increase the number of African-American teachers, we must concentrate on the achievement of African-American children who are at risk. Irvine made the point that children of the African-American middle class are now pursuing careers in medicine, law, and business. Hence, we cannot expect that extensive recruitment efforts targeted at this group will yield significant results. As Irvine (1990) commented:

> Teaching is a profession that has historically attracted the children of minorities, immigrants, and the working poor, who saw it as an entree to the middle class. A large percentage of black teacher education graduates of the sixties fit the broader "at risk" definition of the eighties. These black men and women, who are now in their forties and fifties, came from segregated schools of the South and North, were the first generation to attend college, were mostly low-income in economic terms but middle-class in values, and although bright, scored low on SAT and NTE (National Teachers Examination). If the profession is serious about increasing the numbers of black teachers, it must spend considerable effort to educate low-income black students at the preschool, elementary, and secondary levels. (p. 39)

This idea represents logical and sound reasoning. However, it is rarely mentioned among policymakers and educational reformists who seek simplistic solutions to very serious, complex problems.

Directly related to this issue is the fact that there are too few minority educational researchers and teacher educators in the field (Frierson, 1990; Grant, 1992; Trent, 1992). This is unfortunate, because these researchers could focus on their own experiences in relationship to minority students with presumed learning and behavior problems from a perspective that other researchers and teacher educators could not. Their knowledge of belief systems, values, and ways of thinking about these children could be translated into instructional programs that could be field tested and replicated to improve educational achievement. In addition, these researchers could play a key role in the development of preservice and inservice programs designed to prepare prospective and inservice teachers to better understand the cognitive styles and the culture specific behaviors of children of color.

To accomplish this goal, there must be more federal involvement in programs designed to increase minority participation in practical education research and development. At a minimum, such involvement must take the form of minority scholarships, fellowships, internships, postdoctoral fellowships, early career research grants, and mentoring programs.

Culturally Competent Interagency Collaboration

In general, groups who serve and advocate for culturally diverse children with emotional or behavioral disorders argue that there is a need to develop a community-multidisciplinary approach. According to Cullinan (1992), CCBD's president:

> The community-multidisciplinary approach recognizes that many BD kids have multiple problems that are evident in community, home, and other settings in addition to the school. Services must be located where the problems are evident (community based) and take various forms as indicated by the nature of each problem (multimodal). Residential placements are to be drastically reduced, and most BD kids will not be served adequately by intervention in only one location (e.g., special education at school). Relatedly, there is a commitment to improve the family's ability to take part in intervention (family-friendly service). Prevention and early identification, as well as transition to independent living, will receive much greater emphasis. Central to this approach is the assumption of cooperation among providers of service to children in planning, assessment, implementation, and other activities. (p. 2)

Based on the factors that we have discussed in previous sections of this chapter (e.g., external stressors, socioeconomic factors, current service practices), this conceptual framework for meeting the needs of children with emotional or behavioral disorders is particularly relevant and appropriate for poverty-ridden culturally diverse children who fall under this category. So that services may be rendered in a more appropriate, equitable fashion, service providers such as mental health agencies, public health agencies, social service agencies, and schools must join forces with the families of these children and their communities in a coordinated effort. However, before such interagency collaboration can emerge, service providers within agencies must determine the extent to which they are equipped to serve competently minority families whose children have emotional or behavioral disorders. More specifically, agencies must establish at what stage they fall along a continuum that characterizes attitudes toward minority children with emotional or behavioral disorders and their families. According to Cross et al. (1989), the stages of the continuum include cultural destructiveness, cultural incapacity, cultural blindness, cultural precompetence, cultural competence, and cultural proficiency. These authors also identified those attributes that emerge as agencies progress from cultural destruction to cultural proficiency. As they stated, "The culturally competent system of care values diversity, has the capacity for cultural self-assessment, is conscious of the dynamics inherent when cultures interact, has institutionalized cultural knowledge, and has developed adaptations to diversity" (p. 19).

Hence, culturally competent and proficient agencies would work independently and collectively to:

- Establish policies that focus on services for culturally diverse children with emotional or behavioral disorders, especially those who live in extreme poverty.
- Develop and implement inservice programs designed to move personnel toward cultural proficiency and positive intercultural communication.
- Establish programs that train and retain competent minority professionals and service providers.
- Make resources more accessible to minority families and children who have or who are at risk for developing emotional or behavioral disorders.
- Link natural systems of care (e.g., churches, social clubs, sororities, fraternities) in the communities and homes of these children with professional agencies.
- Conduct research designed to identify intra- and interagency initiatives that are most effective in meeting the needs of these children and their families.

As agencies work to link their services, federal, state, and local governments must provide incentives for such endeavors.

Promoting Access to and Dissemination of Knowledge

Finally, as benefits are reaped from these initiatives, this new knowledge base must be disseminated and incorporated into the curricula of colleges or departments of education, sociology, anthropology, and psychology. Also, these departments must seek ways to connect programs and experiences for students that will enable them to conceptualize service delivery for minority children with emotional or behavioral disorders from a multidisciplinary perspective.

We perceive the need for knowledge dissemination to demystify stereotypes and overgeneralizations that characterize people of color as individuals with deficits. It is time to propose and test different hypotheses (e.g., radical pedagogy, sociological views of special education, discontinuity hypothesis) to explain the construction of failure among minority individuals and to challenge traditional notions in this arena.

CONCLUSIONS

"There is no worse lie than a problem poorly stated" (Bernanos, cited in Cuban, 1989).

In summary, the underlying premise of this chapter has been twofold: First, that the problems exhibited by culturally different children ought to be explained beyond the traditional child deficit view. As evidenced in our review of the literature, factors that are external to culturally diverse children also contribute to their academic and behavioral problems. Second, before we define *how* to solve the dilemmas surrounding this group of students, we need to look more carefully at *what* the basic issues are.

Hence, we need to reframe our understanding of this dilemma by looking meticulously at what we know (or do not know) about the very nature of differences from broader (i.e., multidisciplinary) perspectives. That is, before we continue developing solutions that lack a clear conceptual base and are simplistic in scope, we need to organize and define the basic body of knowledge in various fields (e.g., special education, psychology, sociology, educational anthropology, and policy studies). The interdisciplinary research that emanates from these fields must, at minimum, focus on:

1. The community (e.g., values, relations with home and school).
2. The home (e.g., values and communication and interactive patterns).
3. The educational system (e.g., conceptual issues, policies, procedural issues, and personnel preparation issues).
4. The school (e.g., curricula, policies, and relations with home).
5. The classroom (e.g., teacher, pupils, processes, and outcomes).

Finally, we must use the results of this research to develop interagency partnerships that will create improved and culturally competent systems of care for children of color with emotional or behavioral disorders or who are likely to develop emotional or behavioral disorders. Perhaps then, the Susan Harrises who every day confront a Trevor, a Dianco, a Juan, a Running Wolf, or a Lee will possess the beliefs, perspectives, and resources to meet the needs of these children more appropriately and equitably.

REFERENCES

Abrahams, R. D. (1970). *"Can you dig it?": Aspects of the African esthetic in African-Americans.* Paper presented at the African Folklore Institute, Indiana University, Bloomington.

Achenbach, T. M., Bird, H. R., Canino, G., Phares, V., Gould, M. S., & Rubio-Stipec, M. (1990). Epidemiological comparisons of Puerto Rican and U.S. mainland children: Parent, teacher, and self-reports. *Journal of the American Academy of Child and Adolescent Psychiatry, 29*(1), 84–93.

Akbar, N. (1990). Our destiny: Authors of a scientific revolution. In H. P. McAdoo & J. L. McAdoo (Eds.), *Black children: Social, educational, and parental environments* (pp. 17–31). Newbury, CA: Sage.

Alessi, G., (1988). Direct observation methods for emotional/behavior problems. In E. S. Shapiro & T. R. Kratochwill (Eds.), *Behavioral assessment in schools: Conceptual foundations and practical applications* (pp. 14–75). New York: Guilford.

Anderson, J. A. (1988). Cognitive styles and multicultural populations. *Journal of Teacher Education, 39*, 2–9.

Anderson, W. H. (1988). The behavioral assessment of conduct disorder in a Black child. In R. L. Jones (Ed.), *Psychoeducational assessment of minority group children: A casebook* (pp. 193–223). Berkeley, CA: Cobb & Henry.

Astuto, T. A., & Clark, D. L. (1992). Challenging the limits of school restructuring and reform. In A. Lieberman (Ed.), *The ninety-first yearbook of the National Society for the Study of Education* (pp. 90–109). Chicago: University of Chicago Press.

Bailey, D. B., & Harbin, G. L. (1980). Nondiscriminatory evaluation. *Exceptional Children, 46*, 590–596.

Bell, D. (1987). *And we are not saved: The elusive quest for racial justice*. New York: Basic Books.

Blanton, R. L. (1975). Historical perspective on classification of mental retardation. In N. Hobbs (Ed.), *Issues in the classification of children*. San Francisco: Jossey-Bass.

Brophy, J. E., & Good, T. L. (1986). Teacher behavior and student achievement. In M. C. Wittrock (Ed.), *Handbook of research on teaching* (pp. 328–375). New York: Macmillan.

Brown v. The Board of Education of Topeka Kansas. 347 U.S. 483 (1954).

Carlson, P. E., & Stephens, T. M. (1986). Cultural bias and identification of behaviorally disordered children. *Behavioral Disorders, 11*, 191–199.

Chalphant, J. C., VanDusen Pysh, M., & Moultrie, R. (1979). Teacher assistance teams: A model for within-building problem solving. *Learning Disability Quarterly, 2*, 85–96.

Chinn, P. C. (1984). *Education of culturally and linguistically different exceptional children*. Reston, VA: Council for Exceptional Children.

Chinn, P. C., & Hughes, S. (1987). Representation of minority students in special education classes. *Remedial and Special Education, 8*(4), 41–46.

Clark, D. L. (1989). Emerging paradigms in organizational theory and research. In Y. S. Lincoln (Ed.), *Organizational theory and inquiry* (pp. 43–78). Newbury Park, CA: Sage.

Clark, K. B., & Clark, M. R. (1958). Racial identification and preference in Negro children. In E. Maccoby, T. M. Newcomb, & E. L. Hartley (Eds.), *Readings in social psychology* (pp. 602–611). New York: Holt, Rinehart & Winston.

Clark-Johnson, G. (1988). Black children. *Teaching Exceptional Children, 20*(4), 46–47.

Cohen, R. (1969). Conceptual styles, culture conflict and nonverbal tests of intelligence. *American Anthropologist, 71*, 828–856.

Cooper, H. M. (1979). Pygmalion grows up: A model for teacher expectation communication and performance influence. *Review of Educational Research, 49*, 389–410.

Cooper, H. M., & Tom, D. Y. H. (1984). Teacher expectation research: A review with implications for classroom instruction. *The Elementary School Journal, 85*, 77–89.

Council for Children with Behavior Disorders (CCBD). (1987). *Position paper on definition and identification of students with behavioral disorders*. Reston, VA: Author.

Cowen, E. L., Wyman, P. A., Work, W. C., & Parker, G. R. (1990). The Rochester Child Resilience Project: Overview and summary of first year findings. *Development and Psychopathology, 2*, 193–212.

Cross, T. L., Bazron, B. J., Dennis, K. W., & Isaacs, M. R. (1989). *Towards a culturally competent system of care. A monograph on effective services for minority children who are severely emotionally disturbed* [Monograph]. Washington, DC: CASSP Technical Assistance Center, Georgetown University Child Development Center.

Cuban, L. (1989). "At risk" label and the problem of urban school reform. *Phi Delta Kappan, 70*(10), 780–784, 799–801.

Cullinan, D. (1992, November). President's message. *CCBD Newsletter*, p. 2.

Cummins, J. (1986). Psychological assessment of minority students: Out of context, out of focus, out of control? *Journal of Reading, Writing, and Learning Disabilities International, 2*, 9–18.

Cummins, J. (1989). A theoretical framework for bilingual special education. *Exceptional Children, 56*, 111–119.

Das, J. (1984). Simultaneous and successive process and the K-ABC. *The Journal of Special Education, 18*, 230–238.

Delgado-Gaitan, C. (1991). Involving parents in schools: A process of empowerment. *American Journal of Education, 100*(1), 20–46.

Duffey, J. B., Salvia, J., Tucker, J., & Ysseldyke, J. (1981). Nonbiased assessment: A need for operationalism. *Exceptional Children, 47*, 427–434.

Dunn, L. M. (1968). Special education for the mildly retarded: Is much of it justifiable? *Exceptional Children, 23*, 5–21.

Dusek, J. B., & Joseph, G. (1983). The bases of teacher expectancies: A meta-analysis. *Journal of Educational Psychology, 75*, 347–358.

Edwards, P. A. (1989). Supporting lower SES mothers' attempts to provide scaffolding for bookreading. In J. Allen & J. Mason (Eds.), *Risk makers, risk takers, risk breakers: Reducing the risks for young literacy learners* (pp. 222–250). Portsmouth, NH: Heinemann.

Edwards, P. A. (1990). Strategies and techniques for establishing home–school partnerships with minority parents. In A. Barona & E. E. Garcia (Eds.), *Children at risk: Poverty, minority status, and other issues in educational equity* (pp. 217–236). Washington, DC: The National Association of School Psychologists.

Executive Committee of The Council for Children with Behavioral Disorders. (1989). Best assessment practices for students with behavioral disorders: Accommodation to cultural diversity and individual differences. *Behavioral Disorders, 14*, 263–278.

Ford, A. F. (1992). Multicultural education training for special educators working with African-American Youth. *Exceptional Children, 59*, 107–114.

Forness, S. R. (1988). Planning for the needs of children with serious emotional disturbance: The National Special Education and Mental Health Coalition. *Behavioral Disorders, 13*, 127–139.

Frierson, H. T. (1990). The situation of Black educational researchers: Continuation of a crisis. *Educational Researcher, 19*, 12–17.

Fuchs, L. S., & Deno, S. L. (1991). Paradigmatic distinctions between instructionally relevant measurement models. *Exceptional Children, 57*, 488–499.

Galagan, J. E. (1985). Psychoeducational testing: Turn out the lights, the party's over. *Exceptional Children, 52*, 288–299.

Gelfand, D. M., Ficula, T., & Zarbatany, L. (1986). Prevention of childhood behavior disorders. In B. A. Edelstein & L. Michelson (Eds.), *Handbook of prevention* (pp. 133–152). New York: Plenum.

Gonzales, E. (1989). Issues in the assessment of minorities. In H. L. Swanson & B. L. Watson (Eds.), *Educational and psychological assessment of exceptional children* (2nd ed., pp. 381–402). Columbus, OH: Merrill.

Good, T. (1983). Research on classroom teaching. In L. E. Shulman & G. Sykes (Eds.), *Handbook of teaching and policy* (pp. 42–80). New York: Longman.

Graden, J. L., Casey, A., & Christenson, S. L. (1985). Implementing a prereferral intervention system: Part I. the model. *Exceptional Children, 51*, 377–384.

Grant, C. A. (Ed.). (1992). *Research & multicultural education*. London: The Falmer Press.

Greenberg, J. (1977). How accurate is psychiatry? *Science News, 112*, 28–29.

Hale-Benson, J. E. (1986). *Black children: Their roots, culture, and learning styles*. Baltimore: Johns Hopkins University Press.

Harry, B. (1992). Restructuring the participation of African-American parents in special education. *Exceptional Children, 59*, 123–131.

Hendrick, I. G., & MacMillan, D. L. (1989). Selecting children for special education in New York City: William Maxwell, Elizabeth Farrell, and the development of ungraded classes, 1900–1920. *The Journal of Special Education, 22*(4), 395–417.

Hilliard, A. G. (1984). Democracy in evaluation: The evolution of an art-science in context. In P. L. Hosford (Ed.), *Using what we know about teaching* (pp. 113–138). Alexandria, VA: Association for Supervision and Curriculum Development.

Hilliard, A. G. (1990). Misunderstanding and testing intelligence. In J. I. Goodlad & P. Keating (Eds.), *Access to knowledge: An agenda for our nation's schools*. New York: The College Board.

Hodgkinson, H. (1988). The right schools for the right kids. *Educational Leadership, 45*(5), 10–14.

Hoover, J., & Collier, C. (1985). Referring culturally different children: Sociological considerations. *Academic Therapy, 20*(4), 503–509.

Irvine, J. J. (1988, May). *Preparing teachers for the year 2000.* Paper presented at the southeastern Regional Meeting of the Holmes Group, Washington, DC.

Irvine, J. J. (1990). *Black students and school failure: Policies, practices, and prescriptions.* Westport, CT: Greenwood Press.

Irvine, R. W., & Irvine, J. J. (1983). The impact of the desegregation process on the education of black students: Key variables. *Journal of Negro Education, 52*(4), 410–422.

Isaacs, M. R., & Benjamin, M. P. (1991). *Towards a culturally competent system of care: Programs which utilize culturally competent principles* [Monograph]. Washington, DC: CASSP Technical Assistance Center, Georgetown University Child Development Center.

Jordan, C. (1985). Translating culture: From ethnographic information to educational program. *Anthropology & Education Quarterly, 16*, 105–123.

Kaufman, A. S. (1986a). *Intelligence testing with the WISC-R.* New York: Wiley.

Kaufman, A. S. (1986b). The K-ABC and giftedness. *Assessment Information Exchange* (American Guidance Service Newsletter), 2, 1–2.

Kiesler, C. A. (1992). U.S. mental health policy: Doomed to fail. *American Psychologist, 47*, 1077–1082.

Levine, L. (1977). *Black culture and Black consciousness.* New York: Oxford University Press.

Lieberson, S. (1980). *A piece of the pie: Black and white immigrants since 1880.* Berkeley: University of California Press.

Luetke-Stahlman, B. (1983). Recruiting Black teacher-trainers into programs for the hearing impaired. *American Annals of the Deaf, 128*, 851–853.

MacMillan, D. L., & Hendrick, I. G. (1993). Evolution and legacies. In J. I. Goodlad & T. C. Lovitt (Eds.), *Integrating general and special education* (pp. 23–48). Columbus, OH: Merrill/Macmillan.

Marston, D. B. (1989). A curriculum-based measurement approach to assessing academic performance: What it is and why do it. In M. R. Shinn (Ed.), *Curriculum-based measurement: Assessing special children* (pp. 18–78). New York: Guilford.

McDermott, R. P. (1987a). Achieving school failure: An anthropological approach to illiteracy and social stratification. In G. D. Spindler (Ed.), *Education and cultural process: Anthropological approaches* (2nd ed., pp. 173–209). New York: Holt, Rinehart and Winston.

McDermott, R. P. (1987b). The explanation of minority school failure, again. *Anthropology & Education Quarterly, 18*, 361–364.

McDermott, R. P., & Goldman, S. V. (1983). Teaching in multicultural settings. In L. V. D. Berg-Eldering, F. J. M. de Rijcke, & L. V. Zuck (Eds.), *Multicultural education: A challenge for teachers* (pp. 145–163). Cinnaminson, NJ: Foris Publications.

McLoyd, V. C. (1990). The impact of economic hardship on Black families and children: Psychological distress, parenting, and socioemotional development. *Child Development, 61*, 311–346.

Mercer, J. R. (1973). *Labeling the mentally retarded.* Berkeley, CA: University of California Press.

Mercer, J. R., & Lewis, J. (1978). SOMPA: *System of Multicultural Pluralistic Assessment.* New York: Psychological Corporation.

Nathan, P. E., & Harris, S. L. (1980). *Psychopathology and society.* New York: McGraw-Hill.

National Clearinghouse for Professions in Special Education. (1988). *Information on personnel supply and demand: The supply of minority teachers in the United States.* Reston, VA: Council for Exceptional Children.

Oakes, J. (1985). *Keeping track.* New Haven, CT: Yale University Press.

Obiakor, F. E. (1992, November). *The myth of socio-economic dissonance: Implications for African-American students.* Paper presented at the Council for Exceptional Children (CEC) Topical Conference on Culturally and Linguistically Diverse Exceptional Children, Minneapolis, MN.

Ogbu, J. U. (1992). Understanding cultural diversity and learning. *Educational Researcher, 21*, 5–14, 24.

O'Leary, K. D., & Johnson, S. C. (1979). Psychological assessment. In H. C. Quay & J. S. Werry (Eds.), *Psychopathological disorders of childhood* (2nd ed., pp. 210–246). New York: Wiley.

Ortiz, C. A., & Ball, G. (1972). *The Enchilada Test*. Austin, TX: Institute for Personal Effectiveness in Children.

Patton, M. Q. (1980). *Qualitative evaluation methods*. Beverly Hills, CA: Sage.

Pepper, F. C. (1974). Teaching the American Indian child in mainstream settings. In R. L. Jones (Ed.), *Mainstreaming and the minority child* (pp. 133–158). Minneapolis, MN: Leadership Training Institute/Special Education, University of Minnesota.

Phinney, J. S. (1989). Stages of ethnic identity development in minority group adolescents. *Journal of Early Adolescence, 9*(1–2), 34–49.

Pianta, R. C. (1989). Widening the debate on educational reform: Prevention as a viable alternative. *Exceptional Children, 56*, 306–313.

Ramirez, B. A. (1988). Culturally and linguistically diverse children. *Teaching Exceptional Children, 20*(4), 45–46.

Ramirez, M., III, & Castaneda, A. (1974). *Cultural democracy, bicognition development and education*. New York: Academic Press.

Raven, J. C., Court, J. H., & Raven, J. (1977). *Coloured progressive matrices*. London: Lewis.

Raven, J. C., Court, J. H., & Raven, J. (1986). *Manual for Raven's Progressive Matrices and Vocabulary Scales*, Section 2—Coloured Progressive Matrices (1986 ed. with U.S. norms). London: Lewis.

Reschly, D. J. (1987). Learning characteristics of mildly handicapped students: Implications for classification, placement, and programming. In M. C. Wang, M. C. Reynolds, & H. J. Walberg (Eds.), *Handbook of special education* (pp. 35–58). Oxford, OH: Pergamon.

Rogler, L. H., Cortes, D. E., & Malgady, R. G. (1991). Acculturation and mental health status among Hispanics: Convergence and new directions for research. *American Psychologist, 46*, 585–597.

Rutter, M. (1987). Psychosocial resilience and protective mechanisms. *American Journal of Orthopsychiatry, 57*, 316–331.

Sattler, J. (1988). *Assessment of children* (3rd ed.). San Diego, CA: Author.

Saunders, W., Goldenberg, C., & Hamann, J. (1992). Instructional conversations beget instructional conversations. *Teaching & Teacher Education, 8*, 199–218.

Shade, B. J. (1989). Afro-American cognitive patterns: A review of the research. In B. J. Shade (Ed.), *Culture, style and the educative process* (pp. 94–115). Springfield, IL: Thomas.

Smith, C. R., Wood, F. H., & Grimes, J. (1987). Issues in the identification and placement of behaviorally disordered students. In M. C. Wang, M. C. Reynolds, & H. J. Walberg (Eds.), *Handbook of special education* (pp. 95–123). Oxford, OH: Pergamon.

Smith, M. K. (1988). Effects of children's social class, race, and gender on teacher expectations for children's academic performance: A study in an urban setting. In C. Heid (Ed.), *Multicultural education: Knowledge and perceptions* (pp. 101–117). Bloomington/Indianapolis, IN: Indiana University Center for Urban and Multicultural Education.

Snipp, M., & Sandefur, G. D. (1988). Small gains for rural Indians who move to cities. *Rural Development Perspectives, 5*(1), 22–25.

Spencer, M. B., & Markstrom-Adams, C. M. (1990). Identity processes among racial and ethnic minority children in America. *Child Development, 61*, 290–310.

Spitzer, R. L., & Fliess, J. L. (1974). A reanalysis of the reliability of psychiatric diagnosis. *British Journal of Psychiatry, 125*, 341–347.

Stokols, D. (1992). Establishing and maintaining healthy environments: Toward a social ecology of health promotion. *American Psychologist, 47*, 6–22.

Sugai, G. (1988). *Educational assessment of the culturally diverse and behavior disordered student: An examination of critical effect*. (ERIC Document Reproduction Service ED 298 706).

Sugai, G., & Maheady, L. (1988). Cultural diversity and individual assessment for behavior disorders. *Teaching Exceptional Children, 21*, 28–31.

Swanson, H. L., & Watson, B. L. (1989). Behavioral assessment. In H. L. Swanson & B. L. Watson (Eds.), *Educational and psychological assessment of exceptional children* (2nd ed., pp. 244–282). Columbus, OH: Merrill.

Taylor, R. L. (1989). *Assessment of exceptional students*. Englewood Cliffs, NJ: Prentice-Hall.

Tharp, R. G., & Gallimore, R. (1988). *Rousing minds to life*. New York: Cambridge University Press.

Tomlinson, J. R., Acker, N., Conter, A., & Lindborg, S. (1977). Minority status and school psychological services. *Psychology in the Schools, 14*, 456–460.

Trent, S. C. (1992, May). *Needed: Minorities in educational R&D*. Paper prepared for the Council for Educational Development and Research, Washington, DC.

Vogt, L. A., Jordan, C., Tharp, R. G. (1987). Explaining school failure, producing school success: Two cases. *Anthropology & Education Quarterly, 18*, 278–286.

Weick, K. E. (1979). *The social psychology of organizing* (2nd ed.). New York: Random House.

Weisner, T. S., Gallimore, R., & Jordan, C. (1988). Unpackaging cultural effects on classroom learning: Native Hawaiian peer assistance and child-generated activity. *Anthropology & Education Quarterly, 19*, 327–351.

Weisz, J. R., Suwanlert, S., Chaiyasit, W., Weiss, B., Achenbach, T. M., & Walter, B. R. (1988). Epidemiology of behavioral and emotional problems among Thai and American children: Parent reports for ages 6 to 11. *Journal of the American Academy of Child and Adolescent Psychiatry, 27*, 890–897.

Weisz, J. R., Suwanlert, S., Chaiyasit, W., Weiss, B., Walter, B. R., & Anderson, W. W. (1988). Thai and American perspectives on over- and undercontrolled child behavior problems: Exploring the threshold model among parents, teachers, and psychologists. *Journal of Consulting and Clinical Psychology, 56*, 601–609.

Wilson, W. J. (1987). *The truly disadvantaged: The inner city, the underclass, and public policy*. Chicago: University of Chicago Press.

Ysseldyke, J. E., Algozzine, B., Richey, L. S., Graden, J. L. (1982). Judgment under uncertainty: How many children are handicapped? *Exceptional Children, 48*, 531–534.

CHAPTER

11

Postsecondary Scenarios for Troubled and Troubling Youth

Eugene Edgar
University of Washington

Shepherd Siegel
Puget Sound Educational Service District

The future for youth in the United States is not bright (Hodgkinson, 1991; House of Representatives Select Committee on Children, Youth, and Families, 1989; National Center for Children in Poverty, 1990). Our society is in a period of change and turmoil. Our economy is faltering, special interest groups are in conflict with one another, our political system seems incapable of responding to this crisis, and confidence that "things" will get better is lacking in the minds of our citizens: There is a structural malaise. Amidst this background, youth with troubling behaviors are but another symptom of the problems that are challenging us.

Speculating on the postsecondary scenarios for these youth is a frustrating task. The problems are easy to list, but reasonable proposals for positive action are difficult to generate without sounding foolish and idealist. The general public is reflexively cynical about programmatic solutions touted by political leaders, and such cynicism is not without merit. Regardless, we have proceeded with this task because we believe the problems facing youth with troubling behaviors are resolvable if we as a nation will it.

We begin our discussion with a brief overview of the definition issue, concluding that youth with troubling behaviors need (and deserve) services, regardless of categories of disability. We then discuss the current database on the postsecondary status of youth labeled behaviorally disordered. We move on to the types of services such youth need if we are ever going to begin to meet their needs and improve their quality of life as young adults. The major point we try to make is that these youth (and their families) require a wide range of services exceeding those typically provided by the schools (National Association of State

Directors of Special Education, 1990). Without these extended services, school programs have little chance to be successful. An additional point we make is that many of these services will not be needed by all youth, but these services should be available to all youth who do need them. We then move on to the role that secondary education programs can play in addressing the postschool placements of these youth. We provide several examples of programs that offer some of the services that can meet these diverse needs. As part of the discussion on schools, we address the issues of segregated programs versus integrated programs. We argue for programs that achieve desired outcomes regardless of the degree of inclusion, concede that no one program will ever meet the needs of all students, and advocate for the proactive testing of many program types rather than continued debates on what should be. We conclude with a discussion on the societal factors that we believe need to be considered when developing programs for youth with emotional or behavioral disorders.

If our society is ever to begin to meet the needs of its disenfranchised members, those of us in the helping professions must conduct action research, put aside our disagreements, keep open minds, and assume the larger view of the needs of the people we serve and the role societal institutions play in determining the outcomes we desire. Our hope is that this chapter will assist readers in thinking about these issues and will motivate some of us to risk action in an attempt to improve the quality of the adult lives of troubled youth.

ON THE DEFINITION OF SERIOUSLY BEHAVIORALLY DISORDERED: NECESSARY BUT INSUFFICIENT RESPONSES

There is a major debate on the definition of seriously behaviorally disordered (SBD) or, to be more politically correct, youth with emotional or behavioral disorders for eligibility for special education (Clarizo, 1987; Council for Children with Behavioral Disorders, 1990; Forness, 1992; Kauffman, 1989; Kelly, 1991; Nelson & Rutherford, 1990). Although there is general agreement among mental health professionals that 8% to 10% of youth suffer from serious mental health problems at some time during their school years (Knitzer, 1982), and special education studies have consistently indicated that 2% of all school youth at any given time are in need of special education services for behavioral or emotional disorders, only about 1% of school youth or half of the projected population are so identified (Forness, 1992). One of the reasons for this low incidence rate is the exclusion of students with conduct disorders (social maladjustment) from this category (Maag & Howell, 1992). Individuals with conduct disorders are viewed by the exclusion proponents as individuals who are in control of their behavior and willfully engage in antisocial behavior. Therefore, they do not have a disability and do not "deserve" special education. For example, some states exclude adjudicated youth from special education if their legal problems occurred prior to being identified as eligible for special education (Gonzalez, 1991). Other locales exclude gang members from special education, and drug and alcohol abuse are not considered indicators of behavioral or emotional disorders. Because of court decisions that inhibit suspension of students with individualized education programs (IEPs) from school, some districts prefer to keep their suspension and expulsion options for acting-out students rather than provide special education services.

The inclusion movement, frequently identified with the Regular Education Initiative (REI), has also contributed to the low numbers of youth being identified as eligible for special education services. With the advent of the generic mildly handicapped movement of the 1970s, youth with emotional and behavioral disorders were clumped with learning disabled and mildly mentally retarded youth and regarded as having mild disabilities. The preferred intervention for this group became integration. As mainstreaming became popular, this group of students became candidates for full inclusion in regular classrooms, and prospective special education students who evidenced behavior problems were served by prereferral interventions in an attempt to avoid special education placement. The school reform movement began to speak of pathological systems rather than pathological students. Schools should change to serve all students, they proclaimed. There are no individual student pathologies, only system pathologies (Skrtic, 1991). Youth with emotional and behavioral disorders became even more invisible and easier to exclude from the schools. If no one has a pathology and acting out is self-controlled behavior, then those students who behave in unacceptable ways are choosing to exclude themselves. This debate has important implications for how schools will face the challenge of disruptive students in the future. Ultimately, the impact of the schools' response to these issues will be felt in the entire community and adult world (Rhodes, 1967; William T. Grant Foundation, 1988).

There are multiple causes of serious behavioral or emotional disorders. These youth are not a homogeneous group of individuals; there are multiple etiologies for disturbed behavior that result in a wide range of behavioral manifestations. For example, externalizing behaviors (acting out) may be a result of brain function (attention deficit disorder [ADD]), socialization patterns (exposure to violent behavior, receipt of physical abuse), or temperament. Internalizing behavior (withdrawn behavior) may be a result of brain function (depression), socialization patterns (sexual abuse), or temperament.

Some acting out results in antisocial behaviors (gang activity), violence (fighting), or disruption of classes. Withdrawn behavior may include suicide, drug or alcohol abuse, or decreased activity (depression). Most manifestations include multiple behaviors, often crossing categories. The only common characteristic of these behaviors is that they tend to disturb others (Rhodes, 1967).

A major distinction in what happens to such youth is their involvement with the legal system. A good (but depressing) rule of thumb is that once youths have been adjudicated, there is a low probability they will have any form of positive outcome

(Haberman & Quinn, 1986). The United States incarcerates more of its population than any other country. The rate of incarceration per 100,000 is 455 in the United States, as compared to 311 in South Africa and 268 in the former Soviet Union (Mauer, 1992). For African-American males in the United States, the incarceration rate is 3,370 per 100,000. There are 92,000 youth who are in daily custody in the United States, and 60% of these are minority youth (Allen-Hagen, 1991). Involvement with the legal system is clearly an interaction of behavior with social class and ethnicity. Of youth in juvenile correctional facilities, some 40% are estimated to be classified as eligible for special education services (Rutherford, Nelson, & Wolford, 1985). Some youth who become involved with the justice system are served by special education, although the majority are not. The issue here is to try to understand the circumstances that separate those youth for whom special education is viewed as appropriate as compared to those for whom it is not so determined. Discussion of adjudication rates and interaction with special education, inschool and postschool outcomes for youth with behavioral disorders and those viewed as "at risk" compels discussion of issues of socioeconomic class, ethnicity, and institutional practices, including the delivery of services to youth labeled emotionally or behaviorally disordered.

Some youth with emotional and behavioral disorders evidence good academic skills, but others experience serious academic difficulties (Scruggs & Mastropieri, 1986). In either case, their schooling is seriously jeopardized by their behavior patterns. However, those with academic deficits experience added difficulties and present added challenges to the schools; subsequently, their likelihood of achieving postschool success diminishes.

Clearly, there are no pat answers for such a complex problem encompassing such diverse factors: learning styles, the family, the community, the workplace, and cultural differences. However, there are principles of effective educational program design that can engender the full participation of all the key players, and deliver appropriately sensitive and intense services to every troubled and troubling youth in need of such services. By melding the researcher and practitioner roles, we can complete the search for these principles and develop varying intensity levels of services for students and youth, each receiving according to need, and thus effective and cost-effective educational and postsecondary services will evolve (Wehlage, 1983).

Hobbs (1982) defined *emotional disturbance* as a discord between the behaviors of an individual and the tolerances of that individual's immediate environment. Although this definition is conceptually aligned with the "troubled systems" perspective, a careful interpretation calls for more comprehensive services, not less intensive or fewer services.

The very language we use for definitions shapes our thinking, our perceptions, and our service tendencies. It is a painful irony that the field has developed a set of labels that only the most insensitive would use in the presence of the person so labeled. Does this indicate a problem with the entire mindset of the field and the school–student relationship? Are people fighting for broader inclusion in the SBD category motivated by a desire to upgrade and deliver services more widely, or a desire to paste the stigmatizing label onto more youth? We believe that their intent is the former, and that the limiting of services we described earlier (exclusion of the adjudicated, gang members, and drug-involved youth, and use of the "mild" label) is essentially a defensive reaction intended to reduce costs and commitments, and perhaps to sustain the social standing of the school (Maag & Howell, 1992).

The debate over who should be labeled behaviorally disordered will continue for some time. There is no doubt in our minds that part of the labeling process is used to deny services to some youth who, without some form of specialized services, will fail to become productive citizens in our society. The labeling process becomes a barrier to placements that may be critical to the future of these youth. On the other hand, the labeling process may stigmatize youth with a label that can make appropriate placements (i.e., employment) even more difficult. A new process for determining eligibility should be a priority of the field. This process should be consistent with contemporary social definitions of emotional disturbance, give youth credibility and respect, and provide the foundation for treatment and ongoing support. Finally, such a perspective should encompass the interactive nature of serious behavioral disorders and compel service providers, families, and communities to consider solutions from at least three perspectives: (a) How can troubled and troubling youths modify their behaviors, (b) how can the environment (and ultimately mainstream culture) be modified so that it is more congenial to the idiosyncrasies of a greater range of individuals, and (c) how can ongoing support services be made available to individuals on an as-needed basis?

POSTSCHOOL STATUS OF TROUBLED YOUTH

Regardless of the etiology or behavior manifestations, the outcomes for youth with behavioral disorders are poor. Many fail to finish school, few attend and graduate from any form of postsecondary education program, small numbers find employment that provides a livable wage or health benefits, and many become entangled in the justice system. Although the existing databases may be suspect, enough of a picture is available to draw these gloomy conclusions.

Many of these youth fail to graduate from high school. The National Longitudinal Study (Wagner, D'Amico, Marder, Newman, & Blackorby, 1992) reported a 59% dropout rate for students labeled as behaviorally disordered. These data are consistent with other studies (Blackorby, Edgar, & Kortering, 1991; Bruininks, Thurlow, Lewis, & Larson, 1988; Frank, Sitlington, & Carson, 1991). Data from an ongoing study in Washington state (Edgar, 1992) found that for two school districts the percentage of youth labeled behaviorally disordered who graduated as compared to the total district graduates ranged from .09% to .56% over a 3-year period. During this period of time, 14 students labeled behaviorally disordered graduated and 42 dropped out. Although some of those students who dropped out returned to school (10), only 1 student who had ever dropped out (interrupted their schooling) managed to graduate from school over the 3-year period of the study. These data are clear indications that few students are labeled behaviorally disordered and even fewer graduate.

There are few data available on the status of dropouts, but those data seem to indicate a poor adjustment. For example, Frank et al. (1991) reported an employment rate of 29.9% for youth with behavioral disorders who failed to complete school (dropouts), as compared to 58% for graduates. Similar data were reported by Wagner et al. (1992) for dropouts of all categories of disabilities. These data must be viewed with some degree of caution due to the difficulty of locating dropouts to interview. However, the available data seem to negate the notion that dropouts find employment and manage to find a marginal quality of life. The days when youth could leave school early and find unskilled jobs that provided a reasonable salary are long gone. Dropping out of school (really, failure to graduate from school) is a major risk predictor, and youth with emotional and behavioral disorders have the highest nonschool completion rate of all special education students (Wagner et al., 1992). These data, in and of themselves, are sufficient evidence that major program reform is desperately needed for such youth.

Nor does the quality of life for those who do graduate from high school seem to be high. Employment rates range from 58% (Frank et al., 1991) to 62% (Neel, Meadows, Levine, & Edgar, 1988). The National Longitudinal Study reported an employment rate of 47% for youth out of school for 3 to 5 years and 41% for those out of school for 1 year (Wagner et al., 1992). Although employment rate is an important indicator of quality, weekly income and receipt of health benefits provide a more precise indication of quality. Few youth with emotional and behavioral disorders earn above minimum wage per week, and even fewer receive health benefits from their jobs.

Another indicator of successful transition from school to adulthood is completion of some form of postsecondary education program. Youth who complete college or other degree programs increase their ability to be successful adults. The data on completion of postsecondary education programs for these youth is dismal. Indeed, few youth who were in special education go on to complete any form of postsecondary program; Wagner et al. (1992) reported that only 12% of special education graduates have completed some form of postsecondary education program. For youth labeled as having emotional and behavioral disorders, the completion rate in the National Longitudinal Study was 11%.

An indicator of failure to adjust to adult status is adjudication. Once adjudicated, youth have a greatly decreased likelihood of being successful adults. Youth labeled as behaviorally disordered are adjudicated at a very high rate. For example, Wagner et al. (1992) reported that 57% of emotional and behavioral disorders youth who were out of school for 3 to 5 years and 37% out of school for 1 year had been adjudicated. In a study conducted in Washington state (Institutional Education Legislative Study Committee, 1990), 36% of the 1,822 youth who were incarcerated on March 5, 1990, had *DSM-III-R* classifications, 44% were eligible for special education services, and 29% were classified as behaviorally disordered. Clearly, youth with troubling behaviors tend to populate our juvenile detention centers.

The summary of these findings is that youth with troubling behaviors are not making satisfactory transitions to adulthood. The programs we are currently providing are not meeting the needs of this population. Although we are not certain of the direction in which we need to move, we are certain that the current state of services must change. The one thing we are sure of is that youth labeled behaviorally disordered require a level of service far greater than that currently being provided. Another way to say this is that the current placements are not effective. In the next section we provide a discussion of some possible changes in the service delivery system and the placements of youth with emotional and behavioral disorders that we believe will make a positive difference in the lives of youth who are labeled behaviorally disordered as well as other youth who are troubled but not so labeled.

MODELS FOR INTERVENTIONS

The existing interventions commonly provided to youth with emotional and behavioral disorders (and unidentified youth with troubling behaviors) are totally inadequate. Schools alone will never be able to provide adequate interventions. Only with close collaboration among human service agencies will we ever be able to begin providing acceptable intervention programs. At a minimum, the following services need to be available for youth with emotional and behavioral disorders. This availability needs to be viewed as a potentiality for services (services are readily available on an as-needed basis), because not all youth will need all the listed services at all times, but all the services will be needed by some youth. The notion of potentiality is crucial in that it implies the need for social systems to have the capacity to provide long-term, ongoing support services to these youth. In all probability we are not going to find a cure for many of these problems, and the only other viable alternative to a cure is ongoing support. Without this support the great majority of interventions will, in the long term, fail.

Wraparound Services for Families

Many youth with behavioral or emotional disorders live in families that experience multiple problems (e.g., violence in the home, drug and alcohol abuse, and/or other family members with emotional disorders). A disproportionate number of these youth live in poverty with all its ramifications: lack of health care, poor housing, limited opportunity for social and recreational activities, frequent moving. All this prevents the youth from being able to profit from the school program (and to find their niche in society), regardless of the school program's effectiveness. An array of support services such as housing, access to health care, employment training, individual counseling, drug and alcohol treatment, and day care for infants needs to be made available to these families on an as-needed basis (Burchard & Clarke, 1990; Nelson & Pearson, 1991). Without these services, noneducational problems will continue to overwhelm the families, prevent the families from providing the supportive environment needed by all youth, and stymie the potential success the educational programs might have for individual youth.

Out-of-Home Placements

A large number of youth (Select Committee on Children, Youth, and Family, 1989, reported some estimates to be as high as 500,000 a year) experience emotional and behavioral disorders to the extent that they require out-of-home placements. Most often these youth are placed in hospitals or other forms of residential treatment programs. The prevailing philosophy of these treatment centers is to deal with the acute behavior manifestations and return the youth to their family. Some of these youth live in families that are so dysfunctional that alternative placements need to be located. The only commonly available option in these cases is the foster home system, which is generally acknowledged as inadequate for meeting today's complex needs and harsh circumstances (Tuma, 1989).

Family policy in the United States is myopic on this issue, with the emphasis on family preservation at all costs, that cost often being the life of the child. Some families are beyond repair, and until that fact is acknowledged by human service agencies there is no hope of salvaging the children in these families.

Rather than exploring options for enlarging and improving this system, most efforts are aimed at expanding short-term family preservation programs. Wrap-around services do need to be expanded, but not at the cost of out-of-home placement options. This is a classic example of robbing Peter to pay Paul, shifting funds and priorities in a neverending cycle that refuses to acknowledge the complexities of the issues. This cannot be viewed as a case of either/or, but rather of how to provide a reasonable and comprehensive array of needed services.

An almost forgotten option is long-term group living for youth. Orphanages are considered an artifact of the past and generally unacceptable for out-of-home placements. The sordid histories of group living permeate our consciousness to the point that we don't even consider it an option. Perhaps it is time to revisit group living; we believe that in many cases a superior choice is to create positive group living environments rather than to attempt treatments for these dysfunctional families.

Some youth evidence such disturbed behavior that a 24-hour therapeutic milieu is required for the individual. Although this need flies in the face of the deinstitutionalization movement, the fact remains that under current arrangements some youth require such a program. Ironically, the recommendation for a fresh look at an "old-fashioned" intervention—residential treatment—is one setting ideally suited for the implementation of a relatively recent development, peer support groups (Wolf, Braukmann, & Ramp, 1987). By utilizing the best available professionals and paraprofessionals to bring peer counseling, cooperative learning, support group, and consensus-building processes to youth's group culture, youth with emotional and behavioral disorders can find and provide for each other the support and guidance lacking in their original home environments. They can discover for themselves and "own" the decision-making process that will initiate them into legitimate adult pursuits and sustain them through the concomitant struggles.

As with the other out-of-home programs, when these options are not available the youth are forced to remain in day school programs. These programs become overloaded with extreme cases, resulting in an overall decrease in program quality (these youth consume huge amounts of time and cause frequent disruptions). These youth seldom benefit from the service, usually dropping out or being placed in another program (most often a correctional setting). We do no one a favor by mouthing platitudes about changing systems to meet the needs of all children, or asserting that all children can learn or that everyone has the basic right to live in the community when youth with serious behavioral disorders are continually scrapped in the junk heap of our prisons or left to fend for themselves on our city streets. There is nothing more disturbing than to see a youth who all agree is beyond the help of the available services, wandering the neighborhoods waiting to be adjudicated or killed. We, as the professional community charged with the responsibility of serving this population, must have the vision to create the needed services for these youth in a manner that respects their human dignity and meets their needs. In many instances this will require the development of long-term out-of-home placement options.

Multiple Interventions

Youth with emotional and behavioral disorders require concurrent services from diverse agencies. Although attention needs to be given to increasing collaboration between human service agencies, the real problem is that there simply are not enough "slots" in the services that do exist, and many of the available services are ineffective. There is the need to greatly increase the number of such services and create improved services.

There is little debate that some of our youth are seriously affected by drug abuse, alcohol abuse, or both. What is still open for debate is how our society will respond to this issue. "Just say no" falls short of offering any appealing alternatives to youth, and "cracking down on drug users" only creates greater costs and violence. However, recovery programs that are readily available and address the advertising practices of the alcohol industry are also options that need to be considered. At the present time there are few viable options for youth who are abusing, especially if they do not have adequate health insurance, which at least 20% of all youth lack (Children's Defense Fund, 1989). Until such programs are available, educators will have little success with such youth.

Many youth and their families are in need of intensive and prolonged counseling. Some require individual therapy and others need family therapy. With the exception of those families with the fiscal resources to purchase (and the desire to use) such services, there are few referral options. Teachers faced with providing an educational program for such youth are doomed to failure and often confront a long, frustrating period of dealing with outrageous problems that are impossible to solve with only educational interventions.

Options at the Postsecondary Level

For youth who somehow manage to stay in school through graduation, the struggle is still far from over. The transition to adulthood offers severe challenges. The major options for youth as they leave high school is to go on to some form of postsecondary education (most commonly a 2- or 4-year college), or less frequently, to other forms of formal training such as a vocational or trade school, or to immediately enter the job market. Individuals who require some form of ongoing support are unlikely to find such services. Other choices of acceptable adult lifestyles are few unless the individual has unlimited resources.

Postsecondary educational settings are all too often inflexible in their responses to divergent lifestyles and behavior patterns. Mainstream values rule postsecondary settings, and youth who fail to comply are gladly excluded, especially when enrollment is impacted and they constitute the group most urgently in need of a legitimate chance to succeed. However, there is no educational entitlement beyond high school.

Most youth exiting high school who enter the job market do not have occupational aspirations; rather, they view work as a means to an end (purchasing power). When, for whatever reason, the job does not work out (low pay, hassles from a supervisor, being fired, changes in work hours, etc.), youth with behavioral disorders usually experience few value conflicts and often seek other means to meet their end goal (purchasing power); thus, job hopping, extended periods of unemployment, or even engaging in illegal activities are common. The lack of an occupational self-concept inhibits their ability to delay gratification and stick to a job until advancement and the corresponding improvement in their worklife and standard of living can occur.

One of the main challenges facing society today is to find (or develop) social institutions that can provide meaningful alternatives to youth who seem not to benefit from the available systems (Leone, 1988). This is particularly true for youth who for one reason or another have been disenfranchised from our society (e.g., minority youth, poor youth, or those labeled as troubling or disturbed).

THE ROLE OF EDUCATION

There exists today a unique window of opportunity in the field of education: Society is paying attention to us! Public institutions (such as schools) can only change when someone is paying attention (Bellah, Madsen, Sullivan, Swidler, & Tipton, 1991). Change that is real (as opposed to artificial, quick, and glamorous "band-aids" applied more for the sake of propping up a sagging politician or glamorizing a corporation with an otherwise limp public image) requires open dialogue between the affecting and affected members of society. In a society with diverse cultures and values, this dialogue is difficult to initiate and even harder to maintain. Our diversity provides the dialogue with unlimited possibilities for discussion, but this same diversity also makes real dialogue more difficult. That diversity will either be our salvation or our demise. At this particular point in history we are faced with seemingly insolvable problems, many of which are purported to be of crisis magnitude (population control, world famine, global pollution, a receding ozone layer, a faltering global and national economy). Solutions to these problems will require extended dialogue among diverse peoples. The greater the diversity the more likely a novel and workable solution will emerge—if we can but find a way to facilitate the dialogue.

A good example of such a situation is school reform in the United States. We have entrenched institutions (the public schools) that, by public acknowledgment, are not viewed to be working. There is a multitude of voices shouting directions, most of which are contradictory. The arguments and the data used to fuel this debate are often of questionable validity (Berliner, 1992), and if we are not careful the solutions generated for these perceived problems may be worse than the problems. There is no culturally unified forum to bring the dissenters together, so rather than dialogue there is bellowing. If there were an accepted and acceptable process for synthesizing this information, the richness of diversity would be productive. Without such a process the richness is suffocating. The key issue is how to synthesize multiple viewpoints (ironically, a skill not well thought of in our schools), but this process seems to elude us. If we fail to find a way to come together, the institution of public education, and perhaps our society, will cease to exist. It seems to us there are good reasons to search for "the way" to initiate and support dialogue.

It is now more commonly accepted that the path to the full integration of youth with emotional and behavioral disorders in society is less through methods of "fixing" such individuals, and more through developing ongoing support systems and redesigning our work and adult communities to accommodate diverse behaviors better (Kazdin, 1987). There are several things that our educational communities can do to better prepare youth with emotional and behavioral disorders for the adult world, and to make that adult world more congenial and responsive to the special qualities of these youth. We hope for a world that makes the most of what diversity can offer, and provides youth with emotional and behavioral disorders with maximum opportunities to make the most out of their lives. In the following sections we look at some of the general tasks educators must address to create an environment for this change, and then we offer specific examples of programs in which we believe that this has begun to occur.

Prepare Youth for a Place in Society

From the very beginning of any youth's education, and particularly those with special needs, the fact that they have responsibilities as a citizen in a democracy, and that this democracy will offer them opportunities to develop a legitimate career and assume other roles as a full citizen, should be taken for granted. It is a desperate fact that as the United States moves well into its third century, this is not the case. Youth in inner cities have grown cynical and contemptuous of the options they see for themselves as they reach adulthood (Wilson, 1987). Life itself has been grossly devalued in the most poverty-stricken areas of our nation, and the economic shift to a service and tourist economy has greatly reduced the career choices and the very image of how a self-sufficient adult behaves. Contrast that reality with a school experience that effectively presents a broad array of career choices from a very early age, and convincingly teaches youth that these are within their reach. Consider as well a scenario in which the appeal of a legitimate career is not taught as a way to material wealth but as a critical and required exercise of responsibility to a person's community, regardless of race, class, gender, or disability.

Infuse this curriculum with lessons in democracy, citizenship, effective communication, the development of caring relationships, belief in one's competence, and the exposure to ethical discussions of our society, and you have a very different picture—you have a very different school, one that perhaps can begin to address the needs of a wide range of youth and the reconceptualization of our society. We need to consider the arguments of Jonathan Kozol in his book *The Night Is Dark and I Am Far From Home* and address the open discussion of ethical issues in our schools (Kozol, 1990). How can we hope to prepare youth for life in our society if we do not help them address the inequalities it presents? How can we honestly encourage youth with emotional disorders to "blend in with the system" and comply with societal expectations when we live in a society that overtly oppresses a significant proportion of its citizens? Must we not acknowledge that many of the youth that we have labeled behaviorally disordered have reason to be angry and disturbed with the world they are expected to live in and accept? Is not part of our role as mediators of life for these youth the act of acknowledgement of the world's imperfections?

Collaborate With Other Agencies

Schools are the Grand Central Station where these changes must originate and will first be experienced. However, the participation of collaborating agencies is essential if schools are to move these ideals into a new sense of community that is substantial and pervasive.

For example, vocational rehabilitation can be a critical partner in assisting smooth transitions from school to work for troubled youth. By reassessing their eligibility procedures and creating a way for youth to use services and maintain a sense of control over their own destinies, this agency can provide job search assistance, on-the-job support, accommodation resources, union dues, career-related financial support, support for postsecondary education and training, counseling, and other services. Formalized partnerships with school districts can bring federal dollars to a community that will fund these activities. The current spate of statewide systems-change grants require this collaboration, at least at the state level, as well as the participation of many other agencies.

Among the other agencies needed to be sitting at the table are those that deal with adjudicated youth and correctional institutions and services. Regardless of how many more hours or dollars are expended in the debate of whether adjudication precludes receipt of special education services for youth with behavior disorders (the social maladjustment vs. youth with behavior disorders debate), correctional agencies need to collaborate more closely with educational providers. If special education funds to this population are limited, then the use of other funding sources (Department of Justice, Department of Labor, Joint Training and Partnership Act [JTPA], etc.) could still be better coordinated with school-based services. Programs that carefully monitor the transition from lockup to home and lockup to school can and should be blended with school-to-work transition programs that are in the schools.

Community mental health services are yet another agency with particular relevance to youth with emotional and behavioral disorders. By bringing their services to the school campus, or better yet, staffing a public health-funded counselor as part of a school-sponsored transition program, a concentration of services that will increase the likelihood of success for participating youth is achieved. The status quo alternative of compartmentalized services and low awareness of activities across agency lines results in poor delivery of services.

Experiments in school restructuring have brought schools-as-multiple-service-centers from the blueprint to experimental stage, and the potential for interagency collaboration has never been greater. One example from Woodland, California, is remarkable in its ability to patch together funding from a variety of sources, yet bring that funding into a realized plan of unified service delivery, all within the same school. For example, by using multiple funding sources, they have been able to revive and replenish the idea of school counselors, each with a reasonable number of students to serve.

Provide a Range of Services and Options

Bringing the variety of needed services—social, employment, rehabilitation, correctional, and health—under one roof will be a massive, yet massively rewarding, endeavor. Still, it is not even half of the task. The true coordination of such services requires that they be delivered at levels of intensity that meet the needs of troubled and troubling youth. This means that youth participating in these service options are neither under- nor overserved. Assuming that services are adequately funded, deriving the best level of services for each student will be no simple task. Every youth presents a different profile of needs, and a multitude of factors must be considered by professionals charged with the responsibility of meeting those needs. The nature of the family, the community, the youth, the service providers, and the peer culture all contribute to decisions about how best to serve a youth with behavior disorders participant. Still, there are broad categories under which agencies can be assigned and reasonable predicted ranges of services made available. For example, college- versus employment-bound students would choose from slightly different arrays of services. Adjudicated versus depressed versus drug-involved youth each have some predictability in the types of services they will need. Nonetheless, as needs overlap, and as youth continue to astound us in our attempts to put them into discrete categories, we would be better off to err on the side of overserving in the initial years of such an attempt to coordinate services.

Advocate for Change Outside the Educational Arena

The best efforts of our social, correctional, health, and educational agencies to provide state-of-the-art services will be in vain without the active collaboration of the community at large and the private sector. Children and youth represent everybody's future, not just their parents'. The private sector stands to gain and is also responsible to young citizens. Keep in mind that private enterprises operate only with the permission of the government and the communities in which they reside (Bellah et al., 1991). They are critical partners and servants in our endeavor to attain fuller integration.

Under the Americans with Disabilities Act, employers retain the right to maintain business standards and avoid undue hardship when considering the employment of a person with a disability. In the case of a person with retardation or a serious sensory disability, such calculations of cost and hardship will usually be fairly straightforward and simple to calculate. We predict, however, that it is the accommodation of persons with emotional or behavioral disabilities that will evoke the most controversial, complex, and passionate arguments in the courts. An alternative to a litigious relationship is one in which active public–private collaborations create mainstream opportunities for troubled and troubling youth.

As professionals in the field of special education (and other helping professions), we need to acknowledge that the society in which we live is oppressive and inherently unfair to a rather significant segment of our population; that we, as educators, are preparing youth to enter a capitalistic society that tolerates (some would say encourages) some 25% to 30% of our citizens to live in poverty with little or no hope to escape their fate; and that we, in our professional roles, perpetuate this condition unless we openly and loudly work to change our society as we go about our daily tasks within our chosen roles. We cannot be silent on these issues and pretend to be helping the youth we serve.

POSSIBLE EDUCATIONAL PLACEMENT SCENARIOS

In this section of the chapter we review a number of secondary school options for youth with emotional or behavioral disorders. These options address the educational components of the programs based on possible postschool placements of the students. The wraparound services we discussed earlier need to be in place for these proposed programs to be successful. We believe that schools need to move to the concept of placement rather than graduation. In this manner schools will take on the task of placing youth in situations that are accepted as appropriate for adults in our society. To our way of thinking there are only three possible general placements that could be considered successful: (a) placement in a postsecondary educational program in which the student has a fair chance of succeeding and one that, if completed, will enhance the probability of an enhanced quality of life for the student (colleges, universities, trade schools, vocational colleges, etc.); (b) placement in a job that pays livable wages, provides health benefits, offers some potential for advancement, and is viewed as a desirable occupation by the youth; and (c) placement in an intensive, ongoing treatment program that provides appropriate support to the youth and his or her family and provides placement into one of the other options at the termination of treatment. These are difficult outcomes to achieve, and we acknowledge that at the present time few programs are successful. However, these are the standards we believe should be used to evaluate secondary education programs for youth with behavioral disorders.

Mainstream Programs for College-Bound Youth

Regardless of their risk status, youth who complete a college or university program greatly enhance their life chances. A major goal for youth (including youth with behavioral disorders) should be to attend college. However, that goal must be matched to realistic skills (and attitudes) and appropriate school programs that will adequately prepare the youth for success in college. Although there is some evidence that for each year of school completed there is a corresponding increase in lifelong income (Ashenfelter & Krueger, 1992), completing college (rather than simply attending college) is what most enhances one's prospects.

Youth who are serious candidates for college must evidence both the aptitude and interest for college. Aptitude can be defined as information-gathering skills (reading, listening, interviewing), synthesizing skills (organizing, comparing, contrasting), presenting skills (writing, speaking), content skills (history, science, etc.), and social skills (working with others, following directions, and obeying social rules). These skills need to be present at the beginning of high school (ninth grade) so the students can compete with their age peers in mainstream classes. Such students also must be interested in attending college and probably should have some specific occupational outcome in mind.

These are harsh and stringent criteria for determining who should go on to college. These criteria are, however, the major predictors of success in college. We do no favors by encouraging unprepared youth to go on to college only to fail. Our community college system provides opportunities to reenter higher education at a later period for individuals who develop the interest and aptitudes later in life. This should allow us to make more realistic triage decisions at the high school level, for there is always the opportunity for college at a later time.

During the high school years it is imperative that college-bound youth be mainstreamed in classes with their peers who also plan to go on to college. Within any typical high school curriculum there is a hidden track; courses with the same title and graduation credit are in reality different experiences. There is, for example, the World History course for the college bound. Students are expected to read the text, take lecture notes, engage in group discussion, take essay tests, and rewrite wrong answers. The same course for the general track students has slightly different expectations: at least skim the text, attend classes, and complete a multiple-choice test. The "low" class has the unspoken covenant of "don't disrupt the class and you will pass." Although there are no formal descriptors for these classes the students know which is which. Special education students (and specifically those with behavior disorders) are almost always placed in the low expectation classes. These classes have minimal benefit for any student. If college is the goal the students must take the "real" college prep classes (in lieu of special education or basic classes) for their graduation requirements.

There is more to instruction than merely taking classes. Students headed for college need to learn how to collect information, synthesize this information, and report their findings to others. These skills imply reading and writing, but also include interviewing, organizing ideas, word processing, discussing information with others, debating facts and opinions with others, making verbal presentations, and working in groups. Many of these skills are neglected by regular education programs and, especially for students with troubled backgrounds, these skills need to be directly taught along with content information. Many of these skills fall under the general category of study skills, which are often part of the special education program but not the regular education program. This highlights the need to specify the role of both regular education and special education services in a program geared to prepare youth with emotional and behavioral disorders for college. The overall policy should be to replicate the support systems that are typically available to disabled students in higher education settings. Services provided by special education include instruction in study skills, tutorial assistance, and lessons in self-advocacy.

In addition, special education should provide support for the students in finding appropriate social and recreational activities, including participation in extracurricular activities and formal community groups. Activities that encourage good citizenship skills (volunteering in the community, voting, participating in social action groups) should be part of these activities. Matching students with adult mentors and monitoring out-of-school activities are other possible special education services.

One of the important aspects of any program for youth with emotional and behavioral disorders is to ensure the availability for support and instruction in areas other than traditional academic skills. This potential implies that services are available for youth who need the services but are not, as a rule, offered to every student on an ongoing basis. Each student needs to be assessed on these nonacademic variables in order to determine the need for services. The assessment and provision of these services are the responsibility of the special education program. These services include a wide range of topics dealing with being a good, happy, respected citizen of any community. These basic citizenship and quality of life events are important for all youth, but for youth with emotional and behavioral disorders schools (or some human service agency) must be prepared to provide training and support.

Reasonable accommodation and support is necessary for some students planning to go to college. These supports correspond to support that is also available in the colleges. Tutors, mentors, and special instruction in study skills are such accommodations. Understanding one's abilities and limitations is an important skill that can enable students to get the support they need to be successful in college. These supports need to be provided in a manner consistent with their availability in higher education settings. Financial assistance also needs to be made available to students, so they can have access to college and the needed support services and minimize the complication of working while trying to attend college. Students from affluent families with access to these resources and this type of support find that it often makes the difference between success and failure.

College is a reasonable goal for some youth with behavior and emotional disorders, but only with careful planning and the provision of ongoing support (similar to the needs of all students). In reality, few of these youth will meet the standards noted here. High schools need to engage in reform, and colleges also need to consider increasing their ability to provide reasonable accommodations to youth with such special needs. Perhaps the college of the future will perform its function in a manner not yet conceived. For example, if the social purpose of the university is to develop and direct the best thinking of our society into activities that will improve the economic, environmental, and social systems that we all inhabit, then clearly some element is missing in the interaction between higher education and society at large. Perhaps if colleges dug even deeper into the communities they serve (i.e., serving the youth with emotional and behavioral disorders), then their purpose would be realized. In the meantime, the reality is that for the foreseeable future most youth with behavior and emotional disorders will not be successful in college. Alternative options to college are needed.

Occupational Preparation Programs

Existing occupational preparation programs consist of placement in regular vocational education (a form of inclusion), vocational colleges (placement while the youth is still enrolled in high school), adult community-based programs, government-sponsored programs (Job Corps), and special needs vocational education programs. Although these programs have had success with some students, they have been rather dismal failures with behaviorally disordered youth. They have far too often become dumping grounds for youth who disrupt others, and mere holding tanks until the youth quit school or become adjudicated. They have gained a negative reputation and neither the youth nor teachers feel good about many of these options. We believe new models must be developed that address the myriad needs of these youth and are dedicated to providing the intensity of support services commensurate to the needs of the youth.

Inclusion in Regular Vocational Education Programs. The Pierce County Vocational/Special Education Cooperative, now in a national replication phase, is an example of one such program. Through the formation of a team that includes vocational and special education teachers, and the delivery of on-site technical assistance, inservice training, and the designation of specialized personnel to make adaptations and accommodations in the vocational classroom, many (not all) youth with emotional and behavioral disorders have been able to successfully navigate the mainstream vocational program and continue on to postsecondary training and gainful careers (Gill & Edgar, 1990).

The success of this and other similarly developed inclusion in vocational education programs follows the same guidelines as those we described in the college preparatory programs. The students must be able to compete with their nondisabled peers (this requires advanced academic skills and compliant behavior) with reasonable accommodations by the vocational teachers. Vocational education requires good reading skills (technical manuals) and self-control of behavior by the students. Special education services need to be viewed as supplementary (similar to services provided in vocational colleges by disabled student counseling services) and addressing the social, citizenship, and recreational needs of the students. For students to be successful in this type of program, they need to take a sequence of vocational courses that terminate in a skill level within an occupational field and enables the student to enter the work force or go on to advanced training at a technical college upon graduation from high school. The student, of course, must have an interest in the occupational field of study. Although access to this and the college-bound option must be maintained, we believe that a minority of students labeled behaviorally disordered will be successful in this type of program.

Specially Designed Programs (Segregated Programs). We must develop curricular options with the specific needs of youth with emotional and behavioral disorders in mind. If there were such programs already in place for all youth, we would recommend inclusion for our youth in them. Because there are no such programs, we propose that special education take the lead in developing these programs, but that other nondisabled students would be encouraged to enter them. Some of our colleagues argue that we should spend our efforts assisting the regular education system in developing such programs rather than perpetuating the dual (and segregated) system of special education. We encourage those individuals to attempt that task, but we choose to spend our efforts on working with a smaller system, where quality can be conscientiously monitored and seed money obtained.

We believe these programs will vary considerably as they are developed to meet the needs of youth in different settings and with different needs. However, there seem to be a number of considerations that should be addressed across these programs.

A Triage Process, Driven by Students, Parents, and Teachers, Which Can Also Be Characterized as Futures Planning. This futures planning is based on an ongoing occupational evaluation process that emphasizes matching student interest and aptitudes. This interest and aptitude match requires refinement over time as well as gentle but firm reality feedback that maintains high positive self-concept within realistic boundaries. This process of continually evaluating the match between skills and interests is a lifelong skill needed by all of us. Students need to be afforded the opportunity to match skills to the demands of the career path they are choosing so they can learn how to self-monitor the degree of match. The earlier this process starts, the better for students, because they will have more opportunity to refine the skills they will need for their desired occupation as well as time to reconsider their decision based on related experiences.

Self-Contained Apprenticeship Programs. Such programs emphasize a curriculum that includes citizenship skills and occupationally relevant skills. Intensive occupational awareness activities (job shadowing, speakers, summer employment) should comprise the first part of the program, so as to facilitate the future planning process. Citizenship skills need to be taught throughout the program in an integrated curriculum approach. The desired outcomes are for the students to be productive, respected citizens in their community. Thus, history, civics, and language arts skills could be taught by having the students tutor newcomers to the United States who are preparing for their citizenship test. This matches individuals new to the reponsibilities of citizenship by age with those who are new to it by immigration. It also matches in a friendly alliance people who in another instance—for example, the horror of the Los Angeles riots of 1992—turned against each other.

Instruction by the classroom teachers could consist of helping the students prepare lesson plans for their tutoring sessions, helping them devise remedial activities for those prospective citizens not learning the material, and assisting the students in developing evaluation procedures for their clients. Students could also develop lessons for their peers on the culture of their tutees. This experience demands that the students develop a good understanding of our history and the workings of our government, and skills in interacting with people from diverse cultures. The task of tutoring these immigrants provides a real-life reason for learning this information and skills. Students should also be expected to actively engage in community volunteer activities as well as to meet all standard citizenship responsibilities. These activities become authentic examples of using academic skills to be a good citizen in the students' home community. Academic instruction needs to relate to the current experiences of the students and provide them with opportunities to practice their citizenship skills in a manner that is valued by the adult members of their community. These activities could be part of mainstream classes, but they seldom are. Until such activities are standard fare in the mainstream, special educators should move forward in developing more appropriate instruction for our students.

Concurrent with these academic tasks is the training for a job that is consistent with each student's occupational interest. This training should consist of specific skill training related to a job (e.g., using a word processor, mastering a specific tool, reading a job-related manual) as well as job-related social skills (e.g., dress code, getting along with co-workers, handling criticism, customer relations). The majority of this specific job-related training takes place on the job site by teachers from the program with input from the online supervisor. Students complete paid apprenticeships of varying lengths in job sites related to their occupational interests. At the end of each experience the student completes an in-depth exit interview with the immediate supervisor and the job coach. Detailed feedback is provided on both positive and negative aspects of the student's performance. The student is urged to consider aspects of the job that were enjoyable and unenjoyable.

The final phase of the program needs to be job placement and ongoing support until the student has mastered the job and is integrated into the world of work. When the student experiences high job satisfaction and good job performance in a position that offers a livable wage and health benefits, the student graduates from the program with a high school diploma.

We have included brief overviews of two existing programs that have attempted to address these issues.

Career Ladder Program. From 1985 to 1991, the Career Ladder Program (CLP) provided transition services to youth with mild disabilities exiting San Francisco's public schools. Three underlying concepts informed the development and delivery of this program: (a) taking a comprehensive look at all of the transition needs of the participating youth (i.e., a willingness to look beyond the job environment for barriers to and resources for job success); (b) shaping the service to participants' lives as their needs emerged (i.e., a willingness to improvise services, to venture into an unexpected realm of a youth's life where a problem may be emerging); and (c) basing the delivery of services on the cultivation of authentic relationships with the participants in the program.

The workplace was developed as the setting for the first component of the program, the community classroom: Five to 15 special education youth were offered a half-day supervised work experience 4 days a week, integrated into the employee pool of a single large corporation or employer. This community classroom approach solved many of the problems that accompany either the "place and pray" job placement approach, where the supervising professional is defeated by the need to be in several places at once, or the segregated nature of enclaves.

The second major component was the Employment Skills Workshop, a weekly seminar in which the same youth would come together in a class or conference room to process the work experience. Besides learning the standard and critical survival skills of job search and job interview, and conducting interest and aptitude inventories, the participants engaged in serious team-building activities that included social skills training, peer counseling activities, support groups, and collective analysis of their future prospects as adults. Through these activities, the likelihood of needs for expensive support beyond high school graduation were reduced. The youth learned to rely on each other for support and resources.

The third and most challenging component of the CLP was the provision of transition services beyond graduation. CLP transition specialists posed a novel challenge to the adult service delivery system: What if we never close a case, what if we remain continuously available to any youth who has passed through our initial program (the community classroom)? By thus changing the psychological tenor of the relationship between the provider and the youth, the stage was set for the formation and maintenance of a trusting relationship. That relationship was initiated during the community classroom phase, when the transition specialists would visit the community classroom and the Employment Skills Workshop and familiarize themselves with the program interns. They would also teach them about adult services such as vocational rehabilitation, GED programs, and programs for teen parents. When the interns graduated, they had a familiar person who was able to serve them unfettered by the constraints of eligibility prerequisites or case-closure deadlines. Together, the two could make full utilization of conventional services, fashion a career plan, and ultimately a career ladder.

This means that even when, in the providers' view, the young adult is counted as a success, the transition specialist is still available to that person when boredom or ambition compels the young adult to seek more training or a better job. This means that even when, in the providers' view, the young adult is not counted as a success, the transition specialist is still available to that person (through regular maintenance contacts) when he or she is through with the more free-form floundering, and is ready, after 6 months, 1 year, or 3 years, to get serious about developing a career plan. If the contact has been properly maintained, it is the transition specialist that young adult will call first. The continuous *availability* of services offers a sense of security that grounds the young adults and gives them the courage to pursue a legitimate career.

This commitment led to a case management approach we call "Continuous Cyclical Triage" and "Cohort Service Delivery Model" (Siegel et al., 1993). Continuous Cyclical Triage is a method of monitoring the intensity of each youth's need and measuring out an eclectic array of services to meet those needs. It empowers students to go beyond the need for services without cutting them off. The Cohort Service Delivery model organizes caseloads to allow long-term, trusting relationships to develop between providers and clients, and "cycles back" the provider only when a very high success rate has been assured. The model, as noted previously, was highly successful with a population of youth with mild disabilities. Of the 127 participating youth, longitudinal follow-along substantiated that 92% of them worked, went to school, or engaged in some combination of the two (Siegel, Robert, Waxman, & Gaylord-Ross, 1992).

Belief Academy. The Belief Academy was developed in 1990 in a collaborative effort between the Seattle Public Schools and the University of Washington. The purpose of the Belief Academy is to address the problem of choices for secondary-aged youth in choosing an appropriate secondary program that would prepare them for successful transition after high school. The program proposes to ensure that participants will either go on to college (with appropriate supports in place) or have a job that is consistent with the individual student's occupational interests, pays a livable wage, and provides health insurance.

The seventh- and eighth-grade program focuses on accelerated academics. The notion is to provide each student with appropriate instruction in an attempt to remediate basic skill deficiencies (reading, writing, and math skills are stressed). These skills are taught in a whole language approach that emphasizes culturally relevant information. The program is self-contained and does not use integrated classroom settings, so that the content can be driven by student interests and needs. Basic support services are provided on an as-needed basis to each individual student. These include a mentor or tutor for each student. The role of this individual is to give social support to the student, provide an expanded set of social activities, and be an additional role model for the student. Wraparound services are provided to the families by a case manager based on a Family Plan that is developed for each family. Prevailing throughout the program is the emphasis on belief, the student's belief in him- or herself, the teacher's belief in the student, and the student's, parent(s)'s, and teacher's belief in the program.

At the end of the eighth grade, students, parents, and teachers go through a triage process to determine the type of high school program the student should attend. This futures planning is based on an ongoing occupational evaluation process that emphasizes matching student interest and aptitudes. For those students entering the mainstream high school curriculum, the Belief Academy provides a modified level of services, matching as closely as possible services that will be available to the student when in college.

For those students not moving into the mainstream high school curriculum, a self-contained apprenticeship program is provided. This program emphasizes citizenship and occupationally relevant skills. Concurrent with these academic tasks is the training for a job that is consistent with each student's occupational interest. Students complete paid apprenticeships of varying lengths in job sites related to their occupational interests.

The Belief Academy attempts to provide support services to students on an as-needed basis depending on the individual student and the demands of the environment. There are students, however, with needs that exceed the capability of the Academy. Students with extreme acting-out behaviors (carrying a concealed weapon, sexual assault, ongoing drug and/or alcohol abuse) have not been successful in this program; these students require more intensive services often not available for the majority of students.

SEGREGATED VERSUS MAINSTREAMED VOCATIONAL AND TRANSITION PROGRAMS

Full inclusion of all youth in all aspects of our society is a fundamental principle of the goals and commitments of this chapter's authors. Whenever possible, students should be fully integrated into the mainstream of their family, their neighborhood, their school, their workplace, and their community. However, at some point during a student's school career, likely outcomes must be weighed and balanced. Tradeoffs must be considered. Students with special needs must be fully included in the process of making compromises not unlike those that everyone else must make.

For example, it would benefit no one to maintain a special needs student in a fully mainstreamed program if the likely adult outcome were one where they were excluded from college, employment, or any kind of full engagement in society. We view our K–12 public school system as *the* major entitlement provided to all our citizens, and believe that the outcome of this entitlement should be an improved probability for an enhanced quality of life throughout life. Therefore, the major evaluation criteria of the success of our school programs needs to be the postschool status of the students.

The programs we have described so far can best be described as segregated programs. This type of thinking goes against current thought. The current zeitgeist for inclusion programs is based on a positive value set that emphasizes equity and valuing of all individuals. We concur with these values, but are pessimistic about the tolerance of society in general to make the accommodations required for meeting the needs of these youth without intensive support for both the youth and the institutions serving them. In other words, the distance between the idealistic and inclusive nature of our best schooling and the harsh realities of the world at large is still great enough to create high risks for youth deprived of special options. Although some of our recommendations imply segregation (we prefer *congregation* or simply *alternative option*), we believe that meaningful inclusion in typical activities of all youth is very important. For example, while these youth are participating in the activities we have described, we believe they should also be engaged in a wide variety of extracurricular activities at school. The students should be on athletic teams, working on the yearbook, attending dances, participating in school-sponsored clubs, and involved in student government. The youth should be working in community-based volunteer associations and should have formal affiliation with community-based recreational groups. These forms of inclusion are far more important as a basis of social integration and social acceptance than is inclusion in a history course or eating lunch in the common cafeteria.

The goal of inclusion is for youth with disabilities to be valued by others (Haring, Breen, Lee, Pitts-Conway, & Gaylord-Ross, 1988) and to find their niche in society. This goal implies that youth will have the skills that are valued by others, that opportunities exist that provide youth successful experiences in being viewed as good citizens, and that support is available to assist the youth in these activities. These programs may be described as segregated or they may be viewed as schools within schools. Either way, they should be evaluated on their outcomes, not their appearances. In a naive and overzealous rush to implement fully inclusive school environments, we risk overlooking and discarding the discovery of identity, common will, and support that comes from the opportunity to congregate with those engaged in struggles that share characteristics of ability, culture, status, or environment (Edgar, 1988).

Clearly, a partnership among the youth, the family, and the school must assess a school program and likely adult outcomes. Whenever mainstreaming can serve the need to be included, both now and during the youth's adult life, it should by all means be pursued. However, for students in need of a more intensive intervention we cannot in good conscience recant our support for programs like the

Belief Academy and the CLP. The best interests of integration are served by the programs that make permanent integration into the adult mainstream possible. Full inclusion into the school community is a phony cause if the postschool lives of the students are not positively affected.

In truth, there is the need to develop a wide range of programs (both inclusive and exclusive) and implement these programs with good evaluation and follow-along systems before we will ever be able to assert what does and does not work. There is no one program that will meet the needs of all students; rather, we need to create an array of services that provides incrementally increasing amounts of structure and support. Until this array of services is provided, troubling youth will continue to end up in the trash heaps of society (prisons or the street). Postsecondary options for these youths are directly related to the amount of resources society is willing to invest in comprehensive school programs, health and treatment programs, family support services, employment support programs, and ongoing personal support programs. The alternative to these programs is to build more jails, enlarge our police forces, develop an increased tolerance for poverty and despair in our communities and on our streets, and prepare to live in walled communities of the "haves" that keep us separated and safe from the "have nots." The cost of these alternatives is probably equivalent in terms of dollars, but the consequences of ignoring the needs of these youth are immense in terms of the cost to our spirit, our souls, and our world. By investing substantially in the needs of troubled youth now, we make for ourselves a chance to create a world where such programs are minimal, as are the instances of "have nots."

Regardless, one thing is a given. Youth with disturbing behaviors will not do well in our society unless radical and innovative interventions are implemented. Now is the time for action—enough with the debate of segregated versus integrated programs, enough with the debate of who is and who is not deserving of receiving extra services, and enough with the debate of who (or what) is responsible for the fix we are in. Now is the time to try something!

THE CRITICAL NEED FOR PROFESSIONAL RESPONSIBILITY AND REASONABLE ACCOMMODATION IN THE COMMUNITY

The underlying theme of our discussion thus far is one of society, and really the local community, being more accommodating to all citizens, but especially to those experiencing difficulties. Our political and economic system has provided the majority of our citizens with the opportunity to experience rich and productive lives. The particular form of rugged individualism we practice in the United States serves many of us well. Where we seem to fall short as a society is in the area of supporting those individuals who are not successful in finding their niche. Even more frustrating is the search for a way for individuals to work toward the common good of all people at the community level and lend a hand. As we stated in the opening pages of this chapter, outlining the problems is a far easier task than is creating the solutions. This is most evident in the discussion of how to make individual communities more accommodating to the disenfranchised segment of our population.

Any serious discussion of service options—any serious action for real change—must address three main themes: (a) The need for basic human services to be available to all people on an as-needed basis, (b) the need for special programs to be designed for individuals with needs greater than those typically handled by basic services (e.g., youth with emotional disorders), and (c) the need for communities to be responsive to the needs of the people who reside in them. Special education addresses the middle issue (special programs) but change stands on all three "legs." Without basic human services being available to the youth (and their families) whom we serve, without a responsive and authentically committed community, we cannot expect our programs to be successful.

Communities that include young adults just out of high school do not spontaneously occur at the point when the youth exit the high school program. Human relationships, from business to pleasure and from school to professional, are woven and developed over time. We believe the school-to-adult life transition begins long before high school, and that this transition is dependent on a complex mix of individual characteristics, family dynamics, resource availability, special program options, community receptivity, and luck. School-based programs need to focus on how best to assist the youth in this transition. We professionals who work in these programs need to be held accountable for the content of these programs. With equal responsibility we, along with the other citizens in our communities, need to be held responsible for the support our formal societal institutions provide for this transition and the receptivity of our communities for assimilating all youth.

Unfortunately, many programs do one thing well, but like a macrocosm of the rugged American individualist these programs lack a unifying culture that will guide a youth facing risky circumstances. From the model reading program to the successful sports, wilderness, or support group, from the church or community group to the exemplary job training program, no multiservice oversight and no coalescent community makes real (for large enough numbers of excluded and marginalized youth) the bright futures these services inspire. We lack a seamless arrangement of cooperating services that would truly effect change.

The Belief Academy is an attempt to enlarge what the CLP began, and to address the coordination-of-service issue—it creates long-term program relationships with youth beginning in the middle school. Both these programs attempt to provide wraparound case management services to access, as best as possible, the available human services that together can meet the myriad needs of the youth and their families. To some degree this type of wraparound service has been successful, but there simply are not enough services for the amount of need present in our society. Although these programs provide some short-term relief to a select population, they are not viable long-term solutions. Until our society (that's you, me, and all of us) makes substantial changes in the manner in which we distribute resources, all attempts such as this will be stopgap procedures. We need to continue with these efforts in the short range (if for no other reason than to improve the quality of the lives of a few individuals), but we must always acknowledge the limitedness of these attempts so as not to imply that these methods are permanent solutions. We must not engage in what Bernard Farber (1968) called "progressive status quoism," the appearance that we are solving a problem when in reality nothing is changing.

On the other hand, these two programs have begun to address the issue of community inclusiveness. Mentors recruited from the community have provided long-term relationships between individuals who otherwise would have remained strangers. Community organizations such as church groups, dance clubs, athletic teams, and zoo appreciation groups have found ways to include youth with troubled pasts in their midst in such a way that all involved have profited. Businesses have opened their doors to the youth and have learned to mutually profit from the association. Informal groups, such as hydroplane enthusiasts, have discovered mutual joy in getting to know some of these youth as individuals.

To create an inclusive community, we need all the players at the table. Reform that reaches for these goals in the schools is fine and well, and we support it, but such reform is attained only within the confines of the school building and school-oriented community. Any progress made in a school program that is not integrated with the community at large (and especially the employment community) is at serious risk of unraveling as youth from diverse situations approach the school-to-adult life transition.

Although we know that high-school-to-adult transitions are not automatic, we have structured our schools like holding tanks as if they were. To break down these barriers sooner, programs like the Belief Academy and the CLP have developed job shadowing, mini-internships, corporate partners with schools programs, and, in general, serious attempts to foster caring relationships between the employment community and the youth they will face. The economic system that wants preteenagers basically out of the way so that entrepreneurs can go about the business of making a profit (and a school system that is complicit in this arrangement) creates a chasm. Thus the two populations, youth and employers, understand each other less and less with each passing day. Programs like those we have described attempt to bridge this chasm. Success demands that they occur before high school, continue beyond secondary school exit, and that they be pursued to the level where social change can be detected and measured (as opposed to the level where a school believes that it has done enough, or a corporate sponsor has met its public relations goal).

What is the payoff here for business? Relationships with younger students, complemented by the hosting of more apprenticeship programs for youth facing risky circumstances, provide the underpinnings for business solutions to social problems (Hamilton, 1986). It is the beginning of the end of our social woes. When our diverse youth populations, including youth with behavior disorders, are allowed to have a legitimate role in the employment world, they will have a chance to prove themselves worthy of making a labor and work contribution. When their needs are contemporaneously addressed and their aspirations to challenging career ladders are fulfilled, then we will begin to experience a reduction in the numbers of youth who are incarcerated, alienated, or viewed as disturbed—then the workplace will become the host to more than production and service. It will be one among many community settings where people pursue meaning and identity in their lives. Without abandoning a private sector market economy, employment can fulfill its function as a "basic service." Solutions to the highly specialized problems described herein have implications for us all.

A FUTURE OF OPPORTUNITY

Inclusion means being part of a group to which you want to belong, and having the skills and opportunity to choose from an array of groups. Inclusion in the community, including the school, must be one of the major goals of education and society. How we go about accomplishing this is one of the perplexing riddles of our time. Our approaches must be as comprehensive as possible, address all aspects of our society, and allow for diversity of opinion and vision. We must be inclusionary in our thinking and our acceptance of the ideas of others.

We are tempted to list the programs and services we have enumerated earlier as the example of our vision of the future. We have resisted that idea and the notion of envisioning the future as a society where technology has eliminated the causes of human suffering and a higher moral spirituality has created a society of caring, gentle individuals. Rather, we choose to speculate on the immediate future and a possible scenario of how professionals could come together in some form of common movement to better the lives of youth with troubling behaviors.

Youth in our society are at risk of experiencing a decreased quality of life as compared to their parents. Some youth are at risk of experiencing serious emotional and behavioral disturbances that will greatly decrease their life chances and will cause considerable cost to the larger society. Some youth are at risk of dying before they become adults. The risk factors we know about and agree on are increasing, and more and more youth are affected by these events. The only main known quality of the interventions (including the setting) that are currently available is that they are weak and seemingly ineffective in addressing the range of needs of the youth who are floundering through their lives. The debates that seem to engage us deal with issues that seem detached from the actual lives of the youth who are the reason for the discussion. We continue to chart and count, describe and decry, measure and meditate, and publish and proclaim, but little seems to change for the youth.

An array of services should dominate the agenda and disperse the clutter—our debate should be meaningful. We must do all we can to get national health care to be a reality in our country. We must continue to support the expansion of mental health services, especially those for individuals and families in crisis. We must assert the need for massive increases in drug and alcohol treatment programs that are available to all those in need. We need to push for the development of long-term apprenticeship programs that will give reasonable opportunities for meaningful employment to our youth. None of these recommendations are solely for youth with troubling behaviors; they address real needs for all our citizens. If these services were in place so that the majority of our citizens had ready access to them, the task of developing support services for individuals with serious emotional and behavioral problems would be doable by a group of professionals bound together under a common label, such as special education. However, until such services are commonly available we will continue to be Don Quixotes, dueling the invincible windmills. The issue of placement as a factor in postschool success is but one vane of that windmill.

CONCLUSION

We began this chapter with a recapitulation of the debate over who should and should not be labeled as youth with behavior disorders, and therefore be entitled to special education services. As we conclude our discussion, we would like to suggest that that very debate misses the mark. The antiservice faction of that argument is willing, at a very early age, to let Malthusian tendencies have their way, and allow those showing antisocial behaviors to suffer the unnatural consequences until such time as their numbers constitute a serious threat to the status quo. We shudder to think of what this group might propose at that historical moment.

Our belief is that persons with disabilities and the best of the educational institutions' responses to those persons' needs constitute a leadership movement and the setting of a standard for human services from which all providers can learn and benefit. Instead of getting mired in the distraction of debates over labeling, or wasting precious dollars developing tests calibrated to theoretical constructs, we propose an adequately funded comprehensive social services system for all those with special needs (i.e., persons with disabilities, teen parents, drug-involved youth, sexual minority youth, adjudicated youth, youth in group and foster homes, dropouts, low-income youth, homeless youth, and newcomers) that asks a simple and direct question: Does the individual need services? If the answer is yes, the services (based on an empowerment dynamic, meaning that the recipient's needs will diminish over time) are provided, and no further questions need be asked.

The funds we have spent to ensure that no extra services go to someone "undeserving" are already substantial. The funds that are accumulated in corporate profits, or spent on luxury items and CEOs', professional athletes', and pop musicians' salaries, and the funds spent on our nation's defense and space programs are more than adequate to meet the needs of our neglected populations. In short, services that create independence and interdependence in their clients would not need to be so closely regulated if our system did not make their funding so scarce. Controversy over eligibility is a distraction from the real work of providing services to those in need and reducing their numbers.

How, then, do professional groups (special educators) go about lobbying for these basic services (health care, housing, jobs, day care, etc.) while continuing to play out their professional roles? How do individual citizens go about changing the system of support our society provides to all its citizens? These questions and the issues they represent are "gumption suckers"—events that just make us want to quit thinking about them and ignore the whole issue (Pirsig, 1975). It is responsible for the oft-heard phrase "The problems are so big and the solutions are political—I'm not into politics, I'll do my job the best I can, but I just can't worry about those things I don't control." This is not an acceptable response to the problems. As Kozol (1990) pointed out, "that it remains for anyone to choose to be involved in someone else's desperation—depends upon the prior myth that he is not involved already . . ." (p. 56).

Each of us and our professional organizations must step forward and openly address the issue of the lack of equity in our society and the devastating effects of this on our citizens. Those of us who work with the underbelly of society—those of our citizens for whom the system is not working—have the moral obligation to step to the forefront and advocate for change. If we do not, who will?

Even less obvious than the need to advocate for equitable social services is the need to work at the local community level to make our communities more accommodating to all citizens, including youth with disturbing behaviors. How do we, as individual citizens, go about the task of working for the common good? As described by Bellah, Madsen, Sullivan, Swidler, and Tipton in *Habits of the Heart*, our devotion to the notion of the overriding importance of individual rights, be they "utilitarian individualism" or "expressive individualism," often prevents us from seeing how we can achieve a common good without sacrificing our individual good (Bellah et al., 1986). And just how does one go about convincing employers that it is for the common good to hire youth with past histories of deviant behavior? And what are the procedures that one can use to locate individuals who will be willing to volunteer to be a mentor for a youth who will at times be unlikable? How do we bring together people with diverse values to negotiate our differences and find a common ground on which to coexist? How can educators be expected to not only teach all day (and perhaps engage in serious curriculum reform) but also play a role in national politics and be community activists? These are the real questions that we, as a profession, need to address. Full inclusion into the school community is a superficial cause if our personal and professional actions do not lead to full inclusion for all our citizens at the community level. We must "walk the talk" within both the school systems in which we work and the communities in which we live.

Social services have suffered serious reductions in fiscal commitment by the government and, despite advertising to the contrary, by the private sector. The only advantage of such a period of scarcity has been an opportunity to test on a more modest scale interventions that may work, and a body of research has accumulated. However, before the results of that research become obsolete—history ultimately confounds all social research—and before the tide of violent alienation washes over our country, we would do well to identify programs that do work, calculate the cost of funding those programs to a level that would finally make an impact on the lives of all of our young citizens, and pay the price. If we fail in this endeavor, the greed that created this unhappy situation in our country will surely consume us and levy a far more serious tax on us all.

REFERENCES

Allen-Hagen, B. (1991, January). Public juvenile facilities: Children in custody 1989. *OJJDP Update on Statistics*, pp. 1–10.

Ashenfelter, O., & Krueger, A. (1992). *Estimates of the economic return to schooling from a new sample of twins* (Working Paper No. 304). Princeton, NJ: Industrial Relations Section, Princeton University.

Bellah, R. N., Madsen, R., Sullivan, W. M., Swidler, A., & Tipton, S. M. (1986). *Habits of the heart.* New York: Harper & Row.

Bellah, R. N., Madsen, R., Sullivan, W. M., Swidler, A., & Tipton, S. M. (1991). *The good society.* New York: Knopf.

Berliner, D. C. (1992, February). *Educational reform in an era of disinformation.* Paper presented at the meeting of the American Association of Colleges for Teacher Education, San Antonio, TX.

Blackorby, J., Edgar, E., & Kortering, L. (1991). A third of our youth? A look at the problem of high school dropout among students with mild handicaps. *Journal of Special Education, 25*, 102–112.

Bruininks, R. H., Thurlow, M. L., Lewis, D. R., & Larson, N. W. (1988). Post-school outcomes for students in special education and other students one to eight years after high school. In R. H. Bruininks, D. R. Lewis, & M. L. Thurlow (Eds.), *Assessing outcomes, costs and benefits of special education programs* (pp. 9–111). Minneapolis, MN: University of Minnesota, University Affiliated Program.

Burchard, J. D., & Clarke, R. T. (1990). The role of individualized care in a service delivery system for children and adolescents with severely maladjusted behavior. *The Journal of Mental Health Administration, 17*, 48–60.

Children's Defense Fund. (1989). *Lack of health insurance makes a difference*. Washington, DC: Adolescent Pregnancy Prevention Clearinghouse, Children's Defense Fund.

Clarizo, H. F. (1987). Differentiation of emotionally impaired from socially maladjusted students. *Psychology in the Schools, 24*, 237–243.

Council for Children with Behavioral Disorders. (1990). Policy statement on the provision of service to children with conduct or behavioral disorders. *Behavioral Disorders, 14*, 12–19.

Edgar, E. (1988). Congregate. *Habilitation News, 8*(3), 6–7.

Edgar, E. (1992). *A polymorphic tracking and intervention model for students who drop out or are at risk of dropping out of special education programs in Washington state* (Final Report). Seattle: University of Washington, Experimental Education Unit.

Farber, B. (1968). *Mental retardation: Its social context and social consequences.* Boston: Houghton Mifflin.

Forness, S. R. (1992). Broadening the cultural–organizational perspective in exclusion of youth with social maladjustment: First invited reaction the the Maag and Howell paper. *Remedial and Special Education, 13*(1), 55–59.

Frank, A. R., Sitlington, P., & Carson, R. (1991). Transition of adolescents with behavioral disorders: Is it successful? *Journal of Behavioral Disorders, 16*, 180–191.

Gill, D., & Edgar, E. (1990). Outcomes of a vocational program designed for students with mild disabilities: The Pierce County Vocational/Special Education Cooperative. *Journal for Vocational Special Needs Education, 12*(3), 17–22.

Gonzalez, P. (1991). *A comparison of state policy of the federal definition and a proposed definition of serious emotional disturbance.* Alexandria, VA: National Association of State Directors of Education.

Haberman, M., & Quinn, L. M. (1986). The high school re-entry myth: A follow-up study of juveniles released from two correctional high schools in Wisconsin. *The Journal of Correctional Education, 37*, 114–117.

Hamilton, S. F. (1986). Excellence and the transition from school to work. *Phi Delta Kappan, 68*(4), 239–242.

Haring, T. G., Breen, C., Lee, M., Pitts-Conway, V., & Gaylord-Ross, R. (1988). *The effects of peer-counseling and special friends experiences for nonhandicapped adolescents.* Unpublished manuscript.

Hobbs, N. (1982). *The troubled and troubling child.* San Francisco: Jossey-Bass.

Hodgkinson, H. L. (1991, September). Reform versus reality. *Phi Delta Kappan, 73*, 9–16.

House of Representatives Select Committee on Children, Youth, and Families. (1989). *No place to call home: Discarded children in America.* Washington, DC: U.S. Government Printing Office.

Institutional Education Legislative Study Committee. (1990). *Final report.* Olympia, WA: Institutional Programs, Office of the Superintendent of Public Instruction.

Kauffman, J. (1989). The Regular Education Initiative as Reagan–Bush education policy: A trickle-down theory of education of the hard to teach. *Journal of Special Education, 23*, 256–278.

Kazdin, A. E. (1987). Treatment of antisocial behavior in children: Current status and future directions. *Psychological Bulletin, 102*, 187–203.

Kelly, E. J. (1991). *Differential test of conduct and emotional problems.* Odessa, FL: Psychological Assessment Resources.

Knitzer, J. (1982). *Unclaimed children: The failure of public responsibility to children and adolescents in need of mental health services.* Washington, DC: Children's Defense Fund.

Kozol, J. (1990). *The night is dark and I am far from home.* New York: Touchstone.

Leone, P. (1988). Beyond fixing bad behavior and bad boys: Multiple perspectives on education and treatment of troubled and troubling youth. In R. B. Rutherford, Jr., & S. A. DiGangi (Eds.), *Severe behavior disorders of children and youth* (Vol. 12, pp. 1–10). Reston, VA: Council for Children with Behavioral Disorders.

Maag, J. W., & Howell, K. W. (1992). Special education and the exclusion of youth with social maladjustments: A cultural–organizational perspective. *Remedial and Special Education, 13*(1), 47–54.

Mauer, M. (1992). *Americans behind bars: One year later.* Washington, DC: The Sentencing Project.

National Association of State Directors of Special Education. (1990). NASDSE/SMHRCY adopt resolution on services for children and youth. *Liaison Bulletin, 16*(5), 1–6.

National Center for Children in Poverty. (1990). *Five million children: A statistical profile of our poorest young citizens.* New York: Columbia University.

Neel, R. S., Meadows, N., Levine, T., & Edgar, E. B. (1988). What happens after special education: A statewide follow-up study. *Behavioral Disorders, 13*, 209–216.

Nelson, C. M., & Pearson, C. A. (1991). *Intergrating services for children and youth with emotional and behavioral disorders.* Reston, VA: The Council for Exceptional Children.

Nelson, C. M., & Rutherford, R. B., Jr. (1990). Troubled youth in the public schools: Emotionally disturbed or socially maladjusted? In P. E. Leone (Ed.), *Understanding troubled and troubling youth: Multidisciplinary perspectives* (pp. 38–60). Newbury Park, CA: Sage.

Pirsig, R. M. (1975). *Zen and the art of motorcycle maintenance.* New York: Bantam.

Rhodes, W. C. (1967). The disturbing child: A problem of ecological management. *Exceptional Children, 33*, 449–455.

Rutherford, R., Nelson, C. M., & Wolford, B. (1985). Special education in the most restrictive environment: Correctional/special education. *Journal of Special Education, 19*, 59–71.

Scruggs, T. E., & Mastropieri, M. (1986). Academic characteristics of behaviorally disordered and learning disabled youth. *Behavioral Disorders, 11*, 184–190.

Select Committee on Children, Youth, and Family. (1989). *Where are our children?* Washington, DC: U.S. Government Printing Office.

Siegel, S., Robert, M., Greener, K., Meyer, G., Halloran, W., & Gaylord-Ross, R. (1993). *Career ladders for challenged youths in transition from school to adult life.* Austin, TX: Pro-Ed.

Siegel, S., Robert, M., Waxman, M., & Gaylord-Ross, R. (1992). A follow-along study of participants in a longitudinal transition program for youths with mild disabilities. *Exceptional Children, 58*(4), 346–356.

Skrtic, T. M. (1991). *Behind special education: A critical analysis of professional culture and school organization.* Denver, CO: Love.

Tuma, J. M. (1989). Mental health services for children: The state of the art. *American Psychologist, 44*, 188–199.

Wagner, M., D'Amico, R., Marder, C., Newman, L., & Blackorby, J. (1992). *What happens next? Trends in postschool outcomes of youth with disabilities.* Menlo Park, CA: SRI International.

Wehlage, G. G. (1983). The marginal high school student: Defining the problems and searching for policy. *Children and Youth Services Review, 5*, 321–342.

William T. Grant Foundation. (1988). *The forgotten half: Pathways to success for America's youth and young families.* Washington, DC: Commission on Work, Family, and Citizenship, William T. Grant Foundation.

Wilson, J. W. (1987). *The truly disadvantaged: The inner city, the underclass, and public policy.* Chicago: University of Chicago Press.

Wolf, M. M., Braukmann, C. J., & Ramp, K. A. (1987). Serious delinquent behavior as part of a significantly handicapping condition: Cures and supportive environments. *Journal of Applied Behavior Analysis, 20*, 347–359.

CHAPTER

12

Legal Demands and Constraints on Placement Decisions

Barbara D. Bateman
David J. Chard
University of Oregon

The legal requirements governing placement of students who have emotional or behavioral disorders are the same as for all students who are eligible for benefits and protection under the Individuals with Disabilities Education Act (IDEA; 1990) and §504 of the Rehabilitation Act (1973).[1] However, the applications and issues presented in cases involving students who have emotional or behavioral disorders are often distinctive. For example, these students are more often than others deliberately not identified as having a disability so that they may be excluded from school altogether. When they are in school, administrators frequently attempt to exclude them on disciplinary grounds.

When students with emotional or behavioral disorders are placed in psychiatric residential or day treatment centers, they are sometimes denied IDEA and §504 protections and rights with the rationale that these treatment centers provide medical services and, therefore, are not bound by education law. Private and residential placements of students with emotional or behavioral disorders often lead to lengthy, expensive legal disputes over financial responsibility. This chapter examines the law of special education placement as it applies to all eligible

[1]§504 protects eligible students from discrimination based solely on disability and entitles them to reasonable accommodations or more. Eligibility requires that the student have, have a record of, or be regarded as having a mental or physical impairment which substantially limits a major life activity. All IDEA eligible and ex-eligible students are also covered by §504. If a student has an emotional or behavioral disorder but has been denied IDEA eligibility on the grounds of no adverse immediate effect of educational performance and/or no need for special education, immediate consideration should be given to §504 eligibility, which does not require a need for special education.

students, and presents the special applications and issues that arise with students who have emotional or behavioral disorders.

FUNDAMENTAL LEGAL REQUIREMENTS FOR ALL PLACEMENTS

The basic requirements for placements have been simple and unchanged since IDEA's inception. To comply with federal law placement decisions must be (a) individualized, (b) based on the full continuum of alternative placements, (c) consistent with the principles of the least restrictive environment, and (d) secondary to the primary purpose of special education that is the provision of an appropriate program. Placements are for the purpose of implementing the appropriate program that has been delineated in the student's IEP. The relationship between the law's mandate for an appropriate program and the principle of least restrictive placements is both important and often misunderstood.

Placements Must Be Individualized

One of the fundamental difficulties faced by the discipline of special education in implementing IDEA has been overcoming a history, tradition, and long practice of categorically based placement decisions. A 1987 U.S. Office of Special Education and Rehabilitation Services (OSERS) policy letter spoke to the issue:

> The guidelines ... make explicit what the courts and Congress have stated was intended when P.L. 94-142 was first passed: namely removal from integrated environments must be based solely upon the individual educational needs of the student and not upon ... e.g., category of handicapping condition, configuration of the service delivery system, availability of educational or related services.... (Will, 1987, p. 443)

Again,

> the central and unifying principle expressed in Federal law ... is that each child's educational needs be *individually* evaluated and that an educational plan be *individually* developed and implemented.... Any labelling practice that categorizes children according to their disability in order to facilitate the individual determination of any child's appropriate educational needs or services will be presumed to violate the protections accorded under Federal and State laws. (Richards, 1987, p. 441)

In years past it was common for special educators to identify a child as "being" her or his disability (e.g., "she is mentally retarded") and then to place her automatically on that basis ("and so we will put her in the MR room"). No children with disabilities are more subject to these categorical placements, even after 16 years of legal prohibition, than those students with emotional or behavioral disorders. In some cases these categorical placements reflect a lack of available room or services for children whose behavior is deemed inappropriate. In one of hundreds of similar complaints, the Office of Civil Rights (OCR) investigated a charge that students who were mentally retarded and emotionally disturbed were placed by the district without regard to their individual needs. The investigation found the students had indeed been placed at the segregated facility because of "administrative convenience" and space problems. The district was also returning some students to an integrated setting, but that decision, too, was based not on students' individual needs but was part of an administrative plan to move the program back into districts. Both the nonindividualized placements and the returns to integrated settings were found to violate §504 (*Peru (NY) Central Sch. Dist.*, 1989).

A related problem arises when a program (e.g., a self-contained class) is known as the "SED program" with the erroneous corollary that only children labelled SED can be placed there. Evaluation teams have been rumored to say such things as "We have to change his label from LD to SED so we can get him in the SED room." Unfortunate practices such as this reveal the fundamental failure of the special education system to move from categorical to individualized placement decisions. These unfortunately common practices not only reflect a failure to understand the "central and unifying principle" of the law, as described in Richards (1987), but they also preclude or substantially hamper proper individualized education program (IEP) development.

Placements Must Be Based on the IEP

This principle of individualized placement decisions is tightly linked to the principle of IEP-based placement decisions as discussed by Robert Davila, then Assistant Secretary, OSERS:

> Under Part B, a determination of what constitutes the least restrictive educational placement must be based upon the individual needs of each child, as described and specified in his or her IEP. Placement cannot be based solely on such factors as the category of the child's disability, the availability of appropriate staff, administrative convenience, or the configuration of the service-delivery system.
>
> Part B recognizes, however, that children with disabilities may need to be educated in various types of settings in order to meet their unique educational needs. For this reason, Part B requires public agencies to make available to all students with disabilities a continuum of alternative placements, or a range of placement options, to meet the needs of these students for special education and related services. *See* 34 CFR 300.551(a). The options on this continuum include "instruction in regular classes, special classes, special schools, home instruction, and instruction in hospitals and institutions." 34 CFR 300.551(b)(1). Further, the options on the continuum of alternative placements must be made available to the extent necessary to implement each child's IEP. *See* 34 CFR 300.552(b).

> We emphasize that Part B requires that each child with a disability must be educated in the LRE in which that child's unique educational needs can best be met. In all cases, the determination of what constitutes each child's LRE must be made on a case-by-case-basis in accordance with the requirements outlined above. (Davila, 1991, p. 214)

The legal procedures designed to guarantee an individualized program and placement for every child with a disability are the development of the IEP and the requirement that placement be based on and thus follow the completed IEP. A recent OSERS policy put the matter very succinctly: "... each child's placement must be based on his or her individualized education program (IEP), not on the category of disability" (Davila, 1992, p. 1310).

The Fourth Circuit has held that the district's failure to develop a new IEP prior to proposing a change in placement was per se a failure to provide a FAPE (*Spielberg v. Henrico Co. Pub. Sch.*, 1988). This same procedural error could easily obligate other districts to maintain the student in an expensive program, as it did in *Spielberg*. An exception to the IDEA requirement that placement be based on the IEP [34 CFR 300.552(a)(2)] is made when a private placement is being made and personnel from that placement need to participate in IEP development.

The IEP is the foundation on which the placement structure must be built. This has been better understood by courts than by schools in many cases. The secret, if there is one, to designing an IEP that will justify, uphold, or serve as a foundation for a placement is to delineate clearly the child's unique educational needs or characteristics. We tend to forget that the IEP must contain a statement of the specific special education that is needed [34 CFR 300.346(a)(3)] and that special education is defined as specially designed instruction to meet the child's unique needs [34 CFR 300.17(a)(1)]. Therefore, proper IEP development begins with delineating the child's unique needs and moves to specifying the necessary specially designed instruction (Bateman, 1992). Those two pieces are the heart of the IEP, just as the IEP is the heart of IDEA. Only following development of such an IEP may the placement decision be based on detailed knowledge of the child and the needed instruction.

This intimate connection among the child's needs, the IEP, and the placement is seen in this passage from an early federal case:

> The preponderance of the evidence establishes that Joseph's special educational needs require an environment that would allow for: careful monitoring of his performance in verbal studies and mathematics; immediate correction of his errors; intensive daily programs of remedial training, as opposed to the developmental approach, in reading, spelling, written language expression, and mathematics; small class groups of only learning disabled students, where distractions can be quickly controlled, and where Joseph can receive individual attention to promote his understanding of the contents and concepts of studies in which his functional skills are at a low level; continuing staff interchange as to teaching of each student;

> inculcation in the student of a sense of achievement and accomplishment in the school tasks. Melrose has not provided Joseph with the educational environment to meet these needs, although it has been aware of them for some years. The IEP for 1979–80 was inadequate and inappropriate to meet them, and the educational program outlined for 1980–81 was likewise inadequate and inappropriate.
>
> An acceptable IEP for the years involved in this appeal required Joseph's removal from a regular classroom in order to participate in an educational program having the characteristics and scope of the educational environment suitable to meet his needs. The severity of his specific learning disabilities is such that effective efforts to provide an adequate and appropriate education could not be achieved satisfactorily in regular classes at Melrose, even with the use of supplementary aids and services. (*Norris v. Mass. Dept. of Ed.*, 1981)

Cases such as this, and there are others (e.g., *Laura M. v. Special School District No. 1*, 1980), make one wonder how judges arrive so much closer to the heart of the matter than do so many educators involved in developing IEPs. The answer is that judges start at the beginning, that is, with the students' unique needs and what meeting those needs requires. Too many IEP teams start with the program into which the student will be placed and what services are available there.

Continuum of Alternative Placements

Just as the principle of individualized placements is linked to IEP-based placements, so IEP-based placements are linked to and require a continuum of alternative placements. Every school district must make available instruction in regular classes, special classes, special schools, home instruction, and instruction in hospitals and institutions. Additionally, each district must provide for services supplementary to regular rooms, such as resource room or itinerant instruction (34 CFR 300.551). "If the IEP must be implemented in a special class, special school, or separate facility, that placement is the least restrictive placement for that particular child . . . and must be available to the extent necessary" (Davila, 1989, p. 85). The continuum of placements is fundamental and essential to individualized placements based on individual education programs. Davila stated that his "commitment is to ensure that a full continuum of placement options . . . is available" and that monitoring the states for this availability is key, is done routinely and consistently, and is taken very seriously (Davila, 1991, p. 594).

Segregated Placements

In the midst of current advocacy for the proposition that every child with a disability should be in a regular class in her or his neighborhood school, it is not surprising that some wonder if the law no longer requires individualized, IEP-based decisions about placement. The U.S. Office of Special Education and Rehabilitation Services addressed this issue very directly:

> This Department has not changed its LRE [least restrictive environment] policy . . . public agencies are required to make available . . . a continuum of alternative placements. . . . The Part B regulations require that the educational placement of a child with disabilities must be determined by the contents of that child's IEP. . . . The Department recognizes that some children with disabilities cannot be appropriately placed in regular classrooms. . . . Inherent in a FAPE [free appropriate public education] is a continuum of services, including separate public and private facilities. (*Vergason*, 1991, p. 471)

Earlier, the Office of Special Education Programs (OSEP) ruled that the creation of a separate school for children with emotional disorders would not violate the law, as long as placements there were based on individual needs (*Sachias*, 1986). One of the early cases in which segregated facilities were directly challenged was *St. Louis Developmental Disabilities Treatment Center Parents Association v. Mallory* (1984). The court observed that

> the placement provision, §1412 (5)(B), recognizes the need for separate educational settings both explicitly and implicitly. The section acknowledges that some handicapped children will not be able to receive a satisfactory education in a "regular educational environment" and will need to be placed in "special classes, separate schooling" or otherwise removed from the regular school setting. (p. 1442)

The law—statutory, regulatory, case law, and agency rulings—has consistently and unwaveringly been that special, separate, segregated placements must be available for those students who have been properly and individually determined to need such placements for implementation of their IEPs. Documentation of why a separate placement is necessary has been required by agency interpretations (e.g., *Richland Co. (SC) Sch. Dist. #1*, 1989; *Stevenson*, 1988). There is no obvious regulatory basis for this requirement, but presumably it is grounded in the presumption that every child can be educated satisfactorily in the regular education environment and that the burden is on the party claiming otherwise to provide supporting evidence.

The law aside, the philosophy of inclusion may nonetheless prevail. The risk is substantial:

> If we regard inclusion as a religious principle, if we disregard the differences among the students we consider disabled, if we continue to insist that the least restrictive environment is some absolute standard rather than a continuum of variability that has truth only for each individual in question, we will lose some of the most valuable and creative and lovable citizens in our community. (Diamond, 1993)

And we will lose valuable personnel, programs, and placements that will only have to be replaced when the field returns to individualized placement decisions made within the full continuum of alternative placements.

The Least Restrictive Environment (LRE)

The term *least restrictive environment* (LRE) appears only twice in the IDEA regulations. It is the title of a heading within the larger section called Procedural Safeguards, parallel to such headings as Confidentiality of Information and Additional Procedures for Evaluating Children with Specific Learning Disabilities. The only other place it occurs is in the requirement, often overlooked, that "In selecting the LRE, consideration is given to any potential harmful effect on the child or on the quality of services that he or she needs" (34 CFR 300.552(d)). This requirement has seldom been explicitly invoked or discussed, perhaps because the mandate requires only "consideration." Standing alone, the requirement arguably could allow a team to say "There will be a clear harmful effect on this student if he is removed from placement A and put into B, but we'll do it anyway" or "Placement C lacks the structure, program and teacher expertise of D but it is far less expensive so we'll place Joelle in C."

When "harm to the child" is argued, it is often in the context of whether to remove a child from a successful, ongoing placement. Changing the degree of specialization, intensity, or qualifications of personnel in the delivery of services is most often attempted with a "quality of services" argument. It is also noteworthy that this is the only place the regulations speak to the quality of services, other than in the general requirement of appropriate education.

One district had taken into account the harmful effects of negative staff attitudes toward a student who had emotional and behavioral disorders and had, therefore, placed the student out of the district. However, the State Education Agency (SEA) ruled that the district should have somehow taken the harmful effects into account in a within-district placement (*Dickinson Ind. Sch. Dist.*, 1984). Presumably, taking the negative attitudes into account would mean eliminating them.

Six regulatory provisions, taken together, guide placement decisions and comprise what is commonly called the LRE. Far from being a place or a placement, the LRE is the decision that results from following a set of procedural requirements in IDEA. Three of these LRE requirements are mandatory, absolute, binding, and without an "escape clause":

1. The district must make available a full continuum of alternative placements including resource rooms, special classes, special schools, and so forth.
2. In placement decisions consideration must be given to any potential harmful effect on the child or on the quality of services he or she needs.
3. Placement must be based on the IEP and must be determined annually.

Three other LRE requirements are "qualified," that is, they are preferences to be implemented to an extent indicated:

1. Children with disabilities must be educated with nondisabled children to the maximum extent appropriate.

2. They may be removed from the regular education environment only when the nature or severity of the disability is such that education in regular classes with the use of supplementary aids and services cannot be achieved satisfactorily.
3. Children should attend neighborhood schools unless the IEP requires otherwise, and the nonneighborhood school placement should be as close "as possible" to the child's home.

It is these latter, "qualified" provisions that are the focus of much of the philosophical and ideological debate in the field today. The central issue in the controversy has to do with when, if ever, education cannot be "achieved satisfactorily" in the regular classroom. When it cannot, removal from that classroom is legally appropriate.

Removal Only When Education Cannot Be Achieved Satisfactorily. Some years ago, some of the advocates for what is now called *full inclusion* suggested that the proper test for "achieved satisfactorily" was whether the student's IEP could be implemented in the regular classroom. Under this standard no child would ever have been excluded, which was precisely the intent of the advocates. With a "long enough extension cord" and no concern about efficiency, efficacy, or the remainder of the children in the classroom, they were correct—any IEP could be implemented anywhere.

The first circuit court to address the question of when education was satisfactorily achieved in the regular setting was the Sixth Circuit in *Roncker v. Walter* (1983):

> In a case where the segregated facility is considered superior, the court should determine whether the services which make that placement superior could be feasibly provided in a non-segregated setting. If they can, the placement in the segregated school would be inappropriate under the Act. Framing the issue in this manner accords the proper respect for the strong preference in favor of mainstreaming while still realizing the possibility that some handicapped children simply must be educated in segregated facilities either because the handicapped child would not benefit from mainstreaming, because any marginal benefits received from mainstreaming are far outweighed by the benefits gained from services which could not feasibly be provided in the non-segregated setting, or because the handicapped child is a disruptive force in the non-segregated setting. Cost is a proper factor to consider since excessive spending on one handicapped child deprives other handicapped children. (*See Age v. Bullitt County Schools*, 1982). Cost is no defense, however, if the school district has failed to use its funds to provide a proper continuum of alternative placements for handicapped children. The provision of such alternative placements benefits all handicapped children. (p. 1063)

Six years later, the Fifth Circuit articulated in *Daniel R.R. v. St. Bd. of Ed., El Paso* (1989) what is now generally considered to be the leading analysis of compliance with the least restrictive preference of the law. First, the court very clearly distinguished the law's directives related to the mandated appropriate program from those regarding the strong preference for a mainstream placement and noted the tension between these two provisions. In agreement with two other circuit courts (*Lachman v. Illinois State Board of Education*, 1988 and *Wilson v. Marana Unified Sch. Dist.*, 1984), the *Daniel R.R.* court observed that the "laudable policy objective" of integration must be balanced against the "Act's *principal* goal of an appropriate education" (italics added).

The court then recognized, as had the Sixth and Eighth Circuit Courts before it (Roncker, 1983; *A.W. v. Northwest R-1 School District*, 1987) that the U.S. Supreme Court has spelled out a two-part inquiry for determining whether a district has provided an appropriate program (*Hendrick Hudson Dist. Bd. of Ed. v. Rowley*, 1982), and that that inquiry is not the correct tool for determining mainstreaming compliance. However, it explicitly rejected the *Roncker* analysis, concluding that it intruded too much into the educational policy choices Congress deliberately left to educators and that it departed too far from statutory language.

Based on the language of IDEA, the *Daniel R.R.* court then devised a two-part test for determining compliance with the mainstreaming requirements. This test has also been adopted by the Eleventh Circuit in *Greer v. Rome City School District* (1991) and by the Third Circuit in *Liscio v. Woodland Hills School District* (1990). First, one must ask whether education in the regular classroom can be achieved satisfactorily and then, if not, ask whether the child has been mainstreamed to the maximum extent appropriate. This is to be an individualized, fact-specific inquiry that examines (a) whether the state has taken steps to accommodate the child in the regular class, recognizing that states need not provide every conceivable aid, require regular teachers to devote undue time to one child, or modify the regular program to the extent the child is not required to learn any of the skills normally taught; (b) whether the child will receive educational benefit from regular education (i.e., will grasp the essential elements of the regular curriculum); (c) whether the balance of the benefits to be received favor regular or special education; and (d) whether the presence of the child who has a disability significantly impairs the education of the other children.

The difficult factual questions that recur under these analyses in cases of children who have emotional or behavioral disorders often include the amount of disruption to other children's education that must be tolerated and how harmful it may be to the student to have a one-on-one aide by his or her side in the regular class. (Specific cases are discussed later.)

Removal From the Regular Education Environment. In 1986, Madeline Will, then the Assistant Secretary, OSERS, issued a clarification of the standards for placement in the LRE. At that time, she stated that

> the principle of LRE does not necessarily mean mainstreaming in regular classes. However, it does mean children with the full range of disabilities can and should

> be integrated into regular school *buildings* . . . [and] even those students with the most severe physical and mental disabilities are attending *special classes* in regular public school settings . . . [and] integration means educating all disabled children in regular *schools*. . . . [emphases added] (pp. 6, 7)

The full inclusion movement now supports only regular class placements in neighborhood schools. The role of geography in this movement has been notable. Those states (e.g., Oregon) that had never developed separate special education facilities beyond resource rooms and an occasional regional self-contained class for children with moderate to severe disabilities took integration to mean abolishing those classes and resource rooms and returning all children full time to regular classes. In other states that had extensive special and separate schools the movement initially meant just what Will had suggested, that is, educating all children in the same buildings, and those with disabilities often in special classes or resource rooms, as well as in regular classes.

The entitlement of the child under these LRE regulations is to be removed from the regular education environment (i.e., building) only when education there cannot be achieved satisfactorily. One of the legal effects of this provision is to create a rebuttable presumption that a student may be educated satisfactorily in the regular education environment. Thus, the law presumes this is the case until or unless evidence to the contrary is produced. Some people thought, early on, that this amounted to an entitlement for every child to be placed initially in a regular class. This is not the case, however; there is no "fail-through" requirement that would require a child be placed first in a regular building or class and fail there before being allowed to be placed in a more separate program (*Richards*, 1987; Will, 1986).

In Sum

The LRE is a complex concept that includes both absolute mandates and qualified requirements. The absolute mandates are that placements must (a) be individualized and IEP based, (b) reviewed annually, and (c) selected from the full continuum of alternative placements. The qualified or limited requirements include students' entitlement to be educated (a) with nondisabled children to the maximum extent appropriate and be removed from the regular education environment only when education there cannot be achieved satisfactorily, (b) as close to home as possible, (c) and in the neighborhood school unless the IEP requires otherwise.

These LRE requirements, taken together, constitute guidelines for decision making, not a place. LRE is also a policy preference of the law that must take a secondary role to the primary purpose of the law, that is, to provide a free appropriate public education to every child who has a disability.

In spite of the importance of these LRE guidelines, compliance with them has been minimal at best. This summary of the 1991 federal monitoring of state compliance with LRE provisions was reported to Congress (U.S. Department of Education, 1992):

> OSEP found the following deficiencies:
> (a) *Removal from Regular Education*
> Six of 12 SEAs did not ensure that their public agencies removed children with disabilities from the regular educational environment only when the nature or severity of the disability was such that education in regular classes with the use of supplementary aids and services could not be achieved satisfactorily [§300.550(b)(2)].
> (b) *Continuum of Placement Options*
> Twelve of 12 SEAs did not ensure that each of their public agencies had available a full continuum of alternative placements to meet the needs of children with disabilities [§300.551(a)].
> (c) *Placement Based on IEP*
> Ten of 12 SEAs did not ensure that the educational placement of each of its children with disability was based on his or her fully developed IEP [§300.552(a)(2)].
> (d) *Placement Options Available to Implement IEP*
> Eleven of 12 SEAs did not ensure that each public agency ensures that the various alternative placement options are available to the extent necessary to implement the IEP for each child with disabilities [§300.552(b)].

LRE in Relation to Appropriateness of Program

In the earlier discussion it was seen that the LRE principle allows removal of the student from a regular education environment only when education cannot be satisfactorily achieved in it. However, it does allow removal, and therein is the basic rule that appropriate education always takes precedence over restrictiveness of environment when the two clash. The ideal is that an appropriate program can be delivered effectively in a regular education environment. However, that is not always possible. Under the analyses of the leading circuit decisions in *Roncker v. Walters, Daniel R.R. v. El Paso*, and *Greer v. Rome* it is always possible to conclude that, given specific facts, the regular education environment is not compatible with satisfactory education.

This conflict arose in a Ninth Circuit case (*Wilson v. Marana*, 1984) in which the district wanted to place a 7-year-old student with mild disabilities in an adjoining district 30 minutes away where the special education teacher had different qualifications and in which the district believed the student would receive a better program. The parents wanted her to remain in the neighborhood school, which they believed to be the least restrictive environment. The court was faced with weighing a more appropriate program against a less restrictive one and it concluded that the mainstreaming preference of IDEA must be balanced against the primary objective of providing an appropriate program. The school was therefore allowed to place her in the out-of-district program.

Similarly, the Seventh Circuit has recognized that mainstreaming is to occur only when the child's education can be achieved satisfactorily in the mainstream environment (*Lachman*, 1988). In a very early case the 3rd Circuit held that the concept of least restrictive cannot be applied to cure an otherwise inappropriate placement (*Kruelle v. New Castle County Schools*, 1981). The first principle in defining the relationship between appropriateness of program and least restrictive environment is that appropriateness is central, essential, and takes precedence over LRE should they conflict. LRE is a preference to be exercised when there is more than one appropriate program. For a given child LRE is always the least restrictive environment in which education can be satisfactorily achieved.

Osborne (1992) succinctly summed up the state of the law: "The weight of case law indicates that the least restrictive environment mandate is *secondary* [emphasis added] to the provision of appropriate services and may not be used to deny a student access to needed services" (p. 370).

PLACEMENT ISSUES: STUDENTS WHO HAVE EMOTIONAL OR BEHAVIORAL DISORDERS

Each of the fundamental legal requirements governing placement of students who have disabilities that have just been described—(a) individualized placements, (b) full continuum of alternative placements, (c) LRE based, and (d) primacy of program appropriateness—poses special applications to students who have emotional or behavioral disorders. These are examined in the next section.

Background

One of every five IDEA students identified as having emotional disturbance is presently served in a separate school, residential, homebound, or hospital placement. Fifteen percent are in regular classes, and the remaining two thirds are served in special classes and resource rooms. The numbers of those students who have serious emotional disturbance served in regular schools declined by 4.2% between the school years 1977–78 and 1989–90. A larger decline (5.9%) was seen only for students with multiple disabilities (U.S. Department of Education, 1992).

The factual issues in cases involving placements for students who have emotional or behavioral disorders frequently involve possible or actual disruptiveness, a need for 24-hour structure and continuity of treatment, and acute behavioral episodes requiring immediate, intensive treatment.

Parental role in placement decisions is also often contentious. Although parental involvement is required during the development of the IEP (34 C.F.R. 300.344), IDEA and its regulations do not require districts to consider parental choice in placement decisions. The Office of Special Education and Rehabilitation

Services (OSERS) has stated (*Vergason*, 1990) that districts may consider parental choice in determining an appropriate placement for a child as long as the placement favored by the parent(s) would provide a free appropriate public education (FAPE) and meet all the requirements of IDEA. OSERS encourages parental involvement in placement decisions and suggests that districts could offer parents a choice of appropriate public placements determined in advance by the placement team to meet all of the requirements of IDEA.

Parental preference in placement decisions was the focus of a controversial Seventh Circuit case. At issue was a district court's decision to place Adam, a student with behavior disorders, at a private day school favored by Adam's parents, rather than in an alternative public school for students with severe behavioral disorders, favored by the district and strenuously opposed by the parents. The school district appealed, arguing that parental preference is not a valid factor for evaluating a student's program and placement. The Seventh Circuit concluded that when, as here, parental opposition is so strong that it has "poisoned" the placement and would negatively affect the placement's educational value, the district could not appropriately make the placement (*Board of Education of Community Consolidated School District No. 21, Cook County, Ill. v. Illinois State Board of Education*, 1991). Based on this case, it seems possible that knowledgeable parents could "poison" placements intentionally. Therefore, although parental involvement in placement decisions is not required by law, parental preference may be a factor for districts to consider when determining appropriate placements. Giving parents a choice among placements predetermined by the placement team to be appropriate would seem, when possible, to be ideal.

Students' involvement in placement decisions is also not required by law. However, just as parents may poison a particular placement, students may also reject a proposed placement with such vehemence as to render it inappropriate. In *Brown v. County School Board of Henrico County* (1992), the Virginia Court of Appeals held that a residential placement favored by the parents was not appropriate because the student rejected the placement. In essence, the placement was poisoned by the student.

Placements Must Be Individualized

In remote or otherwise poorly informed (or poorly conforming) areas of this country one still hears such comments as "If we want to put Jason in the SED class we'll have to change his label to SED," or "Our district pays for counseling only if the student is labelled SED," or "If we label him SED we won't be able to expel him." The concept of truly individualized service delivery decisions, including placements, has been nowhere harder to grasp than in special education, and within special education nowhere more difficult than in serving students who have emotional or behavioral disorders. We continue to make categorical decisions—for example, the child is SED, therefore, this service or that placement.

In fact, some children who have emotional and behavioral disorders and who need special education services may thereby need a residential placement, whereas others may need only a clear, implemented behavior management contract in a regular classroom.

An area in which it has been especially difficult to implement individualization is in the discipline of acting-out students who have emotional or behavioral disorders. Too often the inclination of school administrators has been to avoid individual consideration of whether the present placement has played a role in evoking, or causing, the inappropriate behavior, and to simply opt for suspension or expulsion. The practice of disciplinary exclusion for behavior caused by disability will be dealt with later. For now, we observe that according to the U.S. Supreme court in *Honig v. Doe* (1988), during the year preceding passage of P.L. 94-142 (now IDEA) the educational needs of 82% of children with emotional disabilities were unmet. In part this was related to funding constraints, but it also reflected exclusionary practices such as those before the court in this case. The San Francisco Unified School District attempted to expel a 17-year-old emotionally disturbed student who had responded to taunts by choking the offending student and leaving abrasions on his neck and then kicking out a window while being taken to the principal's office. His IEP noted that he could tolerate only minor frustration before exploding, and one of the IEP goals was to learn to cope with frustration without resorting to aggressive acts. Clearly the misconduct was disability related.

The other respondent student's disruptive behavior in *Honig* included stealing, extorting money from other students, and making lewd sexual comments to female students. His IEP and his evaluations all addressed his propensity for verbal aggression. Therefore, the lewd comments for which he was expelled were also disability related. Both students' situations required individualized examination and, consistent with widespread past and present practice, neither received it.

Placements Must Be Based on the IEP

IEP development is the most critical step in ensuring that a successful placement is made. For students with unique emotional and behavioral needs, the concept of an individualized program requires that the IEP team consider more than just academic instruction. In this section, we review two related cases that illustrate what can happen when the IEP does not adequately address emotional and behavioral needs. In practice, IEP teams often fail to address the complete range of a student's unique needs. Fortunately, resources exist that can assist parents and school district personnel to consider all of the emotional, behavioral, and social needs of students.

Good placement decisions depend on IEPs that address the unique needs of each child. In reality, it is common to review files from a school and see IEPs that are nearly identical. This suggests that the programs are less than individualized. Not only is program content sometimes similar, but IEPs may be photocopied with slight changes or the goals and objectives may be computer generated. Failure to individualize an IEP is a clear and serious violation of legal requirements for providing an appropriate program (e.g., *Aaron S. v. Westford Pub. Sch.*, 1987; *Rockford, Ill. Sch. Dist. #205*, 1987; *Tucson, AZ Unified Sch. Dist. #1*, 1987).

For students with behavioral or emotional disturbance, IEPs too often address only the academic portion of their special education needs. Sugai and Colvin (1990) suggested that the IEP process is particularly difficult for students with serious behavior and emotional problems for the following reasons: social behavior targets are more difficult to determine; specific academic curricula are available for placement after academic assessment, whereas similar curricula do not exist for social behavior skills; and academic goals and objectives are easier to write than are social behavior goals and objectives. As a result, behavioral and emotional objectives are often omitted from IEPs altogether, or they lack the level of specificity and clarity necessary to be useful and informative. A memorable example was an IEP from a small Oregon school that stated in its entirety "Levi will improve his behavior 75% of the time." Needless to say, Levi didn't.

Two related cases illustrate the potential educational and legal consequences when school districts fail to address the full range of students' special education needs. In the first case, *Chris D. v. Montgomery Co. Bd. of Ed.* (1990), Chris had not been identified for special education by second grade even though there was evidence that he was "emotionally conflicted." In third grade, Chris was evaluated, found eligible for special education, and placed in a special learning center to address his behavioral needs. After a successful third-grade year the school district returned him to the regular classroom where he then displayed a variety of disruptive behaviors including fighting, swearing, stealing, and beating on walls. He had frequent office referrals and, on occasion, law enforcement officials intervened. He was returned to the special learning center but his behavior did not improve. Chris' mom requested a residential placement but was persuaded by the district that his needs could be met in a full-time special education placement in the regular school. That placement was not successful and police intervention was again needed.

The following year the district maintained Chris' special education class placement despite his mother's repeated requests for residential placement. Finally, Chris was suspended indefinitely, arrested, and removed from school. At the time the parents went to court, both parties agreed that the special education placement in the regular school was not appropriate. The district wanted to place Chris in an isolated room in a separated district building and the parents still sought residential placement. The court found that Chris' behavior had deteriorated because it was left untreated and it ordered that the appropriate placement was a residential program that offered 24-hour, systematic behavioral training.

In a related case by the same name (*Chris D. v. Montgomery County Board of Education*, 1990), a student named Cory entered school with behavioral problems in 1983. After failing the first grade he was socially promoted for the next 3 years. In 1987, the school evaluated Cory for mental retardation in spite of indications of emotional disturbance. He was found ineligible according to mental retardation criteria.

In 1988–89 Cory repeated fourth grade. He was repeatedly disciplined for being verbally abusive, hitting other students, and refusing to comply with directions. He was suspended several times and the police intervened once. In November 1989, Cory was found eligible for special education according to mental retardation criteria and was placed in an educably mentally retarded (EMR) self-contained classroom. Cory's IEP included generic academic goals that were far from individualized (e.g., "Student will participate in reading activities in regular classroom," "Student will read and write numbers 0–999 with __% accuracy"). Meanwhile, Cory's parents hired a specialist who suggested that he might have an emotional disturbance.

The following year, a new IEP was developed, but the objectives remained generic and plans for monitoring progress were vague. In addition, no goals or techniques were specified to teach Cory how to control his behavior. Consequently, Cory's behavior grew worse. He repeatedly cursed at the teacher, refused to sit in his seat or stop shouting, attempted to run away from school, and physically threatened students and teachers. School officials removed Cory from the regular classroom, locked him in a separate class, called his parents, and assigned a special crisis teacher to sit with him. In November 1989, Cory threatened to kill a teacher's daughter. Police intervened, charges were filed, and Cory was removed from the school. He returned in January 1990. In the spring of the year he was restrained to a security desk. At this point Cory's teacher added a behavioral objective to his IEP that aimed to have Cory ignore other students when they exhibited inappropriate behavior. There were no substantial changes in 1990–91 regarding Cory's behavior. In addition, Cory had showed no substantial academic progress since 1987.

The school district in this case failed to develop an adequate program to meet Cory's needs. Repeatedly, the district proposed IEPs that were not truly individualized and did not specify strategies for evaluating Cory's academic progress and the effectiveness of the teaching methods being used. Similarly, the district failed to address Cory's behavioral needs. They attempted to keep him quiet and away from other children without teaching him how to control his behavior and interact appropriately with others. The district's program also failed to counsel and instruct Cory's parents on how to control his behavior. In addition, there was no provision in the district's program to offer Cory the prospect of returning to the regular classroom. In effect, based on the testimony of two expert witnesses, the district's program utterly failed to provide educational benefit and actually may have harmed him.

Although these are extreme cases of how poor programming can turn inappropriate behavior into intolerable, dangerous, and sometimes illegal behavior, it is common for school districts to attend to academic needs while ignoring behavioral and emotional needs. Too often district personnel are not prepared to provide services to students with emotional and behavioral disturbances. In such cases teachers and administrators may choose to punish behaviors. Several studies have documented the inadequacy of IEPs and the lack of relevance of IEP objectives and instruction for students with behavior disorders (e.g., Lynch & Beare, 1990; Smith & Simpson, 1989). Fortunately, resources are available to help IEP teams identify areas of needs for all students, and to improve IEP development (e.g., Bateman, 1992).

One way for IEP teams to improve their identification of the full range of a student's needs is to utilize resources that suggest potential areas of need. In his book *Preventing School Dropouts: Tactics for At-Risk, Remedial, and Mildly Handicapped Adolescents*, Lovitt (1991) detailed 11 different areas in which students with disabilities commonly have special needs. Although this list is not exhaustive, it is an excellent starting point. Under each area, up to 20 focus behaviors are suggested that IEP team members could consider. For example, 1 of the 11 areas of need common to students with behavioral and emotional disturbances is "attitude." Within the area of attitude, Lovitt suggested that some students need to develop, for example, self-management skills in making responsible choices. Still others need to learn to deal with alienation. Tactics for developing these skills are presented. Another area is "compliance," under which time management, reducing hostile-agressive behavior, peer confrontation, and many other specific skills and behaviors are treated. The advantage of a resource such as Lovitt's book is that it offers a wide range of areas from which IEP teams can develop objectives, especially in those areas so often neglected. Use of such a resource may help districts to avoid cases such as those involving Chris and Cory.

Continuum of Alternative Placements

The U.S. Department of Education (1992) reported in 1989–90 that 43.4% of students who have emotional or behavioral disorders were placed in regular classes or regular classes plus resource room, compared to 69.1% of all students with disabilities so placed. The remainder, 56.6% of SED students, were in segregated placements including separate classes (37.1%), separate schools (13.9%), residential facilities (3.6%), and homebound/hospital (2%) placements. Overall, only 30.6% of all students with disabilities were in separate placements, compared to 56.6% of those with emotional or behavioral disorders.

On the one hand, pressures are often great to exclude students who have emotional or behavioral disorders from regular settings, and on the other hand, when these students have been excluded many parents report their states have far too few separate or special facilities available for them.

Nowhere is the "continuum" concept more important than in educational placements of students labeled SED. Interestingly, far less is heard about full inclusion in regular classes of students who have emotional and behavioral disorders than about any other category of disability. Perhaps educators, parents, and other advocates intuitively recognize that some of these children would be impossibly disruptive absent extraordinary behavioral management skills and/or that they need intensive treatment, structure, or continuity that is beyond the capacity of the more ordinary educational settings to deliver.

A large portion of the placement cases involving students who have emotional or behavioral disorders predictably involve the students placed in or seeking placement in separate or residential schools. The issues in these separate school and residential placement cases commonly involve financing the placements and/or whether the LRE principles of the law are being satisfied.

Questions of districts' responsibility to pay for unilateral placements (usually private day or residential placements) made by parents are examined in the framework of *Burlington School Committee v. Mass. Dept. of Education* (1985) and its two-prong test of whether the district's offering constituted an appropriate education as defined in *Hendrick Hudson Dist. Bd. of Ed. v. Rowley* (1982) and, if not, whether the program selected by parents was appropriate under the *Rowley* standard.

Thus, many of the cases that appear on the surface to deal with placement are actually analyzed and decided entirely as program appropriateness questions in which the issues under *Rowley* are whether the program, that is, the IEP (a) was developed in a procedurally correct way and (b) is reasonably calculated to allow the student to receive educational benefit. Many cases involving residential placements raise only these and not LRE issues.

Many cases and rulings speak to residential placements as the LRE in some circumstances. However, the continuum of placements mandates other options as well. For example, in a case of a 13-year-old abused and neglected student whose behaviors included fighting, disrupting the classroom, arson, stealing, lying, and much more, a hearing officer in Massachusetts (*Pittsfield Public Schools*, 1991) ruled that the school district was to provide a day program that contained these components:

> a) therapeutic milieu, b) small, structured classroom, c) extensive individualized programming and one-to-one supervision, d) classroom adjustments to address [ ]'s language difficulties, e) comprehensive behavior modification system, including training in behavioral management for [ ]'s home caretakers, f) school–home liaison to coordinate communication and ensure consistent structure, g) counseling for [ ] and his family, and h) recreational services. (p. 325)

The hearing officer went on to castigate the district for an unfortunately common situation:

> [ ]'s reported "at grade level" performance in Pittsfield, does not make up for Pittsfield's failure to develop an individual education plan geared to this child's acute and varied needs. [ ]'s serious behavioral difficulties were emerging in the classroom, undoubtedly blocking maximum progress. Classroom adjustments and techniques recommended by evaluators were not incorporated into any plan for [ ]. No effort was made to implement a comprehensive behavioral management system in both the home and school, despite [ ]'s critical need for this. Instead, communication ground to a standstill. In spite of [ ]'s severe emotional problems, he was not placed in an intensive therapeutic milieu, and was not receiving group or family counseling. (p. 325)

In one of the "poisoned placement" cases the court upheld a private day school placement (*Bd. of Ed. of Comm. Consolidated Sch. Dist. No. 21 v. Illinois State Bd. of Educ.*, 1991). Another case involved a student who, when angry, pelted his home with eggs, climbed on the roof, used profane language, and spit on his mother. He had physically assaulted other students, choked one, made and threatened to use weapons, and more. In this case the hearing officer ruled that only a secure and locked residential facility was the LRE. The district's offer of other residential placements had not been appropriate because they were not secure. Therefore, under *Burlington* the district was required to pay for the placement at the secure facility (*San Francisco Unified School District*, 1987).

One other illustrative case (*Edward A.F. v. Clint ISD*, 1986) makes several important points. Even though IDEA had been in effect for a decade, the district in this case refused for five years to evaluate the student despite his uncontrollable disruptive behavior, failing grades, two retentions, a history of abuse, and his mother's pleas. Finally the district agreed to an evaluation, but only if the parents paid all costs. The IEP that was eventually provided made no attempt to allow the student to recover educational benefit lost due to the district's inaction, and was found by the hearing officer to be inappropriate under the *Rowley* standard. Finally, the hearing officer ruled on the district's contention that the LRE provisions of the law required placement in the regular classroom and that no other placement could be the LRE. This position was emphatically rejected by the hearing officer:

> With the exception of two isolated and brief periods, Edward's behavior has been unmanageable. Contrary to respondent's attempts to depict Edward merely as a mischievous youth, the record establishes that he has made a shambles of every attempt to control his behavior and make him cooperate with classroom protocol. It is also adequately clear that his antics have so consumed the time and attention of his teachers that the quality of education enjoyed by his classmates has also been diminished. There is absolutely nothing in the record to indicate that a primarily mainstreamed placement for the coming year would be any more successful than prior attempts. To the contrary, the evidence discloses that the only educational settings in which Edward has achieved any degree of success have been those placements where he received structured supervision either under the tutelage of

> a strict disciplinarian or in the form of increased resource assistance. Even in those instances, Edward merely passed his work and was promoted with the rest of his class. As previously stated, in view of the facts and circumstances presented in this appeal, mere promotion is not an acceptable educational goal. It is axiomatic that a highly structured and comprehensive program must be crafted in order for Edward's behavior to be contained to the extent that he will have an opportunity to recapture the lost benefits of the previous years.
>
> As to Edward's growing dependence on his resource teacher, it must be conceded that such represents a legitimate concern. In light of the existing facts and circumstances, however, it is a concern of relatively low priority. The highest priority is Edward's continuing education and the repair of past damage. That priority must be attended to above all else. Edward's education must not be bartered away in exchange for emotional and social independence. Edward has the remainder of his life in which to attain self-reliance. We have but a few more short years in which to provide him an appropriate education. (p. 214)

Some might object that this hearing officer's emphasis on appropriate education is old fashioned or outdated. If so, perhaps that is true of the judicial system as a whole. One cannot help but recall a passage from a case that suggests an equally conservative view of schooling:

> When that "mainstreaming" preference of the Act has been met and a child is being educated in the regular classrooms of a public school system, the system itself monitors the educational progress of the child. Regular examinations are administered, grades are awarded, and yearly advancement to higher grade levels is permitted for those children who attain an adequate knowledge of the course material. The grading and advancement system thus constitutes an important factor in determining educational benefit. . . .
>
> The IEP, and therefore the personalized instruction, should be formulated in accordance with the requirements of the Act and, if the child is being educated in the regular classrooms of the public education system, should be reasonably calculated to enable the child to achieve passing marks and advance from grade to grade. (*Rowley*, 1982, p. 207)

The mandated continuum of placements provides an orderly progression of placements and combinations ranging from ordinary progress in a regular class, as described by the U.S. Supreme Court previously, to a locked and secure residential facility. All placements on the continuum are to be available, as needed, to students who have emotional or behavioral disorders.

Separate Placements

Although most issues involving separate placements arise around residential placement, some disputes have also arisen around other programs. All decisions to place students in separate facilities must be individually justified [*Richland Co. (SC) Sch. Dist No. 1*, 1989]. A tally of the hearings and cases reported in

Individuals with Disabilities Education Law Report (previously *Education for the Handicapped Law Report*) on justification of separate placements for students who have emotional or behavioral disorders is as shown in Table 12.1.

Two recent Office of Civil Rights (OCR) rulings reported consecutively illustrate and summarize the law of separate placement. In the first [*Saginaw (MI) Int. Sch. Dist.*, 1992], OCR ruled that placements of students with SED made by the district at a segregated facility were appropriate because they were based on individual need, not on category of disability, and they provided for appropriate integration opportunities. In the second [*Montgomery Co. (MD) Pub. Sch.*, 1992], similar placements made at a segregated facility violated the LRE because they were made categorically and without consideration of individual needs for nonacademic classes.

Residential Placements. As seen earlier, residential placement issues account for more legal disputes than do other types of separate placements. One of the perplexing issues in providing services for students who have emotional or behavioral disorders is determining when a residential placement is legally necessary. IDEA provides that when placement in a public or private residential program is necessary to provide special education and related services the program, including nonmedical care and room and board, must be at no cost to the parents of the child (34 C.F.R. 300.302). The question is how to know when a residential program is "necessary," under the law, and when the district must therefore pay for it. Because IDEA itself exists for the primary purpose of providing an appropriate education, the courts have been concerned from early on that districts be required to pay for only those residential placements that are for education purposes.

A closely related issue is determining if a residential placement is a related service "required to assist a child with a disability to benefit from special education" (34 C.F.R. 300.16) versus being a "medical treatment," which is excluded from those related services for which a district must pay. Both analyses require distinguishing residential placements that are necessary for educational purposes from those that are not.

TABLE 12.1
Tally of Relevant Hearings and Cases

Type of Separate Placement	*Number of Hearings and Cases*
Residential required	14
Residential not required	6
Residential required, but not for educational reasons	2
Separate day school required	3
Separate class required	4
Separate class not required	1

Kruelle v. New Castle (1981) is one of the leading cases regarding whether a district must pay for residential placement. Under *Kruelle*, the district has the burden of showing that the student's educational needs are "segregable" from other problems that usually do not affect the learning process. Upon such a showing the district's financial responsibility is limited to the education program.

A common scenario is that parents become frustrated and discouraged with the public school program offered or delivered to their child who has emotional or behavioral disorders. They then unilaterally place the child in a private residential program and seek reimbursement from the district. Frequently the unilateral placement is precipitated by violence or acute episodes of out-of-control behavior.

In *Clovis Unified Sch. Dist. v. Cal. Office of Admin. Hearings* (1990), the Ninth Circuit framed the issue of the $150,000 annual hospitalization of a child who had serious emotional disturbance as whether it was either a residential placement under 34 C.F.R. 300.302 or a related service rather than an excluded medial service [34 C.F.R. 300.16(a)] under IDEA. Rather than use the "required to assist the child to benefit" language of the related service regulations, the court examined the purpose of the hospitalization. The plaintiff Michelle was a 10-year-old with severe emotional disturbance who, it was agreed by all, needed a residential placement in order to receive an appropriate program. She was living in Kings View, an acute care psychiatric hospital, at the time her parents' private insurance was exhausted. The school personnel attempted to locate an appropriate residential program, but the family rejected those suggested and instead asked the district to fund Michelle at Kings View.

The district successfully argued that psychiatric hospitalization was not the kind of residential placement envisioned under IDEA and that it is a medical service excludable from related services. The court rejected a simplistic application of the "must be provided only by a physician" test of *Irving Ind. Sch. Dist. v. Tatro* (1984) for defining an excludable medical service. Instead, it also examined, as did *Tatro*, the nature of the service and the burden it would put on the school district. The service included six hours a day of intensive psychotherapy (including pottery and animal care) that "appeared medical" because it addressed a medical crisis. In ruling against the parents the court also relied on the fact that Kings View did not provide its own educational program, but instead used the school district's educational services.

Three months after deciding *Clovis* the Ninth Circuit faced another residential placement case (*Taylor v. Honig*, 1990) involving a student who had an emotional or behavioral disorder. After a tumultuous history of aggression, juvenile detention, and therapeutic placements, a hearing officer ordered Todd be placed in a 24-hour residential facility. The parents proposed San Marcos Treatment Center. The County Mental Health personnel rejected that suggestion and proposed instead five unavailable or unsuitable placements. The issue in the case was whether the school district was obligated to pay for the San Marcos placement or whether it was an excludable medical service.

The court carefully distinguished San Marcos from Kings View in *Clovis* in that the former is a state accredited educational institution and the latter is not. Further, Todd was medically stable, whereas Michelle needed treatment for an "acute" psychiatric crisis. Todd's placement at San Marcos was found necessary to meet his educational as opposed to medical needs. He required a highly structured academic setting where personal and social contacts were ordinary and necessary. This speaks to a school, not a hospital. Thus, the district was financially responsible for his placement.

State Program Approval. Finding an appropriate placement for a student who has a serious emotional or behavioral disorder may be extremely difficult. In one well-known case, the plaintiff was an emotionally disturbed student who had been rejected by six instate residential placements. The school district sought state approval to place the student in the only (according to the lower court) available, appropriate placement—a private placement not approved by the state. The state refused to give its approval and so the father, rather than the district, made that placement and then sought reimbursement. Both the hearing officer and the lower court held for the parents. On appeal, however, the Second Circuit reversed and said the parties should have continued the months-long search for an appropriate and state-approved placement that would admit the student. All reimbursement was denied (*Antkowiak v. Ambach*, 1988).

However, a Massachusetts court held that state approval of a private placement was irrelevant for reimbursement purposes because reimbursement is an equitable remedy. The state would not, however, be able to make a prospective placement in an unapproved facility (*Carrington v. Comm. of Education*, 1989).

In a Fourth Circuit case since decided by the U.S. Supreme court the district had proposed an IEP that was not designed to enable the learning-disabled student to make sufficient progress (*Carter v. Florence Co. Sch. Dist. Four*, 1991). Her parents placed her in a private school that was not, at the time, state approved for special education placements. The Fourth Circuit, in direct conflict with the Second Circuit's ruling in *Antkowiak*, held the district court had correctly applied *Burlington* when it allowed reimbursement for the nonapproved placement.

The IDEA regulatory requirement at issue in these cases is that an "appropriate" education must "meet the standards of the SEA" [34 C.F.R. 300.8(b)]. Some states currently maintain very limited approval lists with few or no out-of-state placements listed. At least some of these states are among those that themselves have very few instate facilities. Should a state be able to protect its districts from ever having to reimburse parents by the simple ploy of not maintaining a list of approved placements? Is it a problem if State A approves Placement C, but State B does not? Should parents in B have to move to A to be reimbursed? Does "meet standards" mean a placement must have been previously determined to have met standards and already be placed on a list, or does it mean that, if investigated, it would be found to currently meet standards? These are the questions the Supreme Court addressed in *Florence Co. Sch. Dist. Four v. Carter* (1993).

The Supreme Court held in *Florence Co. v. Carter* (1993) that unlike public placements, facilities where parents unilaterally place a child need not be under public supervision nor meet state standards in order for parents' expenses to be reimbursable. However, parents still risk the district's program being found appropriate, thus barring reimbursement for the parent-selected program even if it is also appropriate (*Burlington*, 1985).

The Least Restrictive Environment

A variety of factors has been cited in administrative and judicial decisions relative to restrictiveness of placements. In cases of students who have emotional or behavioral disorders these factors often support a decision that a separate placement is the LRE. Some of these factors include previous failure in a "less restrictive" day program, aversion to public school, need for a behavior modification program, disruption to other students in a less restrictive setting, violent behavior, risk of running away, posing danger to others, and unmanageable behavior. In a 1988 hearing (*M. B. v. Teaneck Bd. of Ed.*, 1988) a student was diagnosed as having an emotional and behavioral disorder following an incident in which he stabbed another student and was prevented by bystanders from killing him. The evidence convinced the hearing officer the student needed elimination of frustrating situations, a highly supportive environment, individualized instruction, and psychotherapy as an integral part of his school program. However, the district had no such program. Therefore a private, separate day school was offered. In determining whether that program was in conformance with LRE, the hearing officer observed that LRE

> was never intended to deprive a handicapped child of an appropriate education when his local district does not have a program which accommodates his needs. Determination of least restrictive environment must include consideration of a student's particular handicap. The approach must be tailored to the individual needs of each child. What is too restrictive for one child may be not restrictive enough for another. As the Third Circuit aptly commented, "The goal of placing children in the least restrictive environment does not trump all other considerations: 'Such a setting . . . is selected in light of pupil's special education needs' " (*Geis v. Parsippany–Troy Hills Bd. of Educ.*, 1985). Given the nature of the handicap and the lack of a suitable program in his local district, the least restrictive environment in this case was a private day school offering the type of program described by the child study team. (p. 153)

This issue of the relationship between LRE and appropriateness of program, raised here, will be discussed later. For now the focus is on the reality that many settings can be the LRE for students who have emotional or behavioral disorders or any other disabling condition.

Removal From the Regular Education Environment

As a group, students who have emotional or behavioral disorders do not have cognitive disabilities. Although by definition the disability of an emotional or behavioral disorder has an adverse effect on educational performance, most efforts to remove these students to more restrictive placements (which then become the LRE, if the placement is properly changed) are a result of discipline for inappropriate behavior, rather than of a need for a more restrictive placement to facilitate educational performance.

Discipline

Disciplinary actions are common in dealing with students who have disabilities. IDEA and §504 do not explicitly address discipline of students with disabilities, but federal courts and administrative agencies have outlined procedural guidelines based on their interpretation of both laws. Disciplinary actions constituting significant changes of placement comprise the primary focus of discipline cases to date. Discipline for disability-related misconduct that does not constitute a change of placement remains an unresolved issue for the courts. Because long-term exclusion (more than 10 days unless state law sets a shorter time frame) is a change in placement, as discussed later in this chapter, it is a major concern in disciplinary dealings with all students who have disabilities.

Discipline Constituting a Change of Placement. In a very early case, a child was diagnosed as having a learning disability caused by either a brain disfunction or a perceptual disorder. The student's participation in a schoolwide disturbance resulted in her expulsion. The district court held that the expulsion constituted a change in placement and required the school officials to adhere to the procedural protections of the IDEA (*Stuart v. Nappi*, 1978). The court stated:

> An expulsion has the effect of not only changing a student's placement, but also of restricting the availability of alternative placements. For example, plaintiff's expulsion may well exclude her from a placement that is appropriate for her academic and social development. This result flies in the face of the explicit mandate of the handicapped act which requires that all placement decisions be made in conformity with a child's right to an education in the least restrictive environment. (p. 1243)

This decision foreshadowed later decisions by suggesting that expulsion of students with disabilities should be prohibited altogether. Later, in *S-1 v. Turlington* (1981), nine students with disabilities were expelled from school for a variety of inappropriate behaviors. The Fifth Circuit ruled that prior to such a disciplinary change in placement the students were entitled to a professional team's determination as to whether the misconduct had been caused by the disability. If so, exclusion was not appropriate, although a more restrictive placement may have been.

If the parents object to a proposed change of placement, exclusionary or otherwise, they may trigger the stay-put provision (34 C.F.R. 300.513) of IDEA that "freezes" the student in the present placement by requesting a hearing. In *Honig v. Doe* (1988), the district argued that when students endangered themselves and others, unilateral expulsion should be permissible even if the parents object. The Supreme Court did not recognize such a "dangerousness exception" to the stay-put provision, finding that Congress intentionally omitted any emergency exception to this provision. The Supreme Court stated, however, that school districts are allowed to use normal procedures short of exclusion for dealing with dangerous students, including detentions and timeouts. In an extreme situation, school districts may seek a court-ordered injunction to expel or remove a student from a current placement.

Congress recently reauthorized the Elementary and Secondary Education Act (now the Improving America's Schools Act) and added an amendment that alters IDEA's stay-put provision. Now if an IDEA eligible student brings a gun (no other weapons are covered) to school and a professional team determines there is no relationship between bringing the gun and the student's disability, the student may be placed in an alternative placement for a maximum of 45 days. During this period of time, if the parents request a due process hearing the student will now remain in the alternative placement rather than the original placement. If bringing the gun is related to the disability, IDEA change of placement procedures must be followed or, as before, the school district could seek a judicial injunction to remove the student from school.

A few school districts have sought judicial injunctions to keep allegedly dangerous students from attending school. In one such case, an autistic student with behavior disorders made sexual overtures to female staff and students, engaged in self-abusive behavior, and provoked other physical violence in the school (*Board of Education of Township High School district No. 211, Cook County, Illinois v. Corral*, 1989). The school district determined that the behavior was related to the student's disability, reevaluated the student's program, and recommended a private residential placement. The parents agreed with the recommended placement for the following school year, but requested that the student remain in the current placement for the balance of the school year. The district sought an injunction prohibiting the student from returning to the public school. The court held for the district and issued the injunction. The court found that the potential danger to the staff, students, and the student himself outweighed any inconvenience to the student caused by the change in placement from a program for mildly mentally impaired students at the high school to a private day school.

In a similar case, a Virginia school district sought injunctive relief to keep a teenage student with emotional disturbance from returning to school until reevaluation and review of the student's program could be completed (*School Board of the County of Stafford, Virginia v. Farley*, 1990). In addition to setting fire to a hallway locker, the student had been involved in 44 other incidents that required disciplinary action. The student's parents would not consent to the reevaluation or to homebound instruction during the reevaluation. The Circuit Court of Virginia recognized that the student posed a threat to staff and students and issued the injunction, ordered homebound instruction, and granted a request for reevaluation.

In a contrasting case (*Board of Education of Cherry Hill v. J.D.*, 1989), the Board of Education of Cherry Hill sought injunctive relief for a change of placement for J.D., a student with emotional disturbance, from an alternative school to homebound instruction. J.D. had verbally threatened the principal, expressed suicidal threats, and on one occasion had thrown another student across the room. The district cited J.D.'s large physical size as another reason that his presence in the alternative school posed a danger to staff and students. The New Jersey hearing officer held for J.D. and his parents, stating that J.D.'s behavior was to be expected in an alternative school where some students are difficult to handle. In addition, the hearing officer stated that J.D.'s violations did not constitute the level of "very maladaptive behaviors" that warranted an injunction.

In sum, the Supreme Court in *Honig* restricted the unilateral exclusion options for administrators to use with students who pose a threat to others, but left open the option for injunctive relief via the courts:

> Congress did not leave school administrators powerless to deal with dangerous students; it did, however, deny school officials their former right to "self-help," and directed that in the future the removal of disabled students could be accomplished only with the permission of the parents or, as a last resort the courts. (p. 323)

Although successfully exercising the injunction option will continue to be a challenge to districts, in incidents where students carry guns to school, Congress has acted to offer the 45-day alternative placement described earlier.

Determining the Relationship Between Misconduct and Disability. Since *Turlington*, courts have agreed that in discipline cases involving a change in placement including exclusion from school, it must be determined whether the misconduct is related to the disability. The Ninth Circuit in *Doe v. Maher* (1986) mistakenly stated that the IEP team should determine the relationship between misconduct and disability. At least one State Attorney General's office has said this was simply an error on the court's part and that professionals, not the IEP team, must make this determination (McKeever letter). According to OCR policy the determination may be made by the same group of people that makes placement decisions (Smith, 1988).

The Ninth Circuit also stands alone in its views concerning the behavior–disability relationship. It requires that a direct causal relationship exist between the disability and the misconduct before disciplinary protections apply. A direct causal relationship

> does not embrace conduct that bears only an attenuated relationship to the child's handicap. An example of such attenuated conduct would be a case where a child's physical handicap results in his loss of self-esteem, and the child consciously misbehaves in order to gain the attention, or win the approval, of his peers. (*Doe v. Maher*, 1986, p. 1480)

The other circuit courts have taken the contrasting view that disability-related behavior is any behavior attributable to, or somehow resulting from, a manifestation of the disability. The Fourth Circuit, for example, found that a student's involvement with drugs was indirectly linked to his learning disabilities (*Malone v. School Board of County of Prince William, Virginia*, 1985). It held that even this attenuated relationship between misconduct and disability warranted special protection. "To do otherwise would be to expel a child for behavior over which he may have little or no control" (p. 1217).

Disciplinary Actions Not Constituting a Change in Placement. Any expulsion or suspension of more than 10 days, except when a student brings a gun to school, requires change in placement procedures (*Honig v. Doe*, 1988). However, disciplinary actions that do not constitute a change in placement have not been contested as frequently and, therefore, the law remains unsettled.

The Ninth Circuit, in *Doe v. Maher* (1986), noted that if a district did not propose to exclude a student from a FAPE under IDEA, then informal and reasonable discipline procedures are appropriate. Ideally, before any disciplinary action is taken, the relationship between the student's disability and the misconduct should be determined. If the misconduct is unrelated to the disability, then normal discipline procedures may be appropriate. However, if the misconduct is related to the disability, it would only be reasonable to reevaluate and consider a change in the student's program to address the student's unique needs from both an academic and a behavioral perspective. After all, if the student has little or no control over the behavior, any discipline procedure could be unfair. In our society we do not punish the student who is blind for not seeing the "stay off the grass" sign or the student who is deaf for not hearing the teacher who asked him or her to open the window. But do we punish the student who has an emotional or behavioral disorder when she or he manifests that disability? Too often, yes. Some discipline may in fact be very appropriate and helpful pedagogy. More may not be.

LRE in Relation to Appropriateness of Program

Earlier it was shown that the primary purpose of IDEA is to provide an appropriate program for every child with a disability. The LRE is a preference to be implemented to the extent consistent with the primacy of the law's focus on program appropriateness. A somewhat different approach was taken by the First Circuit where the court in *Roland M. v. Concord Sch. Comm.* (1990) concluded that academic progress is not the only indication of educational benefit, that the superior progress of the student in a private school was not dispositive in determining whether his program complied with the state mandated "maximum possible development" standard, and LRE and program appropriateness operate "in tandem" and "in concert." Finally, the court found:

> Mainstreaming may not be ignored, even to fulfill substantive educational criteria. "Just as the least restrictive environment guarantee cannot be applied to cure an otherwise inappropriate placement, similarly, a state standard cannot be invoked to release an educational agency from compliance with the mainstreaming provisions." *Burlington II*, 736 F.2d at 789 n. 19; *see also Roncker*, 700 F.2d at 1063 ("a placement which may be considered better for academic reasons may not be appropriate because of the failure to provide for mainstreaming")
>
> Correctly understood, the correlative requirements of educational benefit and least restrictive environment operate in tandem to create a continuum of educational possibilities. (*See Rowley*, 458 U.S. at 181 n. 4, 102 S.Ct. at 3038 n. 4; *Burlington II*, 736 F.2d at 785 n. 12; *Abrahamson*, 701 F.2d at 229 n. 10.) To determine a particular child's place on this continuum, the desirability of mainstreaming must be weighed in concert with the Act's mandate for educational improvement. (*See Lachman*, 852 F.2d at 296.) Assaying an appropriate educational plan, therefore, requires a balancing of the marginal benefits to be gained or lost on both sides of the maximum benefit/least restrictive fulcrum. Neither side is automatically entitled to extra ballast. (pp. 992, 993)

In *Roland M.*, the plaintiff, Matthew, was 15 years old, had a learning disability, and attended Landmark, a private residential school for students who have learning disabilities. In a very recent similar case, Christopher, age 14, attended Carroll School, also a private school for students with learning disabilities. The First Circuit followed its *Roland M.* reasoning and found the public school's offering "struck a suitable balance between the goals of mainstreaming and 'maximum possible development' " (*Amann v. Stow Sch. System*, 1992).

The First Circuit is persuaded that attending a school with peers who have similar learning needs is inherently and prohibitively more restrictive than "learning alongside nonhandicapped children" (*Amann*, 1992, at 621). In the value system of this court and others, it appears that children who have disabilities, even mild or invisible ones, are somehow less fit to be "peers" than are nondisabled students.

However, if instead of involving learning disabilities these cases had been brought by students who had emotional and behavioral disorders wanting to stay in separate schools where they performed far better than they did in public schools, the outcomes may have arguably and probably been different. If this is so, why? Is it that the other students in the facility for children who have emotional or behavioral disorders are more appropriate as "peers" than are students who have learning disabilities? Is it that learning alongside the nondisabled is less important for students who have emotional or behavioral disorders than it is students who have other disabilities? Is it that the public school system is better able to accomodate some students and therefore their entitlement is greater?

In sum, it appears that the difficulties inherent in full inclusion of all students with emotional and behavioral disorders may serve to keep alive the fundamental principles of least restrictive environments—individualized placement decisions made according to procedural safeguards, and selected from those on the full continuum of alternative placements.

A Closing Word

The continuum of alternative placements would no longer exist under a full inclusion model. It is extraordinarily difficult to conceive of regular classes able to accommodate the extremes of violent, disruptive, and inappropriate behavior shown by some students who have social and emotional disorders. We must be careful not to allow a situation to evolve where the only placement options for these students are regular classes or locked, secure facilities. If we believe, and surely we do, that many students with emotional and behavioral disorders can and do acquire appropriate behaviors, we must maintain a "ladder" of support via the continuum so that as a student's ability to maintain in increasingly less structured settings improves there are settings to match his or her level. Conversely, if a student's need for structure and support is increasing we must again have settings in between no support and lockup. Those essential in-between settings are exactly what the law now recognizes and mandates.

REFERENCES

A.W. v. Northwest R-1 School District, 813 F.2d 158 (8th Cir. 1987).
Aaron S. v. Westford Pub. Sch., EHLR 509:122 (MA SEA, 1987).
Abrahamson v. Hershman, 701 F.2d 223 (1st Cir. 1983).
Age v. Bullitt County Schools, 673 F.2d 141 (6th Cir. 1982).
Amann v. Stow Sch. System, 982 F.2d 644 (3rd Cir. 1992).
Antkowiak v. Ambach, 838 F.2d 635 (2d Cir. 1988); cert. denied.
Bateman, B. D. (1992). *Better IEPs*. Creswell, OR: Otter Ink.
Board of Education of Cherry Hill v. J.D., EHLR 401:142 (NJ SEA, 1989).
Board of Education of Community Consolidated School District No. 21, Cook County, Ill. v. Illinois State Bd. of Educ., 938 F.2d 712 (7th Cir. 1991).
Board of Education of Township High School District No. 211, Cook County, Illinois v. Corral, EHLR 441:390 (N.D. Ill. 1989).
Brown v. Henrico County School Board, 18 IDELR 670 (Va. Ct. App. 1992).
Burlington School Committee v. Mass. Dept. of Education, 105 S.Ct. 1996 (1985).
Carrington v. Massachusetts Comm. of Education, 535 N.E.2d 212 (Sup.Ct. Mass. 1989).
Carter v. Florence Co. Sch. Dist. Four, 950 F.2d 156 (4th Cir. 1991); cert. granted.

Chris D. v. Montgomery Co. Bd. of Ed., 753 F.Supp. 922 (M.D. Ala. 1990).
Chris D. v. Montgomery Co. Bd. of Ed., 743 F.Supp. 1524 (M.D. Ala. 1990).
Clovis Unified Sch. Dist. v. Cal. Office of Admin Hearings, 903 F.2d 635 (9th Cir. 1990).
Daniel R.R. v. St. Bd. of Ed., 874 F.2d 1036 (5th Cir. 1989).
Davila, R., 18 IDELR 213 (OSERS, 1989).
Davila, R., 16 EHLR 84 (OSERS, 1989).
Davila, R., 18 IDELR 594 (OSERS, 1991).
Davila, R., 18 IDELR 1039 (OSERS, 1992).
Diamond, S. C. (1993). Special Education and the Great God, Inclusion. *Beyond Behavior, 4*(2), 3–6.
Dickinson Ind. Sch. Dist., EHLR 506:395 (TX SEA, 1984).
Doe v. Maher, 793 F.2d 1470 (9th Cir. 1986).
Edward A.F. v. Clint ISD, EHLR 508:204 (TX SEA, 1986).
Florence Co. Sch. Dist. Four v. Carter, 114 S.Ct. 361 (1993).
Geis v. Parsippany–Troy Hills Bd. of Educ., 774 F.2d 575 (3rd Cir. 1985).
Greer v. Rome City School District, 950 F.2d 695 (11th Cir. 1991).
Hendrick Hudson Dist. Bd. of Ed. v. Rowley, 458 U.S. 176, 102 S.Ct. 3034 (1982).
Honig v. Doe, 108 S.Ct. 592 (1988).
Individuals with Disabilities Education Act of 1990, 20 U.S.C. §1401 *et seq.*
Irving Ind. Sch. Dist. v. Tatro, 104 S.Ct. 3371 (1984).
Kaelin v. Grubbs, 682 F.2d 595 (6th Cir. 1982).
Kruelle v. New Castle County Schools, 642 F.2d 687 (3rd Cir. 1981).
Lachman v. Illinois State Board of Education, 852 F.2d 290 (7th Cir. 1988).
Laura M. v. Special School District No. 1, 4-79 Civ. 123 (D. Minn. 1980).
Liscio v. Woodland Hills School District, 734 F.Supp. 689 (W.D. Pa. 1989); aff'd without pub. opinion 902 F.2d 1561 (3rd Cir. 1990).
Lovitt, T. C. (1991). *Preventing school dropouts*. Austin, TX: Pro-ed.
Lynch, E. C., & Beare, P. L. (1990). The quality of IEP objectives and their relevance to instruction for students with mental retardation and behavioral disorders. *Remedial and Special Education, 11*(2), 48–55.
M. B. v. Teaneck Bd. of Ed., EHLR 401:148 (NJ SEA, 1988).
Malone v. School Board of County of Prince William, Virginia, 762 F.2d 1210 (4th Cir. 1985).
McKeever, J. [Letter from the Oregon Attorney General's Office to K. Brazeau, Oregon State Department].
Montgomery Co. (MD) Pub. Sch., 16 EHLR 201 (MD SEA, 1992).
Norris v. Mass. Dept. of Ed., 529 F.Supp. 759 (D. Mass. 1981).
Osborne, A. G. (1992). The IDEA's least restrictive environment mandate: Implications for public policy. *Education Law Reporter, 71*(2), 369–380.
Peru (NY) Central Sch. Dist., 16 EHLR 514 (OCR, 1989).
Pittsfield Public Schools, 17 EHLR 314 (MA SEA, 1991).
Richards, EHLR 211:433 (OSEP, 1987).
Richland Co. (SC) Sch. Dist. #1, EHLR 353:179 (OCR, 1989).
Rockford, Ill. Sch. Dist. #205, EHLR 352:465 (OCR, 1987).
Roland M. v. Concord Sch. Comm., 910 F.2d 983 (1st Cir. 1990); cert. denied.
Roncker v. Walter, 700 F.2d 1058 (6th Cir. 1983).
S-1 v. Turlington, 635 F.2d 342 (5th Cir. 1981).
Sachais, EHLR 211:40 (OSERS, 1986).
Saginaw (MI) Int. Sch. Dist., 19 IDELR 37 (OCR, 1992).
San Francisco Unified School District, EHLR 508:312 (CA SEA, 1987).
School Board of the County of Stafford, Virginia v. Farley, 16 EHLR 1119 (Cir.Ct.Va. 1990).
Smith, S. W., & Simpson, R. L. (1989). An analysis of individualized education programs (IEPs) for students with behavioral disorders. *Behavior Disorders, 14*(2), 107–116.
Smith, W. L., 16 EHLR 491 (OCR Memorandum, 1988).

Spielberg v. Henrico Co. Pub. Sch., 853 F.2d 256 (4th Cir. 1988).

Stevenson, EHLR 312:111 (OCR, 1988).

St. Louis Developmental Disabilities Treatment Center Parents Association v. Mallory, 767 F.2d 518 (8th Cir. 1984).

Stuart v. Nappi, 443 F.Supp. 1235 (D.Conn. 1978).

Sugai, G., & Colvin, G. (1990). From assessment to development: Writing behavior IEPs. *The Oregon Conference Monograph*, University of Oregon, College of Education.

Taylor v. Honig, 910 F.2d 627 (9th Cir. 1990).

Tucson, AZ Unified Sch. Dist. #1, EHLR 352:547 (OCR, 1987).

U.S. Department of Education (1992). *Fourteenth Annual Report to Congress on the Implementation of the Individuals with Disabilities Education Act.* Washington, DC: Author.

Vergason, 19 EHLR 471 (OSERS, 1991).

Will, M. (1986). *Clarifying the standards: Placement in a least restrictive environment.* OSERS, U.S. Dept. of Ed. Vol. 1, No. 2, p. 1–7.

Will, M. EHLR 211:442 (OSERS, 1987).

Wilson v. Marana Unified Sch. Dist. No. 6 of Pima County, 735 F.2d 1178 (9th Cir. 1984).

§504 of the Rehabilitation Act of 1973, 29 U.S.C. §794 *et seq.*

CHAPTER

13

What Less Restrictive Placements Require of Teachers

John Wills Lloyd
James M. Kauffman
University of Virginia

The words *most restrictive placement* probably conjure up different images for different people. When thinking of a restrictive placement, some might imagine a lock-up facility with bars on the windows, hours of seclusion for children, institutional food served through a slot in a door, and so forth. Others might imagine a facility where physicians use Latin terms when they talk about children, and workers dressed in white administer medications that make children docile and seemingly disconnected from their surroundings. Some might envision a classroom within a regular school building where two adults supervise the activities of only a few students and these students work in near isolation for virtually the entire school day. Still others may see a more restrictive placement as characterized by a failure to have immediately available an array of services that a child needs. Surely, others have different views.

Although the meaning of the concept "most restrictive placement" may be unclear, the idea of *least restrictive environment* is more certain. In common parlance, regular classroom placement is the educational setting that is probably most often considered least restrictive. Indeed, in documents that served as the model for PL 94-142, phrases describing least restrictive placements explicitly referred to "regular class placement" (Hocutt, Martin, & McKinney, 1991). Thus, to understand the consequences of placing students with emotional or behavioral disorders in less restrictive environments, we must examine regular classroom environments. What are they like? How do the problems of children and youth with emotional or behavioral disorders align with the characteristics of regular classroom settings? What does it take for students with emotional or behavioral disorders to succeed in them? How likely to be implemented in such settings are the adaptations that are necessary for students' success? As context for these questions, it is important to understand the educational characteristics of children and youth with emotional or behavioral disorders.

PROBLEMS OF STUDENTS WITH EMOTIONAL OR BEHAVIORAL DISORDERS

Estimates of the prevalence of behavior problems vary greatly, depending on factors such as chronicity, severity, age, and gender. Although as many as 20% of children and youth in the general population manifest moderate to severe behavior problems (Brandenberg, Friedman, & Silver, 1990), reasonable estimates of the prevalence of problems great enough to disrupt school performance range from 2% or 3% to 6% of the population (Cullinan, Epstein, & Kauffman, 1984; Juul, 1986; Rubin & Balow, 1978). However, reports from the public schools indicate that fewer than 1% of the school-age population receive services for children and youth with serious emotional disturbance, the U.S. government's designation for emotional or behavioral disorders (Office of Special Education Programs, 1993).

In part, this discrepancy may be caused by the fact that children and youth who receive special education services under other categories of special education (e.g., learning disabilities) often have behavior problems as well. For example, psychiatric disorders and language problems are frequently comorbid conditions (e.g., Gualtieri, Koriath, Van Bourgondien, & Saleeby, 1983). There is substantial disagreement about how to differentiate children with emotional or behavioral disorders from their nondisordered peers and peers with other disabilities (Bower, 1982; Forness & Knitzer, 1990; Kauffman, 1988, 1993). Disagreement about definition contributes, no doubt, to the variation in estimates of prevalence.

Regardless of how many children and youths qualify as students with emotional or behavior problems, they present substantial difficulties for education. Their number may range from those who act violently and aggressively toward others to those who are not noticed by many visitors to a classroom. Further, to qualify for special education services these students must also manifest difficulties in learning.

Problems in Social Behavior

Diverse problems are subsumed under the rubric of "students with emotional or behavioral disorders," and no simple classification of them will satisfy all needs. Although it is difficult to characterize all of the problems of students with emotional or behavioral disorders, there are some legitimate generalizations. To be sure, there are many ways of categorizing behavioral disorders, but those that have the most solid evidentiary basis draw from empirical work on classification (cf. Achenbach, 1985). The highest order or most common general categories of disorder include what are also known as *broad-band factors* (e.g., Achenbach & Edelbrock, 1979). Broad-band factors include the essentially polar problems of externalizing and internalizing syndromes that are also sometimes known as *undercontrolled* and *overcontrolled*, respectively. A third category—mixed syndromes—emerges as well. These problems differ by gender and age. The syndromes are composed of lower-order, more specific problem areas, as reflected in Table 13.1.

The problems shown in Table 13.1 represent the kinds of difficulties that students experience and, hence, those with which teachers must contend. To complicate matters, although empirical work has created these abstractions of types of disorders, there are few prototypical children who would fit a specific category; instead, teachers are confronted with students who sometimes behave appropriately and, at other times, seem tense, restless, and likely to dart from one event or place to another. Such variability in behavior almost certainly adds to the complexity of the classroom environment.

The broad categories of behavior problems are based on more specific descriptions of problems—the items on checklists of behavior problems. These specific items characterize the problems that teachers in less restrictive placements face when students with emotional or behavior disorders are on their rolls. Table 13.2

TABLE 13.1
Syndromes of Behavior Problems Based on Teachers Report Form of the Child Behavior Checklist

Group	*Internalizing Syndromes**	*Mixed Syndromes*	*Externalizing Syndromes**
Boys aged 6–11	Anxious	Unpopular	Aggressive
	Social	Self-destructive	Nervous–overactive
	Withdrawal	Obsessive–compulsive	Inattentive
Boys aged 12–16	Social	Unpopular	Aggressive
	Withdrawal	Obsessive–compulsive	Inattentive
	Anxious	Immature	
		Self-destructive	
Girls aged 6–11	Anxious	Depressed	Aggressive
	Social	Unpopular	Nervous–overactive
	Withdrawal	Self-destructive	Inattentive
Girls aged 12–16	Anxious	Depressed	Aggressive
	Social	Immature	Delinquent
	Withdrawal	Self-destructive	Unpopular
			Inattentive

*Syndromes are listed in descending order of their loadings on the second-order internalizing and externalizing factors.

Note. From *Empirically Based Assessment of Child and Adolescent Psychopathology: Practical Applications* (p. 40) by T. M. Achenbach and S. H. McConaughy, 1987, Beverly Hills, CA: Sage.

TABLE 13.2
Examples of Items That Contribute to the Broad-Band Syndromes of Behavior Disorders

Syndrome	*Examples of Items*
Externalizing	Argues a lot
	Brags, boasts
	Destroys his or her own things
	Destroys property belonging to others
	Has difficulty following directions
	Is disobedient at school
	Gets in many fights
	Physically attacks people
	Steals
	Experiences temper tantrums or hot temper
	Seems preoccupied with sex
Internalizing	Behaves like opposite gender
	Clings to adults or is too dependent
	Cries a lot
	Deliberately harms self or attempts suicide
	Stares blankly
	Is unhappy, sad, or depressed
Mixed	Doesn't seem to feel guilty after misbehaving
	Eats or drinks things that are not food
	Talks out of turn
	Picks nose, skin, or other parts of body

Note. Adapted from Achenbach and Edelbrock (1979).

shows selected items that contribute to the externalizing and internalizing syndromes. These problems represent clear difficulties for teachers working with students who display them, regardless of the restrictiveness of the setting.

Academic Problems

The stereotype that characterizes children and youth with emotional or behavior disorders as tormented by their intelligent insights fades as more evidence about academic and intellectual characteristics emerges. Emotional or behavior disorders almost invariably are accompanied by academic learning problems. Further, students with these disorders are likely to have slightly lower intelligence quotients than are found in the general population (Kauffman, 1993).

Evidence about academic difficulties of children and youth with emotional or behavior disorders began to appear as early as the 1930s, when Fendrick and Bond (1936) reported that adjudicated boys were likely to have severe reading problems. The evidence about such problems has continued to mount, indicating that difficulties in academic learning are a serious problem for students with emotional or behavioral disorders. Indeed, reviews of studies of the academic status of children and youth who have emotional or behavioral disorders reveal that significant underachievement on standardized tests is common (Epstein, Kinder, & Bursuck, 1989; Mastropieri, Jenkins, & Scruggs, 1985).

Summary

The previous paragraphs paint a distressing picture of the school characteristics of children and youth with emotional or behavior disorders. These students display a wide range of inappropriate behaviors. Some not only engage in low-frequency, highly aversive behaviors such as fighting, but they also fail to comply with teachers' directions. Others interact very infrequently, complain when they do interact, and often seem distraught. Added to this, most of these students have academic difficulties. Taken together, these problems imply a substantial burden for teachers in regular classroom environments, particularly if teachers expect students in their classrooms to behave well.

WHAT DO TEACHERS IN LESS RESTRICTIVE SETTINGS EXPECT?

Given the array of social and academic problems that students with emotional or behavioral problems might manifest in a less restrictive setting, it is important to examine what teachers expect of students in their classrooms. Clearly, if teachers did not report problems with such behaviors, some of these characteristics would not be sources of concern, so are there incongruities between teachers' expectations and the behavior of students with emotional or behavior disorders? What are they?

Teachers' expectations have been studied extensively, and teachers in regular classroom environments anticipate that students in their classrooms will have certain competencies and will not behave in certain ways. These expectations may be more or less congruent with the ways in which students with emotional or behavioral disorders behave. Teachers' expectations about student behavior may play a critical role in whether students succeed in less restrictive settings.

Based on an extensive body of work using the *SBS Inventory of Teacher Social Behavior Standards and Expectations* (*SBS*) developed by Walker and Rankin (1983), we can describe what teachers demand and proscribe. Hersh and Walker (1983) and Kerr and Zigmond (1986) identified the student skills deemed critical by teachers in less restrictive elementary and secondary classrooms, respectively. Table 13.3 lists the adaptive behaviors that these teachers reported were most critical for successful adjustment in less restrictive classrooms. Results from other studies (e.g., Kauffman, Lloyd, & McGee, 1989; Walker & Lamon, 1987) corroborate these findings. As can be seen in Table 13.3, teachers place great emphasis on the importance of compliance, application to and completion of appropriate schoolwork, and peaceful interactions with peers.

TABLE 13.3
Ranks of Top 10 Student Behaviors That Teachers at Different Levels Consider Essential for Success in Their Classrooms

Behavior	*Secondary School Teachers**	*Elementary School Teachers***
Student follows established classroom rules.	1	2
Student listens to teacher's instructions and directions for assignments.	2	4
Student can follow teacher's written instructions and directions.	3	<10
Student complies with teacher's commands.	4	1
Student does in-class assignments as directed.	5	9
Student avoids breaking classroom rule(s) even when encouraged by a peer.	6	8
Student produces work of acceptable quality given his or her skill level.	7	3
Student has good work habits, e.g., makes efficient use of class time, is organized, stays on-task, etc.	8	<10
Student makes her or his assistance needs known in an appropriate manner.	9	10
Student copes with failure in an appropriate manner.	10	<10
Student expresses anger appropriately.	<10	5
Student can have normal conversations with peers without becoming hostile or angry.	<10	6
Student behaves appropriately in nonclassroom settings.	<10	7

*Based on Kerr and Zigmond (1986).
**Based on Hersh and Walker (1983).

In both the Hersh and Walker (1983) and Kerr and Zigmond (1986) studies, teachers also identified behaviors they considered intolerable in their classrooms. Table 13.4 shows the behaviors that teachers considered least acceptable in regular education settings. Other research (e.g., Kauffman et al., 1989; Walker & Lamon, 1987) corroborates these findings. Teachers clearly have little tolerance for aggressive and disruptive behavior (regardless of where it is directed) and for noncompliance. Most of the behaviors identified as intolerable fall into the social rather than the academic domain. As Hersh and Walker (1983) noted, these are "child behaviors that are (a) of high magnitude or intensity and (b) occur at an extremely low frequency in most classrooms. . . . One reason that these behaviors may be rated so highly is that teachers feel incompetent to deal with them when they occur" (p. 175). It is more difficult to manage low-frequency, high-intensity behavior problems that are often considered intractable (e.g., stealing) than it is to manage problems such as off-task behavior.

The results of studies of teachers' expectations for appropriate and inappropriate behavior indicate that regular education teachers strongly value appropriate social behavior. Indeed, they may value appropriate behavior and compliance

TABLE 13.4
Ranks of Top 10 Student Behaviors That Teachers at Different Levels Consider Unacceptable in Their Classrooms

Behavior	*Secondary School Teachers**	*Elementary School Teachers***
Student engages in inappropriate sexual behavior.	1	6
Student steals.	2	1
Student is physically aggressive with others.	3	4
Student behaves inappropriately in class when corrected.	4	3
Student damages others' property.	5	8
Student refuses to obey teacher-imposed classroom rules.	6	<10
Student disturbs or disrupts the activities of others.	7	<10
Student is self-abusive.	8	2
Student makes lewd or obscene gestures.	9	5
Student ignores teacher's warnings or reprimands.	10	10
Student refuses to obey teacher-imposed classroom rules.	<10	7
Student has tantrums.	<10	9

*Based on Kerr and Zigmond (1986).
**Based on Hersh and Walker (1983).

with directions from the students in their classrooms more than they value appropriate work-related behaviors. In relation to Doyle's (1986) delineation of the tasks of classroom teaching, regular classroom teachers apparently place greater emphasis on order than they do on learning.

However, students with emotional or behavioral disorders placed in less restrictive settings will enter these classrooms with characteristic academic and social behaviors that we described in the previous section. Such behaviors can make teachers' goals of establishing and maintaining order quite difficult to achieve. Teachers will be substantially burdened by managing these behaviors, and we can expect that the behavior of these pupils will contribute to teacher stress (Forman & Cecil, 1986). What must teachers working in less restrictive settings be able to do if they are to achieve the level of order required to permit instruction and learning?

PRACTICES THAT PROMOTE SUCCESS

Teachers in regular classroom environments must manage both order and learning for students with emotional or behavior disorders. Although the most obvious problems that such students present are in the social domain (e.g., compliance, peer relations), it is clear that individuals with emotional or behavior disorders also have difficulties in academic areas. Consequently, teachers working with these students in less restrictive placements must both manage misbehavior and promote academic competence.

Management of Misbehavior

Perhaps the most effective strategy for managing misbehavior is to implement effective teaching procedures. However, even in classrooms where effective instruction and other preventive measures are practiced, we doubt that all instances of misbehavior will be prevented. Thus, teachers in less restrictive environments would need other means for managing misbehavior. Fortunately, a substantial body of evidence indicates that the technology for doing so is available. The Peacock Hill Working Group (1991, pp. 301–302) described several criteria for establishing effective practices, including these:

> Systematic, data-based interventions. Professionals who deliver services to these students must adopt techniques and procedures that have strong empirical bases. As Carnine (1993) argued, we need to avoid situations in which "untested fads sweep through the profession, gathering authority by the number of schools using them, not by proven gains in learning" (p. 40).
>
> Continuous assessment and monitoring of progress. Programs must include methods for frequent, recurrent assessment to monitor students' academic and behavioral progress; continuation or modifications of programs should be based on whether the programs are producing beneficial effects.
>
> Provision for practice of new skills. Teachers working with students who have emotional or behavioral disorders must provide copious opportunities for practicing both academic and social skills that they have been presenting. Such practice is essential not only for helping students to learn skills (we hardly expect athletes to master complex skills by simply telling them about the skills), but also for promoting transfer or generalization of the skills (practice in multiple settings, with different peer groups, etc.).
>
> Treatment matched to problem. Efforts to educate these students should correspond to their needs; rather than promoting one generic program for diverse problems, teachers must adapt specific procedures that meet the needs of individual pupils.
>
> Multicomponent treatment. Because students with emotional or behavioral disorders usually have multiple, serious problems, special programs must incorporate multiple treatments. Often this means that combinations of remedial, behavioral, psychopharmacologic, or family treatments must be coordinated into a comprehensive program of care.
>
> Programming for transfer and maintenance. The oft-lamented failure to achieve generalization of treatment effects must be treated as an instructional problem. Teachers in least restrictive environments must adopt and execute programs that promote transfer and maintenance.

Commitment to sustained intervention. Educators and others must realize that some emotional and behavioral disorders are most appropriately conceptualized as developmental disabilities; as such, these require continuing intervention rather than applications of one-shot cures.

These principles cut across models or theoretical orientations and examples of packages of materials for preparing teachers to use them are readily available (e.g., Sprick, Sprick, & Garrison, 1992). Further, they should form the core of any educational program, regardless of disability area; their application to students with emotional or behavioral disorders simply underscores their importance. Coupled with effective academic programming (which should probably operate on many of the same principles), effective behavior management programs may make the less restrictive environment even more hospitable to students with emotional or behavioral disorders.

Academic Instruction

The principles of effective instruction described by Rosenshine and Stevens (1986) are probably particularly important for individuals with emotional or behavior disorders. Providing an instructional situation in which there is a high premium on learning and accurate performance should help eliminate many problems. That is, we expect that the results obtained by several researchers (e.g., Ayllon & Roberts, 1974; Kellam, Mayer, Rebok, & Hawkins, 1993) showing that the probability of discipline problems can be reduced by increasing the probability of appropriate academic responding can be replicated in settings that most educators would consider to be less restrictive.

Effective Practices. Rosenshine and Stevens (1986) provided a concise description of important teaching functions:

> In general, researchers have found that when effective teachers teach well structured subjects, they:
>
> - Begin a lesson with a short review of previous, prerequisite learning.
> - Begin a lesson with a short statement of goals.
> - Present new material in small steps, with student practice after each step.
> - Give clear and detailed instructions and explanations.
> - Provide a high level of active practice for all students.
> - Ask a large number of questions, check for student understanding, and obtain responses from all students.
> - Guide students during initial practice.
> - Provide systematic feedback and corrections.

- Provide explicit instruction and practice for seatwork exercises and, where necessary, monitor students during seatwork. (p. 377)

Many teachers in less restrictive classrooms probably practice some of these functions at some times, but for teachers in such settings to be successful with pupils identified as having emotional or behavior disorders (and for pupils who may have other problems, regardless of whether they have been formally identified), they will need to demonstrate most of these components consistently. As Rosenshine and Stevens noted, "The small-step approach which emerges from the research is particularly useful when teaching . . . slower students" (p. 378). This view is shared by Brophy and Good (1986), who argued that evidence about systematic instruction reveals that students who have cognitive and affective deficits "need more control and structuring from their teachers: more active instruction and feedback, more redundancy, and smaller steps with higher success rates" (p. 365). As we stipulated earlier, students with emotional or behavior disorders can reasonably be construed to have difficulties with learning. Thus, this aspect of regular classroom placements or least restrictive environments is very important.

Examples of Effective Models. The features of the instruction recommended by Rosenshine and Stevens (1986) and by Brophy and Good (1986) are represented in some currently available instructional models. For example, two models were clearly found to be effective in evaluations of Project Follow Through (Abt Associates, 1976). The Direct Instruction Model, which was based on the principles described by Engelmann and Carnine (1982), produced a very strong record for raising to middle-class standards the level of academic performance displayed by children who would otherwise be expected to perform in the lowest 20% of students. Not only were these effects apparent on lower level academic measures (e.g., word reading competence), but they were also evident on higher order measures such as reading comprehension, oral expression, and even self-concept. Another model—the University of Kansas Behavior Analysis Model (Ramp & Rhine, 1981)—also produced clearly beneficial effects with similar children. Good, Grouws, and Ebmeier (1983) offered a model for mathematics instruction that has similar characteristics. Taken together, these three models illuminate the characteristics of instruction that are probably necessary for students with emotional or behavior disorders to succeed academically in less restrictive settings.

Although the technology exists for teaching many atypical learners academic skills within less restrictive settings, we should not assume that application of this technology will provide a complete solution. For one thing, some teachers who use highly effective techniques also resist having difficult students placed in their instructional groups (Gersten, Walker, & Darch, 1988). Additionally, the potential for this technology is also influenced by other factors, including current practices in such settings. Unfortunately, the most effective technologies for improving academic performance and social behavior generally are not uniformly held in high esteem by some teachers (Nelson & Polsgrove, 1984).

TEACHER–STUDENT INTERACTIONS IN REGULAR CLASSROOMS

As we have discussed in previous paragraphs, the behavioral and academic characteristics of students with emotional or behavioral disorders are highly problematic for teachers. These students' behavior violates teachers' expectations of teachability and tractability. Nevertheless, classroom management and instructional practices that promote the success of these students have been identified (see Larrivee, 1985). What remains to be demonstrated is the extent to which these practices are and can be employed in regular classrooms. To what extent do teacher–student interactions in regular classrooms approximate those calculated to induce appropriate behavior and learning in students with emotional or behavioral disorders?

As Shores et al. (1993) observed, "behavior disorders are often considered to be monadic phenomena rather than dyadic phenomena involving social interactions between the children with behavior disorders and others in their environment" (p. 27). A substantial body of research now describes the conditions under which students with emotional or behavioral disorders will be expected to learn academic and social skills in most regular classrooms. Much of this research indicates that student–teacher interactions in regular classrooms are not characterized by behavior management or instructional strategies having a high probability of success with difficult students.

Systematic instruction in academic skills has not been a consistent focus in special programs for students with emotional or behavioral disorders (Colvin, Greenburg, & Sherman, 1993; Knitzer, Steinberg, & Fleisch, 1990). However, typical regular classrooms do not offer the direct instruction in academic skills that is most likely to be successful with these students, and the trend toward heterogeneous grouping in American public education does not bode well for their effective instruction (Grossen, 1993). In fact, were regular schools and classrooms to offer effective academic instruction and social skills training for students with emotional or behavioral disorders, very substantial changes would be required in most teachers' instructional methods, and the instructional methods adopted would need to be contrary to those gaining ascendancy in the 1990s school reform movement (cf. Lloyd, Keller, Kauffman, & Hallahan, 1988).

Several studies have shown that in the typical regular classrooms in which students with emotional or behavioral disorders might be placed the rate of teacher–student interaction is quite low, that students receive positive reinforcement for appropriate behavior on a very lean schedule (e.g., Shores et al., 1993; Strain, Lambert, Kerr, Stagg, & Lenkner, 1983; Thomas, Presland, Grant, & Glynn, 1978; White, 1975), and that teachers seldom make necessary accommodations for students' learning difficulties (McIntosh, Vaughn, Schumm, Haager, & Lee, 1993). Consistent findings of low rates of positive teacher consequences for desirable behavior and correct academic responses, in addition to teachers' failure to provide instruction appropriate for individual students' levels and interests, led one research group to suggest that both student and teacher behavior is shaped and maintained primarily by negative reinforcement:

> In a recent naturalistic study of classroom interactions of children with SED [serious emotional disturbance], Shores et al. (1993) found very low rates of teacher positive consequences. Even such prosocial behaviors as compliance to teachers' commands, completion of tasks, or following classroom rules (e.g., hand raising to request help) were on extremely lean schedules of teacher positive attention. The most probable sequence of interactions between teachers and students consisted of the teacher directing (manding) the student to respond, the student complying, followed by another teacher mand. It was suggested that, since students seldom received positive reinforcement for compliance (or other prosocial responses), compliance may have been under the control of negative reinforcement contingencies. That is, the students complied to escape the manding behavior of the teacher. As Sidman (1989) states, "responses that receive little or no positive reinforcement are likely motivated by a history of successful escape from such aversive stimulation" (p. 250). (Gunter, Denny, Jack, Shores, & Nelson, 1993, p. 267)

Gunter et al. (1993) hypothesized that the typical educational setting is aversive for students with emotional or behavioral disorders because the academic tasks they are given are either too easy (leading to boredom) or too hard (leading to frustration), the instructional activities and materials themselves are of little or no interest, the teacher provides ambiguous directions and ineffective instructional help, and the teacher seldom provides positive consequences for appropriate behavior. As a result, these students are motivated primarily by escape or avoidance—getting out of the instructional setting or minimizing its demands. The teacher is also motivated primarily by negative reinforcement—escaping or avoiding negative bouts with students by keeping their interaction rate low and the assigned tasks minimal.

If Gunter et al.'s hypothesis is correct, it might account for much of the inappropriate behavior and academic failure of students with emotional or behavioral disorders in regular classrooms that results in their being identified and placed in other settings. As well, if their hypothesis is correct it suggests that substantial change in regular classroom instruction and management will be required to make it a place that is positively reinforcing for both students and teachers and produce the desired outcomes of more prosocial student behavior and higher academic achievement. Other researchers have found that functional analyses can reveal relationships between problematic behavior and classroom variables, including teacher behavior and academic tasks (Dunlap et al., 1993). These functional analyses suggest that alterations can be made in teacher behavior, presentation of academic tasks, and other classroom variables (e.g., physical proximity to other students, self-evaluation) that effectively improve the behavior of very difficult students.

In short, the available data suggest that the typical classroom environment, whether a special class or a regular class, likely contributes to rather than ameliorates the social and academic problems of students with emotional or behavioral disorders. Both regular classrooms and alternative placements need very substantial change if they are to be made truly therapeutic or habilitative for these students. However, we note two differences between some regular classrooms and some alternative placements that could, if generalizable, prove critical in placement decisions.

First, special classes (regardless of whether students spend all or only a part of a day there), although often characterized by instruction and management that in many respects is inadequate, may offer teacher–student interactions that are more conducive to learning than those occurring in regular classrooms. For example, Shores et al. (1993) found that teachers in special classes were more than twice as likely as teachers in regular classrooms to respond to students' handraises and that "teachers in segregated [special] classrooms were nearly three times more likely to use positive consequences with their student than were the teachers of the integrated [regular] classrooms" (p. 38). Thus, alternative settings may, for many students, provide a closer approximation than regular classrooms of the conditions that foster desirable social behavior and academic learning.

Second, the constraints and culture of regular classrooms may make the adoption of effective, positive methods more difficult than in special classes. High student–teacher ratios in regular classrooms may be a serious obstacle to effective practices. As Dunlap et al. (1993) noted regarding their work in special classes with relatively small enrollments and staffed by a teacher and an aide (not including research personnel), "Admittedly, some of the individualized manipulations [functional analyses] might be a bit difficult to administer in the context of a classroom with one teacher and one aide" (p. 290). Surely, responsibility for more students complicates the task of using the recommended procedures, and regular classroom teachers may find these procedures infeasible. However, Shores et al. (1993) found that student–teacher ratios did not explain completely the differences in positive consequences that they found in regular and special classes. Many teachers of regular classes may find many effective instructional and management procedures infeasible or unacceptable for reasons other than high student–teacher ratios (cf. Von Brock & Elliot, 1987; Witt & Elliot, 1985). Thus, alternative settings may offer a more feasible and hospitable environment than regular classrooms for the needed improvements in instruction.

ADDITIONAL QUESTIONS RAISED BY PLACEMENT OF STUDENTS IN REGULAR CLASSROOMS

Given the characteristics of students with emotional or behavioral disorders and the expectations, demands, and teacher–student interactions that are typical in regular classrooms, what might be the requirements of making the placement of these students in regular classes a success? Regular classrooms are environments in which these students have not often heretofore found academic success or social acceptance, and proposals to place these students in regular classrooms, therefore, prompt several additional questions. These questions are not merely academic; social, academic, and vocational outcomes will be determined in large measure by how these questions are answered. At a minimum, we believe, the following questions must be addressed before arguments for placement of all students with emotional or behavioral disorders in regular classrooms are assumed to be defensible or such placements are adopted as policy (cf. Kauffman, Lloyd, Baker, & Riedel, in press):

1. What are the likely effects of the modifications that are required to manage and teach students with emotional or behavioral disorders in regular classes on their nondisabled peers? More specifically, how will the necessary control and structure required for those with emotional or behavioral disorders affect the educational and social development of students who need far less classroom control and structure?

2. Will schools be able to justify to parents the placement in regular classrooms of students known to exhibit highly volatile, disruptive, and perhaps violent behavior? Will the physical and psychological safety of other students and the benefits of an orderly learning environment be jeopardized? What are the legal liabilities of school personnel involved in the placement of these students?

3. If special schools and classes are eliminated as placement options, what alternatives are most likely to be used for these students? If school personnel are forced to choose between (a) keeping students with emotional or behavioral disorders in regular schools and classes or (b) simply not identifying them for special education (so that they can be suspended and expelled), how will these students be ensured an appropriate education?

4. What are the anticipated benefits to students with emotional or behavioral disorders of being included in regular classrooms? If they have not previously imitated appropriate peer models or benefited from the instructional program in the regular classroom, what assurances can be given that they will now imitate prosocial models and benefit from instruction (cf. Hallenbeck & Kauffman, in press)?

5. What training will allow regular classroom teachers to teach and manage these students successfully? When and by whom will such training be provided? Will teachers and those charged with preparing them to work with students with emotional or behavioral disorders be willing to adopt the kinds of techniques needed to help these students succeed (e.g., Sprick et al., 1992; Walker et al., 1988)?

6. How and by whom will the teachers who are to include more students with emotional or behavioral disorders in their classrooms be selected? Will the most capable teachers be asked to assume disproportionate and unfair responsibility for these students?

7. What additional support services will be provided to regular classroom teachers and to students with emotional or behavioral disorders who are placed in regular classes? Will the necessary number and quality of trained personnel be available before these students are placed in regular classrooms?

8. How will the success of placement in regular classrooms be assessed? What criteria will be used to ascertain that placement in regular classrooms is having positive effects on both nondisabled students and those with emotional or behavioral disorders? What will be done if such criteria are not met?

SUMMARY AND CONCLUSION

The meaning of "more restrictive placement" may be debatable, but the "least restrictive environment" is typically thought to be the regular classroom in a neighborhood school. Students with emotional or behavioral disorders bring very challenging problems of social misbehavior and academic failure to regular classroom teachers. These students violate teachers' standards and expectations, requiring particularly skillful use of behavior management and instructional practices that have been demonstrated to reduce misbehavior and academic failure. These practices are not consistently used in regular classrooms, and the probability is quite low that students with emotional or behavioral disorders will achieve the desired prosocial behavior and academic skills unless marked changes occur in what and how regular classroom teachers instruct and manage their students. A variety of questions must be addressed before placement of all students with emotional or behavioral disorders in regular classrooms can be said to be feasible or justified as policy.

Much is expected of teachers of regular classes in American public schools. Much more will be expected of them if they are assigned the students with emotional or behavioral disorders who are now in alternative placements (Kauffman et al., in press). Research has revealed many of the procedures teachers will need to employ if they are to accommodate such students successfully. Research has not, however, indicated how these procedures can be employed successfully in the setting of the typical regular classroom or how teachers can learn and be induced to use these procedures in the context of present school organization or proposed school reform. Much additional work will be required to establish the conditions under which regular classroom teachers can successfully teach and manage all students with emotional or behavioral disorders.

REFERENCES

Abt Associates. (1976). *Education as experimentation: A planned variation model* (Vol. 3A). Cambridge, MA: Author.

Achenbach, T. M. (1985). *Assessment and taxonomy of child and adolescent psychopathology.* Beverly Hills, CA: Sage.

Achenbach, T. M., & Edelbrock, C. S. (1979). The Child Behaivor Profile: II. Boys aged 12–16 and girls aged 6–11 and 12–16. *Journal of Consulting and Clinical Psychology, 47*, 223–233.

Ayllon, T., & Roberts, M. D. (1974). Eliminating discipline problems by strengthening academic performance. *Journal of Applied Behavior Analysis, 7,* 71–76.

Bower, E. M. (1982). Defining emotional disturbance: Public policy and research. *Psychology in the Schools, 19,* 55–60.

Brandenburg, N. A., Friedman, R. M., & Silver, S. E. (1990). The epidemiology of childhood psychiatric disorders: Prevalence findings from recent studies. *Journal of the American Academy of Child and Adolescent Psychiatry, 29,* 76–83.

Brophy, J., & Good, T. L. (1986). Teacher behavior and student acheivement. In M. L. Wittrock (Ed.), *Handbook of research on teaching* (3rd ed., pp. 328–375). New York: Macmillan.

Carnine, D. (1993, December 8). Facts over fads: Testing out "innovations" might save money, time, and good will. *Education Week,* p. 40.

Colvin, G., Greenburg, S., & Sherman, R. (1993). The forgotten variable: Improving academic skills for students with serious emotional disturbance. *Effective School Practices, 12*(1), 20–25.

Cullinan, D., Epstein, M. H., & Kauffman, J. M. (1984). Teachers' ratings of students' behaviors: What constitutes behavior disorder in schools? *Behavioral Disorders, 10,* 9–19.

Doyle, W. (1986). Classroom organization and management. In M. L. Wittrock (Ed.), *Handbook of research on teaching* (3rd ed., pp. 392–431). New York: Macmillan.

Dunlap, G., Kern, L., dePerczei, M., Clarke, S., Wilson, D., Childs, K. E., White, R., & Falk, G. D. (1993). Functional analysis of classroom variables for students with emotional and behavioral disorders. *Behavioral Disorders, 18,* 275–291.

Engelmann, S., & Carnine, D. (1982). *Theory of instruction: Principles and applications.* New York: Irvington.

Epstein, M. H., Kinder, D., & Bursuck, B. (1989). The academic status of adolescents with behavioral disorders. *Behavioral Disorders, 14,* 157–165.

Fendrick, P., & Bond, G. (1936). Delinquency and reading. *Journal of Genetic Psychology, 48,* 236–243.

Forman, S. G., & Cecil, M. A. (1986). Teacher stress: Causes, effects, interventions. In T. R. Kratochwill (Ed.), *Advances in school psychology* (Vol. 5, pp. 203–229). Hillsdale, NJ: Lawrence Erlbaum Associates.

Forness, S. R., & Knitzer, J. (1990). A new proposed definition and terminology to replace "serious emotional disturbance" in Education of the Handicapped Act. *School Psychology Review, 21,* 12–20.

Gersten, R., Walker, H. M., & Darch, C. (1988). Relationships between teachers' effectiveness and their tolerance for handicapped students: An exploratory study. *Exceptional Children, 54,* 433–438.

Good, T. L., Grouws, D. A., & Ebmeier, H. (1983). *Active mathematics teaching.* New York: Longman.

Grossen, B. (1993). Focus: Heterogeneous grouping and curriculum design. *Effective School Practices, 12*(1), 5–8.

Gualtieri, C. T., Koriath, U., Van Bourgondien, M., & Saleeby, N. (1983). Language disorders in children referred for psychiatric services. *Journal of the American Academy of Child Psychiatry, 22,* 165–171.

Gunter, P. L., Denny, R. K., Jack, S., Shores, R. E., & Nelson, C. M. (1993). Aversive stimuli in academic interactions between students with serious emotional disturbance and their teachers. *Behavioral Disorders, 18,* 265–274.

Hallenbeck, B. A., & Kauffman, J. M. (in press). How does observational learning affect the behavior of students with emotional or behavioral disorders? *Journal of Special Education.*

Hersh, R. H., & Walker, H. M. (1983). Great expectations: Making schools effective for all students. *Policy Studies Review, 2*(1), 147–188.

Hocutt, A. M., Martin, E. W., & McKinney, J. D. (1991). Historical and legal context of mainstreaming. In J. W. Lloyd, N. N. Singh, & A. C. Repp (Eds.), *The regular education initiative: Alternative perspectives on concepts, issues, and models* (pp. 17–28). Sycamore, IL: Sycamore.

Juul, K. D. (1986). Epidemiological studies of behavior disroders in children: An international survey. *International Journal of Special Education, 1*, 1–20.

Kauffman, J. M. (1988). Strategies for the nonrecognition of social deviance. In R. B. Rutherford, C. M. Nelson, & S. R. Forness (Eds.), *Bases of severe behavioral disorders of children and youth* (pp. 3–19). Boston: Little, Brown.

Kauffman, J. M. (1993). *Characteristics of emotional and behavioral disorders of children and youth* (5th ed.). Columbus, OH: Merrill/Macmillan.

Kauffman, J. M., Lloyd, J. W., Baker, J., & Riedel, T. M. (in press). Inclusion of all students with emotional or behavioral disorders? Let's think again. *Phi Delta Kappan.*

Kauffman, J. M., Lloyd, J. W., & McGee, K. A. (1989). Adaptive and maladaptive behavior: Teachers' attitudes and their technical assistance needs. *Journal of Special Education, 23*, 185–200.

Kellam, W. G., Mayer, L. S., Rebok, G. W., & Hawkins, W. E. (1993). *The effects of improving achievement on aggressive behavior and of improving aggressive behavior on achievement through two preventative interventions: An investigation of etiological roles.* Manuscript submitted for publication, Prevention Research Center, Department of Mental Hygiene, Johns Hopkins School of Hygiene and Public Health, Johns Hopkins University, Baltimore, MD.

Kerr, M. M., & Zigmond, N. (1986). What do high school teachers want? A study of expectations and standards. *Education and Treatment of Children, 9*, 239–249.

Knitzer, J., Steinberg, Z., & Fleisch, F. (1990). *At the schoolhouse door: An examination of programs and policies for children with behavioral and emotional problems.* New York: Bank Street College of Education.

Larrivee, B. (1985). *Effective teaching for successful mainstreaming.* New York: Longman.

Lloyd, J. W., Keller, C. E., Kauffman, J. M., & Hallahan, D. P. (1988, January). *What will the Regular Education Initiative require of general education teachers?* Paper prepared for Office of Special Education Programs, U. S. Department of Education, Washington, DC.

Mastropieri, M. A., Jenkins, V., & Scruggs, T. E. (1985). Academic and intellectual characteristics of behaviorally disordered children and youth. In R. B. Rutherford (Ed.), *Severe behavior disorders of children and youth* (Vol. 8). Reston, VA: Council for Children with Behavior Disorders.

McIntosh, R., Vaughn, S., Schumm, J. S., Haager, D., & Lee, O. (1993). Observations of students with learning disabilities in general education classrooms. *Exceptional Children, 60*, 249–261.

Nelson, C. M., & Polsgrove, L. (1984). Behavior analysis in special education: White rabbit or white elephant? *Remedial and Special Education, 5*(4), 6–17.

Office of Special Education Programs. (1993). *Fourteenth annual report to Congress.* Washington, DC: Author.

Peacock Hill Working Group. (1991). Problems and promises in special education and related services for children and youth with emotional or behavioral disorders. *Behavioral Disorders, 16*, 299–313.

Ramp, E. A., & Rhine, W. R. (1981). Behavior Analysis Model. In W. R. Rhine (Ed.), *Making schools more effective: New directions from Follow Through* (pp. 155–200). New York: Academic.

Rosenshine, B., & Stevens, R. (1986). Teaching functions. In M. C. Whittrock (Ed.), *Handbook of research on teaching* (3rd ed., pp. 376–391). New York: Macmillan.

Rubin, R. A., & Balow, B. (1978). Prevalence of teacher identified beahvior problems: A longitudinal study. *Exceptional Children, 45*, 102–113.

Shores, R. E., Jack, S. L., Gunter, P. L., Ellis, D. N., DeBriere, T. J., & Wheby, J. H. (1993). Classroom interactions of children with behavior disorders. *Journal of Emotional and Behavioral Disorders, 1*, 27–39.

Sidman, M. (1989). *Coercion and its fallout.* Boston: Authors Cooperative.

Sprick, R., Sprick, M., & Garrison, M. (1992). *Foundations: Establishing positive discipline policies.* Longmont, CO: Sopris West.

Strain, P. S., Lambert, D. L., Kerr, M. M., Stagg, V., & Lenkner, D. A. (1983). Naturalistic assessment of children's compliance to teachers' requests and consequences for compliance. *Journal of Applied Behavior Analysis, 16*, 243–249.

Thomas, J. D., Presland, I. E., Grant, M. D., & Glynn, T. L. (1978). Natural rates of teacher approval and disapproval in grade-7 classrooms. *Journal of Applied Behavior Analysis, 11*, 91–94.

Von Brock, M. B., & Elliot, S. N. (1987). The influence of treatment effectiveness information on the acceptability of classroom interventions. *Journal of School Psychology, 25*, 131–144.

Walker, H. M., & Lamon, W. (1987). Social behavior standards and expectations of Australian and U.S. teacher groups. *Journal of Special Education, 21*, 56–82.

Walker, H. M., & Rankin, R. (1983). Assessing the behavioral expectations and demands of less restrictive settings. *School Psychology Review, 12*, 274–284.

Walker, H. M., McConnell, S., Holmes, D., Todis, B., Walker, J., & Golden, N. (1988). *The Walker social skills curriculum: The ACCEPTS Program.* Austin, TX: Pro-Ed.

White, M. A. (1975). Natural rates of teacher approval and disapproval in the classroom. *Journal of Applied Behavior Analysis, 8*, 367–372.

Witt, J. C., & Elliot, S. N. (1985). Acceptability of classroom management strategies. In T. R. Kratochwill (Ed.), *Advances in school psychology* (Vol. IV, pp. 251–288). Hillsdale, NJ: Lawrence Erlbaum Associates.

CHAPTER

14

Appropriate Placement of Students with Emotional or Behavioral Disorders: Emerging Policy Options

Peter E. Leone
Margaret J. McLaughlin
University of Maryland

Students with emotional or behavioral disorders (EBD) challenge the abilities of public school systems and local communities to provide appropriate services for them. Evidence suggests that our current ways of providing services to many children with EBD are ineffective (Knitzer, Steinberg, & Fleisch, 1990; Koyanagi & Gaines, 1993) and that a large number of these youths drop out of school prior to graduation (Valdes, Williamson, & Wagner, 1990).

In this chapter we discuss policies related to education for youth with emotional or behavioral disorders, and we describe a policy framework for developing placement options for children with emotional or behavioral disorders. As other chapters in this volume have indicated, the quality and availability of services for children with EBD are highly variable across the United States. (See, e.g., chap. 3, this volume.) Further, social, emotional, educational, and employment outcomes for many adolescents and young adults with EBD are dismal. We begin by posing questions related to policies for students with emotional or behavioral disorders and briefly discuss the evolution of policies for this group in the public school. Next we examine beliefs that support our current practices and policies, and discuss recent studies of adolescents and young adults after leaving specialized placements. We conclude by presenting a schema or framework for placement policies that was derived from an investigation of the Center for the Study for Policy Options in Special Education, and we briefly discuss policies and practices associated with providing effective services to youth with emotional or behavioral disorders.

POLICY DEVELOPMENT AND YOUTH WITH EMOTIONAL OR BEHAVIORAL DISORDERS

Policies guide agency or school actions. Well-articulated policies provide a consistent response to the needs of some client group, the perceived interests of an agency or organization, or specific problems. Often policies emerge as agencies codify practices that are commonplace but perhaps not written down. Policy discussions about placement options for children with EBD typically involve descriptions of child or adolescent characteristics including the intensity and/or topography of specific behaviors, and the capacities of teachers, schools, or programs to provide services.

Many of our current policies concerning the education of children with emotional or behavioral disorders have developed over time in response to specific problems or crises, legislation, or litigation. The Individuals with Disabilities Education Act (IDEA) and corresponding legislation and regulations have, since the mid-1970s, shaped many school districts' policies concerning students with emotional or behavioral disorders. Landmark litigation, *Honig v. Doe et al.* (1988), has shaped school policies concerning suspension and expulsion of children with emotional or behavioral disorders. In most jurisdictions, policy development has proceeded pell-mell, in an incremental rather than a holistic fashion.

Since the mid-1980s, mental health professionals, educators, and advocates have struggled with the failure of communities and agencies to meet the needs of children and youth with emotional or behavioral disorders. In addition to high rates of school failure and dropout (Koyanagi & Gaines, 1993), the overrepresentation of children with serious mental health problems in the juvenile justice system is an ongoing concern (Cocozza, 1992). In response to the inability of current education and mental health systems to meet the needs of youth with EBD, new policies and initiatives have been developed to move away from static, microlevel responses to troublesome behaviors, and toward comprehensive, child- and family-centered services (Nelson & Pearson, 1991; Stroul & Friedman, 1986). New initiatives in this area suggest the need to rethink and perhaps reconsider policies for children and youth with EBD.

Evolution of Policies

Since the late 1800s, public schools have developed policies for educating students who were different and/or disabled, although the quality of services provided has been highly variable. The idea that troublesome youngsters require a different school program than other students was developed more than 100 years ago with the establishment of the first separate classes in New York and other big-city school systems (Hewett & Forness, 1977). When compulsory attendance laws were enacted during the late 19th and early 20th centuries, a more diverse group of young people enrolled in schools and special classrooms for "unmanageable, incorrigible, defective pupils" were established (Tropea, 1987). Professional beliefs at that time constructed emotional disorders as intrapsychic, rooted in emotional conflicts existing within the child. Placement policies and options for children with EBD were ostensibly motivated by a desire to protect children from academic failure and social rejection (Leinhardt & Pallay, 1982). However, a competing perspective on early policies and options is that special classes reflected institutional priorities that allowed schools to exclude students from the regular classroom while complying with compulsory attendance legislation (Carrier, 1990; Tomlinson, 1982; Tropea, 1987). In the latter view, the growth of special programs for troublesome pupils was facilitated by tacit understandings that schools could maintain order by isolating certain pupils.

During the first half of the 20th century, many school districts developed special class programs for one or more groups of children with disabilities. However, programs developed for children with emotional or behavioral disorders during this time were most often special schools or were associated with hospital settings (Coleman, 1986; Kauffman, 1989). Special day school and psychiatric hospital placements reflected popular and professional beliefs about both the etiology of disturbed behavior and the role and function of public schools. Only in the 1950s and 1960s did classes for children with EBD become commonplace in the public schools (Morse, Cutler, & Fink, 1964) and instructional practices move from a psychodynamic focus to an academic and behavioral emphasis (Haring & Phillips, 1962; Hewett, 1968).

During the past 30 years the number of programs for children and youth with emotional or behavioral disorders has increased dramatically; many new programs have been created since 1975 and the passage of P.L. 94-142 (Grosenick, 1991). With the passage of P.L. 94-142 Individuals with Disabilities Education Act (IDEA), states, regional education agencies, and local education agencies have, among other things, developed new policies for funding services, and parents now have procedural protections in assessment, identification, and placement. Yet, a perennial issue for those concerned with the education of students with emotional or behavioral disorders involves developing appropriate placement policies. Several factors influence school districts' policies and decision making concerning educational placements of students with EBD. They include beliefs about deviant behavior and the purposes of schooling, the role of the school in the community, and legislation and litigation.

Beliefs About Deviant Behavior

Although many school policies concerning children with emotional or behavioral disorders are driven by the mandates of the IDEA and related litigation, popular and professional beliefs about the nature of emotional or behavioral disorders, the purposes of schooling, and the role of the school in the community guide the implementation and interpretation of policy. Although federal legislation set parameters for who is entitled to services, it also reinforced person-centered or person-as-problem-centered perspectives and policies by providing additional financial support to school districts for each student identified as seriously emotionally disturbed. Such person-centered perspectives have the same effect on placement practices as the medical model of deviance and disability (Glennon, 1993). From person-centered perspectives, those concerned with troublesome behavior attempt to fix deviant behavior (Leone, 1989), and devote minimal attention to problems that create disturbance within school settings or to rectifying maladaptive relationships between students and teachers or students and families. Policies concerning children with emotional or behavioral disorders devote minimal attention to the contexts of deviant behavior and the culture of the schools.

In addition to reinforcing person-centered perspectives, the definition and terminology in many policies contain restrictive language that excludes students who are "socially maladjusted." In some jurisdictions this exclusionary clause has enabled schools to label some troublesome behavior as externalizing disorders or conduct disorders and use disciplinary policies to isolate and exclude those who violate school rules (Cline, 1990; Forness & Knitzer, 1992). Evidence suggests that researchers have been unable to distinguish reliably between emotionally disturbed and socially maladjusted youth for the purposes of special education eligibility (Nelson, Center, Rutherford, & Walker, 1991).

Although beliefs about disordered or deviant behavior influenced the development of placement policies for youth with EBD, school districts' beliefs about the purposes of school and the history of noneducational services in the public schools also contributed to the evolution of current policies.

The Purpose of Schooling and Noneducational Services in the Schools

The purpose of public schooling in the 20th century has been dominated by a cultural-transmission ideology. From this perspective, the primary work of the schools is transmitting knowledge, skills, and social and moral rules of the culture. Meeting the needs of students with EBD, helping children and adolescents develop self-sufficiency, social skills, and independent problem-solving behavior is more consistent with romantic and progressive ideologies of schooling (Kohlberg & Mayer, 1972). When individualized education programs specify mental health and other related services for students, the psychologists, therapists, social workers, and other professionals who provide those services may experience an environment that does not value their skills or services, nor see what they do as central to the mission of the school.

Noneducational services in school settings have a long and variable history that began in late 19th century with social reformers who were concerned about poor health and social conditions of many urban and immigrant children. Robert Hunter, writing in 1904, stated that a new conception of the responsibilities of the school was needed: "Parents . . . bring up their children in surroundings which make them in large numbers vicious and criminally dangerous" (Hunter, 1905, p. 209, cited in Tyack, 1992, p. 19). Hunter and other reformists of his time believed that a single agency, specifically the school, should assume responsibility for the whole life of the child.

Some public schools, with the help of philanthropic groups and foundations, began to provide noneducational services. Meals, recreation programs, counseling and vocational training, and dental and other health care were just some of the services that were provided in urban schools in the early part of this century. Some schools providing services to children and adults became the social centers of their communities, and the expanded role of the school often promoted cooperation among agencies and collaboration among professionals (Tyack, 1992).

Not all educators were uniformly supportive of these reforms. Some, consistent with the cultural transmission model of schooling, believed that the only mission of schools was to provide instruction in basic academic areas. Other school administrators, who embraced a broader concept of schooling, were concerned about the economic implications when outside sources of philanthropic support for noneducation services left. Nonetheless, many noneducational services—including immunizations, physical exams, and dental exams—became institutionalized in the schools. However, many other noneducational functions—such as social services, mental health services, and meals—were phased out over time and have only gradually reemerged in some schools during the past 30 to 40 years (Tyack, 1992).

In general, public schools did not endorse a broad view of their responsibilities toward students nor of the mission of public education. As Tyack (1992) noted, even as schools hired social workers and other noneducational personnel, they redefined their roles to serve the schools' mission. Thus, many of these individuals became attendance monitors and enforcers of school standards.

Policy Basis for Current Placements

Current policies regarding the location of services for students with EBD, as well as for other students with disabilities, are influenced by the statutory and regulatory language of IDEA that calls for educating students in the least restrictive environment (LRE). IDEA expresses a clear preference for educating students with disabilities in the regular classroom. The statute provides that:

> to the maximum extent appropriate, handicapped children, including children in public or private institutions or other care facilities, should be educated with children who are not handicapped, and that separate schooling, or other removal of handicapped children from the regular educational environment should occur only when the nature or severity of the handicap is such that education in regular classes with the use of supplementary aids and services cannot be achieved satisfactorily. (20 U.S.C. 1412(5)(B); 34 C.F.R. 3000.551)

The accompanying regulations, however, further define *least restrictive environment* in terms of a continuum of placements moving from the regular classroom to more restrictive placements, including hospitals and homebound instruction. The LRE provision, as part of the 1975 statute, was in large part a statement of the principles of normalization (Rostetter, Kowalski, & Hunter, 1984) and an assertion about the value of integrated education for individuals with and without disabilities. The regulations represent an attempt to make those beliefs and principles operational in light of what was then current knowledge and practice in the schools. For many students with EBD, access to public education was the primary battle; placement was a secondary concern.

Despite changes in orientation regarding what constitutes good education for students with EBD, there was a prevailing belief in the early 1970s in the need for psychiatric and psychological services and the value of medical intervention, including hospitalization. Thus, LRE-based policies designed to provide appropriate education to those students had to encompass the existing placement options, such as public and private special day schools, residential institutions, and hospitals.

The Implementation of LRE Policy

The use of differing placement options has varied over time and across jurisdictions. Danielson and Bellamy (1989), using data from the *Tenth Annual Report to Congress*, demonstrated considerable variation among states in the placement of students with disabilities in more restrictive settings, such as special schools and hospitals. Several studies suggest that states' relative wealth, as defined by per capita income as well as proportion of nonrural population, are related to use of more restrictive placements for students with EBD (McLaughlin & Owings, 1993; Noel & Fuller, 1985).

Other studies shed light on the impact of special education funding on placement of students with disabilities. For example, researchers have demonstrated a link between restrictiveness of placements and the mechanisms that generate funds for those services (Dempsey & Fuchs, 1993; Moore, Walker, & Holland, 1982; Singer & Raphael, 1988). In general, use of a funding formula that weighs or accounts for more intensive or expensive placements (e.g., self-contained classes, special schools, etc.) results in greater use of those placements. Dempsey and Fuchs (1993) analyzed the changes in placements over time in one state that moved from a funding formula based solely on child count to one that provided additional support for restrictive placements. The results clearly indicated a shift in services from partial resource room and other integrated placements to a greater use of more restrictive placements with the change in formula.

Contextual factors have been shown to be generally influential in the implementation of LRE policy in other studies as well (Rostetter, Kowalski, & Hunter, 1984; Turnbull, 1983). Most recently, a study by Hasazi, Johnston, Liggett, and

Schattman (1994), provided a broader more comprehensive view of the local variability in use of various placements. Specifically, this multisite qualitative study of school districts that differed in use of restrictive versus inclusive settings indicated the influence of several important factors. Lack of fiscal resources in general, specifically for moving toward more integrated service delivery, was cited as a chief barrier. Also critical to the movement toward more integration was the perceived intractability of the special education service system and regulatory base that had institutionalized a continuum of placements and put in place procedures that maintained that continuum. In terms of facilitators for changing district policies, the knowledge and values of those within a local district were considered critical, as were parents, advocates, and state-level leadership.

THE IMPETUS TO CHANGE

Within the past few years a number of studies and reports have compelled educators to reexamine the manner in which services are provided to children and youth with emotional or behavioral disorders and the policies supporting current practices. Data from the *14th Annual Report to Congress on the Implementation of IDEA* (U.S. Department of Education, 1992) indicate that students with serious emotional disturbance or EBD are half as likely to be accommodated in regular classes as other children with disabilities. They are also less likely than other children enrolled in special education to receive services in a resource room or regular classroom setting. They are over twice as likely to be placed in separate day schools, residential schools, and home and hospital settings as any other student with a disabling condition. Analysis of annual report placement data for youths in various disability categories over the 1977–78 to 1989–90 school years indicates a decrease of almost 4% over time in the placement of students with EBD in regular schools. In contrast, for that same period, there was a 6% increase in placements in regular schools for all disabilities combined and varying increases for all other disabilities, with the exception of students with mental retardation who showed only a slight decline (Sawyer, McLaughlin, & Winglee, 1994).

Moreover, within these specialized placements, the curricula and experiences offered students with EBD are typically very narrow. According to Knitzer, Steinberg, and Fleisch (1990), programs focus primarily on behavior management and control and devote minimal attention to building academic, vocational, or social skills. After visits to numerous sites across the United States, Knitzer and her colleagues concluded, "Too often, the classroom life is, at best barren, and at worst, punitive and not oriented toward either academic or social learning" (p. 116).

Recently, school districts have begun to increase the use of home instruction as a placement option for children and youth with emotional or behavioral disorders. While attempting to identify an appropriate placement, local education agencies frequently use home instruction as a temporary placement for those youth who don't fit the current range of options available within the school district and for whom an out-of-district placement has not been located. According to the *14th Annual Report to Congress on the Implementation of IDEA* (U.S. Department of Education, 1992), states report using homebound instruction most often with students identified as seriously emotionally disturbed. Thirty percent of all children and youth aged 6 to 21 receiving homebound instruction during the 1989–90 school year were identified as EBD; this represents 2% of all youth children and youth identified as EBD. In some jurisdictions home instruction is no longer used as a crisis-stabilization procedure for many youth with EBD, but rather as a long-term, albeit inadequate, service delivery system that provides approximately six hours of instruction per week (*Cordero et al. v. PA Department of Education*, 1991).

The meager educational experiences offered students with EBD is associated with their bleak educational outcomes. The National Longitudinal Transition Study (NLTS) of Special Education Students (Wagner, 1991) sheds light on the school experiences and outcomes of students with varying disabling conditions, including those with emotional or behavioral disorders. The study, based on a nationally representative sample of more than 8,000 students, gathered information on students' characteristics, school careers, and postsecondary education or employment. Data suggest that among secondary school students with disabilities ages 13 to 21 during the 1985–86 school year, the highest percentage receiving failing grades and the lowest percentage promoted were identified as emotionally disturbed. With regard to leaving school, 55% of the secondary school youth identified as emotionally disturbed in the 1985–86 and 1986–87 school years in the NLTS sample dropped out, a larger percentage than in any other disability classification. Further, 44% of students identified as having an emotional or behavioral disorder had been arrested within two years after leaving school (Valdes, Williamson, & Wagner, 1990).

Findings from the Washington Statewide follow-up study (Neel, Meadows, Levine, & Edgar, 1988) and the Iowa State follow-up study (Frank, Sitlington, & Carson, 1991) broaden and confirm the findings of the NLTS on the postsecondary adjustment of students with emotional or behavioral disorders. Neel and his colleagues (1988) found that only 60% of the youth who had graduated or aged out of 21 school districts in Washington between 1978 and 1986 were employed; in contrast, 73% of a comparable nondisabled cohort were employed at the time of their study. They also found that although only 8% of the nondisabled former students were unengaged (i.e., not working nor pursuing postsecondary education or training), 31% of the former students identified as having a behavior disorder were unengaged. Frank and his colleagues (1991) compared former students with behavior disorders who had dropped out of school with those who had graduated. They found that among former students from the classes of 1985 and 1986 that they studied, 58% of the graduates versus 30% of the dropouts were employed full or part time.

The poor educational outcomes for students with EBD, coupled with criticism of the educational programs designed for those students, have focused professionals' attention on placement policies and the settings in which services are provided. In addition, the national movement toward inclusion of all students within neighborhood schools is creating tensions and ambiguities within special education regarding how and where to best serve students with EBD.

The LRE Mandate and Inclusion

The impetus to develop more responsive education programs for students with EBD can be examined within the context of inclusion. During the past half decade, the discussions surrounding the LRE or least restrictive environment requirement of IDEA have taken on a new focus often referred to as *inclusion*. The push for inclusion, the education of students with disabilities within regular classroom and instructional settings, has gained tremendous momentum from two different groups. The first group, those who advocate on behalf of students with developmental disabilities, particularly students with severe cognitive and multiple disabilities (Biklen, 1985; McDonnell & Kiefer-O'Donnell, 1992; Sailor, 1991; Sailor, Gee, & Karasoff, 1993; Thousand & Villa, 1989), calls for an end to educational segregation of students with disabilities on both a moral as well as an educational basis. Those advocates believe that the development of valuable social and communication skills among students with disabilities in integrated settings will promote their ability to be part of the larger adult community of nondisabled people. Further, advocates argue that long-term postschool success for many of those students will depend on developing natural support networks among co-workers and others in the community, and such networks can only emerge when students with disabilities are educated with their peers (Stainback & Stainback, 1989).

Others, such as Gartner and Lipsky (1989); National Association of State Boards of Education (NASBSE; 1992); Stainback and Stainback (1984, 1989); Skrtic (1991); and Reynolds, Wang, and Walberg (1987) suggested that the current special education system, including both the differential diagnoses and labelling and use of separate placements, is neither efficacious nor producing desired educational outcomes and should be dismantled in favor of a unified or single system that is driven by individual child needs and favors flexible service delivery. These proposals are not without critics (e.g., Davis, 1989; Fuchs & Fuchs, 1988; Kauffman, 1989; Kauffman, Gerber, & Semmel, 1988; Learning Disabilities Association of America, 1993) who cite lack of receptivity and ability on the part of regular educators to educate students with significant academic and behavioral problems effectively. In addition, those same critics question the motives of those who are advocating change, particularly the call for increased flexibility in use of fiscal resources and program design (Fuchs & Fuchs, 1994).

McLaughlin and Warren (1992a) recently investigated a number of school districts engaged in educational restructuring to determine the anticipated effects on special education programs and on students with disabilities. They found that in districts that were including special education programs in restructuring efforts, the changes were being made to remove the service and administrative barriers among regular education, special education, and other categorical programs (such as Title I) to promote the education of all students within regular education classrooms. However, across districts where such innovation was underway, there were questions regarding how students with EBD would fare within an inclusive system if that meant only education within regular classrooms and comprehensive schools.

Discussion about inclusion and students with emotional or behavior disorders is just beginning to emerge (Diamond, 1993; Landrum & Kauffman, 1992). In some respects because EBD, unlike other categories of exceptionality, is a social disability, inclusion of youngsters with EBD in regular classrooms and programs presents particular challenges. At the present time, "a viable continuum of services including both school and community-based options does not exist" (Grosenick, 1991, p. 13). Since Morse et al.'s analysis in 1964, the separate classroom continues to be the most frequently employed setting for providing educational services to youth with emotional or behavioral disorders.

Capacity Versus Will

Although several factors contribute to the movement toward inclusion of students with disabilities into the general education system, the impetus for change may have outpaced the capabilities of local schools and agencies. Recent litigation and a due process hearing illuminate some of the problems associated with identifying appropriate placements for youths with emotional or behavioral disorders. In one state, uncontested facts presented by plaintiff special education students in a class action lawsuit indicate that a state department of education policy designed to promote least restrictive placements has capped the number of out-of-district, within-state placements. Simultaneously, local districts failed to develop less restrictive local options, with the result that scores of children including many with EBD have been inappropriately placed on home instruction (*Cordero et al. v. PA Department of Education*, 1991). In another state, inflexible local school policies resulted in the attempted expulsion of an eligible student who entered a new school district midyear. Timelines associated with a rigid prereferral intervention policy resulted in severe disciplinary sanctions against a youth prior to his enrollment in special education (*U.D. v. School Board of Orange Co., FL*, 1992).

Both the variability in the use of different placements as well as the factors contributing to those differences are not surprising in light of what is known about implementation of education policy in general. A vast amount of implementation research (Berman & McLaughlin, 1977; Fullan & Stieglebauer, 1991; Mclaughlin, 1990) suggests that contextual variables, such as local beliefs and values

(McLaughlin & Warren, 1994), as well as fiscal and human resources are major determinants of how specific policies are interpreted and shaped into programs.

A FRAMEWORK FOR DEVELOPING PLACEMENT POLICIES

Having considered some of the forces that have shaped current placement options for students with EBD, we now present a framework for developing service options for those students and their families. This framework was developed as part of a more general investigation of programs and services for students with EBD conducted by the Center for Policy Options in Special Education at the University of Maryland. This center was charged with identifying the critical policy issues confronting the field in providing services to students with EBD. In addition, the center was also to identify and analyze options that address those issues. The center has conducted a series of focus group meetings with a variety individuals from the fields of education, mental health, social service, and juvenile justice who are concerned with the current service delivery options available to children and youth with EBD. In addition, center staff have interviewed parents and have visited programs considered by leaders in the field to be innovative approaches to educating students with EBD. From this investigation, issues that embodied concerns about services for students and their families emerged and options that represented responses to those issues were identified. The following framework emerged from those focus group meetings, site visits, and interviews.

Two issues were central to the discussions about changing service delivery options. First, our research identified that school systems needed to embrace a broader vision and mission for students with emotional and behavior problems that included attention to noneducational needs of students and their families. A second related issue was that service systems could no longer be constrained by narrow conceptualizations of eligibility and services. Current policies respond to individual children or family members without a view toward improving the overall effectiveness of the system (Glennon, 1993). In general, a conclusion drawn from the discussion was that what is needed at this juncture is a cohesive and defensible framework for defining available service options for students and their families, including consideration of where those services shall be delivered. Placement options cannot be considered separate from larger questions regarding what the service system should look like. As previously discussed, current placement options exist as a result of uneven policy development and confusion or contradictory beliefs about EBD students as well as institutional missions. Therefore, a new framework must be grounded on certain assumptions and provide a template for policymakers and program developers.

Several assumptions underlie the architecture of a new policy framework:

Students must be served in the context of their families. Family composition must be broadly defined and accepted; policies should support stable, nurturing home environments. (This may mean supporting biological parents or other family members as well as stable but nonrelated family units.)

Services should be provided closest to the educational and community settings of nondisabled peers. This does not mean that alternatives to "regular" schools cannot exist, but the use of highly restrictive, residential, or other alternative settings must be systematically linked to the student's anticipated home community.

Placement options should not be dependent on specific definitions, program regulations, or histories; rather, they should be based on student need. Students may need services at different times, intensity, and duration throughout their educational lives and should not be subjected to artificial and contradictory eligibility decisions in order to receive needed services. However, high-cost or highly specialized services need to be restricted and some form of gatekeeping needs to be established.

If policymakers are able to accept these assumptions about programs and services for students with EBD, a new configuration for programs can be developed. Following is a framework that elaborates a set of principles that can guide policy development and program design with regard to services for students and their families. The framework does not suggest specific policies, but rather creates the basis for making decisions about how programs are structured and where students are educated.

Outcome-Driven Systems

Currently, education as well as other systems providing services to students with EBD and their families are process-driven systems. That is, agencies and service providers define what they do by a set of procedures or processes, such as assessment for service eligibility or development of treatment plans. As discussed earlier in the chapter, many of the procedures have been defined in part by conceptual models and beliefs and historical precedents, and through formal policy mechanisms such as legislation. The more formal policies have been pieced together over time in response to specific societal problems and with differing objectives. The result is a patchwork of educational and other services, guided by regulations and processes and driven by objectives that may be vague and contradictory.

As noted earlier, there has been little attention to the outcomes of students with EBD. Too often, research and program evaluations have focused more on demonstrating the effectiveness of specific interventions or packages of interventions relative to a finite set of skills or behaviors. In addition, agencies may spend extraordinary amounts of time and other resources documenting process (e.g., numbers of clients served, dollars expended), but pay almost no attention to the outcomes of those processes. Further, at present there is no unified or commonly agreed-on set of outcomes that can be used to assess program effects or guide program development.

Policies supporting process-driven systems rely primarily on prescriptive procedures. The requirements for developing individualized educational plans are examples of some extreme process oriented policies. In contrast, outcome-driven systems require the definition of client outcomes across agencies and demand that service plans be evaluated in terms of those outcomes. How plans are written can be interpreted more flexibly.

Students with EBD are not doing well; they are not staying in school and they are not doing well after they leave school. Although some may argue that segregated placements have contributed to those poor outcomes, it is equally likely that the programs developed to serve those students do not respond to a consistent set of education outcomes and would yield no better results if offered in more integrated settings. Not only is each discipline or agency delivering services according to its own, often implicit, beliefs about appropriate outcomes for clients, but there has been little or no accountability on the part of schools and other agencies or systems for those outcomes (Gerry & Certo, 1992).

The absence of a framework for defining and assessing outcomes is a problem confronting all of special education. For too long, many special educators have focused on providing services to individual students based on narrowly defined individualized education program (IEP) goals objectives without a sense of how those objectives contribute to the long-term success of the students (Pugach & Warger, 1993). The lack of connection between IEPs and actual student programs has been documented by Smith (1990), who asserted that the IEP has evolved into little more than a tool for monitoring the school's compliance with specific mandated procedures. The attention to outcomes for students with disabilities is relatively new and long overdue (McLaughlin & Warren, 1992b; National Center on Educational Outcomes [NCEO], 1991) and has resulted in a number of approaches to defining those outcomes. Perhaps the most comprehensive set of outcomes is being developed by the NCEO (1993) at the University of Minnesota. The NCEO has, through broad national consensus, identified a set of exit outcomes for all students with disabilities that encompass both acquisition of knowledge and skills in traditional academic areas as well as competencies in social and personal areas. These efforts may lead to building a more outcome-oriented system.

Outcomes and Accountability. Although identification of outcomes is important as a guide to program development, it is most useful if linked to system accountability. That is, if the outcomes are used to monitor the success of programs, not just students. The concept of outcome-based accountability is becoming increasingly important in today's atmosphere of reduced resources and educational restructuring (Gerry & Certo, 1992; Kirst, 1990; McLaughlin & Warren, 1994). For special education, student educational outcomes should replace process variables as the driving force for determining appropriateness of educational programs.

For students with EBD, questions about where services should be delivered must be driven by students' progress toward the broad educational outcomes. This assumes that (a) a set of such outcomes can be developed that are acceptable to all stakeholders (e.g., students and families, educators, and providers of other services), and (b) all systems involved in the education of the student will endorse those outcomes. At present, neither assumption is met.

The concept of using educationally defined outcomes as a basis for determining interdisciplinary program success may be foreign to other service providers. Similarly, the important outcomes for mental health or social services may appear to be irrelevant to educators. Thus, it is likely that some compromise set of outcomes may need to be constructed that accommodates orientations and perspectives of different disciplines. A core set of agreed-on outcomes can unify programs and services and provide benchmarks for determining when there is a need for program improvement or change. What is more, building consensus around the definition of important outcomes for students and families provides an opportunity to develop and strengthen communication among professionals and to broaden the often narrow perspectives on students with EBD and their families.

Beyond holding schools and other service agencies accountable, educational outcomes also need to be translated into curriculum standards and experiences that students with EBD must have. For example, if vocational and employability skills are important for long-term adjustment, then programs that serve those students, regardless of where they are located, must provide opportunities to learn those skills and competencies. As Knitzer and her colleagues (1990) stated, "We are challenging any easy interpretation that the spirit of the law is better met if a child is in a 'less restrictive' rather than a more restrictive placement unless equal attention is paid to the quality of programming" (p. 34).

System-Linked Services

The second principle in the policy framework involves linking services across systems. The need for interdisciplinary services delivered by different professionals is integral to the design of any system of services for students with EBD (Knitzer et al., 1990; Nelson & Pearson, 1991; Stroul & Friedman, 1986). The needs of many students with EBD and their families transcend the manner in which services are organized and the ways in which professionals are trained (Leone, 1990). Appropriate placement and services often require cooperation from mental health, social services, health, and juvenile justice agencies as well as education.

Accordingly, policies must ensure a continuum of services for students and their families that is cross-disciplinary, coordinated, and guided by a common core of outcomes. Gerry and Certo (1992) pointed out that the current federal and state system of categorical programs is a primary barrier to creating a more fluid and integrated continuum of services. Among the policy problems cited are:

No single point of community access to services.

Lack of a unified or holistic approach to meeting family needs.

Conflicting program rules and administrative procedures.

Disincentives within some categorical programs for self-help or self-determination.

No single point of accountability.

A flexible continuum of services neither requires nor restricts specialized placements. However, policies should not direct the use of certain placements. At present, many education placement decisions are still based on only a slice of the problem. For example, students may be placed in hospitals or residential facilities because there is a lack of specialized foster care, respite care, or consistent in-home support for families. Without system-linked services, education must use resources to craft an imperfect and costly solution to what is a complex student and family problem. Placements in settings away from the home school and community may also be governed by other factors such as professional convenience, insurance benefits, state reimbursement formulae, and program history and tradition (Stroul & Friedman, 1986). As noted earlier, within the special education programs, state funding formulae of special education services tends to support reimbursements for more restrictive placements (Dempsey & Fuchs, 1993; Goertz, 1993). Also, federal regulations require that states maintain a continuum of placements as opposed to a continuum of services. The emphasis on settings in the regulations, as opposed to services, perpetuates segregation and requires states to maintain and use high-cost settings instead of attempting to use funds more creatively and flexibly to meet specific needs within community settings.

Finally, professional beliefs and attitudes also dictate where services are delivered. Typically, those beliefs and attitudes are not based on either the desired outcomes of the services or what might meet the needs of clients and their families more efficiently and cost effectively. Rather, professional attitudes "come naturally" and are based on the need for punitive or medical responses to troublesome behaviors (Glennon, 1993). Nonetheless, many school districts are rethinking the range of services they provide to all students and are collaborating with mental health, social services, and other public agencies to serve youth with EBD (Leone, McLaughlin, & Meisel, 1992; Melaville, Blank, & Asayesh, 1993; Nelson & Pearson, 1991). Some of the options involve moving noneducational services into the public schools and developing new collaborative relationships with social services, mental health, and juvenile justice agencies.

Creating comprehensive, coordinated systems requires a number of policy changes, both within the larger federal and state program infrastructures as well as the more specific operational policies that govern how agencies function. The former will require legislative changes, whereas many operational changes can be accomplished with some changes in program administrative policy. For example, although funding structures need to promote more flexible service provision (including more emphasis on prevention and less reliance on deep-end crisis-oriented service provision), there are also a number of what Melaville et al. (1993) called "technical tools of collaboration" (p. 59) that need to be implemented.

These tools include case management as a key strategy for ensuring interagency service delivery, common intake and assessment forms, common or complementary eligibility requirements that ensure that there are no gaps in service, and a management information system that ensures client confidentiality but provides for consistent flow of information across service providers. Each of these tools will require changes in policy at the agency levels; many of the necessary changes can be implemented without changes in the larger policy structures.

There are a number of barriers that thwart the creation of flexible service systems. These include a limited array of services within communities; an emphasis on specialized case management that responds only to specific problems and fails to focus on broader child and family outcomes (Morrill, 1992); the inability of professionals to move beyond their own knowledge and experiential base (Morrill, 1992); program rules and regulations that restrict flexible use of funds and personnel (Farrow & Joe, 1992; Nelson & Pearson, 1991); lack of a universal entitlement to services (Bernstein, 1993; Gerry & Certo, 1992); restrictions on confidentiality and use of information (Nelson & Pearson, 1991); and professional training, licensure, and culture (Morrill, 1992).

In spite of these problems, a number of examples of successful collaborative efforts are underway (Knitzer et al., 1990; Melaville et al., 1993; Morrill, 1992; Nelson & Pearson, 1991; Norfolk Youth Network, 1989; Stroul & Friedman, 1986). Systems such as the Alaska Youth Initiative, Bluegrass Impact, and the Ventura Model (Nelson & Pearson, 1991) may use specialized settings; however, services are based on the beliefs that students with EBD need a community identity and that there should be stability over time among the adults who interact with those students. For example, in a community described by a participant in one of our focus groups, a student who was placed in a psychiatric hospital had developed a relationship with one of the counselors. After discharge, the interagency team that was overseeing that child's program arranged for the counselor to continue to work with the child within the home as part of a wraparound service plan designed for the family. Policies need to be crafted that support this type of service system, including flexible use of personnel and funds as well as the creation of interagency planning and service teams.

Family-Responsive Services

The third principle, family-responsive services, is closely related to creating system-linked services. However, even well-coordinated systems can fail to meet the needs of families. Currently, agencies and systems are organized around a professional, bureaucratic culture that assumes certain roles and power relationships with clients and has particular traditions about the use of time and how one conducts business (Skrtic, 1991). Decisions about services for children and families are often made by professionals prior to the arrival of these participants at the meetings. The relationships between parents and professionals are influenced by longstanding attitudes on both sides. School personnel bring their stereotypes about emotional disabilities, their causes, and the types of services needed. According to Glennon (1993), parents themselves may hold many of these same stereotypes. "In addition, parents may blame themselves for their children's problems, and they may not feel entitled to receive help from the schools" (p. 353). Too frequently, as schools involve families in the decision-making process, friction develops concerning the rights and safeguards guaranteed to families (Karp, 1993). Although some parents may be unaware of their rights under the law, others defer to the judgment of professionals when making decisions about educational placements. Professional judgment, although ostensibly driven by the best interests of the child, is strongly influenced by traditions, beliefs about punishing or treating bad behavior, and knowledge of existing services (Glennon, 1993; Karp, 1993).

Another problem is that professional cultures promote the concept of a 9-to-5 work day and assume that services to clients will be provided during those hours. Further, each agency has its own system for managing information as well as places for delivering client services. These professional traditions or conveniences that are major barriers to providing family responsive services (Jehl & Kirst, 1992; Sugarman, 1991) are also barriers to providing comprehensive and collaborative service systems.

Being responsive to families means providing services at times and in places convenient to family members as well as services that are sensitive to their needs. Supportive family services are frequently delivered outside professional offices, often in the home or community. For instance, The Norfolk Youth Network (1989) provides services for children and youth with EBD and their families in a number of settings. In addition to traditional school and mental health services, the Youth Network provides preventative home-based services, a preschool prevention program, therapeutic respite care, and transitional home-based services for youth returning to the community from residential placements. Other services include therapeutic family homes for youth at risk for residential placement and intensive probation services for adjudicated youths. Community Assessment Teams, with representatives of education and other human service agencies, provide a single point of entry for children and youth and their families.

Providing stable treatment to families will require a blurring of professional roles and a focus on building a network of support, joint communication, and mutual goal sharing. Services cannot be delivered by separate and concerned individuals working in isolation. Case management services are essential to building a network of support. A case manager might be an educator, social worker, or juvenile service employee. However, such an individual's commitment is not to a particular agency but rather to supporting a stable relationship with a family and timely information about services to the family. Further, professionals from different agencies need to trust one another and to support and respect the relationships among professionals and individual families (Schorr, 1988).

Policies governing personnel, such as licensing and certification, as well as those that define roles and responsibilities can stand in the way of creating such supportive climates. Further, services that are crisis oriented and fail to address prevention, or services that are not sensitive to cultural differences are not family oriented. Yet, much of the current policy framework does just that.

A policy framework that does not include alternative placements, such as specialized foster care, group homes, or short-term crisis support or respite care, fails to recognize the diversity among families and children and youth with EBD. Alternative living arrangements or placements may be required as part of a continuum of services. However, decisions regarding the use of those placements must be uncoupled from decisions about where education and other services should be provided. For example, school attendance policies need to be established that allow individual students with EBD to attend schools outside of their attendance area when the student's living situation changes to ensure continuity in education. Educational outcomes applied to public school programs for students with EBD must also be used to provide instructional continuity across nonpublic or specialized educational programs in hospitals or residential settings in order to ease transition back into community schools. Service providers need to be empowered to make decisions about treatment and resources necessary to respond to most family needs quickly.

Responsive family services also shift the locus of power and decision making from professionals to families. Learning to respect the positions and viewpoints of even the most unsophisticated family members requires a change in attitudes and a belief in the importance of families in the long-term success of the students with EBD (Karp, 1993).

Implementation of the Policy Framework

The proposed policy framework represents a major shift away from the current policy infrastructure supporting services to students with EBD and their families. Thus, it will not be easy to shift existing policies and practices, nor will implementation of the new ways of doing business be consistent across various jurisdictions. However, as noted, a number of states and local communities have already begun to install outcome-driven, family-responsive, system-linked services. Lessons learned from these various prototypes suggest several key factors related to successful implementation. These include institutional commitment or the willingness to change the current service delivery system, flexibility in the use of resources, and professional competencies.

Institutional Commitment. Among the factors that have been identified to support new service systems, a critical one stands out. Our research at the Center for Policy Options in Special Education, as well as the professional literature, emphasize the importance of institutional commitment to the proposed changes in service delivery (Glennon, 1993; Melaville et al., 1993). In almost every instance, individuals involved in our focus groups spoke of the need to motivate policymakers and agency directors to critically examine their missions and beliefs in light of their current policies. Some participants indicated that institutional commitment followed a mandate to change, usually as a result of some legislative action or directive from general government. Others developed a cadre of concerned administrators at the community level who were willing to take risks and begin to operate in new ways. In any case, institutional commitment will ultimately require both mandate for change as well as resolve by administrators and service providers.

Within education, there will be a need to broaden the current mission and underlying beliefs that guide much of what schools do. There must be a willingness on the part of educational policymakers to endorse a broader view of what schools will need to become to support the increasingly diverse students and families. As Tyack (1992) noted, endorsement of such a broader mission has not historically been supported by educators. Nonetheless, for a new policy framework to emerge, new views of what schools should become will be necessary.

Flexibility

Another barrier to the development of outcome-driven, system-linked, family-responsive services is the inflexibility in current policy governing the use of resources (Bernstein, 1993; Joe & Farrow, 1992; Schorr, 1988). Although lack of adequate funding for programs has been a perennial problem, so too has been the restrictions on how existing funds can be used. Policies that govern the allocation of resources must be created that facilitate changes in services and accommodate differing circumstances (Bernstein, 1993; NASBE, 1992). As noted earlier, current restrictive approaches to funding result in major service gaps as well as overutilization of high-cost crisis-oriented services.

Changing to a more flexible system of resource allocation will permit attention to prevention and can open the doors to a wider interpretation of who might be served. In systems with flexible resource allocation, multiagency community-based teams often pool some funds from multiple agency budgets to support flexibility. The team is empowered to make decisions within broad parameters about who might receive services. Several states, such as Kentucky (Nelson & Pearson, 1991) and Virginia (Comprehensive Services Act, 1992), have enacted legislation mandating interagency collaboration and removing the barriers for sharing funds and other resources.

Although new approaches stress prevention and suggest that more students and families can receive services, the reality is that current funds are insufficient regardless of how efficiently they are used. Melaville et al. (1993) cautioned that focusing on broad institutional changes should not distract policymakers from increasing the funds for family services. Thus, within a climate of increased flexibility there remains a need for gatekeeping to ensure that high-cost services are not used indiscriminately. Gatekeeping seems to suggest the need for eligibility criteria. This is not to be interpreted as rule-bound processes; rather, this suggests the need for service triage, based on behavioral assessments or some other system of structured service provider evaluations (C. M. Nelson, personal communication, July 1, 1993; H. Walker, personal communication, January 14, 1993).

Professional Development

A major part of implementing any new set of policies or programs is the degree to which all those charged with that implementation have the requisite knowledge and skills. Fullan and Stiegelbauer (1992), in their discussion of how to change educational systems, noted that teachers will always be the most critical factor in any new educational endeavor because, ultimately, it is their support and actions with children that will make the difference. The same can be said for other service providers. Any reconceptualization of services will require a rethinking of the roles and responsibilities of those who will administer and deliver the services (Jehl & Kirst, 1992; Kauffman & Hallahan, 1993; Nelson & Pearson, 1991; Schorr, 1988). This redefinition of roles must occur for middle management as well as those who are on the front lines of service. Melaville et al. (1993) and Stroul and Friedman (1986) believed that an ethos of collaboration is absolutely necessary if the concept of system-linked services is to prevail.

Creating such a culture will require comprehensive professional development at the preservice levels as well as ongoing support and development of current staff. Individuals will need to develop common language and begin to understand the perspectives of differing disciplines. Support for professional development should be integral to changes in the service systems. Cross-disciplinary training and opportunities to share issues and strategies should receive substantial support in any systemic change effort. In addition, the various professional disciplines will ultimately be challenged to redefine roles and responsibilities required of staff in new systems and reconstruct professional training programs.

SUMMARY

This discussion highlights some of the significant issues affecting how and where students with EBD are served. In addition, a framework for constructing new policies was proposed with an intent to create more of a child and family orientation to services. Our discussion has focused on broad contextual changes needed in order to develop more effective services for children with emotional or behavioral disorders and their families. We have chosen not to focus on specific policy debates (e.g., definitions, inclusion, punishment, funding alternatives). Although other issues are related to the overall design of services, they represent very specific policy areas and narrow conceptualizations of the issues and are insufficient for creating the changes we are proposing.

Educators concerned with the well being of youth with emotional or behavioral disorders need to work with colleagues in related disciplines to redefine our beliefs about the troublesome behavior and the purposes of schooling, and reconstruct policies to reflect our new beliefs. This will require a commitment to the principles embedded in the framework and a willingness to act on those principles.

REFERENCES

Berman, P., & McLaughlin, M. (1977). *Federal programs supporting educational change: Vol. VIII. Implementing and sustaining innovations.* Santa Monica, CA: Rand Corporation.

Bernstein, C. D. (1993). Financing the educational delivery system for special education. In J. I. Goodlad & T. C. Lovitt (Eds.), *Integrating general and special education* (pp. 73–102). New York: Merrill.

Biklen, D. P. (1985). *Achieving the complete school.* New York: Teachers College.

Carrier, J. G. (1990). Special education and the explanation of pupil performance. *Disability, Handicap & Society, 5*, 211–226.

Cline, D. H. (1990). A legal analysis of policy initiatives to exclude handicapped/disruptive students from special education. *Behavioral Disorders, 15*, 159–171.

Cocozza, J. J. (Ed.). (1992). *Responding to the mental health needs of youth in the juvenile justice system.* Seattle, WA: National Coalition for the Mentally Ill in the Criminal Justice System.

Coleman, M. C. (1986). *Behavior disorders: Theory and practice.* Englewood Cliffs, NJ: Prentice-Hall.

Comprehensive Services Act for At Risk Youth and Families, Virginia Acts of Assembly, Chapter 837. Code of Virginia, Title 2.1, Chapter 46 (1992).

Cordero et al. v. Pennsylvania Department of Education. (1991). (M.D. PA, No. 3: CV-91-0791).

Danielson, L. C., & Bellamy, G. T. (1989). State variation in placement of children with handicaps in segregated environments. *Exceptional Children, 55*, 448–455.

Davis, W. E. (1989). The regular education initiative debate: Its promises and problems. *Exceptional Children, 55*, 440–446.

Dempsey, S., & Fuchs, D. (1993). "Flat" versus "weighted" reimbursement formulas: A longitudinal analysis of statewide special education funding practices. *Exceptional Children, 59*, 433–443.

Diamond, S. C. (1993). Special education and the great god, inclusion. *Beyond Behavior, 4*(2), 3–6.

Farrow, F., & Joe, T. (1992). Financing school-linked, integrated services. *The Future of Children, 2,* 56–67.

Forness, S. R., & Knitzer, J. (1992). A new proposed definition terminology to replace "seriously emotionally disturbance" in the Individuals with Disabilities Education Act. *School Psychology Review, 21,* 12–20.

Frank, A. R., Sitlington, P. L., & Carson, R. (1991). Transition of adolescents with behavioral disorders—is it successful? *Behavioral Disorders, 16,* 180–191.

Fuchs, D., & Fuchs, L. S. (1988). An evaluation of the adaptive learning environment models. *Exceptional Children, 55,* 115–127.

Fuchs, D., & Fuchs, L. (1994). Inclusive schools movement and the radicalization of special education reform. *Exceptional Children, 60,* 294–309.

Fullan, M. G., & Stiegelbauer, S. (1991). *The new meaning of educational change.* New York: Teachers College Press.

Gartner, A., & Lipsky, D. K. (1989). *The yoke of special education: How to break it.* Rochester, NY: National Center on Education and the Economy.

Gerry, M. H., & Certo, N. J. (1992). Current activity at the federal level and the need for service integration. *The Future of Children, 2,* 118–126.

Glennon, T. (1993). Disabling ambiguities: Confronting barriers to the education of students with emotional disabilities. *Tennessee Law Review, 60,* 295–364.

Goertz, M. E. (1993). *School reform and education finance.* Unpublished paper prepared for Office of Special Education and Rehabilitative Services, U.S. Department of Education.

Grosenick, J. K. (1991). Public school services for behaviorally disordered students: Program practices in the 1980s. *Behavioral Disorders, 16,* 87–96.

Haring, N. G., & Phillips, E. L. (1962). *Educating emotionally disturbed children.* New York: McGraw-Hill.

Hasazi, S. B., Johnston, A. P., Liggett, A. M., & Schattman, R. A. (1994). A qualitative policy study of the Least Restrictive Environment provision of the Individuals with Disabilities Education Act. *Exceptional Children, 60,* 491–507.

Hewett, F. M. (1968). *The emotionally disturbed child in the classroom.* Boston: Allyn & Bacon.

Hewett, F. M., & Forness, S. R. (1977). *Education of exceptional learners* (2nd ed.). Boston: Allyn & Bacon.

Hoenig v. Doe et al., 108 S.Ct. 592 (1988).

Hunter, R. (1905). *Poverty.* New York: Harper & Row.

Jehl, J., & Kirst, M. (1992). Getting ready to provide school-linked services: What schools must do. *The Future of Children, 2,* 95–106.

Karp, N. (1993). Collaborating with families. In B. Billingsley (Ed.), *Program leadership for serving students with disabilities* (pp. 64–101). Blacksburg, VA: Virginia Technical University.

Kauffman, J. M. (1989). The regular education initiative as Reagan–Bush education policy: A trickle-down theory of education of the hard to teach. *Journal of Special Education, 23,* 256–278.

Kauffman, J. M., Gerber, M. M., & Semmell, M. I. (1988). Arguable assumptions underlying the regular education initiative. *Journal of Learning Disabilities, 21,* 6–11.

Kauffman, J. M., & Hallahan, D. P. (1993). Toward a comprehensive delivery system for special education. In J. I. Goodlad & T. C. Lovitt (Eds.), *Integrating general and special education* (pp. 73–102). New York: Merrill.

Kirst, M. (1990). *Accountability: Implications for state and local policymakers.* Washington, DC: U.S. Department of Education.

Knitzer, J., Steinberg, Z., & Fleisch, B. (1990). *At the schoolhouse door: An examination of programs and policies for children with behavioral and emotional problems.* New York: Bank Street College of Education.

Kohlberg, L., & Mayer, R. (1972). Development as the aim of education. *Harvard Educational Review, 42,* 449–496.

Koyanagi, C., & Gaines, S. (1993). *All systems failure: An examination of the results of neglecting the needs of children with serious emotional disturbance.* Alexandria, VA: National Mental Health Association.

Landrum, T. J., & Kauffman, J. M. (1992). Characteristics of general education teachers perceived as effective by their peers: Implications for inclusion of children with learning and behavioral disorders. *Exceptionality: A Research Journal, 3*, 147–163.

Learning Disabilities Association of America. (1993, January). *Position paper on full inclusion of all students with learning disabilities in the regular education classroom.* Pittsburgh, PA: Author.

Leinhardt, G., & Pallay, A. (1982). Restrictive educational settings: Exile or haven? *Review of Educational Research, 52*, 557–578.

Leone, P. E. (1989). Beyond fixing bad behavior and bad boys: Multiple perspectives on education and treatment of troubled and troubling youth. In R. B. Rutherford & S. A. DiGangi (Eds.), *Severe Behavior Disorders Monograph, 12* (pp. 1–10). Reston, VA: Council for Children with Behavior Disorders.

Leone, P. E. (1990). Toward integrated perspectives on troubling behavior. In P. E. Leone (Ed.), *Understanding troubled and troubling youth* (pp. 15–22). Newbury Park, CA: Sage.

Leone, P. E., McLaughlin, M. J., & Meisel, S. M. (1992). School reform and adolescents with behavior disorders. *Focus on Exceptional Children, 25*, 1–15.

McDonnell, J., & Kieffer-O'Donnell, R. (1992). Educational reform and students with severe disabilities. *Journal of Disability Policy Studies, 3*, 54–74.

McLaughlin, M. (1990). The Rand change agent study revisited: Macro perspectives and micro realities. *Educational Researcher, 19*, 11–16.

McLaughlin, M. J., & Owings, M. R. (1993). Relationships among states' fiscal and demographic data and the implementation of P.L.94-142. *Exceptional Children, 59*, 247–261.

McLaughlin, M. J., & Warren, S. H. (1992a). *Issues and options in restructuring schools and special education programs.* College Park, MD: Institute for the Study of Exceptional Children and Youth, University of Maryland.

McLaughlin, M. J., & Warren, S. H. (1992b). Outcomes assessment for students with disabilities: Will it be accountability or continued failure? *Preventing School Failure, 36*, 29–33.

McLaughlin, M. J., & Warren, S. H. (1994). Restructuring the special education programs in local school districts: The tensions and the challenges. *Special Educational Leadership Review, 2*(1), 2–21.

Melaville, A. I., Blank, M. J., & Asayesh, G. (1993). *Together we can: A guide for crafting a profamily system of education and human services.* Washington, DC: U.S. Government Printing Office.

Moore, M. T., Walker, L. J., & Holland, R. P. (1982). *Finetuning special education finance: A guide for state policymakers.* Princeton, NJ: Educational Testing Service.

Morrill, W. A. (1992). Overview of service delivery to children. *The Future of Children, 2*, 32–43.

Morse, W. C., Cutler, R. L., & Fink, A. H. (1964). *Public school classes for the emotionally handicapped: A research analysis.* Washington, DC: Council for Exceptional Children.

National Association of State Boards of Education (NASBE). (1992). *Winners all: A call for inclusive schools.* Alexandria, VA: Author.

National Center for Educational Outcomes (NCEO). (1991). *Assessing educational outcomes: State activity and literature integration.* Minneapolis, MN: College of Education, University of Minnesota.

National Center on Educational Outcomes (NCEO). (1993). *Educational outcomes and indicators for students completing school.* Minneapolis, MN: College of Education, University of Minnesota.

Neel, R. S., Meadows, N., Levine, P., & Edgar, E. B. (1988). What happens after special education: A statewide follow-up study of secondary students who have behavioral disorders. *Behavioral Disorders, 13*, 209–216.

Nelson, C. M., Center, D. B., Rutherford, R. B., & Walker, H. M. (1991). Do public schools have an obligation to serve troubled children and youth? *Exceptional Children, 57*, 406–415.

Nelson, C. M., & Pearson, C. A. (1991). *Integrating services for children and youth with emotional and behavioral disorders.* Reston, VA: Council for Exceptional Children.

Noel, M. M., & Fuller, B. C. (1985). The social policy construction of special education: The impact of state characteristics on identification and integration of handicapped children. *Remedial and Special Education, 6*, 27–35.

Norfolk Youth Network. (1989). Booklet. Norfolk, VA: Author.

Pugach, M. C., & Warger, C. L. (1993). Curriculum considerations. In J. I. Goodlad & T. C. Lovitt (Eds.), *Integrating general and special education* (pp. 125–148). New York: Merrill.

Reynolds, M. C., Wang, M. C., & Walberg, H. J. (1987). The necessary restructuring of special and regular education. *Exceptional Children, 53*, 391–398.

Rostetter, D., Kowalski, R., & Hunter, D. (1984). Implementing the integration principle of P.L. 94-142. In N. Certo, N. Haring, & R. York (Eds.), *Public school integration of severely handicapped students* (pp. 293–320). Baltimore, MD: Brookes.

Sailor, W. (1991). Special education in restructured schools. *Remedial and Special Education, 12*, 8–22.

Sailor, W., Gee, K., & Karasoff, P. (1993). Full inclusion and school restructuring. In M. E. Snell (Ed.), *Instruction of students with severe disabilities* (4th ed., pp. 1–30). New York: Merrill.

Sawyer, R. J., McLaughlin. M. J., & Winglee, M. (1994). Is integration of students with disabilities happening? An analysis of national data trends over time. *Remedial and Special Education, 15*, 204–215.

Schorr, L. (1988). *Within our reach.* New York: Doubleday.

Singer, J. D., & Raphael, E. S. (1988). *Per pupil expenditures for special education: To whom are limited resources provided?* (Report to the Office of Special Education, U.S. Department of Education, Grant No. GOO8630147). Cambridge, MA: Harvard University.

Skrtic, T. (1991). *Behind special education: A critical analysis of professional culture and school organization.* Denver, CO: Love Publishing.

Skrtic, T. M. (1991). The special education paradox: Equity as the way to excellence. *Harvard Educational Review, 61*, 148–206.

Smith, S. (1990). Individualized education programs (IEPs) in special education—from intent to acquiescence. *Exceptional Children, 57*, 6–14.

Stainback, S., & Stainback, W. (1984). A rationale for the merger of special and regular education. *Exceptional Children, 51*, 102–111.

Stainback, S., & Stainback, W. (1989). Integration of students with mild and moderate handicaps. In D. K. Lipsky & A. Gartner (Eds.), *Beyond separate education: Quality education for all* (pp. 41–52). Baltimore, MD: Brookes.

Stroul, B. A., & Friedman, R. M. (1986). *A system of care for severely emotionally disturbed children and youth.* Washington, DC: CASSP Technical Assistance Center, Georgetown University Child Development Center.

Sugarman, J. M. (1991). *Building early childhood systems: A resource handbook.* Washington, DC: Child Welfare League of America.

Thousand, J. S., & Villa, R. A. (1989). Enhancing success in heterogenous schools. In S. Stainback, W. Stainback, & M. Forest (Eds.), *Educating all students in the mainstream of regular education* (pp. 89–104). Baltimore, MD: Brookes.

Tomlinson, S. (1982). *A sociology of special education.* London: Routledge & Kegan Paul.

Tropea, J. L. (1987). Bureaucratic order and special children: Urban schools, 1890s–1940s. *History of Education Quarterly, 27*, 29–56.

Turnbull, H. R. (1983). A policy analysis of "least restrictive" education of handicapped children. *Rutgers Law Journal, 14*, 489–540.

Tyack, D. (1992). Health and social services in public schools: Historical perspectives. *The Future of Children, 2*, 19–31.

U.D. v. School Board of Orange County Florida. (1992). (State of Florida, Division of Administrative Hearings, Case No. 92-4014E).

U.S. Department of Education. (1992). *Fourteenth Annual Report to Congress on the Implementation of The Individuals with Disabilities Education Act.* Washington, DC: Author.

Valdes, K. A., Williamson, C. L., & Wagner, M. M. (1990). *The National Longitudinal Study of Special Education Students statistical almanac: Youth categorized as emotionally disturbed.* Menlo Park, CA: SRI International.

Wagner, M. (1991). *The transition experience of youths with disabilities: A report from the National Longitudinal Transition Study.* Menlo Park, CA: SRI International.

PART IV

CODA

CHAPTER

15

SPECIAL EDUCATION CAN WORK

Douglas Fuchs
Lynn S. Fuchs
George Peabody College of Vanderbilt University

On December 9, 1993, special education was mugged in a dark alley. The thugs were Joe Shapiro and his gang at *U.S. News and World Report* (cf. Shapiro et al., 1993). Their brass knuckles and tire irons were the half-truths and full-blown distortions they patched together (with the finesse of a Mike Tyson) into a cover story entitled "Separate and Unequal: How Special Education Programs Are Cheating Our Children and Costing Taxpayers Billions Each Year."

Were this an isolated case of mayhem, we might shake our heads, cluck our tongues, and assume the dismissive attitude of "Well, too bad, but life goes on." However, the *U.S. News* piece is not an isolated case. Rather, it is another in a lengthening line of attacks on special education, which includes position papers of major general education groups (e.g., Council of Chief State School Officers, 1992; National Association of State Boards of Education [NASBE], 1992), professional books (e.g., Stainback & Stainback, 1992), editorials, including one in *The Wall Street Journal* ("Special Ed's Special Costs," 1993), and many journal articles (beginning, perhaps, with Dunn, 1968, and Milofsky, 1974).

Failure to see the *U.S. News* article as the latest in special education bashing is dangerous right now. In 1995, Congress is expected to review the Individuals with Disabilities Education Act (IDEA) as part of its reauthorization process. As Jost noted, "U.S. Education Secretary Richard Riley and Tom Hehir, the department's director of special education, said they will urge Congress to make fundamental changes in the . . . law" (1993, p. 1099). Riley and Hehir must hear from more than the special education bashers; those who believe the field is worth perserving must respond vigorously to persons outside and inside the profession who would have special education dismantled and hauled off to the town dump. And each of us must assume this responsibility personally because our so-called leaders appear to have a terminal case of the shakes.

RESPONDING TO SPECIAL EDUCATION CRITICS

The *U.S. News* article contained the following accusations: "Imprecise state and federal regulations . . . drive up the size and cost of the special education system"; "Special education programs often operate in ways specifically designed to attract state and federal dollars—not to best serve students"; "Black students are overrepresented"; "Special education labels are so ambiguous that classifications vary from state to state"; and in "special education classrooms . . . academics . . . takes a back seat." In this chapter, we take up the last two charges, but our main purpose is to debunk the notion that special education can't strengthen children's school performance.

Disability Is in the Eye of the Beholder

Some critics say special education is damaging to children in part because most who are identified as "special needs" are not really disabled (cf. Skrtic, 1991). The labeling process, therefore, is viewed as unnecessary, costly, and presumably stigmatizing for those to whom the labels are assigned. Whereas the notion that most special education students are nondisabled may strike many lay people and professionals as unlikely, it is fast becoming fashionable, thanks in part to a popular perspective on disability, referred to as "social constructivism."

Applied to disabilities, social constructivism holds that "disability" does not reside within the person, but rather is invented by society for societal reasons (Skrtic, 1991). For example, Sleeter (1986) argued that "learning disabilities" (LD) was "caused" by our nation's anxious reaction to Sputnik: "After Sputnik, standards for reading achievement were raised and students were tested more rigorously and grouped for instruction based on achievement level. Students unable to keep up with raised standards were placed into one of five categories. Four . . . were used . . . to explain the failures of lower class and minority children; learning disabilities was created to explain the failures of white middle class children" (p. 46).

Ysseldyke, Algozzine, Shinn, and McGue's (1982) research also challenged the legitimacy of the LD construct. It did so by claiming an absence of important differences on school-related tasks between children labeled LD and nondisabled low-achieving children. (The empirical basis for this claim recently has been reviewed by Kavale, Fuchs, & Scruggs, 1994.) A more recent and extreme example of the social constructivist perspective was Biklen's (1990) assertion that people with autism are not disabled. Thompson (1994) stated,

> Biklen targets people with the most severe cognitive disabilities . . . to show that they function like everyone else linguistically, given proper tools (i.e., facilitated

> communication). According to Biklen's reasoning, if people with autism can be shown to function linguistically like everyone else, it must follow that only superfical appearances distinguish people with autism (and by extension, others with less severe disabilities) from those who have no identifiable disability. (p. 671)

Just as Jacques Derrida, the celebrated French philosopher, deconstructed texts in search of ways in which they failed to make the points they seemed to be trying to make, those like Sleeter, Ysseldyke, et al., and Biklen attempt to deconstruct "disability" to show the impossibilities and dangers inherent in believing in such a notion. Special education deconstructionists are not to be confused with the likes of Bill Rhodes (1970) and his community participation analysis, or Nettie Bartel and Sam Guskin (1980) and their work on handicap as a social phenomenon. Rhodes and Bartel and Guskin never denied the existence of disability even as they attempted to show how society may contribute unwittingly to it.

We must leave to others (e.g., Hallahan, 1992; Hallahan & Kauffman, 1994; Kavale & Forness, 1987) the task of arguing the fine points of the limitations of deconstruction and social constructivism as applied to "disability" and special education. Suffice it to say, one need not deny that there are children in special education who are not disabled to hold that some indeed have very serious special needs and require (by law if nothing else) special—and effective—assistance. Bateman (1994), Gottlieb, Alter, Gottlieb, and Wishner (1994), and Hallahan and Kauffman (1994) went further: As a consequence of poverty, drugs, family instability, and so forth, there may be more, not fewer, students requiring special education, and they may have increasingly serious problems that special educators will be required to address. Later in the chapter we suggest that the prospect of greater numbers of special-needs children is particularly problematic for special education in these times.

Special Education Can't Work

A second rap against special education is that it does not help students academically or otherwise who are placed in its charge. To wit:

> There is no compelling body of evidence that segregated special education programs have significant benefit for students. (Gartner & Lipsky, 1987, p. 375)

> [Special education] pulls students from general education classrooms and places them in small, segregated classes, in which they . . . are given a watered-down curriculum, and receive less rather than more instructional time. (Wang & Walberg, 1988, p. 131)

> Indeed . . . in one special ed classroom in Ohio, students learned how to bake a frozen pizza in an oven. (Shapiro et al., 1993)

> It is now time to ask, are children currently classified as "special education students" achieving what they are capable of? Are they being prepared for life after school?

> Are current mainstreaming practices producing their intended outcomes? [We] answer, "No!" (National Association of State Boards of Education, 1992)

Compliance, Not Outcome, Data. At least two factors contribute to the view that special education can't work. The first is that for the past two decades special education at federal, state, and local levels has been overly concerned about compliance with the Free Appropriate Public Education dimension of the Individuals with Disabilities Education Act, and insufficiently interested in student outcomes (Hehir, 1994). As a consequence, special educators at all levels typically have not produced the necessary database to document their worth, even when their programs may have been successful in all respects.

Efficacy Studies. Adding significantly to the "special education can't work" view are the so-called efficacy studies. It is well known that these studies, conducted during the past 60 years, generally show that students with mental retardation in mainstream classrooms perform as well as, or better than, their counterparts in special education settings. It also is well known that nearly all these investigations are seriously flawed: The study groups (students in special education classes versus those in mainstream classes) rarely were constituted by random assignment. Rather, they tended to be intact groups, with the consequence that the mainstreamed special-needs students typically were stronger academically and otherwise at the study's start than the children in the special education classes. Nevertheless, critics like Gartner and Lipsky (1989) never tire of trumpeting the failure of the efficacy studies to demonstrate the superiority of student performance in special education classes. (For more on critics' misuse of the efficacy studies as "proof" of special education's ineffectiveness, see Hallahan & Kauffman, 1994; MacMillan, Semmel, & Gerber, 1994.)

Fallout From the "Special Education Can't Work" Belief. The conviction that special education can't work seems to be growing and is exerting a corrosive effect. As suggested by Hallahan and Kauffman (1994), it feeds a zeitgeist that special education is harmful, not helpful; evil, not good (see National Association of State Boards of Education, 1992; Shapiro et al., 1993). A few special education academics have bought this proposition so completely that they have left their own departments for others, or have worked to diminish the visibility and importance of their academic units by helping to subsume them under other entities like "curriculum and instruction" or "educational psychology," or they have succeeded in eliminating special education as both a department and a program. Recent data from the Higher Education Consortium on Special Education (HECSE) may reflect this trend. Of 45 colleges and universities granting a doctoral degree in special education and forming the HECSE group, 39 responded to a recent survey. In 1987, 36 of the 39 institutions claimed special education departments; in 1992, the number of institutions with special education departments was only 25, a 31% drop in 5 years (H. J. Rieth, personal communication, February 1, 1994).

Moreover, "the low esteem in which the conceptual bases of special education and its practices are now held by many advocates of reform may contribute to the fact that special education teachers leave the profession in droves" (Hallahan & Kauffman, 1994, p. 497). Some special education leaders are beginning to wonder how long the field can hold out—whether it can avert a complete collapse (cf. Hallahan & Kauffman, 1994).

SPECIAL EDUCATION CAN WORK

Are all the critics full of hot air? Is there no basis for their charge that special education does not work? Of course not. In some places special education is indeed in disrepair. The cascade of services, for example, often fails to work in a manner prescribed in the statutes and regulations. In one large school district with which we are familiar, fewer than 2% of all students with learning disabilities, mild/moderate intellectual disabilities, and emotional and behavior disorders are decertified yearly. Moreover, in this same district, instances of students progressing "up the cascade"—from special day schools into self-contained classes in neighborhood schools, or from self-contained classes into regular classes—are few and far between. There are many reasons for this: Creating a dynamic cascade is difficult to accomplish without concerted effort (e.g., D. Fuchs, Dempsey, Roberts, & Kintsch, in press; D. Fuchs, Fuchs, Fernstrom, & Hohn, 1991); there is an absence of empirical work to guide reintegration efforts, a little-known fact because such work typically is confused with the "mainstreaming" literature (D. Fuchs, Fuchs, & Fernstrom, 1993); and the leadership of our profession (e.g., Council for Exceptional Children) gives the cascade of services lip service, but does little to improve it through offers of technical assistance or opportunities for professional development.

But if it is true that some things do not work in special education, it is also true that the field knows how to serve many children with disabilities, a fact that certain critics ignore. Just as the Sandia report (Carson, Huelskamp, & Woodall, 1993; Huelskamp, 1993)—a generally positive evaluation of the state of general education in America—was quashed by those in the Reagan and Bush administrations whose policies required widespread belief that all general education was bad (see Tanner, 1993), there are some who work overtime to help ensure that special education looks equally bad.

Successful Interventions

Critics' efforts notwithstanding, many academic and social–behavioral interventions for school-age children with disabilities have been shown to be effective, thanks to the hard work of and close collaboration between special education researchers and teachers. The following, largely lifted from Mastropieri and

Scruggs (1987), hardly qualifies as an exhaustive list; rather, it is meant to be suggestive of the impressive knowledge base that exists in special education.

Primary Studies of Interventions That Promote Academic and Behavior Improvement. In the area of reading, Deshler, Alley, Warner, and Schumaker (1981), Pany and Jenkins (1978), Pany, Jenkins, and Schreck (1982), and others provided evidence for the effectiveness of a direct instructional, phonics-based approach; Bos (1982), Jenkins, Stein, and Osborne (1981), and Schumaker, Deshler, Alley, Warner, and Denton (1982) described effective teaching of reading comprehension; Palinscar and Brown (1984) and Graves (1986) demonstrated the importance of metacomprehension training as a facilitator of prose recall; Scruggs, Mastropieri, McLoone, Levin, and Morrison (1987) provided evidence for the effects of pictures and prose learning with learning-disabled students; and Osguthorpe and Scruggs (1986) and others demonstrated the effectiveness of peer tutoring.

In spelling, the following techniques have been shown to be effective with students with disabilities: cumulative rehearsal/distributed practice (Gettinger, Bryant, & Fayne, 1982); grouping words with similar spellings (Gettinger, 1984; Neef, Iwata, & Page, 1980); self-monitoring and self-checking procedures (Beck, Matson, & Kazdin, 1983); peer tutoring (Rieth, Polsgrove, & Eckert, 1984); and rehearsal techniques (Weaver, 1984).

Regarding handwriting, successful self-instruction and self-correction techniques were developed by Graham (1983) and Kosiewicz, Hallahan, Lloyd, and Graves (1982). Instructional interventions for strengthening the written language of students with disabilities were developed by Isaacson (1985), Thomas, Englert, and Gregg (1987), Chatterjee (1983), and others.

The following classroom management strategies have been found effective: tangible reinforcement, including token systems, in special education classrooms (Baker, Stanish, & Frazer, 1972); time-out procedures (Rutherford & Nelson, 1982; Spencer & Gray, 1973); self-monitoring techniques (Broden, Hall, & Mitts, 1971; D. Fuchs, Fuchs, & Bahr, 1990; D. Fuchs, Fuchs, Bahr, Fernstrom, & Stecker, 1990; Glynn, Thomas, & Shee, 1973; Hallahan, Lloyd, Kosiewicz, Kauffman, & Graves, 1979); cognitive–behavioral interventions (Kerr & Nelson, 1983); and group contingencies (Wolf, Hanley, & King, 1970).

Quantitative Syntheses. Moreover, quantitative syntheses of multiple and sometimes hundreds of studies of instructional techniques with students with disabilities have shown the effectiveness of the following teaching approaches: delayed prompt procedures (Handen & Zane, 1987); direct instruction (White, 1988); use of mnemonic strategies and activities-oriented curricula in science (Mastropieri & Scruggs, 1992); peer tutoring (Britz, Dixon, & McLaughlin, 1989; Cook, Scruggs, Mastropieri, & Casto, 1985–86); language intervention (Nye, Foster, & Seaman, 1987); computer-assisted instruction (McDermid, 1990;

Schmidt, Weinstein, Niemic, & Walberg, 1985–86); self-management procedures (Hughes, Korinek, & Gorman, 1991; Rock, 1986); reinforcement and feedback (Skiba, Casey, & Center, 1985–86); and systematic formative evaluation (Fuchs & Fuchs, 1986).

Successful Interventions Validated in Special, Not General, Education

For the most part, the just-mentioned interventions were developed and validated in special education settings. How come? For starters, and as mentioned, a majority of the developers are special educators with strong interest in improving practice for students with disabilities. Such students are often found in special education classrooms. However, special education settings are also where special education teachers are—many of whom have a particular training and a unique willingness to implement instructional or behavior-related procedures that are sometimes complex and demanding. Also, special education settings are more likely than mainstream classrooms to be places where student–teacher ratios are favorable to individualized and small-group instruction (Leinhardt & Pallay, 1982), which characterizes many of the most successful interventions.

Another reason why exemplary academic and behavior strategies have been validated in special education is because many general educators are unable or unwilling to incorporate them into their classes. Commenting on the infrequency with which general educators employ prereferral intervention strategies, Gottlieb et al. (1994) wrote:

> It is not even clear what forms of support would be required to retain children in general education classes . . . to prevent referrals. In our survey of 206 referring teachers in two separate urban school districts, other than indicating that children need one-to-one instruction, classroom teachers were not certain what support they needed to [help] the children. Almost two-thirds (63%) could not indicate what resources they would need. Only 16% indicated they could be trained with the necessary skills to retain the referred children in their classes. Only 10% presented activities that could reasonably be described as curriculum adaptations. (p. 462)

Our recent work, which brings curriculum-based measurement into regular classes, indicates that whereas many teachers will look at group and individual performance data, few will use the data to make teaching adaptations when given evidence that individual students are not learning. Additionally, this refusal to make changes in instruction is seemingly so ingrained (see Baker & Zigmond, 1990; L. S. Fuchs, Fuchs, & Bishop, 1992; McIntosh, Vaughn, Schumm, Haager, & Lee, 1993; Schumm, 1994; Zigmond & Baker, 1993) that the training, material resources, and technical assistance we have provided to encourage such adaptations have had only marginal effects. The apparent perspective of many (most?) general educators is that their job is to teach subject matter, not children; their loyalty is to a class of undifferentiated students, not individuals; and order, not learning, is of greatest importance (Lloyd & Kauffman, this volume).

General Education Practices for Special-Needs Students: Popular and Unvalidated

Not only are most exemplary special education practices unvalidated in general education, but general education practices often described as effective means of educating students with disabilities have not been validated in either special or general education. Team teaching, collaborative consultation, and cooperative learning are examples of popular, but inadequately validated, practices for students with disabilities.

Team Teaching. In team teaching (or co-teaching), a special educator and his or her students move from a resource room, or self-contained class, to a regular classroom. The special and general educators decide what role the special education teacher will play. He or she might assume half the teaching responsibilities, lead small instructional groups in the back of the class, function as a teacher's aide, or play out some combination of these. Although team teaching is described frequently in recent books and teacher-oriented magazines, we know of no empirical explorations of its effectiveness. We do know, however, that Zigmond and Baker (1993) recently visited "exemplary inclusive schools" in Minnesota, Pennsylvania, Kansas, Virginia, and Washington, in which team teaching was a popular "inclusive" strategy. Zigmond and Baker's running record of their classroom observations indicated that team teaching was associated with infrequent individualized instruction and teaching modifications, an absence of formative and summative evaluative data, and a tendency to relegate the special educator to the role of a teacher's aide.

Consulting Teacher. Even a generally well-accepted approach like the consulting teacher model, which, for two decades (e.g., Egner & Lates, 1975), has been presented as a reasonable approach to (a) providing support to classroom teachers, (b) addressing many teachers' reliance on the special education referral, and (c) helping to bring special and general education closer together, has scant data on its effectiveness (see D. Fuchs, Fuchs, Dulan, Roberts, & Fernstrom, 1992).

Gottlieb et al. (1994) claimed there are many ways to operationalize the consulting teacher model: The special educator works exclusively with the general educator, providing indirect service; the special educator works directly with at-risk children in the mainstream; and a blending of the two. Said Gottlieb et al.:

> The premise underlying the consultant teacher model is that 2 or 3 hours weekly of special education small group instruction for LD children will be sufficient to compensate for the depressed level of academic performance. We do not believe this to be true. The needs of . . . inner city children . . . referred to and placed in

> special education are so severe that 2 or 3 hours of weekly instruction will not likely be sufficient. (p. 461)

Moreover, "when the consultant teacher [model] is used to accommodate special education learners in the regular classroom, it costs about 33% more than the resource room program, but [it] does not yield any demonstrable improvement in academic achievement beyond what resource rooms yield" (Gottlieb et al., 1994, p. 462; see also Gottlieb, Alter, & Yoshida, 1990).

Cooperative Learning. Unlike team teaching and consulting teacher models, cooperative learning has considerable student outcome data, but few data on students with disabilities. Further, data on the effectiveness of cooperative learning with special-needs students have been inconsistent (e.g., D. Fuchs, Fuchs, Jenkins, & Jenkins, 1991; Lloyd, Crowley, Kohler, & Strain, 1988; Tateyama-Snizek, 1990), the claims of some cooperative learning proponents notwithstanding (e.g., Slavin et al., 1991; Stevens & Slavin, 1992).

O'Connor and Jenkins (1993) observed 12 children with disabilities and 12 average-achieving peers in the same regular classroom during two to six hours of reading instruction, which used the Cooperative Integrated Reading and Composition (CIRC) program developed by Stevens and colleagues (e.g., Stevens, Madden, Slavin, & Farnish, 1987). They commented:

> How well did this form of cooperative learning work for these special education students? For some students, admirably; for others, not so well; for the group overall, probably less well than most would have liked. Using quality judgements of the help given by teammates, of students' contribution to the group's work, and of progress on assigned task, we classified fewer than 40% of the students with disabilities as successfully participating in cooperatively structured reading activities. (O'Connor & Jenkins, 1993, p. 27)

Team teaching, teacher consultation, and cooperative learning may eventually prove effective for many special-needs students in regular classrooms. We support continued work in these areas by researchers and practitioners dedicated to determining their value. At this juncture, however, it would seem foolish, if not professionally irresponsible, to sacrifice the instructional techniques validated in special education—requiring one-to-one or small-group arrangements—for team teaching, collaborative consultation, cooperative learning, and so forth about which we do not know enough.

GETTING FROM "CAN BE EFFECTIVE" TO "IS EFFECTIVE": DOWNSIZING THE SYSTEM

Stating that special education teachers have access to potent instructional and behavioral interventions—claiming, in effect, that special education can be effective—is not the same as declaring that it is. Critics get political mileage by charging that special education can't work because, in many places, it doesn't. What, then, is needed for special education to work? A partial solution, we believe, is that the system must be downsized.

The answer to most of general education's problems is not special education reform, although the reverse may be considerably more true. If special education got its act together (however one wishes to define this), general education would still have major problems, especially in the big cities of this nation. Special education must improve itself not primarily to help general education, but to help itself; to preserve itself as a viable option and profession in these days of special education bashing (like the recent article in *U.S. News*), of radical proposals for reform (like full inclusion), and of Congress's reauthorization of the Individuals with Disabilities Education Act.

More specifically, special education must seriously reconsider for whom it should exist. Traditionally, it has acted in accordance with a "Statue of Liberty" mentality ("Give me your tired, your poor, your huddled masses"). Bateman (1994), an acknowledged leader in the field, exemplified this spirit when she wrote, "We are . . . seeing an actual increase in the proportion of children who have categorical disabilities. Let us hope that 25 years further down the education road no one has to write that we ignored these warnings or the children's needs" (p. 513). Such a point of view is understandable. In many school systems, the only way to provide extra services to young children in educational difficulty is to refer them to special education (see Bateman, 1994; Fafard, in press; Gottlieb et al., 1994).

However, special education pursues its "Statue of Liberty" approach at its own peril. Downsizing is necessary, which should result in fewer children in special education. Such a reduction need not, and probably should not, occur equally across categories of exceptionality. For example, considerable evidence suggests that too many students are being identified as LD; that is, many who are not LD are being assigned the label anyway (e.g., Gottlieb et al., 1994). The number of students in this category should probably be reduced substantially. On the other hand, data indicate that children with emotional and behavioral problems may be underserved (National Mental Health Association, 1986) and, therefore, modest increases in this category might be expected and tolerated.

Whereas we believe there needs to be a sizable net decrease in numbers of students in special education, the number of special education teachers should remain constant. This will achieve at least two important ends. First, it will reduce student–teacher ratios in many places, maximizing opportunities for teachers to become more effective. Such an accomplishment is more important now than ever, because the days of proving one's worth by simply producing an up-to-date IEP are fast coming to an end. "Accountability" and "student outcomes" will soon become synonymous terms. Special education administrators must support the movement for better student outcomes, hold special educators to the highest standards, and, importantly, produce conditions necessary for the teachers to meet them.

Second, reducing student–teacher ratios should permit special educators to spend more time in general education, working to ensure better responsiveness to and accommodations of mainstreamed students with disabilities, as well as low-achieving, nondisabled students who might otherwise flounder. This second potential benefit of downsizing reflects the political reality that, for special education to win support from general education for lower student–teacher ratios, it must be capable of sharing with general education the challenge represented by increasing numbers of difficult-to-teach nondisabled students.

In sum, downsizing the number of students, but not teachers, in special education can pave the way for three systemic and timely changes: (a) Special education can better explain who it serves—and strengthen its credibility—by reducing "false positives" (i.e., children labeled "disabled" who are not); (b) special education can better demonstrate its effectiveness and justify its cost by decreasing student–teacher ratios and assuming an "outcomes-based" mentality; and (c) special education can work closely with general education by encouraging more special educators to work part time in mainstream classrooms with students who are in trouble, academically or otherwise, but not disabled. In short, we suggest special education follow a policy of "reverse triage": Students with some coping skills (with some chance of making it in the mainstream) should be sent to general education, despite a discouraging prognosis for them there. Special education should continue to work with only the most academically needy, socially vulnerable, and behaviorally inappropriate. Yes, such a proposal may be interpreted as showing a callous disregard for those earmarked for a precipitous return to general education, but times appear such that if the field does not follow some version of a "reverse triage" plan, it may soon be robbed of the resources to serve any students, including those who are most in need of its expertise.

REFERENCES

Baker, J. G., Stanish, B., & Frazer, B. (1972). Comparative effects of a token economy in a nursery school. *Mental Retardation, 10*, 16–19.

Baker, J. M., & Zigmond, N. (1990). Are regular education classes equipped to accommodate students with learning disabilities? *Exceptional Children, 56*, 515–526.

Bartel, N. R., & Guskin, S. L. (1980). A handicap as a social phenomenon. In W. M. Cruickshank (Ed.), *Psychology of exceptional children and youth* (4th ed., pp. 45–73). Englewood Cliffs, NJ: Prentice-Hall.

Bateman, B. D. (1994). Who, how and where: Special education's issues in perpetuity. *The Journal of Special Education, 27*, 509–520.

Beck, S., Matson, J. L., & Kazdin, A. E. (1983). An instructional package to enhance spelling performance in emotionally disturbed children. *Child and Family Behavior Therapy, 4*, 69–77.

Biklen, D. (1990). Communication unbound: Autism and praxis. *Harvard Educational Review, 60*, 291–314.

Bos, C. S. (1982). Getting past decoding: Assisted and repeated readings as remedial methods for learning disabled students. *Topics in Learning and Learning Disabilities, 1*, 517–555.

Britz, M. W., Dixon, J., & McLaughlin, T. F. (1989). The effects of peer tutoring on mathematics performance: A recent review. *B. C. Journal of Special Education, 13*, 17–33.

Broden, M., Hall, R. V., & Mitts, B. (1971). The effect of self-recording on the classroom behavior of two eighth grade students. *Journal of Applied Behavior Analysis, 4*, 191–199.

Carson, C. C., Huelskamp, R. M., & Woodall, T. D. (1993). Perspectives on education in America: An annotated briefing. *Journal of Educational Research, 86*, 259–310.

Chatterjee, J. B. (1983). A comparative analysis of syntactic density and vocabulary richness in written language of the learning-abled and learning-disabled children at third- and fifth-grade levels. *Dissertation Abstracts International, 44*, 2436A.

Cook, S. B., Scruggs, T. E., Mastropieri, M. A., & Casto, G. C. (1985–86). Handicapped students as tutors: A meta-analysis. *The Journal of Special Education, 19*, 483–492.

Council of Chief State School Officers. (1992, March). Special education and school restructuring. *Concerns, 35*, 1–7.

Deshler, D. D., Alley, G. R., Warner, M. W., & Schumaker, J. B. (1981). Instructional practices for promoting skill acquisition and generalization in severely learning disabled adolescents. *Learning Disability Quarterly, 4*, 415–422.

Dunn, L. M. (1968). Special education for the mildly retarded: Is much of it justifiable? *Exceptional Children, 34*, 5–22.

Egner, A., & Lates, B. J. (1975). The Vermont consulting teacher program: Case presentation. In C. Parker (Ed.), *Psychological consultation: Helping teachers meet special needs* (pp. 31–53). Reston, VA: Council for Exceptional Children.

Fafard, M. B. (in press). Twenty years after Chapter 766: The backlash against special education in Massachusetts. *Phi Delta Kappan*,

Fuchs, D., Dempsey, S., Roberts, H., & Kintsch, A. (in press). Peabody Reintegration Project: Case-by-case mainstreaming into reading classrooms. In J. Grimes & A. Thomas (Eds.), *Best practices in school psychology—III*. Washington, DC: National Association of School Psychologists.

Fuchs, D., Fuchs, L. S., & Bahr, M. W. (1990). Mainstream Assistance Teams: A scientific basis for the art of consultation. *Exceptional Children, 57*, 102–108.

Fuchs, D., Fuchs, L. S., Bahr, M. W., Fernstrom, P., and Stecker, P. M. (1990). Prereferral intervention: A prescriptive approach. *Exceptional Children, 56*, 493–513.

Fuchs, D., Fuchs, L. S., Dulan, J., Roberts, H., & Fernstrom, P. (1992). Where is the research on consultation effectiveness? *Journal of Educational and Psychological Consultation, 3*, 151–174.

Fuchs, D., Fuchs, L. S., & Fernstrom, P. (1993). A conservative approach to special education reform: Mainstreaming through transenvironmental programming and curriculum-based measurement. *American Educational Research Journal, 30*, 149–177.

Fuchs, D., Fuchs, L. S., Fernstrom, P., & Hohn, M. (1991). Toward a responsible reintegration of behaviorally disordered students. *Behavioral Disorders, 16*, 133–147.

Fuchs, D., Fuchs, L. S., Jenkins, J. R., & Jenkins, L. (1991, April). Peer-mediated strategies. In M. Kaufman (Chair), *Dangerous liaisons: Emerging themes from six studies of schoolwide interventions for integrating students with learning disabilities into general education*. Symposium presented at the annual meeting of the American Educational Research Association, Chicago.

Fuchs, L. S., & Fuchs, D. (1986). Effects of systematic formative evaluation: A meta-analysis. *Exceptional Children, 53*, 199–208.

Fuchs, L. S., Fuchs, D., & Bishop, N. (1992). Teacher planning for students with learning disabilities: Differences between general and special educators. *Learning Disabilities Research and Practice, 7*, 120–128.

Gartner, A., & Lipsky, D. K. (1987). Beyond special education: Toward a quality system for all students. *Harvard Educational Review, 57*, 367–395.

Gartner, A., & Lipsky, D. K. (1989). *The yoke of special education: How to break it. Working paper.* Rochester, NY: National Center on Education and the Economy. (ERIC Document Reproduction Service No. ED 307 792)

Gettinger, M. (1984). Applying learning principles to remedial spelling instruction. *Academic Therapy, 20*, 41–47.

Gettinger, M., Bryant, N. D., & Fayne, H. R. (1982). Designing spelling instruction for learning-disabled children: An emphasis on unit size, distributed practice, and training for transfer. *The Journal of Special Education, 16*, 439–448.

Glynn, E. L., Thomas, J. D., & Shee, S. M. (1973). Behavioral self-control of on-task behavior in an elementary classroom. *Journal of Applied Behavior Analysis, 6*, 105–113.

Gottlieb, J., Alter, M., Gottlieb, B. W., & Wishner, J. (1994). Special education in urban America: It's not justifiable for many. *The Journal of Special Education, 27*, 453–465.

Gottlieb, J., Alter, M., & Yoshida, R. K. (1990). *Evaluation of consultant teacher program* (Report submitted to New York State Education Dept., Office of Children with Handicapping Conditions). Larchmont, NY: Center for Educational Research.

Graham, S. (1983). The effect of self-instructional procedures on LD students' handwriting performance. *Learning Disability Quarterly, 6*, 231–234.

Graves, A. W. (1986). Effects of direct instruction and meta-comprehension training on finding main ideas. *Learning Disabilities Research, 1*, 90–100.

Hallahan, D. P. (1992). Some thoughts on why the prevalence of learning disabilities has increased. *Journal of Learning Disabilities, 25*, 523–528.

Hallahan, D. P., & Kauffman, J. M. (1994). Toward a culture of disability in the aftermath of Deno and Dunn. *The Journal of Special Education, 27*, 496–508.

Hallahan, D. P., Lloyd, J., Kosiewicz, M. M., Kauffman, J. M., & Graves, A. W. (1979). Self-monitoring of attention as a treatment for a learning disabled boy's off-task behavior. *Learning Disability Quarterly, 4*, 413.

Handen, B. L., & Zane, T. (1987). Delayed prompting: A review of procedural variations and results. *Research in Developmental Disabilities, 8*, 307–330.

Hehir, T. (1994). Special education: Successes and challenges; A memo from the Director of the U.S. Office of Special Education Programs. *Teaching Exceptional Children, 26*(3), 5.

Huelskamp, R. M. (1993). Perspectives on education in America. *Phi Delta Kappan, 74*, 718–721.

Hughes, C. A., Korinek, L., & Gorman, J. (1991). Self-management for students with mental retardation in public school settings: A research review. *Education and Training in Mental Retardation, 26*, 271–291.

Isaacson, S. L. (1985). Assessing written language skills. In S. Simon (Ed.), *Communication skills and classroom success: Assessment methodologies for language-learning disabled students* (pp. 403–424). San Diego: College-Hill Press.

Jenkins, J. R., Stein, M. L., & Osborne, J. R. (1981). What next after decoding? Instruction and research in reading comprehension. *Exceptional Education Quarterly, 2*, 27–39.

Jost, K. (1993, December 10). Learning disabilities. *CQ Researcher, 3*, 1083–1099.

Kavale, K. A., & Forness, S. R. (1987). History, politics, and the general education initiative: Sleeter's reinterpretation of learning disabilities as a case study. *Remedial and Special Education, 8*(5), 6–12, 27.

Kavale, K., Fuchs, D., & Scruggs, T. E. (1994). Setting the record straight on learning disabilities and low achievement: Implications for the policymakers. *Learning Disabilities Research and Practice, 9*(2), 70–77.

Kerr, M. M., & Nelson, C. M. (1983). *Strategies for managing behavior problems in the classroom.* Columbus, OH: Merrill.

Kosiewicz, M. M., Hallahan, D. P., Lloyd, J., & Graves, A. W. (1982). Effects of self-instruction and self-correction procedures on handwriting performance. *Learning Disability Quarterly, 5*, 71–78.

Leinhardt, G., & Pallay, A. (1982). Restrictive education settings: Exile or haven? *Review of Education Research, 52*, 557–578.

Lloyd, J. W., Crowley, E. P., Kohler, F. W., & Strain, P. S. (1988). Redefining the applied research agenda: Cooperative learning, prereferral, teacher consultation, and peer-mediated models. *Journal of Learning Disabilities, 21*, 43–52.

MacMillan, D. L., Semmel, M. I., & Gerber, M. M. (1994). The social context of Dunn: Then and now. *The Journal of Special Education, 27*, 466–480.

Mastropieri, M. A., & Scruggs, T. E. (1987). *Effective instruction for special education.* Boston: Little, Brown.

Mastropieri, M. A., & Scruggs, T. E. (1992). Science for students with disabilities. *Review of Educational Research, 62*, 377–411.

McDermid, R. D. (1990). A quantitative analysis of the literature on computer-assisted instruction with the learning-disabled and educable mentally retarded. *Dissertation Abstracts International, 57*, 1196A.

McIntosh, R., Vaughn, S., Schumm, J. S., Haager, D., & Lee, O. (1993). Observations of students with learning disabilities in general education classrooms. *Exceptional Children, 60*, 249–261.

Milofsky, C. (1974). Why special education isn't special. *Harvard Educational Review, 44*, 437–458.

National Association of State Boards of Education. (1992, October). *Winners all: A call for inclusive schools.* Washington, DC: Author.

National Mental Health Association. (1986). *Severely and emotionally disturbed children: Improving services under the Education of the Handicapped Act (P.L. 94-142).* Washington, DC: Author.

Neef, N. A., Iwata, B. A., & Page, T. J. (1980). The effects of interspersal training versus high-density reinforcement of spelling acquisition and retention. *Journal of Applied Behavior Analysis, 13*, 153–158.

Nye, C., Foster, S. H., & Seaman, D. (1987). Effectiveness of language intervention with the language/learning disabled. *Journal of Speech and Hearing Disorders, 52*, 348–357.

O'Connor, R. E., & Jenkins, J. R. (1993, April). *Cooperative learning as an inclusion strategy: The experiences of children with disabilities.* Paper presented at the annual meeting of the American Educational Research Association, Atlanta, GA.

Osguthorpe, R. T., & Scruggs, T. E. (1986). Special education students as tutors: A review and analysis. *Remedial and Special Education, 7*(4), 15–25.

Palinscar, A. S., & Brown, A. L. (1984). Reciprocal teaching of comprehension-fostering and comprehension-monitoring activities. *Cognition and Instruction, 1*, 117–175.

Pany, D., & Jenkins, J. R. (1978). Learning word meanings: A comparison of instructional procedures. *Learning Disability Quarterly, 1*, 21–32.

Pany, D., Jenkins, J. R., & Schreck, J. (1982). Vocabulary instruction: Effects on word knowledge and reading comprehension. *Learning Disability Quarterly, 5*, 202–215.

Rhodes, W. C. (1970). A community participation analysis of emotional disturbance. *Exceptional Children, 36*, 309–314.

Rieth, H. J., Polsgrove, L., & Eckert, R. (1984). A computer-based spelling program. *Academic Therapy, 20*, 49–56.

Rock, S. L. (1986). A meta-analysis of self-instructional training research. *Dissertation Abstracts International, 46*, 3322A.

Rutherford, R. B., & Nelson, C. M. (1982). Analysis of the response-contingent time-out literature with behaviorally disordered students in classroom settings. *Behavior Disorders, 5*, 79–105.

Schmidt, M., Weinstein, T., Niemic, R., & Walberg, H. J. (1985–86). Computer-assisted instruction with exceptional children. *The Journal of Special Education, 19*, 493–501.

Schumaker, J. B., Deshler, D. D., Alley, G. R., Warner, M. M., & Denton, P. H. (1982). Multipass: A learning strategy for improving reading comprehension. *Learning Disability Quarterly, 5*, 295–304.

Schumm, J. (1994, February). *Classroom teachers' standards for students with disabilities: Findings from a decade of research.* Paper presented at the meeting of the Pacific Coast Research Conference, La Jolla, CA.

Scruggs, T. E., Mastropieri, M. A., McLoone, B. B., Levin, J. R., & Morrison, C. (1987). Mnemonic facilitation of text-embedded science facts with LD students. *Journal of Educational Psychology, 79*, 27–34.

Shapiro, J. P., Loeb, P., Bowermaster, D., Wright, A., Headden, S., & Toch, T. (1993, December 13). Separate and unequal: How special education programs are cheating our children and costing taxpayers billions each year. *U.S. News and World Report, 115*(23), 46–60.

Skiba, R. J., Casey, A., & Center, B. A. (1985–86). Nonaversive procedures in the treatment of classroom behavior problems. *The Journal of Special Education, 19*, 459–481.

Skrtic, T. M. (1991). *Behind special education: A critical analysis of professional culture and school organization.* Denver: Love.

Slavin, R. E., Madden, N. A., Karweit, N. L., Dolan, L., Wasik, B. A., Shaw, A., Mainzer, K. L., & Haxby, B. (1991). Neverstreaming: Prevention and early intervention as an alternative to special education. *Journal of Learning Disabilities, 24*, 373–378.

Sleeter, C. E. (1986). Learning disabilities: The social construction of a special education category. *Exceptional Children, 53*, 46–54.

Special ed's special costs. (1993, October 20). *The Wall Street Journal*, p. A-14.

Spencer, R. J., & Gray, D. F. (1973). A time-out procedure for classroom behavioral change within the public school setting. *Child Study Journal, 3*, 29–38.

Stainback, S., & Stainback, W. (1992). *Curriculum considerations in inclusive classrooms: Facilitating learning for all students.* Baltimore: Paul Brookes.

Stevens, R. J., Madden, N. A., Slavin, R. E., & Farnish, A. M. (1987). Cooperative integrated reading and composition: Two field experiments. *Reading Research Quarterly, 22*, 433–454.

Stevens, R. J., & Slavin, R. E. (1992). *The cooperative elementary school: Effects on students' achievement, attitudes and social relations.* Baltimore, MD: Center for Research on Effective Schooling for Disadvantaged Students. (ERIC Document Reproduction Service No. ED 349 098)

Tanner, D. (1993). A nation 'truly' at risk. *Phi Delta Kappan, 75*, 288–297.

Tateyama-Snizek, K. M. (1990). Cooperative learning: Does it improve the academic achievement of students with handicaps? *Exceptional Children, 56*, 426–437.

Thomas, C. C., Englert, C. S., & Gregg, S. (1987). An analysis of errors and strategies in the expository writing of learning disabled students. *Remedial and Special Education, 8*, 21–30.

Thompson, T. (1994). [Review of the book *Communication Unbound: How Facilitated Communication Is Challenging Traditional Views of Autism and Ability/Disability*]. *American Journal of Mental Retardation, 98*, 670–673.

Wang, M. C., & Walberg, H. J. (1988). Four fallacies of segregationism. *Exceptional Children, 55*, 128–137.

Weaver, T. L. (1984). The effects of training strategic behaviors on the spelling performance of learning disabled children. *Dissertation Abstracts International, 45*, 1720A.

White, W. A. T. (1988). A meta-analysis of the effects of direct instruction in special education. *Education and Treatment of Children, 11*, 364–374.

Wolf, M. M., Hanley, E. L., & King, L. A. (1970). The timer game: A variable interval contingency for the management of out-of-seat behavior. *Exceptional Children, 37*, 113–118.

Ysseldyke, J. E., Algozzine, B., Shinn, M. R., & McGue, M. (1982). Similarities and differences between low achievers and students classified learning disabled. *The Journal of Special Education, 16*, 73–85.

Zigmond, N., & Baker, J. (1993, October). *An examination of the meaning and practice of special education in the context of full-time mainstreaming of students with learning disabilities.* Paper presented at the Policy Conference on the Meaning and Practice of Special Education in the Context of Inclusion, Nemacolin Woodlands, PA.

CHAPTER

16

Toward a Sense of Place for Special Education in the 21st Century

James M. Kauffman
John Wills Lloyd
University of Virginia

Terry A. Astuto
New York University

Daniel P. Hallahan
University of Virginia

The preceding chapters suggest that placement issues are complex, frequently misunderstood, and not open to easy resolution. Placement decisions and policy options are informed by few reliable data that explain how placement is related to the desired outcomes of education or treatment. Many factors and people with very different perspectives influence both the making of individual placement decisions and the making of rules about placement decisions.

The clearest message emerging from the preceding chapters is that much more work is needed to answer many of the questions one might ask about the place of special education in a system of public education, and about the use of various placement options for students with emotional or behavioral disorders. How does the place a student occupies determine his or her construction of a social environment, and how does that environment, in turn, shape the student's social behavior? How does a student's social environment interact with instructional methods? How does the structure of the system for delivering special education services affect the social environment of professionals, and how do they, in turn, reshape the structure of the system? The answers to these questions require insights not yet attained.

If 20th-century social scientists have achieved an insight about human social environments, however, it is that people's responses to a given environment are highly individualistic (cf. Gallagher, 1993). Plomin (1989) noted that the shared environment of a family is often perceived very differently by siblings, and that the family environment does not make children in the same family similar. The individual characteristics of the child and slight differences in patterns of interaction among family members can account for major differences in the behavioral outcomes of being reared in the same family. If families are known to provide environments with such highly personalized effects on siblings, then we might guess that the other environments in which children are placed will not have uniform effects. Specific to the present discussion, any school or classroom is likely to be perceived very differently by and have very different effects on the individual students placed in it. For students with emotional or behavioral disorders, as well as those in other categories, no single type of educational place will be perceived as supportive, habilitative, or self-enhancing for or by all. As Morse (1994) said, "The impact of being special turns out to be an individual person–ecology matter" (p. 535). And, as Gallagher noted, "an everyday setting that inclines one individual to feel and function well can push another in the opposite direction" (p. 18).

We might expect also that no single service delivery structure with its attendant social environments will be seen as adequate by all special education professionals. Those who framed federal special education law in the 1970s appear to have structured placement decisions in the knowledge or anticipation of findings regarding the individualistic responses of children and youth to given environments (Hocutt, Martin, & McKinney, 1991). Whether the congruity of law and science on this matter was intentional or fortuitous does not matter; what matters is that the placement procedures called for by the law are consistent with the finding that any single type of placement will inevitably be a bad fit for some and a good fit for others. The continuum of alternative placements, the preference for placement in the least restrictive alternative environment, and the case-by-case determination of placement—three requirements codified in the Education for All Handicapped Children Act of 1975 (EHCA: P.L. 94-142) and amendments now known as the Individuals with Disabilities Education Act of 1990 (IDEA)—were intended to preclude category-based placement decisions and ensure the availability of the placement option judged most appropriate for each individual student. As one legal scholar commented after reviewing U.S. appeals court decisions involving mainstreaming,

> It would be premature for school districts to provide all special education services in mainstream classes, just as it would be intransigent to refuse to provide individualized support services there. Although separate services have done an injustice to too many students, forcing all students into mainstream regular education classrooms will also be an injustice. Students with disabilities need options based on their individualized needs—not just a shift from a separation paradigm to an inclusion paradigm. Of course, that is part of the great challenge for both regular and special educators: how to serve a diversified student body with a variety of needs that do not respond to one administratively imposed model. The individualized and flexible legal standard of least restrictive environment serves students

> with disabilities well. We need to pay it more than lip service. (Huefner, 1994, p. 52)

Those who framed federal special education law in the 1970s did so in a social environment that was supportive of their efforts. In the mid-1970s, special education was perceived by most as an important service to students with special needs, and its continuum of alternative placements was seen as an invaluable feature of policy and practice in which nearly all special educators took pride. Two decades later, however, criticisms in the professional literature of the continuum of alternative placements (e.g., Laski, 1991; Lipsky & Gartner, 1991; Taylor, 1988) had found their way into the popular press (e.g., "Into the Mainstream," 1993; Shapiro et al., 1993). Placing students with emotional or behavioral disorders in environments defined as more restrictive had become quite difficult, regardless of the obviousness of students' needs for supports that are extremely difficult if not impossible to provide in regular classrooms and neighborhood schools (cf. Idstein, 1993).

In a sociopolitical context in which "the dominant myth in American politics . . . was that government programs didn't work" (Freedman, 1993, p. 4), special education was said by some to be not just another failed social program but an enterprise fundamentally flawed in conception and structure (cf. Lipsky & Gartner, 1991). To some critics, special education reflected not only basic structural flaws but empire building by special educators (cf. Wang & Walberg, 1988). However, it is important to recognize that "regardless of the motives imputed, an increasingly obvious fact is that burgeoning enrollments and crowded classrooms in many places . . . are making a mockery of special education's historic and noble intent to differentiate and enhance instruction for students with disabilities" (Fuchs & Fuchs, 1994; see also Morse, 1994).

Special education—merely receiving it in any form (and being thereby labeled), but especially receiving special services outside the regular classroom—became, in the opinion of many in the mid-1990s, the school-based curse of students not responding well to general education (cf. Morse, 1994). The congregation of students with disabilities for nearly any reason became suspect, and some called for maintaining a "natural proportion" of students with disabilities in each school and classroom (cf. Brown et al., 1989). The continuum of alternative placements mandated by IDEA and the sense that placements outside regular classrooms and neighborhood schools are appropriate for some students appeared to be endangered by the rhetoric of some reformers (e.g., Laski, 1991; Stainback & Stainback, 1991), and some attacked the very concept of the continuum (e.g., Taylor, 1988). Special education appeared to be at risk of losing its place in the structure of American public education (Kauffman & Hallahan, 1993), much as teacher education had lost its rightful place in American colleges and universities—through absorption into the more general enterprise, diffusion of focus, lack of authority, and loss of protected resources (cf. Goodlad, 1990).

How can one explain the shift in thinking from support to attack, from optimism to pessimism, from pride to shame about special education that occurred within two decades following the enactment of EHCA? And how might we forge a sense of place for special education in the 21st century—a renewed sense of support, optimism, and pride? How can one explain the change from consensus that a continuum of alternative placements is essential to the preservation of the rights of students with disabilities to attacks on the very notion of the continuum? And how might we renew the commitment of advocates, legislators, and program administrators to maintaining and refurbishing a continuum of alternative placements? There are many possible answers to these questions. Hirschman's (1986) economic analysis of late 20th-century views of the welfare state suggested answers consistent with the history of special education since the early 1960s (particularly since the enactment of EHCA) and relevant to controversies of the 1990s regarding the radical restructuring of special education (cf. Fuchs & Fuchs, 1991, 1994; Kauffman, 1991, 1993; Lipsky & Gartner, 1991).

Hirschman (1986) noted that some persons are prone to gloss over important flaws in a social enterprise, always suggesting very minor and inadequate responses to critical problems. Others tend to find fundamental structural errors behind every problem and prescribe radical restructuring, speaking always of fundamental change, deep malady, or final crisis of the system, even for problems that will resolve themselves with time and good management, or certainly with less than fundamental change or radical reform. In the last decade of the 20th century, many if not most government social welfare programs are viewed as failures (cf. Freedman, 1993), and structuralist calls for reform have become the norm (e.g., see Lipsky & Gartner, 1991, for a structuralist commentary on special education). However, contempt for social welfare programs may not have a single origin, and identifying the nature of the sources of derogation may be critical to addressing the problem effectively.

In the case of the social welfare programs of government, of which special education is a pertinent example, unhappiness with services may arise from two groups: those who pay for the services and those who are the intended beneficiaries. Hirschman suggested that the most significant contributor to the disgruntlement of both payors and beneficiaries is the rapid expansion of services that brings with it a deterioration in their quality in relation to expectations. If rapidly expanding demand alters what is put into the services, then the substitution of inputs results in quality of output that is not up to expected standards. If, in addition, the market is noncompetitive and consumers are slow for whatever reason to recognize the deteriorating quality, then it may appear that fundamental change is necessary, although a less radical response to the problem is in fact most appropriate.

Hirschman also noted that the same misapprehension of the problem—the mistaken notion that something fundamental or structural must change—can be created without an actual decline in quality of the services in question. When services are intended for newly emerging groups of consumers or when demand arises in advance of knowledge of how to satisfy it (Hirschman noted that day-care and psychotherapeutic services are examples), both the providers of the services and consumers of them may have inappropriate expectations of the quality or effects of the services.

Hirschman's analysis fits the rapid expansion of special education services since the late 1960s, particularly the very substantial expansion of quantity and diversity of services following the enactment of EHCA. In fact, the growth of special education services was so rapid that many special education teachers were poorly prepared (if at all prepared) to teach students identified as having disabilities, and a large number of teachers were only provisionally certified. Neither teacher training nor the instruction of students with disabilities have been guided consistently by the available knowledge of effective practices. Moreover, some of the critical features of special education practices were mandated by the law in advance of actual knowledge of how to satisfy its requirements, with individualized education plans (IEPs), and placement in the least restrictive environment (LRE) being prime examples.

Given these conditions, it is not surprising that the quality of these services declined as predicted by economic theory. If Hirschman's analysis is correct, then the fundamental restructuring of special education is likely to be counterproductive. A better approach to refurbishing special education's place in American public education—at least if one believes that students with disabilities should have the free and appropriate education sought by IDEA—would be the patient, deliberate restoration of quality through careful attention to inputs within the present structure (cf. Carnine, 1993; Kauffman, 1993; Kauffman & Hallahan, 1993, for commentary on this approach).

Unhappiness with government social welfare programs such as special education, and calls for their radical restructuring, are predictable responses of conservative politicians and ideologues. Given the liberal sympathies of those who gave special education its current structure and the liberal bent of most special education reformers, how does one explain the calls of reformers for radical restructuring (cf. Kauffman, 1989)? Hirschman (1986) offered the following hypothesis:

> I wish to raise a question in the sociology of knowledge: why have the various conceivable nonstructural arguments not been coherently put forward so far, with the result that we could only choose between various kinds of structuralist explanations? The reason, I think, lies in a rather odd ideological asymmetry. . . . Structuralist thinking about a problem or crisis comes easily to those who dislike the institution that experiences the problem or finds itself in crisis. For example, right-wing and conservative people dislike the welfare state and oppose its expansion: they are naturally prone to interpret any difficulties it encounters as symptoms of a deep-seated malady and as signals that radical retrenchment is in order. For similar reasons, left-wing and liberal opinion has traditionally opted for structuralist

> explanations when it came to account for difficulties experienced by capitalism. But with the debate about capitalism and the market economy having stood in the center of public discussion for so long, this tradition appears to have created on the Left something of an unthinking structuralist reflex: Left-liberal people are automatically partial to structuralist explanations, even though ideological self-interest ought to make them diagnose some difficulties—those that affect structures they themselves have promoted—as self-correcting or temporary. As a result of this strange ideological trap into which the Left has been falling, there has been a marked lack of balance in the analysis of current difficulties of the welfare state. (p. 169)

At the close of the 20th century, the place of special education in American public education is a topic for heated debate. Whether structuralist or nonstructuralist arguments will carry the day is an open question. Whether one takes a structuralist or a nonstructuralist view of special education's late 20th-century problems, it is clear that the "implementational sins" to which Redl (1966; see also chap. 2, this volume) referred are still with us; in practice, we too often do not see a reliable match between knowledge and implementation. Regardless of how special education is structured and regardless of the place in which special education services are provided, the central task of reform remains bringing the practice of special education into line with reliable data on the effects of two variables: First, the instructional methods and materials used to teach academic and social skills; second, the environments in which instruction is delivered (cf. Carnine, 1993; Grossen, 1993; Kauffman, 1993). Ultimately, special education's place in American public education, as well as the alternative placements that are available for the practice of special education, will be determined by how we respond to the central task of reform that, so far, has been largely ignored—improving the inputs that determine the quality of services (reforming our "implementational sins").

ACKNOWLEDGMENTS

We are indebted to Michael M. Gerber for calling the work of Albert O. Hirschman to our attention, and to Loretta Giorcelli for her review of this chapter.

REFERENCES

Brown, L., Long, E., Udvari-Solner, A., Davis, L., VanDeventer, P., Ahlgren, C., Johnson, F., Gruenewald, L., & Jorgensen, J. (1989). The home school: Why students with severe intellectual disabilities must attend the schools of their brothers, sisters, friends, and neighbors. *JASH, 14*, 1–7.

Carnine, D. (1993, December 8). Facts over fads. *Education Week*, p. 40.

Freedman, J. (1993). *From cradle to grave: The human face of poverty in America.* New York: Antheneum.

Fuchs, D., & Fuchs, L. S. (1991). Framing the REI debate: Abolitionists versus conservationists. In J. W. Lloyd, N. N. Singh, & A. C. Repp (Eds.), *The regular education initiative: Alternative perspectives on concepts, issues, and models* (pp. 241–255). Sycamore, IL: Sycamore.

Fuchs, D., & Fuchs, L. S. (1994). Inclusive schools movement and the radicalization of special education reform. *Exceptional Children, 60*, 294–309.

Gallagher, W. (1993). *The power of place: How our surroundings shape our thoughts, emotions, and actions.* New York: Poseidon.

Goodlad, J. I. (1990). *Teachers for our nation's schools.* San Francisco: Jossey-Bass.

Grossen, B. (1993). Focus: Heterogeneous grouping and curriculum design. *Effective Teaching Practices, 12*(1), 5–8.

Hirschman, A. O. (1986). *Rival views of market society and other recent essays.* New York: Viking.

Hocutt, A. M., Martin, E. W., & McKinney, J. D. (1991). Historical and legal context of mainstreaming. In J. W. Lloyd, N. N. Singh, & A. C. Repp (Eds.), *The regular education initiative: Alternative perspectices on concepts, issues, and models* (pp. 17–28). Sycamore, IL: Sycamore.

Huefner, D. S. (1994). The mainstreaming cases: Tensions and trends for school administrators. *Educational Administration Quarterly, 30*, 27–55.

Idstein, P. (1993). Swimming against the mainstream. *Phi Delta Kappan, 75*, 336–340.

Into the mainstream. (1993, April 21). *USA Today*, pp. 7D–9D.

Kauffman, J. M. (1989). The regular education initiative as Reagan–Bush education policy: A trickle-down theory of education of the hard-to-teach. *Journal of Special Education, 23*, 256–278.

Kauffman, J. M. (1991). Restructuring in sociopolitical context: Reservations about the effects of current reform proposals on students with disabilities. In J. W. Lloyd, N. N. Singh, & A. C. Repp (Eds.), *The regular education initiative: Alternative perspectives on concepts, issues, and models* (pp. 57–66). Sycamore, IL: Sycamore.

Kauffman, J. M. (1993). How we might achieve the radical reform of special education. *Exceptional Children, 60*, 6–16.

Kauffman, J. M., & Hallahan, D. P. (1993). Toward a comprehensive service delivery system. In J. I. Goodlad & T. C. Lovitt (Eds.), *Integrating general and special education* (pp. 73–102). Columbus, OH: Merrill/Macmillan.

Laski, F. J. (1991). Achieving integration during the second revolution. In L. H. Meyer, C. A. Peck, & L. Brown (Eds.), *Critical issues in the lives of people with severe disabilities* (pp. 409–421). Baltimore, MD: Paul H. Brookes.

Lipsky, D. K., & Gartner, A. (1991). Restructuring for quality. In J. W. Lloyd, N. N. Singh, & A. C. Repp (Eds.), *The regular education initiative: Alternative perspectives on concepts, issues, and models* (pp. 43–57). Sycamore, IL: Sycamore.

Morse, W. C. (1994). Comments from a biased viewpoint [Special issue, Theory and Practice of Special Education: Taking Stock a Quarter Century After Deno and Dunn]. *Journal of Special Education, 27*, 531–542.

Plomin, R. (1989). Environment and genes: Determinants of behavior. *American Psychologist, 44*, 105–111.

Redl, F. (1966). Designing a therapeutic classroom environment for disturbed children: The milieu approach. In P. Knoblock (Ed.), *Intervention approaches in educating emotionally disturbed children.* Syracuse, NY: Syracuse University Press.

Shapiro, J. P., Loeb, P., Bowermaster, D., Wright, A., Headden, S., & Toch, T. (1993, December). Separate and unequal. *U.S. News and World Report, 115*(23), 46–60.

Stainback, W., & Stainback, S. (1991). A rationale for integration and restructuring: A synopsis. In J. W. Lloyd, N. N. Singh, & A. C. Repp (Eds.), *The regular education initiative: Alternative perspectives on concepts, issues, and models* (pp. 226–239). Sycamore, IL: Sycamore.

Taylor, S. J. (1988). Caught in the continuum: A critical analysis of the principle of the least restrictive environment. *Journal of the Association for Persons with Severe Handicaps, 13*, 41–53.

Wang, M. C., & Walberg, H. J. (1988). Four fallacies of segregationism. *Exceptional Children, 55*, 128–137.

AUTHOR INDEX

Page numbers in *italics* denote complete bibliographical citations.

A

B

C

D

G

I

J

K

N

S

T

U

V

W

Y

Z

Subject Index

O

P

Q

R

S

T

W